Where to wat

Southern & Western Spain

Ernest Garcia and Andrew Paterson

Second edition

Christopher Helm
A & C Black • London

Acknowledgements
We are most grateful to the following for their help, advice, information and, on
occasions, their company; Steve Abbott, John Bartley, Andy Chapell, Francisco Chiclana,
Judy Collins, P.F.Cooper, Colin Davies, William Davies, Bruce Forrester, Joan Garcia,
Nacho García Paéz, Richard Gunn, Robert Haigh, Martin Henry, Eduardo de Juana, Eileen
Marsh, Juan Luis Muñoz, Jan Nordblad, Andrés Paterson, Charlie Perez, Tania Roe, Gene
Skelton, Ann Small, Roy Smith, Chris Smout, G.F. Trowmann, Jesús Valiente and Ivor
White.

First edition 1994

© 2001 Ernest Garcia and Andrew Paterson
Reprinted 2003
Illustrations by Stephen Message
Maps by Andrew Paterson

Christopher Helm (Publishers) Ltd, a subsidiary of
A & C Black (Publishers) Ltd, 37 Soho Square, London W1D 3QZ

ISBN 0-7136-5301-9

A CIP catalogue record for this book is available from the British Library

A & C Black uses paper produced with elemental chlorine-free
pulp, harvested from managed sustainable forests.

www.acblack.com

Printed and bound in Great Britain by Creative Print and Design (Wales), Ebbw Vale

CONTENTS

Contents

FOREWORD

Visitors to Spain in search of birds naturally gravitate to the south and west, to Andalucía and Extremadura. They are attracted by the spectacular assemblages of breeding and migrant raptors, by the exotic wetland species and by the colourful passerine communities of the Mediterranean. But there is much more on offer. Here are some of the best unspoilt wildlife habitats surviving in Europe supporting a wide range of species which are uncommon or absent elsewhere. Nowhere else in Europe can you find Little Button-quail (Andalucían Hemipode), Red-knobbed Coot, White-rumped Swift, Little Swift or Trumpeter Finch. The bulk of the world population of Spanish Imperial Eagle inhabits Extremadura and western Andalucía. Here too there are excellent and, in many cases, unparalleled opportunities for seeing a large range of Iberian and Mediterranean species. The proximity to Africa, the migration routes, the combination of mountain, steppe and maritime habitats and, of course, the superb year-round climate are all extra ingredients which will make an ornithological visit to southern and western Spain memorable and rewarding.

The Mediterranean countries do not have a good name in conservation circles. By and large, there is the impression that they are peopled by hordes of callous hunters, intent on blasting or netting everything that moves. There certainly are notorious blackspots but, in Spain at least, there have been great improvements over recent years accompanied by a widespread increase in interest and awareness among the Spaniards themselves. We are all fortunate that there is still a great deal left to conserve in Spain. Conservation, though, has its price and the case for preserving important areas is strengthened if they can be seen to attract tourists as well. We hope that this book will contribute to conservation of Spanish birds and their habitats by encouraging visits to areas which deserve to be protected. Do tell hoteliers and other local people why you are visiting. By doing so you will be helping to ensure that Spanish wildlife remains the spectacle that it is.

This book has been written to help you to get the most out of your stay in southern and western Spain, whether as a visitor or as a longer-term resident. We hope you find it useful. Please let us know if it is or if it isn't! Your comments and suggestions will be most welcome and will of course be acknowledged in any future revised edition. *Buen viaje!*

Ernest Garcia & Andy Paterson
2001

Addresses for correspondence

Dr E.F.J. Garcia, Woodpecker House, 2 Pine View Close, Chilworth, Guildford, Surrey, GU4 8RS, UK.

A.M. Paterson, Edificio San Gabriel 2–4°A, c/.Escritor Adolfo Reyes, 29620 Torremolinos, (Málaga) Spain.

INTRODUCTION TO THE
SECOND EDITION

This book was first published in 1994, under the title *Where to watch birds in Southern Spain*. The new title gives a better indication of the area covered and also shows that it complements the sister volume, *Where to watch birds in North and East Spain*, by Michael Rebane and published in 1999, which covers the rest of Spain. We have fully revised and updated the original text and, in particular, the maps. We have taken note of changes in the status of many species and of the latest crop of rarities. This edition also includes nine completely new sites, as well as an expanded treatment of many of the original locations.

The interval of only six years since the appearance of the first edition has nevertheless been enough for some quite important changes to have occurred and we draw your attention to some of the most interesting ones here. Some are developments of conservation significance, both positive and negative. Others have involved changes in numbers and geographical distribution of certain species. Yet others arise from alterations to bird names and from the revisions of the classification system.

Conservation issues

The good news is very real. Interest in Spanish birds and wildlife, and in the environment generally, continues to grow as evidenced by the rising membership of the Sociedád Española de Ornitología (Spanish Ornithological Society — also known as SEO/BirdLife) and other organisations, by the expansion of the network of protected areas established and maintained by both official bodies and voluntary organisations and, not least, by the ever-increasing number of visitors who come to the region in search of its rich natural heritage.

There are, however, a number of serious problems. Some catch the news headlines for short periods because of their dramatic nature. Of these, the list is headed by the toxic spillage in the Doñana area in April 1998, described in the site account (H4) on p. 60. The full immediate potential for ecological disaster inherent in this incident was averted, but the long-term effects may yet have to be felt. More insidious and pervasive has been the recurrent upsurge in the laying of poison baits for the control of foxes and other 'vermin', which is having a severe effect on the population of Spanish Imperial Eagles and other raptors.

Changes in land use often have implications for the environment which give cause for concern. The extension of irrigated areas in Extremadura and elsewhere may have incidentally provided additional wetland habitats, for example by the ongoing expansion of rice cultivation, but some of this has involved the loss of steppe habitats which formerly accommodated bustards and other threatened birds. The same habitats are threatened locally by the expansion of afforestation; large tracts of open country now sport plastic tree-guards protecting (yet more) olive trees especially. Conversely, the grubbing-out of the evergreen oak woodlands of Extremadura especially is causing significant loss of habitats for wintering Cranes and many breeding species. Cork-oak forests, vital habitats for some of the best of our area's wildlife, may also be threatened if demand for cork continues to decline, something to remember when choosing wine; plastic stoppers are definitely not 'green'.

Wind-power has been féted for its environment-friendly credentials; wind is pollution-free after all. However, a visit to the Strait of Gibraltar makes the concept of visual pollution starkly real since hundreds upon hundreds of wind turbines now disfigure the hillsides in what used to be an area of outstanding, nay exceptional, natural beauty. The windmills chop up birds too, but we do not yet know whether this is having an impact on any populations. Wind-farms are expanding in the Strait area (site CA2) and have gained a foothold near the Sierra Crestellina (site MA11) and we must fear that they will continue to proliferate.

Less disfiguring, but still hideous, is the increasing use of polythene strips as cloches, which shelter beans and other crops and conserve water. The result is not only that some 'lakes' turn out to be made of plastic on closer inspection but also that trees and bushes nearby are soon festooned with the tattered remnants of those strips which, inevitably, fly away.

Increased urbanisation and road-building has affected our area quite noticeably, especially perhaps along the Atlantic shoreline, where the formerly pristine beaches have attracted a swathe of tourist developments and holiday homes.

Voluntary agencies and others in Spain are working to ensure that the issues raised by the above and other developments are properly addressed. Spain has been slow in meeting its responsibilities, under European Union agreements, to designate a full network of Important Bird Areas (IBAs), which identify key regions and provide a basic level of regulation of the land use there. Pressure is being brought to encourage the establishment of the IBAs, which are invaluable in providing essential protection to key habitats and their species. A considerable number of IBAs, or ZEPAs (Zonas de Especial Protección para las Aves) as they are known in Spain, have already been designated but the network is far from complete. Extremadura is particularly poorly served in this respect as are the steppe habitats generally.

Changes in the avifauna

The bird populations of such a large region as ours are bound to fluctuate in the long-term but even the short period of the last decade has seen significant changes.

There have been very large increases in the population of White Storks. They have benefitted from the increased provision of food handouts at landfill garbage dumps, to the extent that some have become virtually resident in Spain and no longer risk the hazards of the annual return trip to Africa. White Storks are censused periodically and the results speak for themselves. There were 14,513 pairs counted in 1948 but these had declined to 6,753 by 1984. However, by the time of the 1994 census the population was at a record high of 16,643 pairs and numbers have continued to increase since, with recent expansion into new areas such as Málaga province.

Spectacular increases have also occurred among Griffon Vultures, also beneficiaries of the sloppiness of human waste-disposal but also in response to a reduction of direct persecution, now that raptor-shooting is universally prohibited in Spain. The vulture population has burgeoned from 3,240 pairs in 1979 to over 17,000 pairs in 1999.

Other breeding species showing significant and ongoing increases in numbers and geographical spread include Grey Heron, Glossy Ibis, White-headed Duck (with eastward range expansion), Black-shouldered Kite, Purple Gallinule, Yellow-legged Gull (alas!), Collared Dove, White-rumped Swift and Red-rumped Swallow.

There have been increases among wintering species too. White Storks undoubtedly overwinter to a much greater extent than used to be the case. There are increasing winter records of a number of raptor species, such as Black Kites, Short-toed Eagles and Booted Eagles, which were formerly regarded as fully migratory, but this may simply reflect greater observer activity. The increase in wintering by Ospreys, especially around Cádiz Bay (site CA12) seems real, however. Hirundines are being recorded in spectacular numbers in the Guadalquivir valley in midwinter but they may simply be returning from Africa very early. Swallows moult in their winter quarters and sub-Saharan Africa provides plenty of food while they do so. Genuine wintering in Spain would mean moulting there too and this has yet to be found to happen.

There is a debit list too, unfortunately. Perhaps the greatest concern attaches to the fall in the Spanish Imperial Eagle population from 148 pairs in 1994 to 131 pairs in 1999. These are the global population figures since the bird now breeds exclusively in Spain, and chiefly within our region. The decline has been attributed to poison baits, laid for mammalian predators, but a lot of birds are electrocuted on power lines. The re-design of pylons, with the addition of raised perches, has helped to reduce the latter losses but the poisoning problem could be the coup-de-grace for this flagship species unless prompt measures are taken. The same poison baits also threaten Egyptian Vultures, Red Kites and Ravens in particular.

Other significant decreases within our area have been shown by Marbled Duck (habitat loss), Montagu's Harrier (nest destruction by early harvesting of wheat), Bonelli's Eagle (disturbance and displacement by Golden Eagles), Lesser Kestrel (pesticides; now recovering), Little Button-quail (habitat loss), Little and Great Bustard (habitat loss) and Black-bellied and Pin-tailed Sandgrouse (habitat loss).

Recent developments have included colonisation by two or three potential breeding species and the establishment of a whole range of exotics, derived from escaped cagebirds. Imagine a day's birding in which the list includes Great White Egret, Rüppell's Griffon Vulture, Little Swift, Red-billed Quelea, Red Bishop and Black-rumped, Common and Orange-cheeked Waxbills. A tropical African venue no doubt, but the picture is confused by the appearance of Monk Parakeet (South America) and Red Avadavat (Asia). In fact, all these species could be seen in Cádiz province right now, and many of them breed there.

Rüppell's Griffon Vulture was first seen in Spain in May and June 1992, when a subadult was seen in Extremadura (Cáceres). What may have been the same bird turned up in Doñana in October of the same year. These records would have been regarded as 'escapes' were it not that in autumn 1997 at least three individuals were in the vicinity of the Strait and at least five were present there by late 1998, with further records subsequently. It seems likely, therefore, that wild birds have reached Spain, perhaps having become incorporated in flocks of Eurasian Griffons wintering in tropical west Africa and having travelled back north with the latter. The species is certainly one to look out for in our area.

Little Swifts colonised northernmost Morocco at least 50 years ago, and were nesting in Tangier by 1952. They are quite common in Tangier, where they are resident, but until recently this species has been very rarely seen in Spain. Frequent sightings in the region of the Strait, at the Sierra de la Plata behind Bolonia (site CA5), occurred from 1995 onwards and it is quite likely that a few are now settling to breed there, most probably squatting in House Martin nests in the caves. This is at present the only site with a good chance of producing Little Swifts, in spring and summer at least, with the added bonus of the simultaneous presence of White-rumped Swifts and even the other three European swift species. Can it be long before there's a roadside billboard proclaiming 'Bolonia! Swift capital of Europe'?

The Great White Egret is in a different category, occurring mainly as a winter visitor, with increasingly frequent records from major wetland sites. Its presence coincides with an increase in the breeding populations of central Europe, which has produced some westward spread. It is quite likely that it will soon breed within our area.

The list of exotic species is long and ever-growing. The regulars include stray Lesser Flamingos at Fuente de Piedra (MA1), established populations of Monk and Ring-necked Parakeets, breeding Red-vented Bulbuls at Torremolinos (in 1999 and 2000) and a long and ever-growing list of tropical finches (see the Systematic List). These latter find the Spanish wetlands very much to their liking, and indeed the Guadalquivir valley on a hot summer afternoon puts on a very convincing impression of an African river scene. Two species, Common Waxbill and the Red Avadavat, are especially well established and may be regarded as naturalised. Fortunately, both are attractive creatures which do not seem to be causing any problems.

Changes in classification status and names

The whole issue of bird names and, especially the defining of species-boundaries, is a highly controversial area and one in which the exigencies of fashion sometimes seem to play at least as big a part as the objective analysis of evidence. We have followed recent practice here in recognising the splitting of Mediterranean Shearwater into two species: Balearic Shearwater (*Puffinus mauretanicus*) and Levantine Shearwater (*P yelkouan*), the separation of the Mediterranean form of Great Grey Shrike into a separate species, Southern Grey Shrike (*Lanius meridionalis*), and the similar elevation of Iberian Chiffchaff to full species status (*Phylloscopus brehmii*).

The vernacular names used in this book remain those which will be familiar to all. The only changes from the first edition, apart from the above, are Little Buttonquail (for Andalusian Hemipode), Red-knobbed Coot (for Crested Coot) and Zitting Cisticola (for Fan-tailed Warbler). We retain Rufous Bush Chat (instead of Rufous Bush Robin), purely on grounds of personal preference.

HOW TO USE THIS BOOK

The core of the book is the site accounts but we hope that you will find the preliminary chapters helpful in planning your visits. They describe the area and its birds. The Systematic List (p. 316) gives the status of all the species which occur with any regularity in the region. It is the principal reference for those widespread species which do not often receive a mention in the site accounts. The index is cross-referenced with the site accounts to help you to track down those species which are likely to be of particular interest to you. For example, to see White-headed Ducks you can look up that species in the index and find a reference to all those sites where they regularly occur. Rarities do turn up and 'Rare birds in Southern Spain' (p. 338) is an account of the vagrants which have been recorded so far; needless to say, new ones are added every year.

In many ways, southern Spain is one big birding site. Certainly you do not have to travel far to find a great deal of interest, especially if the Mediterranean region is new to you. Almost every town seems to have its rooftop population of White Storks and Lesser Kestrels, not to mention legions of screaming swifts. A drive through the countryside reveals Bee-eaters, Woodchat Shrikes, Zitting Cisticolas and many others. By British standards especially, birds of prey are everywhere: Montagu's Harriers quarter the fields and soaring Griffon Vultures and other large raptors are omnipresent. Still, there is a lot more to see and we have tried to provide a dossier of the principal sites of the area, selecting those which we know are accessible and can be relied upon to provide the main regional specialities. We also suggest areas which are likely to repay closer investigation but for which there is less information available. Southern Spain is both fun and rewarding to explore and there remains a great deal of scope for birding in little known corners of both Andalucía and Extremadura.

PROVINCE CHAPTERS

Site accounts are grouped by provinces into ten chapters. Each province chapter has an introductory section giving, in order, a brief description of the province, a list of the sites with their code numbers, general information and useful addresses, a summary of relevant maps, an outline of access to the province and advice on where to stay. A map shows the position of individual sites within the province, in relation to main towns and access roads, for ease of location.

The sites themselves are coded by letters and numbers. The former are the national provincial abbreviations, which are:

Andalucía (8 provinces): Huelva (H), Sevilla (SE), Cádiz (CA), Córdoba (CO), Málaga (MA), Granada (GR), Jaén (J) and Almeria (AL).

Extremadura (2 provinces): Cáceres (CC) and Badajoz (BA).

Gibraltar is treated separately (p. 308).

Map 1 shows the locations of the provinces of Andalucía and Extremadura in relation to the Iberian peninsula as a whole.

The provincial abbreviations appear on local vehicle number plates so a useful rule-of-thumb is that you have arrived in a particular province when most of the cars show the relevant letters.

Map 1: Provinces of Andalucía and Extremadura with Gibraltor
AL (Almería), BA (Badajoz), CA (Cádiz), CC (Cáceres), CO (Córdoba),
GR (Granada), H (Huelva), J (Jaén), MA (Málaga), SE (Sevilla)

SITE ACCOUNTS

Each site account gives the following information.

Site map

Showing the main features of the site, and the access roads and paths. The map scales should be noted carefully. The smaller wetland sites have smaller-scale maps. The extensive sites covering the plains and mountains (sierras) are necessarily drawn on a larger scale.

Key to maps

	towns, villages and built-up areas		water
	autovías/motorways		marsh
	1st class road (eg. N-340)		trees
	2nd class road (eg. EX-330)		reeds
	country roads/tracks		cliffs
---	paths		sierra/mountain range
---	reserve boundary		mirador/lookout point
		P	parking

13

Site description

The principal structural and botanical features of the area.

Species

The major bird species typical of the site. Species of other wildlife are also mentioned briefly where appropriate.

Timing

The best times of year to visit and any other factors to consider.

Access

How to get to, enter and explore the site.

Calendar

The main bird species are listed under all or some of the following headings: all year, breeding season, winter, passage periods. 'All year' often means 'Resident' but for some species (Red Kite, Crag Martin etc.) there is actually a great deal of turnover among the populations involved. The lists are sometimes extensive but they are not exhaustive. In particular, they usually omit species such as Woodchat Shrike, Stonechat and Corn Bunting, which are widespread and common throughout southern Spain.

VISITING SOUTHERN AND WESTERN SPAIN

The region is such a well-known holiday destination that there are literally dozens of published tour guides offering ample, and usually reliable, advice on planning a visit. You may wish to obtain a recent edition of the *Guide Michelin* or one of its many surrogates; public libraries often have copies. Such a guide provides far more information on hotels, prices and general holiday information than we can include here, although we can offer some general guidelines. Best of all, the Internet is a invaluable tool to planning and booking a holiday and we advise on key websites below.

PLANNING YOUR VISIT

This book can be used in a variety of ways, depending on the nature of your visit or, indeed, if you live in the region. As far as visitors are concerned, there are two main options:

Touring
This is the best option for a birding holiday. Most touring birders fly to a suitable airport (see below) and then travel widely in a hired car, staying at a variety of hotels. Clearly, the amount of time available will dictate what is feasible. An idealised two-week trip, with a good chance of producing 200 or more species and all or most of the regional specialities, would involve flying to western Andalucía in late April or early May. From here you would spend three or four days visiting sites in Cádiz, including at least one day watching raptor migration at Gibraltar or Tarifa, four or five days based at Doñana and visiting that area, and then five or six days in Extremadura visiting the best sites of both provinces.

The key sites to include on such an itinerary are: **Gibraltar**; **Cadiz province**: Tarifa (CA1 & CA2), La Janda (CA4), Sierra de la Plata (CA5), Ojén valley (CA6), Laguna de Medina (CA15), East bank of the Río Guadalquivir (CA17) and Grazalema (CA19); **Sevilla province**: Brazo del Este (SE1 — whatever you do don't miss this one!); **Huelva Province**: Doñana (H5) and Odiel (H4); **Badajoz province**: Western Sierras (BA2), La Serena (BA9), Northeastern rice fields (BA10) and Eastern Badajóz reservoirs (BA11); **Cáceres province**: Cáceres-Trujillo steppes (CC3), Las Villuercas (CC4), Valle del Jerte (CC8) and (also not to be missed) Monfragüe (CC6)

Centre-based visits
This is the option for those who have a family in tow or who simply don't want to drive very far. Most typical family holidays will be based on the coastal resorts but many of these are well placed for visiting a wide range of sites.

Almería can be very interesting and Roquetas de Mar makes a very good centre. Direct flights and package tours are available to here. From Roquetas you are within three hours of all the Almería sites as well as

the eastern end of the Sierra Nevada (Granada). The centre is accordingly well placed for seeing waders, seabirds and steppe species, including
the 'desert' specialities such as Dupont's Larks and Trumpeter Finches.

The section of the Costa del Sol between Málaga and Almería, for
example the resort of Nerja, is not recommended as a base, although it
provides good access for the Sierra Nevada. Wetlands are particularly
lacking here.

The western Costa del Sol, from Torremolinos south to Gibraltar, is a
much better base. Even from Torremolinos you are within a three-hour
drive of parts of Cádiz, such as Tarifa and La Janda, the southern Córdoba lakes and most of the Málaga sites. Inland resorts to consider in
this sector are Ronda, Benaoján, Grazalema and Jimena, all of which
are good centres for walking holidays.

Gibraltar itself is an excellent base and provides easy access to all the
sites in Cádiz province and most of those in Málaga province. The border
can be an obstacle since queues may build up there during busy periods.
However, leaving Gibraltar in the mornings and returning in the evenings
is usually straightforward; the commuters are heading in the opposite
direction then. Gibraltar is a particularly good site for raptor and seabird
watching. (It is also the ONLY place in our entire region where you can
get a decent cup of tea; be warned, the Spanish offerings in this respect
are unspeakably awful — tea addicts, bring your own with you.)

The Atlantic coast of Cádiz has comparatively few hotels and is only
served directly by a few package tour companies but it is rapidly gain-
ing in popularity. A base at Zahara de los Atunes has all the essentials
for a sun, sea and sand family holiday in abundance (and no raucous
night-life) and is on the shore of the Strait itself, within easy striking
range of all of Cádiz province and Sevilla as well. The airports at Gibraltar and Jerez provide access to the area.

The Huelva coast has more hotels and, naturally, the Doñana area is
an obvious base for a birding holiday. Matalascañas offers the usual sea-
side amenities but is also an excellent centre for touring the area.

It is obviously possible to establish a base-camp at any of the inland
localities but none of these would prove a good choice for family holidays. A single-base visit to Extremadura could be organised around an
hotel in Mérida, Cáceres or Trujillo. You would need to fly to Madrid or
Sevilla first.

INTERNET BIRDING IN SOUTHERN AND WESTERN SPAIN

Seasoned travellers will have discovered long ago that there is no better
preliminary to foreign travel these days than to indulge in a spot of surf-
ing on the internet. A little judicious searching will mean that you arrive
at your destination very well briefed. You may also have booked your
travel and all your accommodation on-line. Where birding is concerned, many sites offer maps, pictures of the birds themselves and
even live images via webcams. So, if you really want to, you can do all
your birding from the comfort of your own home and never trouble to
set foot in Spain or wherever at all! The chances are though that your
appetite will have been whetted and you will be all the keener to visit.

Websites are forever being changed and updated. New ones appear
and others drift away into the void of cyberspace. All the addresses

given here were active (i.e. working) in 2000. Your search engines should help you to re-establish links with any sites which become elusive in future.

The sites considered here are those which may help to make your visit to our area more interesting or complete. They are all among those which we have made use of recently ourselves. We haven't been paid or bribed (alas) to include any of them and of course we are not responsible for the accuracy or otherwise of their content. The selection is very far from being exhaustive, as a search with a keyword such as 'Doñana' will quickly reveal.

General travel arrangements (flight booking, car hire etc.)

Ever more sites do this, including the airlines' own websites. A useful service is Expedia (www.expedia.co.uk).

Searching for information

We all have our favourite search engines but we like Copernic 2000, which makes use of 15 or more search engines all at once. Download the free software from www.copernic.com.

Accommodation

Hotels and other accommodation can easily be located, inspected and often booked on-line. There are a number of sites which allow you to enter the name of a town or village and see a list of all the available hostelries. Details of each place, including the tariffs, can then be viewed and a booking made by email or telephone. We recommend:

For Andalucía and Extremadura, www.hotelsearch.com; general site, in English, www.parador.es; homepage for the Paradores, providing better class accommodation. Gives details and on-line reservation facilitiies.

For Andalucía, Turandalucía is a very professional-looking site with optional English text as well as Spanish; www.turandalucia.com (omit the accent in Andalucía when contacting site).

For Extremadura, Alex Vende Turismo, www.alextur.net. Email info@ alextur.net. An excellent site and highly recommended. In Spanish (but probably intelligible to English speakers). Booking is free, by email, and the customer service is first-rate. An English-language version is planned.

General tourist information

Accommodation apart, many sites provide information about tourist attractions, ranging from sites of historic interest to such trivia as beaches and theme parks, and also such essential information as lists of restaurants, city plans and road maps. They include:

Andalucía Tourism (www.andalucia.com)
Extremadura Naturalmente (www.turismoextremadura.com)
Gibraltar Tourist Board (www.gibraltar.gi)
Andalucían Environment Agency/Consejería de Medio Ambiente (www.cma.junta-andalucia.es)
Extremaduran Environment Agency/Consejería de Medio Ambiente (www.juntaex.es)

Weather

It's always useful to know what the weather may be doing and the five-day forecasts offered by Yahoo Weather (http://weather.yahoo.com) are often a good place to check.

Birds and birding

All of the following sites provide useful, relevant information. Most of them have versions in English as well as Spanish.

Sociedad Española de Ornitología (www.seo.org). The Spanish Ornithological Society's website provides a great deal of information about the Society and its activities as well as links to kindred organisations. Useful pages on this site include 'El Escribano Digital': SEO/birdlife's online bulletin board with details of current issues and activities; 'Programa Migres': about the autumn raptor counting programme at the Strait of Gibraltar, with on-line registration for would-be participants; 'Medmaravis': the Mediterranean Seabird Group; 'Rarezas': the Rarities Committee site, including the proforma for submitting details of rare birds; and 'Listas', the Spanish bird list.

The postal address of the society is SEO/BirdLife, C/Melquiades Biencinto 34, 28053, Madrid (email: seo@seo.org).

ADENEX (http://mastercom.bme.es/adenex). Website of la Asociación para la Defensa de la Naturaleza y los Recursos de Extremadura. Extensive and informative. It includes an English version which EG recently revised on the Society's behalf.

Gibraltar Ornithological and Natural History Society (www.gibnet.gi/~gonhs). Information on birds and other wildlife of Gibraltar. Bird news is updated fairly regularly. Includes details of how to book accommodation in the Upper Rock nature reserve and bird observatory.

Balearic Shearwater site (www.life-puffinus.org). Specifically devoted to the on-going studies of both Balearic and Levantine Shearwaters, with good identification guidelines and pictures.

Rare birds in Spain (www.terra.es/personal3/gutarb/). Essential reading for news and often photographs of recent rarities from throughout Spain. Updated very frequently by rarities committee member Ricard Gutiérrez. In English.

Delta del Llobregat (www.gencat.es/mediamb/rndelta). There are many good sites of birding interest from parts of Spain outside our area. This one is so good that we urge you to have a look at it, even though the delta itself is in Catalonia. It includes some lovely photographs, whose number is ever increasing. You can also download the latest version of the Spanish national bird list, complete with A, B, C and D category indications and both Spanish and English names. Rarities Committee member Ricard Gutiérrez is also a driving force behind this site.

Avesforum. The newsgroup used by Spanish birders in Spain. In Spanish of course but, if you can read it, this is an excellent way of getting tuned-in to current news and concerns. Avesforum is run by SEO/BirdLife and is accessed via their website (see above) which tells you how to subscribe.

Birdwatch Spain. An English-language newsgroup about Spanish birds. Postings tend to be rather sparse compared with Avesforum however. Contact birdwatch-spain-owner@egroups.com

MAPS

In general our own maps are sufficient to guide your access to the various sites. You will need to inspect the provincial header map, at the start of each chapter, perhaps in conjunction with a published road map, to establish the exact location of the sites covered. A large-scale road map (*Firestone, Michelin* or equivalents) is essential to give an overview of your journey. Best of all is the official road atlas — *Mapa Oficial de Carreteras* — published by the Spanish Ministry of Information. The latest version can be purchased from any bookshop (Librería) or large newsagent anywhere in Spain. The 2000 edition costs 2,300 ptas (£9). The atlas maps are excellent and up-to-date and there are legends in English and French.

We also recommend the maps issued by the Spanish publisher Plaza & Janes, which can be obtained from most sizable book stores in Spain. The relevant ones are *Andalucía*, which also includes southern Extremadura, and *Madrid-Centro*, which covers most of Extremadura except the far west. Equivalents to the Plaza & Janes maps and obtainable at British bookshops are maps published by Geocenter International in their Euromap series. The relevant ones are Spain 7/8: *Costa del Sol and Andalucía*, and Spain 5: *Central Spain*. The Official Atlas, the Euromaps and the Plaza & Janes maps are all on a scale of 1:300,000.

The maps in this book are designed to meet the requirements of visitors. However, regulars and residents will know that by far the best maps are the single-province maps produced by the Instituto Geografico Nacional (I.G.N.) in Madrid, on a scale of 1:200.000 or 2 km: 1 cm. You will wish to obtain those covering the provinces which you visit frequently or extensively. Like all maps, however, even these are sometimes slightly out of date and fail to show the new roads, especially the motorways (autovías) which have been opening like sunflowers recently.

Provincial maps apart, the I.G.N. also publishes a few special maps, on a scale of 1:50.000, of the Doñana area, Odiel, Bahía de Cádiz, Montes de Málaga, Sierra Nevada, Grazalema and Cabo de Gata, all of which are extremely detailed and very highly recommended.

The Province maps and the others are obtainable in Britain from Edward Stanford Ltd. Current maps may be in stock but delivery may take six to ten weeks if they need to be ordered specially. The address is: Edward Stanford Ltd, 12–14 Long Acre, LONDON, WC2E 9LP (tel: 0207-836-1321/Fax: 0207-836-0189).

The I.G.N. maps may also be obtained in Spain from the following: Centro Nacional de Información Geográfica, c/. General Ibañez de Ibero 3, 28071 MADRID (fax ex UK: 010-34-15532913), and La Tienda Verde, Maudes 23 y 38, 28003 MADRID (fax ex UK: 010-34-1533.6454).

An additional source of information are the *Guías Prácticas* (Practical Guides) to the Natural Parks produced by the Consejería de Medio Ambiente (environment agency) C.M.A. These are free leaflets incorporating a map and a fund of useful information and addresses, the latter including hotels and campsites. The text is in English, French and German, as well as Spanish. The Guías Practicas can usually be obtained in the information offices in the Parques Naturales and also from the Consejería de Medio Ambiente in both Andalucía and Extremadura. The latter is best contacted via its web addresses (see above) since its reputation for response to snail-mail is a conspicuous endorsement of that charming sobriquet for the postal services. ADENEX provides ample information on Extremadura with its excellent website (see above) and its own information leaflets.

WHEN TO COME

All times of year are of interest. However, spring (March–May) is generally best for seeing a wide range of species. Visits in early spring (March–April) allow you to find many of the wintering species as well as some of the arriving migrants. The attractions of springtime include the birdsong, which can be spectacular and also makes it much easier to find passerines, the aerial displays of raptors, which make species such as Goshawks much more visible than usual, and the splendid displays of wild flowers.

Summer (June–August) has the disadvantages of high temperatures, dried-up lakes and large numbers of tourists along the coasts but there is still plenty to see at most sites.

Autumn (September–November) is a pleasant season, especially once the rains arrive. There are plenty of birds, including migrants, although these are not as visible as in spring.

Winter (December–February) has the attraction of the wintering species, including great numbers of Cranes, raptors and waterfowl, although summer visitors are naturally then absent.

The amount of daylight available varies significantly according to the season and is of obvious importance. Spain and Gibraltar run on Central European Time: GMT plus 1 hour in winter and GMT plus 2 hours in summer. In summer, birding is possible from about 6 am to 10 pm local time. In winter the days are noticeably longer than in northern Europe; birding is possible from about 8 am until 6 pm, local time.

WHAT TO WEAR

We realise that birders are not trend-setters in the world of sartorial elegance. What you wear is largely up to you but sombre colours are obviously a good idea. Our main purpose here is to caution against assuming that the weather is always sweltering in southern Spain. It often is but, then again, it is often literally freezing cold.

Visitors in summer will get away with light clothing, although a sweatshirt or cardigan is useful when seawatching or when visiting high mountains. At other times of year it is necessary to pack some warm clothing, especially when visiting inland and mountain sites. Winter can be very cold, with frost and snow in many areas away from the coast. Hence, Barbour jackets and their equivalents will be invaluable, not least because the cooler times of year are often very wet as well. In general, you can rely on hot weather anywhere between June and September but you should be prepared for something cooler at other times of year.

GETTING THERE

By air

Many visitors travel by air, either to take advantage of one of the many relatively inexpensive one-centre package holidays or as a preliminary to touring the country in a hire-car. Package holidays are mainly centred on Malaga (for the Costa del Sol) and Almería and often involve charter flights. Scheduled flights are also available to these destinations as well as to Sevilla, Jerez and Gibraltar. Madrid is also a handy starting point for a visit to Extremadura, an easy four-hour drive from Madrid airport. Flights originate from many parts of Europe, including all the main British airports.

As ever, scheduled flights, although more expensive, have certain advantages over charters: roomier planes, greater punctuality and more sociable hours of travel. Charters are cheaper but be prepared for last-minute changes in flight times. Perhaps the best available value is that provided by the low-cost airlines, such as Easyjet, Go and Buzz, which serve Málaga, Almería and Jerez between them.

By car

A car is not absolutely essential for enjoying southern Spain; you can spend enjoyable visits walking in the Serranía de Ronda or just sitting and watching migration at Gibraltar, for example. It is, however, impossible to visit many of the sites in this book without using a vehicle and you would be severely limited in your options without one.

Flying out and hiring a car is probably the best strategy for the short-term visitor. Car-hire is available at all the airports and resorts but it often pays to make arrangements beforehand through a travel agency. Visitors from Britain have a choice of UK-based companies which will

Map 2: Routes to Andalucía and Extremadura from the rest of Spain

arrange car-hire at very competitive rates. Unlimited-mileage rental is the norm and is essential; you will probably cover many hundreds of miles in a week or so. Hiring a car avoids the cost of travelling to Spain by road and saves your own vehicle from the undoubted wear-and-tear of a birding holiday. British visitors will also avoid the risks of driving a right-hand drive car on the Continent.

If you do come in your own vehicle, several choices are on offer. Travellers from Britain will find that the easiest option is to take the ferries from Plymouth to Santander or from Portsmouth to Bilbao. Otherwise you can drive down through France, taking in the Pyrenées on the way if desired. Map 2 provides a route guide for access to the region.

For travellers from Santander, the quickest way to reach Extremadura is to drive south as far as Burgos on the N-623 and then on to Madrid on the E-5/N-1 (393 km in total). From Bilbao, head first for Burgos on the E-805 and E-5/N-1. From Madrid take the E-90/N-V for both Cáceres and Badajoz provinces. For direct access to Andalucía from Madrid take the E-5/N-IV south as far as Córdoba and then Sevilla or turn off at Bailén for Málaga and the eastern provinces. Travellers following the Mediterranean coast from France will usually enter Andalucía on the E-15/N-340, which provides good access to all the coastal provinces, following the shoreline as far west as Cádiz.

DRIVING

Cities apart, our area offers pleasant and varied driving on often traffic-free roads. A few words of caution, however:

Roads

These are often excellent. Nowadays, even most minor roads have been very much improved, often with the assistance of extravagant European Community funding. However, since we are often guiding you off the beaten track, it is as well to be aware that such roads are often not at all good and driving on the dirt tracks mentioned in many of our site accounts is an acquired art. Common sense should suffice but remember that unsurfaced roads are gritty and slippery, needing great care when braking or cornering. Speeds should be kept down on such roads, not least because of the dust cloud which you will otherwise raise. Dirt roads are best avoided altogether in wet weather unless you have an all-terrain vehicle.

You will soon notice that ditches and roadsides generally often present a major hazard: the ditches are often deep and there are often no crash barriers to protect the unwary or unfortunate from sheer drops down precipices. If you go off the road you will stay off and, especially in the mountains, the experience can easily prove terminal. All the sites mentioned in this book are safely accessible, given reasonable care, but we naturally cannot accept any liability for any mishaps which may occur.

Traffic police (Guardia Civil) and driving regulations

We realise that traffic police have no friends, but they can be very helpful here and in some cases will go to considerable trouble to help stranded motorists. On the other hand, they will deal briskly with lawbreakers and they do have the power to inflict on-the-spot fines. If caught it is no use pleading ignorance of traffic regulations as they take the view that when driving on Spanish roads you should know Spanish traffic rules (even if many locals appear not to!). Note that fines, particularly for speeding, can be large (up to £500), although a 20% discount is available for prompt payment. Ask for a receipt (recibo). The traffic police usually operate in pairs on motorcycles and often use unmarked radar cars.

Several points are worth remembering to avoid any trouble.

Drinking and Driving: We need hardly say this but, quite simply, don't do it. Do not underestimate the combined effects of a little booze and a hot sun. They don't mix overly well. The police will breathalyse and a positive result could give your holiday a memorable and involuntary extension at His Majesty's pleasure, and Spanish judicial processes are s-l-o-w.

Speed Limits: Watch out for these very carefully as in some areas the police are red-hot in enforcing them. The usual speed limit is 120 kph on motorways (autovías) and 100 kph on major roads, unless otherwise shown. In towns the limits are considerably lower, usually 40–50 kph.

Turning Left: Turning left on a main road often means filtering right into a holding lane. You then cross both carriageways when these are clear. Such crossings are often controlled by traffic lights. They are indicated by Cambio de Sentido (change of direction) signs. Stopping in the centre of the road in heavy traffic is a fairly good recipe for a shunt up the stern and it will certainly earn you a cacophony of horns from irritated drivers.

Seat Belts: Use is obligatory at all times.

Traffic Lights: Some visitors have difficulty in getting accustomed to overhead traffic lights and the orange flashing warning lights which precede them. The lights themselves can be very easy to miss, particularly in bright sunlight.

Parking: Illegal parking in towns is not a good idea. The tow truck (grúa) may swoop like a marauding hawk at the slightest infringement in some areas. Similarly, stopping and parking to watch birds, even along country roads, should be undertaken with some care. Always try to pull right off the road into a farm-track entrance or similar lay-by. If there isn't a suitable place then don't stop at all.

Traffic densities

Traffic is refreshingly light by the sorry standards of northern Europe and southeast England in particular. Nevertheless, cities and their outskirts are often busy at peak periods and trunk roads may become painfully congested at holiday times, notably during the four days (Thursday–Sunday) of the Easter weekend, at Christmas, at New Year and at weekends during the summer months (July–September). The holiday travel periods, when Spaniards flock en masse to and from the coasts, are also best avoided; they comprise the middle of July and beginning and end of August especially. Traffic problems occur along the main trunk roads; country roads are not greatly affected but note that congestion occurs around particular towns and villages during their local festivals (fiestas). The 'mother of all fiestas' is probably that of El Rocío in Doñana (H5); over a million people descend on the local church in a massive outburst of religious fervour and festivities. This occurs on the seventh weekend after Easter, at Pentecost (Whitsun), and we very strongly recommend total absence during the preceding week and on the following two days. Birding is impossible.

Signs

It is always useful to know what signs mean as it could save you a great deal of trouble. The following are likely to be noticed during a birding holiday.

Entrada Prohibida/Paso Prohibido	No Entry
Incendio Prohibido	No fires
Basura Prohibida	No dumping of rubbish
Privado/Particular	Private
Camino Privado/Particular	Private road (i.e. keep out)
Coto Privado de Caza	Hunting rights reserved — usually also indicated by little rectangular signs, diagonally split black and white and often peppered with shotgun pellet holes (presumably by frustrated hunters)
Ganado Bravo	Fighting cattle (see below)

Protected areas generally have green signs headed C.M.A or A.M.A (Consejería or Agencia de Medio Ambiente — environment agency) and giving the status of the site, e.g. Reserva Natural.

NATURAL HAZARDS

The Spanish countryside is a great deal wilder than that of northern Europe and certain hazards need to be kept in mind.

Bulls: Southwest Andalucía and parts of Extremadura are the land of the fighting bull. These beasts are big (half a ton or more), remarkably rapid for their size, and boast a set and spread of horns equipped for dealing with the unexpected (you). A set of these in the wrong place could really ruin your day and would be the ultimate catharsis. The cows of the breed are every bit as nasty as the bulls, particularly if they have calves at heel. Note that fighting cattle are not necessarily black. Therefore, a strong word of warning: these animals are killers and they will kill you if they get hold of you. Never enter fenced fields containing cattle, especially if there are 'GANADO BRAVO' signs. Quite a few of the local varieties (vacas retintas) of 'ordinary' cattle also have impressive horns and should also be treated with respect, again especially if they are with their calves.

Mosquitoes: These are present in many areas year round and can be a nuisance. Fortunately malaria is not a hazard in Spain. If you are susceptible to insect-bites you would be well advised to come equipped with your favourite repellent and anti-histamine cream. The Spanish anti-histamine cream Fenergan is very effective at alleviating bites and can be obtained from any pharmacy (farmacia). Since most mosquitoes strike at night we also heartily recommend the use of anti-mosquito 'plugs'. These fit into an electrical socket and burn a repellent tablet, usually to great effect. Bring one with you or obtain one at any pharmacy or supermarket in Spain; Fogo or Evapor are common brands.

Scorpions and Spiders: There is some risk of falling foul of these, especially in rocky country. Campers may need to check clothing and footware in the morning 'just in case'.

Venomous Snakes: A few species such as Lataste's viper are venomous. Leave all snakes alone unless you are familiar with all of the local species. A rapid visit to the nearest doctor, clinic or Casa de Socorro (first-aid post)of the Cruz Roja (Red Cross) would be in order in the unlikely event of a snake-bite.

Dogs: The sheep flocks in Extremadura are accompanied by equally woolly, large, white sheep dogs, which seem to be particularly unfriendly. Elsewhere the numerous strays are generally too emaciated to pose any direct threat but they are a definite menace on the roads. They show a total lack of road sense and have a suicidal knack of turning up in the middle of the carriageway even on the busiest stretches. Drivers beware! Main roads are littered with dog corpses in various stages of mummification but there always seem to be some live ones left.

Sunburn: Sunny Spain often lives up to its name, even in midwinter. Always wear a hat and use a good sunblock to prevent sunburn or worse. Remember that the cooling effect of coastal sea-breezes may well disguise the onset of sunburn; the painful reckoning will come later. Sunglasses are a boon when driving, in snowy conditions, when birding near water and, especially, when scanning high clouds for raptors.

SECURITY

Tourist areas worldwide are a happy hunting ground for thieves but our area is no worse in this respect than most other similar regions. The cities and coastal resorts are the high-risk areas, the countryside usually being quite safe, but commonsense precautions to guard your belongings are always advisable. Pickpockets are rife in towns and theft from cars is a major hazard in built-up areas. The cities of Sevilla and Córdoba are notorious blackspots in this respect. The obvious rule is never to leave valuables unattended in vehicles, especially in full view. It is even unwise to drive through cities like Sevilla with bags or belongings on the seats; there are plenty of cases of smash-and-grab thefts by youths on motorbikes who use bricks to break windows when their target is stopped at traffic lights.

LANDSCAPE AND CLIMATE

Andalucía and Extremadura together include a broad range of terrain, habitats and climatic regimes, allowing them to accommodate an impressive range of bird species, including some not found elsewhere in Europe. Habitat characteristics are an important part of our site descriptions but there are general landscape features which we summarise here.

LANDSCAPE

The Andalucían mountains

Andalucía is dominated by the mountains of the Betic Cordillera, running northeast from the Strait to and beyond Almería. They include the Sierra Nevada, whose principal peak (Mulhacén, 3478 m) is the loftiest in Spain. In the west many of these ranges are heavily wooded, with extensive forests of cork oak and pine. The harvesting of cork is of great importance both economically and from the point of view of conservation. The trunks are stripped every seven years or so, revealing the bright red inner bark. Between times the forests are largely undisturbed and shelter a thriving community of passerines, raptors and other wildlife. The drier eastern ranges are relatively barren, as are the highest tops. The many cliffs and the gorges along watercourses provide secure nest sites for raptors and others. To the north of the Guadalquivir, the older mountains of the Sierra Morena, also extensively wooded, separate Andalucía from Extremadura and Castilla la Nueva (La Mancha).

The Atlantic coastlands

The coast running from Gibraltar westwards to the Portuguese Algarve is the Costa de la Luz (Coast of Light). The Atlantic beaches are broad and sandy, often with a backing of large and sometimes massive dunes. The tides sustain well-developed saltmarshes in the river mouths and there are extensive areas of active and abandoned salt pans, important as a habitat for waders. This coast has a succession of noteworthy wetland habitats, ranging from scattered small freshwater lagoons to the large inlets and marismas of the Huelva coast, most notably those of the Coto Doñana. All these are of the greatest interest and importance ornithologically. Forests of maritime pines and stone pines are characteristic and there are areas of heathland and low scrub, including the palmetto scrub dominated by the dwarf fan palm. Much of the hinterland is cultivated; orange and olive groves are characteristic of the region. The Costa de la Luz is better preserved than the Costa del Sol despite having superior beaches. Strong winds are a factor discouraging greater touristic exploitation.

The Mediterranean coastlands

The Costa del Sol (Sun Coast) runs from Gibraltar eastwards to Cabo de Gata (Almería), where you turn the corner into the southern part of the Costa Blanca (White Coast — not apparently a reference to the initial condition of northern sun-seekers!). The coastal strip is familiar as a notorious tourist trap and there are certainly lengthy stretches of extensive development ranging from the tasteful to the unspeakably awful. Until the 1960s the beaches were largely inhabited by Kentish Plovers but these have had to give way to the hordes of visitors and new residents who have colonised the area.

The mountains sweep down very close to the coast but there are stretches where alluvial deposits in the river mouths have produced the fertile and intensively cultivated, if narrow, coastal plain. The central portion of the Costa del Sol lacks the coastal plain and large beaches. Here the mountains reach the sea as high cliffs.

Conditions become progressively more arid as one moves east until in Almería there are areas of true steppe and semi-desert. Tidal activity is limited in the Mediterranean and the beaches are relatively narrow. Unlike on the Atlantic shore, wetland habitats are relatively few but there are some interesting small estuaries and important expanses of salt pans.

The river valleys

Three important rivers, the Tajo (Tagus), Guadiana and Guadalquivir cross the area. The Guadalquivir valley is the main feature of the plain of Andalucía, the broad fertile lowlands which flank the river from the Atlantic eastwards across the provinces of Sevilla, Córdoba and Jaén. Water is at a premium in Spain and the valleys are intensively cultivated. Irrigation schemes extend the influence of the rivers across a wide region and natural habitats are limited. Nevertheless, dams have created new wetlands, especially in Extremadura, and a number of important freshwater lagoons also occur.

Minor watercourses abound although many of these, especially in eastern Andalucía, are seasonal and completely dry for months on end. Heavy rains in the mountains, including summer thunderstorms, can produce unexpected and sometimes dangerous flash flooding in even the driest-looking stream beds. The watercourses often hold concentrations of breeding birds, notably colonies of egrets and Bee-eaters and numbers of Nightingales, Cetti's Warblers, Olivaceous Warblers and other passerines.

The Extremaduran plateau

Extremadura is the western part of the central Spanish plateau. Much of the area is gently undulating country with more mountainous areas to the east (Sierras de Guadalupe) and to the north (Sierra de Gredos, just outside the region). Cultivation of the Iberian holm oak or encina is characteristic of the sierras here. The trees are a source of animal fodder, the acorns especially being a staple of the numerous pig herds.

The large expanses of open country are barren and steppe-like, with huge areas of rough pasture interspersed with cereal fields. The remaining natural vegetation is, strictly speaking, a garrigue or low Mediterranean scrub. True steppe, such as is found in Almería and other areas of minimal rainfall (below 300 mm annually), is lacking in Extremadura but the plains still attract a thriving community of bustards, sandgrouse and other steppe birds.

CLIMATE

Southern Spain has a Mediterranean climate with hot, dry summers and mild, wet winters, but there are important variations in temperature and rainfall across the region. In addition, the rains themselves are not always reliable and some recent years have seen prolonged droughts (sequías) with only a fraction of the normal rainfall and serious consequences for wetland habitats especially (not to mention for crops and drinking water supplies).

The Atlantic region has the mildest temperature regime: summer daytime temperatures on the Huelva and Cádiz coasts reach 28°C, cooling by a few degrees at night. The Mediterranean coastlands are several degrees warmer than the Atlantic shores in summer. In winter, all the coastal regions are extremely mild with average daytime temperatures above 10°C and a virtual absence of frost or snow. Almería is the warmest part of southern Spain in winter, with mean temperatures averaging 18°C. Inland in Andalucía temperatures are more extreme. Sevilla and Córdoba in the Guadalquivir valley are notoriously hot in summer, regularly achieving maximum temperatures over 40°C. Away from the coasts in winter, the days are cool and frosts are not uncommon, especially in eastern Andalucía.

Most rain arrives from the Atlantic and is deposited on the western Andalucían mountains. The result is the relative lushness of Huelva and Cádiz provinces and the extreme dryness of eastern Andalucía, with semi-arid conditions in southeastern Almería. Grazalema (Cádiz), in the western part of the Serranía de Ronda, has a massive annual rainfall of 2000 mm (nearly 80 inches), the highest in Spain. In contrast, Cabo de Gata (Almería), in the rain-shadow of the Sierra Nevada, receives only some 200 mm (under 8 inches), the lowest annual rainfall of anywhere in Europe.

Extremadura is drier than western Andalucía and often hotter in summer, when daytime temperatures regularly exceed 35°C and occasionally rise above 40°C. Nights are some 10°C cooler. Winters in Extremadura average below 10°C during the day and nights are cold, with frequent frosts.

Temperatures drop rapidly with altitude and the higher mountain ranges are snow-capped in winter. Snow also affects intermediate ranges, such as the Serranía de Ronda, during cold snaps. Some snow lingers in hollows on the north side of the Sierra Nevada throughout the summer.

CLIMATE AND BIRDS

The climate of southern Spain (and the relatively limited application of pesticides) encourages invertebrate life and the wide range of insectivorous birds dependent on it. Spring comes early in southern Andalucía, where Swallows lay their first clutches in February. The hot dry summers do affect birds however, especially aquatic species which have to fledge their young and move on before their breeding lagoons dry up in the annual drought. Very dry years may mean a complete failure of nesting by the Flamingos at Fuente de Piedra, for example.

The mild winters of the coastal lowlands make them attractive to many species at that time. There are enough flying insects to support

Crag Martins, and even some Swallows and House Martins, in winter in western Andalucía. Large numbers of larks, pipits, thrushes, warblers and finches winter in southern Spain and there are notable populations then of Greylag Geese, other waterfowl, Cranes and waders.

Wind has an important influence on birds, especially in the coastal regions. It must be taken into account by anyone hoping to see the migrations of storks and raptors in the Gibraltar area; in general, these happen at the downwind end of the Strait. Broadly speaking, westerly winds (vientos de poniente) dominate in winter and easterlies (vientos de levante) in summer. Westerly and southwesterly gales bring seabirds onshore along the Huelva coast, especially in winter and early spring. They also force seabirds into the Mediterranean through the Strait. The easterly winds blow down the Mediterranean coast usually as a result of anticyclonic weather over Iberia. These easterlies get stronger as they approach the Strait where they can blow with some ferocity (reaching force 10+) for days on end. Levanter conditions during migration periods often cause passerines and other migrants to descend in droves along the coasts. These falls of migrants are especially likely if easterly winds are accompanied by rain or thunderstorms.

BIRDS AND OTHER WILDLIFE OF
SOUTHERN AND WESTERN SPAIN

BIRDS

Southern Spain offers many special bird species. It is a key place — and in some cases the only place — in Europe in which to find Marbled Duck, White-headed Duck, Black-shouldered Kite, Spanish Imperial Eagle, Barbary Partridge, Little Button-quail (Andalusian Hemipode; if you are exceptionally fortunate!), Purple Gallinule, Red-knobbed Coot, Lesser Crested Tern, Black-bellied Sandgrouse, Red-necked Nightjar, White-rumped Swift, Little Swift, Black Wheatear, Iberian Chiffchaff, Azure-winged Magpie, Spotless Starling, Common Waxbill, Red Avadavat and Trumpeter Finch. In addition, the region provides ample opportunities to see Squacco Heron, Black Stork, Black Vulture, Little Bustard, Great Bustard, Slender-billed Gull, Audouin's Gull, Gull-billed Tern, Pin-tailed Sandgrouse, Great Spotted Cuckoo, Dupont's Lark, Lesser Short-toed Lark, Thekla Lark, Rufous Bush Chat, Olivaceous Warbler and Southern Grey Shrike, all of which have a restricted range in other parts of Europe.

The rich bird communities of the region result from the combination of the strategic location and extensive favourable habitats. Details of all the species which occur are in the Systematic List (p. 316). Many species can be seen all year round but there is a great deal of movement affecting the populations of these nominally resident birds. Waterbirds, such as Greater Flamingos and White-headed Ducks, move around as and when their regular haunts dry up. Mountain raptors, such as Bonelli's and Golden Eagles, often hunt in the adjacent lowlands in winter. There are some species, as diverse as Mallards, Common Buzzards and Blackcaps, where the large breeding population is greatly increased by individuals from northern Europe during migration times and in winter. In addition, there are a number of species which make the usual definitions of 'resident' or 'winter visitor' more or less meaningless. Such itinerant birds typically leave southern Spain for Africa as soon as they finish nesting but they return with the arrival of the winter rains. White Storks are a classic example of this: most of them cross the Strait to Africa in July and August but they return in numbers from November onwards. Similar movements are carried out by Lesser Kestrels, many Hoopoes, Great Spotted Cuckoos and significant numbers of Barn Swallows and House Martins. Among the conventional migrants, some return very early in the year: Black Kites, Egyptian Vultures, Short-toed Eagles, Pallid Swifts and Subalpine Warblers seen in February are usually new arrivals and not wintering birds.

Resident species
Typical residents include Little and Cattle Egrets, many White Storks, Spoonbills, Greater Flamingos, White-headed Ducks, 13 raptor species among which Griffon and Black Vultures are especially obvious, Eagle Owls and numerous passerines, among which special mention can be made of Calandra Larks, Thekla Larks, Crag Martins, Stonechats, Black

Wheatears, Blue Rock Thrushes, Cetti's Warblers, Zitting Cisticolas, Crested Tits, Short-toed Treecreepers, Southern Grey Shrikes, Azure-winged Magpies, Red-billed Choughs, Ravens, Spotless Starlings, Spanish Sparrows, Rock Sparrows, Serins, Cirl Buntings, Rock Buntings and Corn Buntings. The steppe-like habitats of Extremadura have a typical community which includes Great Bustards, Little Bustards, Stone Curlews, Black-bellied Sandgrouse and Pin-tailed Sandgrouse, with Dupont's Larks and Trumpeter Finches in the true steppes of Almería.

Wintering species

In winter (loosely defined as November to February) there are notable concentrations of waterfowl, including internationally significant numbers of Greylag Geese in Doñana. Resident raptors are joined by Hen Harriers and Merlins and, locally, Ospreys. Waders and gulls winter in large numbers along the coasts where there are also significant local concentrations of Common Scoters, Caspian Terns and Sandwich Terns. Extremadura is a major wintering zone for Cranes; over 40,000 are regularly present then. The conspicuous wintering passerines include very large numbers of Skylarks, Meadow Pipits, White Wagtails, Song Thrushes, Blackcaps, Common Chiffchaffs, Starlings and finches. Penduline Tits are also widespread at this season.

Summer visitors

These are the species which breed in Andalucía or Extremadura but which spend the winter in Africa. Some, such as Black Kites and Barn Swallows, return as early as February. Most are back by April but a few, such as White-rumped Swifts, do not appear until May. Departures begin from July onwards and few individuals are seen after late October, although there are quite a number of records of occasional wintering by such species. The typical 'summer' visitors include Little Bitterns, Purple Herons, Black Storks, Black Kites, Short-toed Eagles, Montagu's Harriers, Booted Eagles, Hobbies, Quails, Collared Pratincoles, Little Ringed Plovers, most terns, Turtle Doves, Cuckoos, Scops Owls, nightjars, swifts, Bee-eaters, Rollers, Short-toed Larks, Tawny Pipits, Rufous Bush Chats, Nightingales, Black-eared Wheatears, Rock Thrushes, many warblers, flycatchers, Golden Orioles, Woodchat Shrikes and Ortolan Buntings.

Passage migrants

Bird migration is a prominent feature of southern Spain and it occurs in some form in every month of the year. Northern European populations wintering in Africa cross the region twice annually and seabird movements are prominent along the coasts and through the Strait. The enormous numbers of birds which occur as summer or winter visitors also contribute prominently to the migratory movements of the region. Visible migration is the highlight of the Gibraltar area but is often seen elsewhere. Wetlands especially attract a steady turnover of ducks and waders on migration.

Apart from those species which are represented by breeding or wintering populations, the typical migrants include Honey Buzzards, Little Stints, Curlew Sandpipers, phalaropes, Pomarine Skuas, Lesser Crested Terns, Tree Pipits, Whinchats, Grasshopper Warblers, Sedge Warblers, Wood Warblers and Willow Warblers. In addition, there is an extensive and ever-lengthening list of vagrants (see p. 338), all of which are strays from their normal ranges.

THE BIRDWATCHING CALENDAR FOR ANDALUCÍA AND EXTREMADURA

July Tarifa: White Stork southward migration begins. Strait: westward movement of Audouin's Gulls and Gull-billed Terns. Passage waders.

August Strait: southward passage of White Storks and raptors, mainly Black Kites. Westward passage of Audouin's Gulls. Black Tern passage along coasts. Black Stork flocks at Extremaduran reservoirs.

September Strait: main passage month for raptors and Black Storks. Migrants widespread generally. First wintering seabirds arrive.

October Strait: passage of Red Kites, Griffon Vultures, Hen Harriers and Buzzards, as well as finches and other passerines. Balearic Shearwaters re-enter Mediterranean. White-rumped Swifts depart. Waterfowl numbers increase. Lesser Crested Terns leave Mediterranean.

November Strait: small numbers of raptors crossing south. Passerine migration continues. White Storks begin to return north. Wintering seabirds obvious. Cory's Shearwaters leave Mediterranean. Cranes arrive in Extremadura. Wintering waterfowl numbers high.

December Strait: northward passage of White Storks. Wintering seabirds present. Peak numbers of most wintering species generally.

January Strait: northward passage of White Storks. Wintering seabirds present. Peak numbers of most wintering species generally. First Barn Swallows arrive.

February Strait: northward passage of White Storks, Black Kites and Short-toed Eagles begins. Hirundines and other passerines move north. Raptors displaying over breeding sites. Cranes leave Extremadura. Waterfowl numbers decline.

March Strait: northward passage of Black Kites and other raptors. Migrants generally obvious. Cory's Shearwaters and Audouin's Gulls enter Mediterranean. Gannets and other seabirds leaving winter quarters. Main arrivals of Pallid Swifts.

April Strait: large variety of raptors and Black Storks on passage north. Best month for falls of passerine migrants. Common Swifts arrive. Breeding season in full swing for most species.

May Strait: massive arrival of Honey Buzzards. Passage of Melodious Warblers, flycatchers and other late migrants. Arrival of White-rumped Swifts, Rufous Bush Chats and Olivaceous Warblers. Lesser Crested Terns enter Mediterranean. Breeding season in full swing generally.

June Strait: small numbers of raptors still arriving. Balearic Shearwaters leave Mediterranean. Breeding birds the main attraction everywhere.

OTHER ANIMALS

Invertebrates

It is quite impossible for us to do justice here to the huge diversity of terrestrial and aquatic invertebrates of the region. They range in form from the numerous dragonflies and damselflies, to the bizarre praying mantises, the lumbering rhinoceros and dung beetles, an assemblage of often large spiders, the cacophonous cicadas, the hordes of grasshoppers and crickets and the ever-present ants and flies. Special mention must be made, however, of the butterflies.

The whole of the region is a paradise for butterflies and Andalucía itself constitutes a significant reservoir for species, such as clouded yellow *Colias crocea,* which migrate to northern Europe. The variety of available habitats ensures a pleasing diversity of species and there are butterflies in all places and, at least in the warmer areas, at all seasons. The list is a long one: over 130 species, and includes some 30 species of blues alone! If you are interested you will find a copy of Chinery (1998) or some other similar fieldguide invaluable. The many striking species which are readily noticed include swallowtail *Papilio machaon,* scarce swallowtail *Iphiclides podalirius,* Spanish festoon *Zerynthia rumina,* Moroccan orange tip *Anthocaris belia,* Cleopatra *Gonepteryx cleopatra* and, perhaps the most impressive of all, two-tailed pasha *Charaxes jasius.* Painted lady *Cynthia cardui* is common and, occasionally in some springs, after suitable winters in Morocco, there are enormous invasions when great numbers cross the Strait and Sea of Alborán and move north. To be 'attacked' by territorially minded fritillaries around the head and blues around the ankles (both probably of 'unknown' species) whilst watching raptors overhead is a delightful experience.

Amphibians and reptiles

Members of these two groups are not only interesting in their own right but also important as food for many storks, herons and raptors. Waterside margins everywhere are home to quantities of frogs, notably marsh frog *Rana ridibunda,* whose strident croaking commands attention. One species, the tiny, green tree frog *Hyla meridionalis* inhabits the taller vegetation, in which it climbs adeptly. A range of newts, toads and salamanders completes the amphibian list.

Reptiles are much more widespread than amphibians, unsurprisingly given the aridity of many areas. Lizards are everywhere. They range from the sometimes massive, almost iguana-like, ocellated lizard *Lacerta lepida* — the Jolly Green Giant — which can grow up to half a metre long, down to the abundant wall lizards and geckoes. The latter are obvious at night when they emerge to haunt balconies and walls, especially those which are illuminated by electric lights and so attract insects. The southern provinces of the area are the haunt of the strictly protected Mediterranean chameleon *Chamaeleo chamaeleon.* The bizarreness of the latter is easily eclipsed by a much less obtrusive reptile, the legless and burrowing amphisbaenian *Blanus cinereus,* a worm to the uninitiated but a fully-qualified vertebrate to the discerning. Waterside margins are commonly covered in the basking bodies of terrapins; both European pond terrapin *Emys orbicularis* and stripe-necked terrapin *Mauremys caspica* occur, splashing noisily into the water when approached. Their relative, spur-thighed tortoise *Testudo graeca,* can be found lumbering through the scrub. Marine turtles also occur offshore but are seldom seen from land.

Snakes are common, as evidenced by the numbers of Short-toed Eagles. The eagles have eight species to choose from, ranging from the familiar grass snake *Natrix natrix* to the venomous Lataste's viper *Vipera latasti* and Montpellier snake *Malpolon monspessulanus,* the latter occasionally reaching impressive lengths of some two metres.

Mammals

The region is home to a substantial variety of mammals. The continued if precarious survival of wolf *Canis lupus* testifies not only to the quality of the wilderness but also to the skill which these wary creatures have in hiding themselves. You will be most unlikely to see one nor even that other local speciality, the Spanish lynx *Lynx pardina*. The otter *Lutra lutra* is common in many rivers but is again seldom seen. Small carnivores are quite frequently picked up by car headlights as they cross roads at night; the spotted ones are the genets *Genetta genetta* and the brown ones with a tuft on the tail are the Egyptian mongooses *Herpestes ichneumon*.

Herbivores are locally abundant and both red deer *Cervus elaphus* and fallow deer *Dama dama* are especially readily observed in Doñana, together with wild boars *Sus scrofa*. The Spanish ibex *Capra pyrenaica* is quite easily seen in the Andalucian mountains, notably in the Sierra de las Nieves (MA10) and the Sierra Bermeja (MA12). The mouflon or wild sheep *Ovis musimon* has been introduced locally.

The many smaller mammals include the tiniest known, Savi's pygmy shrew *Suncus etruscus*; a big one is 60 millimetres long (including 8 millimetres of tail) and 2 grammes in weight. The vagrant or Algerian hedgehog *Erinaceus algirus* occurs along the Costa del Sol at least, as does the more widespread common hedgehog *Erinaceus europaeus*. In both cases, most specimens seen are those which have failed to make a road crossing. There are moles around in areas which have soil and their hummocks can occasionally be seen. The local species is the blind mole *Talpa caeca*.

Rabbits *Oryctolagus cuniculus* and brown hares *Lepus capensis* are both reasonably common, despite heavy hunting. Red squirrels *Sciurus vulgaris* occur in pines, although the distribution appears to be very patchy. The days when it was said that a squirrel could go from the Pyrenées to Tarifa without touching the ground are long gone; the destruction by man of the original Mediterranean forests was achieved centuries ago.

Bats are common, even numerous at times in some areas. They fall into three general groups: the small or medium-sized pipistrelle types, the long-eared ones, and the big, high-flying ones which appear in the summer months. These last are noctules *Nyctalus noctula* or the even larger European free-tailed bats *Tadarida teniotis*. It is normal to see pipistrelles even during winter, when in northern Europe they would be hibernating. Then they may be seen during full daylight up to an hour after sunrise and two hours before sunset, occasionally even at midday in bright sunshine during midwinter. There are frequent records of these day-flying bats being hunted by kestrels.

Cetaceans are well represented offshore and they are a particular feature of the Strait and Bay of Gibraltar. Large pods of dolphins, chiefly common dolphins *Delphinus delphis* but also striped dolphins *Stenella coeruleoalba* and bottle-nosed dolphins *Tursiops truncatus*, are readily seen by seabird watchers from Europa Point (Gibraltar) and similar vantage points. The waters of the Strait also produce regular sightings for on-shore observers of pods of pilot whales *Globicephala melaena* and occasionally such larger species as fin whales *Balaeonoptera physalus*, sperm whales *Physeter catodon* and killer whales *Orcinus orca*.

PLANTS

The botanical diversity of the area fully merits the production of a specialist book along the lines of this one. The Iberian peninsula is one of the major plant-hunting regions of Europe and the southern portions include quantities of endemic species in such regions as the Sierra Nevada (GR1) and Cazorla (J1). Only the most single-minded of birders would fail to remark upon the spectacle of the spring flowers and many will want to identify at least some of the species involved. Although we have commented upon the vegetation of all our sites in the site descriptions, interested visitors will require a suitable fieldguide. An excellent and highly-effective introduction, with photographs of over 200 of the more obvious species, has been produced by Molesworth Allen (1993). Enthusiasts are catered for by Polunin & Smythies (1973) and Polunin (1969). The flora of Gibraltar has most recently been covered by Linares *et al.* (1996).

WATCHING SEABIRDS AND THE MIGRATION OF RAPTORS AND STORKS

General birding apart, southern Spain offers particular opportunities in two specific areas: seabird watching and seeing the impressive migration of soaring birds. The general advice here will help you to make the most of these.

WHERE TO WATCH SEABIRDS

A large part of this guide is obviously devoted to landbirds but there are also some very interesting seabirds to be observed along both the Atlantic and Mediterranean coasts of Andalucía, some of which are extremely rare in other parts of Europe. A few species of what are technically seabirds also winter in significant numbers inland, including in Extremadura.

Seawatching still has relatively few addicts in Spain, in spite of the enormous possibilities of some areas, and the only sites that have been intensively watched in our region are the Strait of Gibraltar and Málaga Bay. As a result, there is little in English about seabird observation in Iberia in general and the English summaries in *Aves Marinas de Iberia, Baleares y Canarias* (Paterson, 1997) provide the only guide in English to the regional situation of seabirds in Andalucía and Extremadura.

You can, of course, seawatch from any point on the coast between Huelva and Almería but clearly some areas, such as headlands, are

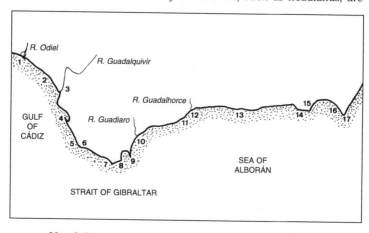

Map 3: Important seabird observation sites in Andalucía

1 Odiel estuary	7 Tarifa beach	13 Granada coast
2 Huelva coast	8 Punta Secreta	14 Punta Entinas
3 Doñana	9 Gibraltar	15 Salinas de Roquetas
4 Cádiz Bay	10 Sotogrande	16 Salinas de Cabo de
5 Cape Trafalgar	11 Benalmádena	Gata
6 Barbate estuary	12 Guadalhorce estuary	17 Cabo de Gata

rather more productive than others, although some of the bays are also good for watching resting gulls and terns. River mouths, of which there are very few, exercise a strong attraction, as do the equally few areas of standing fresh water along the coast and also the salt pans (salinas). This section highlights the more productive sites (see map 3); details of each are given in the relevant province chapter. More specific information on each species is given on p. 316–327 and in Paterson (1997).

At sea

There has been relatively little observation carried out at sea either off the Atlantic or Mediterranean shores of Andalucía, except in the western approaches to the Strait of Gibraltar and within the Strait itself. Several migrant petrels and shearwaters almost certainly occur offshore far more commonly than shore-based observations suggest. There are acceptable records of Wilson's Storm-petrels, Great Shearwaters, Sooty Shearwaters and Little Shearwaters, as well as all the skuas, within this area and especially in Atlantic waters. European Storm-petrel is common at sea. There is a possibility of finding Madeiran Storm-petrel, as there are isolated late autumn/winter records of beached birds from Huelva and Cádiz provinces.

Ferry crossings between Spain and North Africa provide opportunities for making observations at sea. One of us (EG) made over 50 crossings of the Strait between Gibraltar and Tangier in the early 1970s. These observations, as well as work by Hashmi (in Finlayson, 1992), revealed the regular presence there of a wide range of seabirds, including skuas, shearwaters, storm-petrels, auks and many of the gulls and terns, including one of the very few Iberian records of Forster's Tern. Anybody crossing the Strait from Gibraltar or Algeciras to Tangier or Ceuta would be well advised to keep a weather eye open, both for seabirds and for landbirds overhead. For birding purposes, the diagonal crossings of the Strait, Algeciras/Tangier, are best since the trip takes about 2.5 hours; the Ceuta trips are only one hour.

Ferries also serve the Spanish North-African enclave of Melilla from Málaga and Almería. These are much longer crossings, 8 hours or so. Most of the available observations from here have been made in summer, when usually the only species to be seen are a few Cory's and Balearic Shearwaters, European Storm-petrels — which are usually around fishing vessels or near cetaceans — and occasional Great Skuas, Yellow-legged Gulls and Audouin's Gulls. Winter crossings may well prove more interesting here.

Watching from ships is an acquired art. It is usually best to find an observation point towards the front of the ferry and as high up as possible. Conventional ferries are a must. Some services are provided by hydrofoils which are next to useless for seabird watching since they are too fast, too noisy, raise a lot of spray and have most of the passenger accommodation enclosed.

The Atlantic coast

The entire coast of Huelva province is most interesting, and all the region between the Portuguese border and the mouth of the Guadalquivir is worth visiting. The Odiel marshes (H4) are a notable site. In particular, the causeway (El Espigón) which runs along the west side of the river opposite Huelva city attracts thousands of gulls as well as large numbers of terns and waders, both in winter and during migration periods. The wintering community includes hundreds of Great Cormorants, dozens of Caspian Terns and some Slender-billed Gulls. Black Terns are often numerous on passage in August and September. The tip of El Espigón offers an obvious vantage point for seawatching. Wintering Caspian Terns are also a feature of the Guadiana estuary, in the far west (H1), which also attracts a good range of seabird species.

Further east, the beach at Matalascañas (H5), holds large numbers of wintering and migrant gulls and terns, including Audouin's Gulls. Offshore there are regular winter concentrations of up to 5,000 Common Scoters. The scoter flocks are worth close inspection since other sea-ducks also occur occasionally.

Within the Doñana region itself there are breeding populations of Gull-billed Terns and Slender-billed Gulls, the latter more or less resident. Both species also occur commonly across the river in the salinas at Bonanza and Trebujena (CA17) , which also attract migrant and wintering Caspian Terns.

Balearic Shearwaters

From the mouth of the Guadalquivir southwards to Tarifa, the beaches are heavily used by migrant and wintering gulls, notably Yellow-legged Gulls and Lesser Black-backed Gulls and to a lesser extent by Black-headed Gulls. There are always some wintering Mediterranean Gulls here and there is the possibility of finding scarce wintering species such as Common Gulls and Great Black-backed Gulls.

The salt pans and wetlands complex of Cádiz Bay (CA12) is important and harbours breeding colonies of Black-headed and Yellow-legged Gulls, as well as Little Terns and several species of waders. The bay itself is one of the very few areas in Andalucía where there is a good possibility, in winter, of seeing divers, normally Great Northern and Red-throated Divers and occasionally also Black-throated Divers. It also holds a wintering flock of up to 200 Great Crested Grebes. Cape Trafalgar (CA10) has some potential for seawatching even though the Cape itself is rather low and the light is against you in the afternoons. AP has seen Great Shearwaters here and Audouin's Gulls occur regularly. Further south, at Barbate (CA10), there is a large colony of Yellow-legged Gulls on the cliffs, and the beaches and the tidal mudflats along the river, together with the rubbish tip to the south of the town, attract enormous numbers of gulls, especially in winter.

Audouin's Gulls turn up with ever-increasing frequency near the Strait. The best site on the Atlantic coast to see them is Tarifa beach (CA1), which is a must at any time of year. This same site is also one of the likely places to see Lesser Crested Terns, which may appear in May or at any time between August and late October or early November, especially after easterly winds. The very rare Royal Tern is also recorded here occasionally in late summer or early autumn. The beach also holds a considerable wintering population of Sandwich Terns, with some non-breeders remaining all summer. Grey Phalaropes may occur onshore in winter after westerly gales.

The Strait of Gibraltar

Access to the northern shore of the Strait between Tarifa and Punta Secreta is very limited because of the presence of the Spanish army, who are not sympathetic to birders. Seawatching from the harbour wall at Tarifa (CA2) or from Punta Carnero and Punta Secreta (CA3) may produce some good results. Audouin's Gulls may be seen at Punta Secreta during most of the year but especially in late summer and autumn. Lesser Crested Terns occur here too in the autumn and there is also an autumn record of Royal Tern. It is worth noting that there are enterprises in both Tarifa and Gibraltar that take people out on whale- and dolphin-watching trips and an expedition on one of these boats, amply primed with dramamine where necessary, might well prove fruitful, seabird-wise, in September or October.

Gibraltar itself offers much for the seabirder. Apart from the very substantial colony of Yellow-legged Gulls (5,000 pairs at least) and the very few pairs of Shags, its claim to fame is the excellent seawatch site at Europa Point. This the best place by far for observation of seabird migration in the area and it is possible to obtain very close views at times of such species as Balearic and Cory's Shearwaters. In particular, it can be very good for the observation of Audouin's Gulls from July to September (several thousand pass) and it offers the whole range of migrant and wintering seabirds.

The Sea of Alborán

The Alborán basin is the part of the Mediterranean off the Costa del Sol, from Cabo de Gata (Almería) in the east to the Strait of Gibraltar in the west. The mouth of the River Guadiaro at Sotogrande (CA8) is an excellent site for watching a wide variety of gulls and terns. Razorbills and occasional grebes also occur in winter. Yellow-legged Gulls are always present, along with numbers of Lesser Black-backed Gulls and some Audouin's Gulls during most months of the year. In winter there are usually Sandwich Terns. This is one of the best places to see Lesser Crested Terns, which may appear between August and late October. Caspian Terns also occur during migration periods.

The western side of Málaga Bay, between Benalmádena and the River Guadalhorce, is a very productive area which has been extensively watched by AP. As a result it boasts a very fair share of the seabird rarities seen in Andalucía, including Masked and Brown Boobies, three species of Nearctic Gull; Franklin's, Laughing and Ring-billed, Little Shearwater, Bulwer's Petrel and all four species of skua. Seawatching from the harbour wall of the Puerto Deportivo (marina) at Benalmádena is often particularly fruitful for Gannets, fly-by gulls and, at times, for close views of Balearic Shearwaters. The attractiveness of this area is probably a result of a combination of the change in coastal direction and the presence of fresh water at the mouth of the River Guadalhorce.

The river mouth and ponds of the Río Guadalhorce (MA8) are always interesting and often host a good variety of gulls and terns. The presence of fresh water attracts significant numbers of non-breeding Audouin's Gulls in late spring and early summer, as well as Mediterranean Gulls and all the common gull species, plus occasional Slender-billed Gulls. There is often a conspicuous spring passage of several hundred Little Gulls but this varies greatly from year to year. Caspian Terns and Lesser Crested Terns occur on passage, most frequently in autumn. The Royal Tern has occurred here on three occasions. Common and Little Terns occur only on migration and there is an unusual early autumn report of an Arctic Tern. The Roseate Tern has been recorded three times in the 1980s. There are large numbers of migrant marsh terns, notably Black Terns with some Whiskered Terns in spring, and Black Terns in late summer and early autumn. Occasional White-winged Black Terns occur in autumn after prolonged easterlies.

The eastern Málaga coast from Rincón de la Victoria to Nerja attracts large numbers of Yellow-legged Gulls all year and numerous Black-headed and Lesser Black-backed Gulls in winter. Mediterranean Gulls also occur here in numbers between December and February.

There appears to be little of particular interest off the Granada coast, apart from a few pairs of breeding Yellow-legged Gulls, although numbers of gulls and terns occur along the shores at the appropriate times of year. The river mouth to the west of Motril, and the fishing port at that town, may repay some attention.

In Almería there are records of large numbers of gulls and terns at various sites, notably at Punta Entinas and the salinas at Roquetas (AL2) and, especially, at the salinas at Cabo de Gata (AL1). The most interesting species at this last site is again Audouin's Gull and flocks of up to 1,000 birds have been recorded there. Seawatching from the tip of Cabo de Gata should be good during migration periods, for Cory's and Balearic Shearwaters as well as for the migrant and wintering gulls and terns, which occur in large numbers just around the corner at the salinas.

Inland sites

There are also several inland sites where gulls and terns can be seen. The whole of the Doñana region (H5) and the Guadalquivir valley as far north as Sevilla offer interesting species, as do both the wetlands of southern Córdoba (CO1–7) and the Laguna de Fuente de Piedra (MA1). The last attracts migrant marsh terns and there are sizable breeding numbers of Black-headed Gulls and Gull-billed Terns in suitable years, with Slender-billed Gulls as occasional breeders. These sites are of particular interest during passage periods but they may also attract seabirds in winter; the frequent occurrence of large numbers of Mediterranean Gulls at the Laguna de Medina (CA15) and several thousand Lesser Black-backed Gulls at Fuente de Piedra (MA1) are cases in point.

Seabirds are obviously less prominent in Extremadura but in recent years there have been notable increases of wintering Great Cormorants, Black-headed Gulls and Lesser Black-backed Gulls, all of which are locally abundant. Marsh terns occur on passage and Gull-billed Terns breed at the Embalse de Orellana (BA11) and several other localities.

WATCHING RAPTOR AND STORK MIGRATION

Soaring birds migrating in large numbers are an unforgettable spectacle and one which can only be observed regularly in a limited number of localities. Flocks of raptors and storks on the move may be encountered anywhere in southern Spain but the Strait of Gibraltar is where the fly-paths converge and the largest assemblages take place. The Strait offers the shortest sea-crossing between Africa and western Europe: only 16 kilometres at its narrowest point. As such it is useful to those species, notably storks and broad-winged raptors, which rely on soaring flight since thermals and updrafts are largely lacking over the sea.

When to watch

The migration season at the Strait is a long one. Significant movements of raptors occur from mid-February until early June (northbound) and from late July until early November (southbound), although different species are involved at different times. White Storks are on the move from November to May (northbound) and July to September (south-bound). Black Storks pass from February to April and again from September to late October mainly. In all, there is seldom a time when passage cannot be observed and no visit to southern Andalucía can be regarded as complete if it has not included a day or two watching the activity across the Strait. Residents in the area will need no encourage-ment from us; raptor watching is an addictive fixture which claims many hours from those fortunate enough to live close to the action.

Where to watch

Watching the migration at the Strait requires a modicum of planning and it is absolutely essential to pay due regard to the wind direction. We have often seen birders scanning the skies disconsolately and in vain

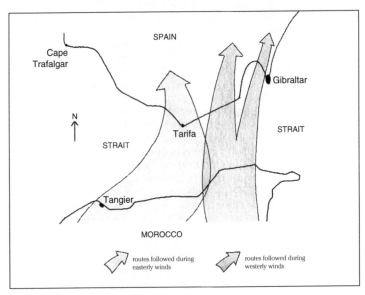

Map 4a: Northward passage of soaring birds in relation to wind direction

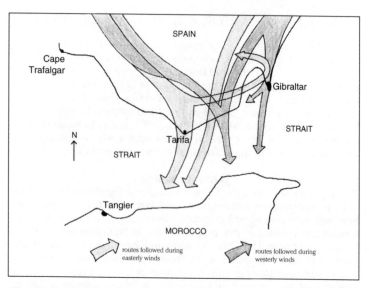

Map 4b: Southward passage of soaring birds in relation to wind direction

from totally unsuitable watchpoints and have (usually) been able to redirect them to more fruitful positions sometimes only a couple of kilometres away. A place which is overflown by streams of raptors on one occasion may be useless the next day, or even later the same day, if the wind changes. At the Strait the winds have generally got either an easterly or a westerly component. The rule of thumb is that **movements take place at the downwind end of the Strait**.

Soaring birds are prone to lateral drift by the wind As a result, westerly winds will drift birds towards the eastern (Gibraltar) end of the Strait. Easterly winds will drift them towards the western (Cape Trafalgar) end. The effect is most marked during the northward migration, i.e. in 'spring'. Then birds will have crossed the open sea from Africa to Europe and will have been fully exposed to any lateral effects of the wind. In the southward migration, i.e. in 'autumn', birds tend to accumulate at the downwind end of the Strait and they will either cross there or move into the wind towards the shortest crossing point near Tarifa. If the winds are very strong, however, the birds will overshoot Tarifa and return inland to await better conditions. Strong easterlies between August and October regularly result in large numbers of birds flying east from Tarifa, into the wind, even as far as Gibraltar, where they mill about for some time before virtually always returning northwards again.

Maps 4A and 4B, which show the principal flight paths in the region of the Strait, and the table below will help you to decide where to watch. Our site descriptions for CA1, CA2, CA3 and Gibraltar give details of access to the various vantage points which need to be used. Finally, there is no substitute for experience and local advice should be sought and heeded whenever possible. The observatory at Jews' Gate (Gibraltar) is regularly manned at migration times and the observers are an indispensable source of up-to-the-minute information. Visitors are always welcome there.

Table: Where to watch raptor and stork migration in relation to wind direction

WIND	SITES	SITE CODE
Strong westerly	Gibraltar, Punta Secreta	Gibraltar, CA3
Light/moderate westerly	Gibraltar, Punta Secreta, El Bujeo	Gibraltar, CA2D, CA3
Calm	Tarifa. El Bujeo	CA2B, CA2D
Light/moderate easterly	Tarifa	CA2B
Strong easterly	Tarifa, Los Lances	CA2B,CA1

The situation is never entirely straightforward. Honey Buzzards are the most determined migrants and are least affected by the wind. They do drift but they allow themselves to do so since they are powerful fliers which can employ flapping flight for long periods over the sea and so can afford to deviate far from the regular flightpaths across the Strait. Strong winds which will ground all storks and most raptors may produce Honey Buzzard movements into and from the Costa del Sol and into and from the Cape Trafalgar/Doñana region.

White Storks are strongly attracted to the short sea crossing in the centre of the Strait and tend not to cross at all if they cannot do so there. Hence White Storks are comparatively irregular at Gibraltar itself, even during westerlies. Black Storks, on the other hand, are less reliant upon soaring flight and occur at Gibraltar together with raptors.

During the southward passage, Booted and Short-toed Eagles especially tend to avoid Gibraltar even during westerly winds. They prefer to follow the mountains down to Tarifa and use the short crossing there. By contrast, they are among the most likely raptors to turn up at Gibraltar during strong *easterlies* in autumn, having aborted an attempt to cross at Tarifa and having coasted instead towards the Rock. These occasions regularly result in the impressive sight of up to several hundred eagles in view at once circling over Gibraltar. During the northward passage both species are common at Gibraltar in westerlies, after drifting there when crossing the Strait.

Watching migration

Despite the numbers involved, there is not a continuous flow of raptors across the Strait, even if you happen to have found the right spot to watch from. Some points to consider are:

- Larger raptors and storks are not on the move until well after dawn and they settle to roost well before sunset. (Honey Buzzards are often an exception.) The peak times for watching are from 10 am to 6 pm, local times, approximately.
- Gaps in the flow of up to a couple of hours are quite usual, especially at the extremes of the season. If the gaps are any longer check that the wind direction has not changed.
- Birds which have crossed the Strait have often lost a great deal (or all) of their height and may arrive flapping low over the sea.
- Birds leaving the Spanish coast will often soar to a great height beforehand, in order to try and glide across.
- Raptors flier higher in hot weather. An 'empty' sky may reveal hundreds of birds when scanned carefully. We have seen Honey Buzzards which could only just be picked up through binoculars from a

watch point on the top of Gibraltar and the radar there has picked up raptors to altitudes of over 3000 metres. Most migration is low enough to be visible however.

- Persistent heavy rain will stop movements but showery, blustery weather does not deter most species.
- Counting the movements is difficult since they are usually on a broad front and a large team of observers is necesary. Counting the movement over a particular point is possible but allow the birds to pass you before you count them and don't contemplate counting soaring flocks; wait until they level off into a stream.
- It is a good idea to scan ahead. Raptors can be seen some kilometres before they arrive and it is best not to be taken by surprise. Rear views are always frustrating.
- The gulls at Gibraltar provide an early-warning service. An explosion of alarm calls often means that raptors have arrived.
- Porter *et al.* (1981) remains as one of the best available guides to raptor identification, but there are more recent contenders for the title.

Honey Buzzards coasting south, Tarifa

Programa Migres

Regular coordinated counts of migrating soaring birds take place in the area of the Strait each autumn, from mid-July to mid-October, under the auspices of Programa Migres, a project funded by the regional government (Junta de Andalucía) and organised by the Spanish Ornithological Society (SEO/BirdLife). Volunteer observers are always in demand and should contact the organisers at Programa Migres, Centro de Vistantes Huerta Grande, El Pelayo, 11390 Algeciras, Cádiz (tel: 956-679156, email p.migres@teleline.es). There is also an on-line registration form at the SEO website (www.seo.org). Participants receive free board and lodging. This is an excellent way to get acquainted with the area and to make a useful contribution to an important long-term programme. The Huerta Grande includes an information centre and is south of Algeciras at Km 96.2 on the N-340, south side.

What to expect

Pages 318–321 give details of the species involved but a short summary is provided here. Veteran watchers, who took part in the pioneering counts in the 1960s and 1970s, remark on the enormous increases since then in the numbers of both stork species and also of Sparrowhawks and Griffon Vultures. The relative scarcity of Common Buzzards is an ongoing trend, probably reflecting changes in winter quarters, but the visible declines in Montagu's Harriers and Egyptian Vultures especially probably result from real decreases in their populations.

Regular migrants: Black Stork, White Stork, Honey Buzzard, Black Kite, Red Kite, Egyptian Vulture, Griffon Vulture, Short-toed Eagle, Marsh Harrier, Hen Harrier, Montagu's Harrier, Sparrowhawk, Common Buzzard, Booted Eagle, Osprey, Lesser Kestrel, Kestrel, Merlin, Hobby, Peregrine.

Scarce or irregular migrants: Black-shouldered Kite, Black Vulture, Goshawk, Spanish Imperial Eagle, Golden Eagle, Bonelli's Eagle, Eleonora's Falcon.

Vagrants: Lammergeier, Rüppell's Griffon Vulture, Pallid Harrier, Long-legged Buzzard, Lesser Spotted Eagle, Spotted Eagle, Red-footed Falcon, Lanner.

ANDALUCÍA

The eight provinces of Andalucía cover a broad expanse of territory and a full range of habitats: marine, littoral, wetland, lowland and montane, with their associated birds. As we have suggested, there is ample scope for wide-ranging touring, perhaps taking in Extremadura as well, or visits concentrated in just a small part of the region.

The autonomous regional government, La Junta de Andalucía, through its environment agency, La Consejería (formerly Agencia) de Medio Ambiente (C.M.A.) has been assiduous in giving protected status of some sort to most of the key wildlife sites (but still with the notable exception of the 'steppe' habitats). These now comprise a network of reserves covering some 20% of the territory of Andalucía. The green C.M.A/A.M.A. signs will become a familiar sight to users of this book. Reserves apart, much of the countryside of the region is relatively unspoilt, especially by north-European standards, and birds are an obvious feature wherever one travels.

There are four different types of classification of the protected sites:

Reserva Natural (Nature Reserve) This is the lowest level of protection and is roughly equivalent to that of an S.S.S.I. (Site of Special Scientific Interest) in Britain. Nature Reserves are intended to protect specific ecosystems or communities. These are mainly small sites, many of them lagoons. Only activities compatible with the survival of the sites are permitted there; for example, fish-farming is banned at wetland sites. It is also forbidden to introduce alien species to the sites.

Paraje Natural (Natural Locality) This is a similar status to Nature Reserve and protects mainly restricted areas of general scenic or biological interest. Traditional activities (not hunting) are permitted to continue.

Parque Natural (Natural Park) A Natural Park is an extensive area, often of sierras and woodlands, which offers well-preserved natural or semi-natural habitats. The designation protects the area from further unsuitable development, while still allowing compatible traditional activities to continue. A feature of a Natural Park is that it aims to provide educational and recreational facilities for the general public. The protection of traditional architecture and cultural aspects is included. Many of the parks have information centres which provide leaflets (Guías Prácticas) and other information about the region.

Parque Nacional (National Park) A National Park enjoys the highest level of protection. The designation protects extensive areas of international importance within which all human activities are strictly controlled. Access too is limited where this is in the interests of the fauna and flora. There are only nine National Parks in Spain and only one, Doñana, in Andalucía. Moves are afoot to designate a new National Park in the Sierra Nevada.

The above reserves protect entire habitats and all the wildlife there, not just the birds. Some have additionally been designated as Important Bird Areas (IBAs; called ZEPAs in Spain), as explained on p. 9. The relevant protection status is given under each site account.

HUELVA PROVINCE

Huelva province is best known for the remarkable habitats and birds of the Coto Doñana (H5) but in fact Doñana is only one (and the best) of a series of wetland sites which extend the entire length of the provincial coastline. The province is accordingly of the greatest importance for waterbirds and waders of all kinds, and also for seabirds. Inland, Huelva offers the mountains of the western end of the Sierra Morena, a relatively unspoilt region of wooded hills and open country, supporting a good variety of raptors and other birds.

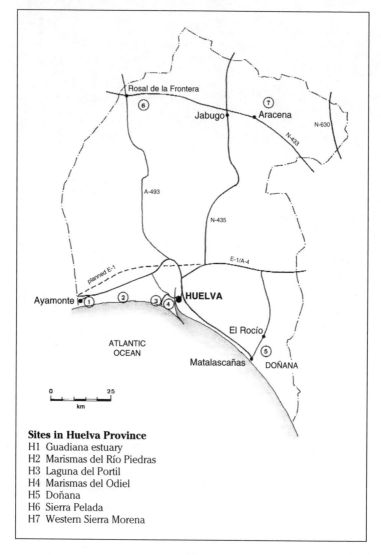

Sites in Huelva Province
H1 Guadiana estuary
H2 Marismas del Río Piedras
H3 Laguna del Portil
H4 Marismas del Odiel
H5 Doñana
H6 Sierra Pelada
H7 Western Sierra Morena

Maps

Mapa Provincial Huelva, IGN, 1:200,000.

Mapa Guía Parque Nacional de Doñana, IGN, 1:50,000; detailed map of the National Park (site H5).

Mapa Guía Marismas del Odiel, IGN, 1:50,000; detailed map of the Paraje Natural (sites H3 & H4).

(Both mapas guías are available at the shop at El Acebuche in Doñana.)

Getting there

Most of the sites listed are to the south of the E-1/N-431 Sevilla/Portugal trunk road, which crosses the province east/west. This is a motorway as far west as Huelva city and a motorway extension to the Portuguese border is planned. Visitors from further east may travel via Sevilla using the E-15/N-340 Cádiz-Almería coast road and the E-5/A-4 Cádiz–Sevilla motorway. The motorway charges a modest toll but is excellent value; speedy transit and no lorries (they prefer the free trunk roads). The centre reservation is a model of its kind: resplendent in season with the yellows of genistas and retamas, the pinks and whites of oleanders and the sober greens of stone pines; it is popular with Hoopoes among others. The A-381 is an excellent and recently improved short-cut across Cádiz province connecting the motorway at Jerez (exit 5 — Jerez Sur/Medina) and Algeciras. Some sections of the A-381 are being upgraded to motorway status. The N-433 Sevilla–Portugal trunk road is the obvious access to the northern half of the province and connects with the N-630 road, linking western Andalucía with Extremadura.

Where to stay

Coastal Huelva has many tourist resorts, although fortunately it is still nowhere near as developed as the Costa del Sol. The accommodation ranges from the Paradores at Ayamonte in the west and Mazagón in the east — both of them modern buildings and offering exemplary facilities and service — to a diversity of campsites and hotels. The coastal resort of Punta Umbría is a useful central location which offers a number of hotels.

The whole coastal area is within easy access of Matalascañas and El Rocío, which are the obvious bases for visitors to Doñana. Matalascañas has a range of hotels and campsites and there are more campsites just to the west at Mazagón. However, our first preference is for the Hostal Cristina in El Rocío, which offers good simple food and clean and inexpensive accommodation. It seems purpose-built for the birders who seem to make up most of the clientele. Pre-booking is advisable. The address is: Hostal Cristina, Real 36, El Rocío, Almonte, Huelva. (tel: 959-442413).

There a number of other hostales in El Rocío and a newish three-star hotel; all of these are ideally situated for Doñana and the hinterland. The address of the latter establishment is: Hotel Puente del Rey, Avenida de la Carraliega, 21750 El Rocío, Almonte, Huelva (tel: 959-442575).

Elsewhere in the province, there are small hotels and hostales in most of the towns. Visitors to the Western Sierra Morena (H7) may find convenient accommodation in Aracena. In this area we can particularly recommend: Hotel Galaroza Sierra, Carretera Sevilla-Lisboa Km 69.5, 21291 Galaroza, Huelva (tel: 959-123237, fax 959-123236); 2-star, on the north side of the N-433, immediately west of Galaroza.

GUADIANA ESTUARY
(MARISMAS DE ISLA CRISTINA)   H1

Status: Includes the Isla Cristina Paraje Natural (2145 ha).

Site description

This is the southwesternmost corner of Andalucía, the River Guadiana marking the border with Portugal. Tidal activity has produced sand spits sheltering extensive areas of saltmarsh and abandoned salt pans, dominated by glassworts. The xerophyte community is well developed. The low sand dunes have extensive covering vegetation, including areas of stone pine and juniper woodland. Wide sandy beaches comprise the coastline and flank the principal mouth of the Guadiana. This is an excellent site in that it offers a range of well-preserved and relatively accessible habitats within a reasonably confined area, even though much of the littoral and dune habitat has been lost to the ever-expanding tourism developments.

Species

The area is attractive all year round to a good variety of waders, gulls and terns. The largest numbers occur during passage periods and in winter but many species are represented even in summer. Caspian Terns are present in small numbers, even in summer when some nonbreeders occur. Spoonbills are regular visitors from the Marismas del Odiel (H4) and occur in flocks of up several hundred birds. Among the waders, Kentish Plovers occur in good numbers all year round; winter counts of over 300 are on record. The whole area is liable to hold significant numbers of a variety of passerine and other landbird species during passage periods.

Timing

Visits during passage periods and in winter are recommended but there are interesting birds here all year round. The sandy beaches, and the rapidly expanding hotel complexes at Isla Cristina, Playa del Moral and Playa de Canela, attract large numbers of tourists in summer when the area may get very congested; however, the saltmarshes are not part of the regular tourist haunts. Visits in hot weather should be timed to avoid the heat of the day with its attendant glare and haze.

Access

A visit to the area should include the saltmarsh proper, the dune vegetation and the beaches. The coast road leading south from Ayamonte to Isla de Canela gives access to the estuary and the beaches at Playa de Canela. Driving eastwards the road rises near a stone tower, the Torre de Canela, affording views over the saltmarsh. Continuing east towards Isla del Moral, a sandy track leads north immediately west of the village. This connects with a causeway which allows exploration of the southern marshes for a distance of several kilometres. Entry is only possible on foot but there is a short access track and limited parking available near the gate which blocks the causeway to vehicles. The causeway follows the main creek of the saltmarsh and skirts areas of dense glass-

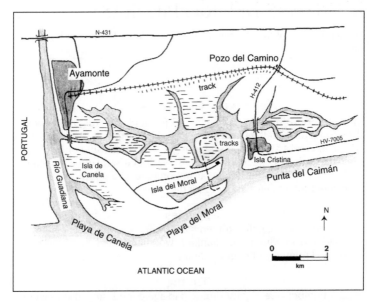

worts and other xerophytes as well as giving close views over the abandoned salt pans, which attract waders.

The shore at Playa del Moral gives views across the marsh entrance. Sandbanks and rocky breakwaters here attract gulls and terns especially. A stone jetty provides a suitable vantage point for scanning for seabirds offshore.

The eastern side of the marsh is accessible from the Pozo del Camino/Isla Cristina road which crosses the creeks. Views of the main creek and marsh inlet are also available from Isla Cristina. A cycle and walking track (signposted Via Verde del Litoral) following the disused railway line between Pozo del Camino and Ayamonte allows views across the saltmarshes and an area of salt pans from the northern bank. A sand bar to seaward immediately south of Isla Cristina encloses a shallow inlet attractive at times to waders. A rickety but safe wooden bridge crosses the inlet, giving access to the beach at Punta del Caimán. The inlet is reached by following signs to the Faro (lighthouse) through Isla Cristina town.

Calendar

All year: Little Egret, White Stork, Marsh Harrier, Black-winged Stilt, Kentish Plover, Redshank, Yellow-legged Gull, Caspian Tern, Zitting Cisticola.

Breeding season: Montagu's Harrier, Collared Pratincole, Little Tern, Pallid Swift, Bee-eater, Hoopoe, Yellow Wagtail.

Passage periods and winter: Spoonbill, waterfowl, waders; including Oystercatcher, Ringed Plover, Grey Plover, Sanderling, Little Stint, Dunlin, Black-tailed Godwit, Bar-tailed Godwit, Whimbrel, Curlew, Spotted Redshank, Greenshank, Green Sandpiper, Common Sandpiper, Turnstone; gulls and terns. Gannets, Common Scoters and other seabirds offshore.

MARISMAS DEL RÍO PIEDRAS

Status: Paraje Natural (Marismas del Río Piedras y Flecha del Rompido)
2530 ha.

Site description

The curious sandy spit (La Flecha del Rompido) across the mouth of
the Río Piedras shelters an area of saltmarsh. Mudflats are exposed in
the main creeks at low tide and along the landward side of La Flecha.
The spit itself has exceptionally well-developed sand-dune vegetation
and is of considerable botanical importance. Coastal pinewoods are
prominent to both east and west of the estuary.

Species

Waterfowl, waders, gulls and terns occur in some numbers, chiefly on
passage and in winter. The flanking woodlands and the dune scrub
hold good numbers of migrants at times.

Timing

Wader numbers are highest during passage periods and also in winter,
when visits are recommended. There would seem to be considerable
potential for seawatching off the beach; the coastal dunes along the
southern edge of La Flecha provide an elevated viewpoint. The beach
gets busy in summer and is best avoided then.

Access

The site is reached from the N-431, driving south from Lepe (west bank)
or Cartaya (east bank). On the western side, the main creek of the saltmarsh is viewed from the fishing village of Puerto de El Terrón. South of

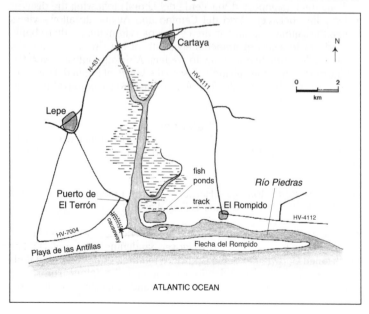

here a causeway leads across a minor creek and an area of salt flats to the beach. You can explore La Flecha on foot from this point.

On the eastern side there is good access to the central channel and also to extensive salt flats and coastal dune vegetation, as well as an expanse of salt pans and fish farms. Follow the wide signposted road 'Camino del Lancon' which leads west for 4 km off the El Rompido/Cartaya road, just north of El Rompido. The entrance is almost directly opposite a Campsa petrol station. The road is poor tarmac which soon becomes a sandy dirt track of indifferent quality

Kentish Plovers in the sand

and with some sticky patches during wet conditions. It is perfectly passable with care, nevertheless. The salt pans and fish farms are on the seaward side of the coastal pine belt, and are reached by a branch track about 3 km from the entrance. Ask for permission before entering the fish farms which are obviously private and are guarded by a collection of unpleasant looking (though chained) dogs.

Good views over the main inlet to the marsh and La Flecha are obtainable from the village of El Rompido itself, where there are sizable mudflats. The coast road rises east of El Rompido where a viewpoint (mirador) gives panoramic views of La Flecha and the mouth of the estuary.

Calendar

All year: Marsh Harrier, Black-winged Stilt, Avocet, Little Ringed Plover, Kentish Plover, Redshank, Southern Grey Shrike, Dartford Warbler.

Breeding season: Spoonbill, Collared Pratincole, Little Tern, Hoopoe, Yellow Wagtail.

Passage periods and winter: Balearic Shearwater, Leach's Storm-petrel, Gannet, Great Cormorant, Little Egret, Red-crested Pochard, Common Scoter, Red-breasted Merganser, Osprey, waders, including Knot; Arctic Skua, Great Skua; gulls, including Little Gull; terns, including Caspian Tern, Bluethroat.

LAGUNA DEL PORTIL

H3

Status: Reserva Natural, 16 ha, plus 1300 ha of peripheral protection.

Site description
This is a substantial freshwater lagoon, fringed with reeds and bulrushes and surrounded by a protected expanse of stone pine and cork oak woodland. The lake is situated adjacent to the coast, immediately east of the resort village of El Portil.

Species
The lagoon attracts waterfowl and gulls, especially on passage and in winter, many species visiting occasionally from the adjacent Marismas del Odiel (H4). It is a reliable site for Ferruginous Ducks, especially in winter.

Timing
Visits during passage periods and in winter are most likely to be productive but some waterfowl are always present. This is a site which you bound to pass when travelling along the Huelva coast and it always deserves a look.

Access
The lake may be inspected quickly and easily from the service road which follows its southern boundary and gives good elevated views. A telescope is useful. The service road is best entered at its eastern end, which is almost opposite the lake itself. For closer scrutiny, park in the village and walk along the surrounding footpaths. There is a hide on the west bank but it is rather distant from the water's edge.

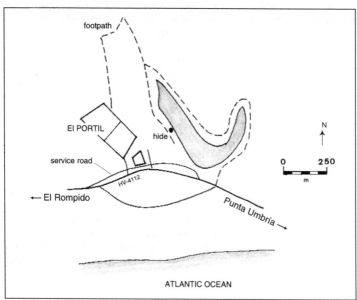

Calendar

All year: Little Grebe, Great Crested Grebe, Mallard, Purple Gallinule, Coot, Moorhen.

Breeding season: Little Bittern, Reed Warbler.

Passage periods and winter: Black-necked Grebe, Grey Heron, Spoonbill, ducks, including Gadwall, Teal, Shoveler, Red-crested Pochard, Common Pochard and Ferruginous Duck; gulls.

MARISMAS DEL ODIEL (RIA DE HUELVA)   H4

Status: Includes the Parajes Naturales of the Marismas del Odiel (7185 ha; also a ZEPA), Lagunas de Palos y Las Madres (693 ha), Estero de Domingo Rubio (480 ha) and Enebrales de Punta Umbria (162 ha).

Site description

The provincial capital of Huelva lies at the confluence of the rivers Odiel and Tinto surrounded by a complex of broad tidal dykes fringed by salt flats and saltmarshes. There are areas of fresh marsh and a number of small freshwater lagoons nearby. The spit of Punta Umbría encloses the marismas and is an extension of the sandy beaches of the central Huelva coast. An even longer spit, El Espigón, extends from the centre of the delta, southeastwards parallel to the coast, for some 10 km.

Species

The area is noteworthy for the large colonies of Spoonbills, at least 400 pairs, reputedly about a third of the European population. It is indeed an excellent site to see this species. Spoonbills are scattered singly and in flocks across the whole region, foraging in the tidal creeks and salt pans as well as in the freshwater marshlands. They are confiding and give excellent views at close quarters. Spoonbills are very much a familiar part of the local landscape; the town of Punta Umbría even has a Spoonbill street (Calle Espátula)!

The region also holds good numbers of breeding Purple Herons (20 pairs) as well as nesting Grey Herons and Little Egrets. Black-winged Stilts, Kentish Plovers and Redshanks are among the breeding waders and there is an important nesting population of Little Terns (400 pairs).

Very large numbers of waders and up to 1,000 Greater Flamingos occur on passage and in winter. The area is attractive to gulls and flocks of thousands accumulate there. In summer these are mostly non-breeding Yellow-legged Gulls but a diverse range of species occurs at other seasons. There are excellent opportunities for scanning gull flocks and, in view of the numbers present, good chances of finding something unusual. Terns are also attracted to the area and the wintering species include numbers of Sandwich Terns and small flocks of Caspian Terns. Hundreds of Cormorants are present in winter. Ospreys occur regularly in winter, when up to 15 individuals may be present. There is potential for sea-watching from Punta Umbría and, especially, from the end of El Espigón.

Timing
The site is of interest at all times of year. However the resort areas, notably the beaches extending west from Punta Umbría, are crowded with human visitors in summer and during the Easter holidays.

Access
The core of the Marismas del Odiel is strictly protected and not gener-ally accessible. The region still offers a number of points from which the key species of the area can be readily observed.

A Punta Umbría
The village and resort of Punta Umbría is reached from the coast road west of the estuary. It is possible to follow the road through the town for good views of the western channel and the islets beyond. Continuing south the road ends in a stone jetty, accessible only on foot, offering views of the estuary and the open sea. West of the town there are pine-woods and well-preserved dune vegetation, partly comprising the Paraje Natural of Los Enebrales de Punta Umbría. This site is worth searching for passerine migrants and holds numbers of the ubiquitous Azure-winged Magpies. It also gives northward views of the western salt pans and lagoons of Odiel, an area attractive to waterfowl and Flamingos especially.

B El Portil/Aljaraque
This road (A-497) passes along the western flanks of the Marismas del Odiel, adjacent to lagoons and disused salt pans. The northern part of this road is a dual carriageway with a central reservation and few chances for stopping. The southern part is a single carriageway and offers opportunities for pulling off the road and inspecting the marismas and the nearby pools. Also, it is possible to pull off the dual carriageway from the northbound side, just before it passes under a blue-painted overpass, on to a spit which overlooks the area. Two disused stone storehouses mark the spit. Remember to turn right only, when rejoining the dual carriageway from the spit! The light favours viewing in the after-noons especially.

C The central causeway
This road is clearly marked at its northern end. It is signposted with the rather grand title of 'Carretera de las Islas. Dique Juan Carlos I, Rey de España'. The road travels down the centre of the reserve and beyond for a total of over 20 km. It branches south from the Aljaraque/Huelva road (A-497) just west of the two road bridges across the Rio Odiel. The ear-lier part of this road passes through salt flats and salt pans before cross-ing the main western creek of the marshes and turning southeastwards to follow the southern bank of the river, opposite the city of Huelva. The road continues through saltmarshes and by shallow sandy lagoons, affording good views of the Odiel mudflats at low tide.

The final 10 km is a spectacular drive along the narrow and tapering spit, El Espigón, which stretches seemingly endlessly parallel to the

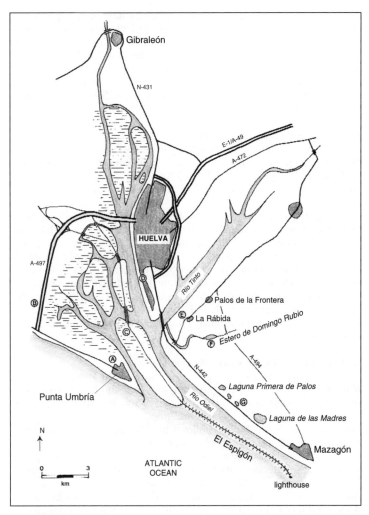

coast, to end eventually at a lighthouse. The whole road allows close inspection of the Odiel mudflats and the sandy beaches to seaward. The end of El Espigón is a good site for seawatching, with seabirds passing close by during favourable, chiefly westerly, winds.

D Huelva city waterfront

The waterfront road follows the course of the Río Odiel, giving good views over the river and its muddy fringes, The area attracts large numbers of gulls and some waders, chiefly in winter and during passage periods. The road is a dual carriageway and so access to the waterfront is easiest from the southbound side. There are many places to stop all along this road. View in the mornings to avoid staring into the sun.

E La Rábida

Huelva displays abundant monuments celebrating the discoveries of Christopher Columbus and the Spanish contribution to the colonisation of the Americas. A large statue of Columbus himself dominates the point of confluence of the Río Odiel and Río Tinto. Other monuments, and a renowned monastery, are concentrated at Columbus' point of departure on the eastern bank of the Río Tinto at La Rábida, which accordingly is heavily signposted throughout the area. Follow signs to La Rábida and continue down to the river, where a jetty (Muelle de la Reina) gives good views over the channel and mudflats. Large flocks of gulls often gather here.

F El Estero de Domingo Rubio
This is a creek which enters the estuary just southeast of La Rábida (see above). The fringing saltmarsh attracts Spoonbills, herons, waterfowl and waders.The road to La Rábida follows the creek and gives good views over the western portions. The creek is tidal only along its lower reaches.

The upstream portions include a freshwater lagoon with fringing freshwater marshes, bordered by stone pine woods. Access to the freshwater sector is from the Palos/Mazagón road (A-494). There is a signposted walking track just south of the bridge which crosses the creek itself and parking is available under the trees on the west side of the road nearby. The track itself is one kilometre long, giving good views of the lagoon and marshes. It is also possible to walk upstream from the bridge. Breeding species include Purple Herons, Little Bitterns, Purple Gallinules and Whiskered Terns. Wintering waterfowl include White-headed Ducks.

G Lagunas de Palos y Las Madres
A total of four lagoons (De Palos, de la Jara, de la Mujér and de las Madres) make up a reed-fringed complex along the N-442 coast road, immediately southeast of the oil refineries and industrial complexes south of La Rábida. The lagoons are fringed by stone pine woodland and numerous, often boggy, hollows thickly vegetated by tamarisks. Strawberry fields are also a feature of the area. The natural vegetation often holds numbers of migrants and the lagoons attract waterfowl and waders. Little Bitterns, Night Herons and Squacco Herons and Purple Gallinules breed. White-headed Ducks are often present and may breed. Access to the lagoons is via short, drivable, sandy tracks leading directly off the north (inland) side of the N-442; those at kilometres 12, 13 and 15.6 are best.

Calendar
All year: Little Grebe, Great Crested Grebe, Black-necked Grebe, Cattle Egret, Little Egret, Grey Heron, White Stork, Spoonbill, Greater Flamingo (sometimes breeds), Gadwall, Mallard, Red-crested Pochard, Common Pochard, Marsh Harrier, Common Kestrel, Water Rail, Moorhen, Purple Gallinule, Coot, Oystercatcher, Black-winged Stilt, Avocet, Kentish Plover, Grey Plover, Sanderling, Dunlin, Black-tailed Godwit, Bar-tailed Godwit, Whimbrel, Curlew, Redshank, Arctic Skua, Great Skua, Black-headed Gull, Lesser Black-backed Gull, Yellow-legged Gull, Hoopoe, Lesser Short-toed lark, Crested Lark, Cetti's Warbler, Zitting Cisticola, Dartford Warbler, Spectacled Warbler, Sardinian Warbler, Southern Grey Shrike, Azure-winged Magpie, Magpie, Jackdaw, Raven, Spotless Starling, Corn Bunting.

Breeding season: Little Bittern, Night Heron, Purple Heron, Squacco Heron, Black Kite, Collared Pratincole, Little Tern, Whiskered Tern, Yellow Wagtail, Savi's Warbler, Reed Warbler, Great Reed Warbler, Melodious Warbler, Golden Oriole, Woodchat Shrike.

Winter: Red-throated Diver, Balearic Shearwater, Gannet, Great Cormorant, Glossy Ibis, Greylag Goose, Shelduck, Wigeon, Teal, Pintail, Shoveler, Tufted Duck, Common Scoter, Red-breasted Merganser, Whiteheaded Duck, Osprey, Hen Harrier, Golden Plover, Snipe, Caspian Tern, Razorbill, Skylark, Meadow Pipit, Water Pipit, Grey Wagtail, White Wagtail, Blackcap, Common Chiffchaff, Firecrest, Penduline Tit, Common Starling, Reed Bunting.

Passage periods: Balearic Shearwater, Knot, Curlew Sandpiper, Purple Sandpiper, Common Sandpiper, Turnstone, Little Gull, Common Tern, Roller, Crag Martin, Tawny Pipit, Tree Pipit, Common Redstart, Whinchat, Northern Wheatear, Black-eared Wheatear, Grasshopper Warbler, Sedge Warbler, Olivaceous Warbler, Subalpine Warbler, Orphean Warbler, Whitethroat, Garden Warbler, Bonelli's Warbler, Willow Warbler, Spotted Flycatcher, Pied Flycatcher, Rock Bunting, Ortolan Bunting.

DOÑANA   H5

Status: Parque Nacional and ZEPA, 50,270 ha. The surrounding areas comprise a buffer zone, Parque Natural del Entorno de Doñana, of a further 56,930 ha.

The survival of this area as a natural wilderness owes a great deal to its history as a hunting preserve, or Coto, of the dukes of Medina Sidonia. One of the dukes married a Doña Ana, and it is after her that the region is still called the Coto de Doña Ana; Doñana for short.

The Dukes played host to hunting parties of the Kings of Spain for over 300 years. These were grand outings, with the royal parties accompanied by large retinues of courtiers and camp followers. As many as 12,000 people assembled for the visit by Felipe IV in spring 1624, enough, one would imagine, to have scared off the game for miles around! Such hunting spectaculars were rare events and did nothing to detract from the importance of Doñana as a refuge for wildlife. Today that importance has been recognised and Doñana is one of the five mainland national parks of Spain.

The Coto de Doñana National Park is administered by the Ministry of Agriculture, Fisheries and Food through ICONA, the National Institute for the Conservation of Nature. It is run, very well we must say, by a director and staff based at El Acebuche. There is also an independent biological research and bird-ringing station at El Palacio, which is not open to the public.

Site description

Doñana is immense. The national park and its protected margins (pre-parques) cover over 1300 square kilometres (500 square miles) of near-virgin habitat, most of it the flat marshlands or marismas. The park comprises the western edge of the Gualdalquivir estuary. Here, the actions of sea and river have combined to build up a large sand bar sheltering an inland sea of shallow lagoons and seasonally-flooded salt flats. To seaward lie some 35 km of unspoilt sandy beach, its waters paddled not by thousands of holiday-makers but by a few dozen fishermen allowed by licence to compete for the cockles with the Scoters and Oyster-catchers which flock there. Moving inland there is an extensive system of sand dunes giving onto open woodlands of stone pine and extensive stretches of low scrubland, dominated by the cistus-like yellow sunroses. Areas of cork oaks support some of the major heronies of the park. Rock roses, lavenders, junipers, tree heaths and a rich variety of other flowering plants provide an aromatic understorey in the woodlands.

Large clearings interrupt the woodlands and here the herds of browsing ungulates suggest a scene from the African veldt. Herds of fallow and red deer are scattered around, browsing contentedly and untroubled by the customary presence of human visitors. Parties of wild boars, elsewhere shy and retiring, snuffle for roots in the mud in broad daylight, the rangy adults accompanied in spring by groups of striped piglets. By contrast, the mammalian predators remain unobtrusive and mainly nocturnal; you are unlikely to see the Spanish lynxes which are also characteristic of the park.

Much of Doñana is a large segment of the Marismas del Guadalquivir, a shimmering expanse of shallow water with islets and reedy lagoons providing cover for a multitude of waterfowl. At one time too one of the oddest sights in Europe could be seen here: a herd of wild camels splashing incongruously through their watery home. These were the descendants of 80 beasts brought to Cadiz in 1829 for use as pack animals. The camels proved useless. Every time they went into towns the local horses panicked and havoc resulted. In the end the camels were released in Doñana where their numbers dwindled away by the early 1950s, not least because of poaching. Apparently the meat used to be sold as venison!

Doñana is above all a wetland site and without doubt it is the number one such reserve in Europe. Only the Danube delta in Romania rivals it. The marismas are bounded to the north and west by salt pans and rice paddies and large areas of low scrub dominated by glassworts, fleshy plants capable of standing periodic washing by salt water at high tides. This huge expanse of watery habitats attracts birds in great numbers, especially in winter.

In recent years, the park has been at the centre of controversy. Proposed golf courses and tourist developments at Matalascañas have threatened to lower the water table and destroy much of the wetland interest of Doñana. These plans have been shelved for the time being but similar threats are likely to recur. In addition there have been damaging incidents of mass deaths of waterfowl attributable partly to outbreaks of botulism but also to the indiscriminate and illegal use of pesticides in adjacent rice fields.

These threats were eclipsed by the ecological catastrophe which struck the region on 25 April 1998, with the sudden rupture of a retaining wall holding back toxic residues from the Aznalcóllar mine, north of Doñana. This sent five million cubic metres of acidic sludge and waste water, generously laced with cadmium, zinc and other metals, into the drainage basin of the River Guadiamar, a key feeder stream for the wetlands of the national park. Conservation organisations had been ringing alarm bells for years over what was clearly a disaster-in-waiting. Indeed the Spanish Ornithological Society raised the issue with the European Commission in 1988, who were fobbed off with reassurances from the relevant authorities. In the event, nothing was done.

The aftermath of the disaster was met with the construction of three dykes, which diverted the toxic flow away from the core of the national park, and a massive clean-up operation. Six thousand hectares of farm-land have been permanently 'decommissioned' and fleets of lorries spent two years ferrying the contaminated topsoil back to the mine. Remarkably, the mine itself is back in operation, after further reassurances that 'it can never happen again'.

Visitors to the national park will not notice any obvious conse-quences of the Aznalcóllar spillage. Even the Zona de Entremuros, the important wetland site to the east (see SE2) through which much of the contaminated water was diverted, was alive with birds in 2000. The long-term effects may be harder to foresee, however. Zinc residues in many plants remain very high and are liable to pass to their consumers. An unprecedented spate of White Storks born with beak deformities was seen in 2000 and gives cause for concern.

Species

Doñana is one of the major wetlands of Europe and holds internation-ally important concentrations of wildfowl in winter and during passage periods. Principal among these are the Greylag Geese, some 60,000 of which cross Iberia to spend the winter in the park. They are accompa-nied by some 250,000 ducks; chiefly Teal, Wigeon, Mallard, Shoveler, Pintail and Pochard, as well as thousands of Coots. Large numbers of waders, notably godwits, Ruffs, Black-winged Stilts and Avocets also occur both in winter and on passage.

The park is also of the greatest importance for the species which breed there. There are large heronies, supporting Cattle and Little Egrets, Grey Herons, Night Herons, Purple Herons and the otherwise elusive Squacco Herons, as well as Spoonbills and White Storks. Glossy Ibises have bred successfully in increasing numbers in recent years and are an established feature of the park. Raptors occur in great numbers; there are hundreds of pairs of Black Kites. Red Kites also breed commonly as well as Short-toed Eagles, Marsh Harriers, Booted Eagles, Buzzards, Kestrels and Peregrines. Some 15 pairs of Spanish Imperial Eagles nest within the boundaries, typically in the crowns of stone pines.

A site of this importance cannot fail to attract scarce and elusive species. The Andalusian Hemipode appears to survive in the north of the park (Coto del Rey). Spotted Eagles have been recorded in several recent successive winters. Vagrants discovered in Doñana have includ-ed such disparate birds as African Marabou, Rüppell's Griffon Vulture, Surf Scoter, Grey-headed Gull and Pallas's Warbler.

Timing

The park is always of interest but the combination of low water levels (or no water at all!) and the influx of tourists to the nearby beaches makes summer a time to avoid. Water levels fluctuate with the rains, and there have been some very dry years in the 1970s, 1980s and 1990s. However, in an average year the park lives up to its wetland status and large numbers of wintering and passage aquatic birds can be seen from October to May. The activity and sound of birds settling to breed and the steady through-flow of migrants, makes visits in spring (March–May) particularly pleasant.

For birding purposes at least, it is also a good idea to avoid Doñana at Pentecost (seven weekends after Easter), when up to one million pilgrims converge on El Rocío for the celebration, over several days, of the Fiesta de Nuestra Señora del Rocío (Our Lady of the Dew). This is a statue of the Virgin Mary, venerated locally for over 500 years, which is housed in the large church at El Rocío. The pilgrims include gipsies in caravans and many horsemen with their colourful señoritas sitting behind them.

Access

Doñana is run principally with the interests of the fauna and flora in mind. As a result, most of it is closed to the general public. Entry to the core of the national park is strictly controlled. Basically you can't get in here at all except as part of an organised visit and these need to be booked well in advance at popular times. The visits are run by private companies under licence. There are generally two trips a day, morning and afternoon. The standard visit takes four hours, during which you travel in a Land Rover or a 'safari' bus, which generally drives south along the beach from Matalascañas before cutting inland to cross the

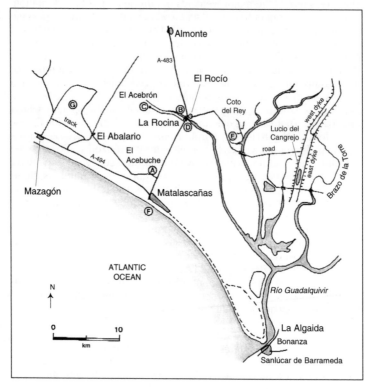

dunes. The route then visits the pinewoods and the southern fringes of the marismas, before returning towards Matalascañas along the beach. The buses stop from time to time but they aren't an ideal way to see birds, particularly if your party chances to include some of the more raucous members of the general public. Still the visit is worthwhile if only because it allows you to experience the full range of habitats in the area, and there aren't many places in Europe where such large expanses of unspoilt terrain remain. The crossing of the dunes, a veritable sand-sea, is particularly memorable, especially if your bus gets bogged down. Fortunately if it does there really will be another one along 'in a moment'. It is possible to hire a vehicle with (obligatory) guide for the whole day, for a more leisurely stay and this would seem a good idea for visiting groups.

Prospective visitors to the park need to contact a tour company in advance. They include: Doñana Ecuestre SL, Avenida la Canariega 1, El Rocío, Almonte, Huelva (tel: 959-442474) and Guías de Doñana SA, C/Real 38, El Rocío, Almonte, Huelva (tel/fax: 959-442035). Information on tours may also be obtained from the National Park Offices, Centre Administrativo El Acebuche, 21760, Matalascañas, Huelva (tel: 959-448739/fax: 959-448576).

Although much of Doñana is relatively inaccessible (and there is surely scope for improving public access without damaging the environment), the park periphery offers a number of first-rate sites which alone make a visit more than worthwhile. Try them all!

A Centro de Recepción 'El Acebuche' (tel: 959-448711)

A good place to start is the Information Centre at El Acebuche, which lies 1.5 km west of the Almonte–Matalascañas road at Km 29. The centre offers displays and other information about Doñana as well as coffee and souvenir shops, the latter selling the usual car-stickers, T-shirts, books and similar material which may be of interest. Excellent maps are available here too. The centre is adjacent to the large (33 ha) lagoon of El Acebuche, which although a kilometre or so long is no wider than 200 metres and is overlooked in comfort from eight large wooden hides. A telescope will be useful here and elsewhere for first-rate views of waterfowl at close quarters. The lagoon is a good site to see Ferruginous Ducks and Purple Gallinules, among other waterfowl. The last three hides overlook an enclosed section of the lagoon, which

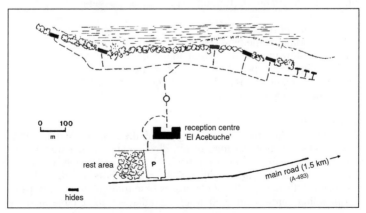

houses pinioned exhibits of such species as Ruddy Shelduck and White-headed Duck; not tickable except by the most unconscionable of birders! The surrounding nature trail through the Mediterranean scrub and pinewoods offers a chance to see passerines. The flocks of Azure-winged Magpies are simply unmissable and there are always raptors overhead. A pair or two of photogenic, and much-photographed, White Storks nest on the picturesque roof of the centre.

B Centro de La Rocina (tel: 959-442340)
The information centre at La Rocina lies across the road from the village of El Rocío. The centre itself offers general information. The main interest lies in the associated nature trail, 2.5 km long, which includes three hides overlooking the marshy Charco de la Boca, a slow stream flowing

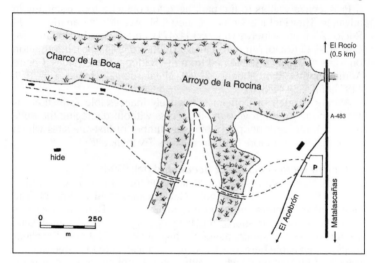

into the Madre de las Marismas at El Rocío and with numerous boggy inlets and reedbeds as well as small areas of open water. This is a reliable site to see Savi's Warblers. Purple Gallinules and other waterfowl are present and the surrounding woodlands and scrub are worth searching for resident and migrant passerines. The diversity of habitats means that anything can turn up, especially on passage.

C Palacio del Acebrón
A 'stately home' in the pinewoods, 7 km from La Rocina. A permanent exhibition showing traditional human life and exploitation of the marismas is of interest, especially if it's raining outside. A nature trail, which visits the adjacent woods and the pool of El Charco del Acebrón, is well worth the short walk.

D El Rocío
Much of the village of El Rocío, lying just off the Almonte/Matalascañas road (A-483), is a living relic of the days when Doñana was almost wholly inaccessible except on horseback. The sand streets and white houses, these last complete with hitching rails for horses, suggest the set for a spaghetti western. The only posses here though are the groups of scope-toting birders since El Rocío is adjacent to a large shallow

lagoon, a northward extension of the marismas proper, called La Madre de las Marismas (mother of the marshes). Water levels permitting this is a superb site, the whole area thronged with herons, egrets, waterfowl and waders, notably Black-winged Stilts, Avocets, Ruff and Black-tailed Godwits and the attendant kites, Marsh Harriers and other raptors. Glossy Ibises turn up here with some regularity. This site can produce 70 or more species before breakfast, which can be achieved if you spend a night or two in the village.

The Sociedad Española de Ornitología (SEO) have an information centre at El Rocío, which will undoubtedly be valuable as a guide to what has turned up recently. Address: Observatorio Madre del Rocío, Pº Marismeño, 21750 El Rocío (tel/fax: 959-506093).

E The Northern Marismas
A dirt road leads east from El Rocío through the stone pinewoods of the Coto del Rey before entering the northern boundary of the park and continuing east through the northern part of the marismas. The road through the pines is rutted and is a problem in wet weather. In particular, it crosses a shallow ford just east of El Rocío which only drivers of 4WD vehicles will wish to attempt except in the driest of conditions. Once into the marismas the road is good and offers a slightly elevated view across the marshes and salt flats. The woods are good for raptors, including views of Imperial Eagles over the park proper. The scrub of the Coto del Rey offers at least a chance of finding the Little Buttonquail (Andalusian Hemipode) but the birds are highly elusive and it should be regarded as a major triumph if you see or hear one! The marismas show concentrations of ducks and waders, except in the dry season. The passerines here must not be overlooked; Lesser Short-toed Larks and Spectacled Warblers breed commonly for example.

F The Beach
The beach at Matalascañas is a busy resort in summer but at other times it is quiet. Like others on the Costa de la Luz, the beach is broad, sandy and tidal. The portion within the park boundary is accessible on foot from Matalascañas. Seabirds are visible offshore, especially in winter. They include large rafts of Common Scoters in winter, worth scanning carefully since both Velvet and Surf Scoters have turned up among them.

G The Western Pinewoods
Huge tracts of stone pine woodland and intervening tracts of open heathland, comprise the western borders of Doñana. There are also plenty of boggy hollows and temporary lagoons. Access is from the tarmac road which leads inland opposite the Parador of Mazagón, 22 km west of Matalascañas on the A-494. Alternatively, take the turn off from A-494 signposted for El Abalario, on the western boundary of the park, where a good dirt road leads inland through the woodlands. Both roads interconnect via a network of sandy dirt roads, offering plenty of opportunities for exploration on foot or by vehicle. It is easy to get somewhat lost here so a compass would be useful to anyone with a poor sense of direction. Characteristic species include Spanish Imperial and Short-toed Eagles, Red-necked Nightjars and Azure-winged Magpies, as well as most of the woodland passerine species of Doñana.

Calendar

All year: Little Grebe, Great Crested Grebe, Black-necked Grebe, Cattle Egret, Squacco Heron, Little Egret, Grey Heron, White Stork, Spoonbill, Greater Flamingo, Gadwall, Mallard, Marbled Duck, Red-crested Pochard, Pochard, Red Kite, Egyptian Vulture, Griffon Vulture, Black Vulture, Marsh Harrier, Common Buzzard, Spanish Imperial Eagle, Booted Eagle, Lesser Kestrel, Common Kestrel, Peregrine, Red-legged Partridge, Quail, Andalucian Hemipode, Water Rail, Spotted Crake, Baillon's Crake, Little Crake, Moorhen, Purple Gallinule, Coot, Red-knobbed Coot, Little Bustard, Oystercatcher, Black-winged Stilt, Avocet, Stone Curlew, Little Ringed Plover, Ringed Plover, Kentish Plover, Grey Plover, Lapwing, Sanderling, Little Stint, Dunlin, Ruff, Black-tailed Godwit, Bar-tailed Godwit, Whimbrel, Curlew, Spotted Redshank, Redshank, Marsh Sandpiper, Greenshank, Green Sandpiper, Arctic Skua, Great Skua, Black-headed Gull, Slender-billed Gull, Lesser Black-backed Gull, Yellow-legged Gull, Caspian Tern, Sandwich Tern, Pin-tailed Sandgrouse, Woodpigeon, Barn Owl, Little Owl, Tawny Owl, Long-eared Owl, Hoopoe, Green Woodpecker, Great Spotted Woodpecker, Calandra Lark, Lesser Short-toed Lark, Crested Lark, Thekla Lark, Woodlark, Barn Swallow, House Martin, Stonechat, Blackbird, Mistle Thrush, Cetti's Warbler, Zitting Cisticola, Dartford Warbler, Spectacled Warbler, Sardinian Warbler, Crested Tit, Short-toed Treecreeper, Southern Grey Shrike, Azure-winged Magpie, Magpie, Jackdaw, Raven, Spotless Starling, Spanish Sparrow, Tree Sparrow, Common Waxbill, Cirl Bunting, Corn Bunting.

Spanish Imperial Eagle

Breeding season: Little Bittern, Night Heron, Purple Heron, Garganey, Black Kite, Short-toed Eagle, Montagu's Harrier, Hobby, Collared Pratincole, Gull-billed Tern, Little Tern, Whiskered Tern, Black Tern, Turtle Dove, Great Spotted Cuckoo, Cuckoo, Red-necked Nightjar, Bee-eater, Short-toed Lark, Sand Martin, Red-rumped Swallow, Yellow Wagtail, Rufous Bush Chat, Nightingale, Savi's Warbler, Reed Warbler, Great Reed Warbler, Melodious Warbler, Golden Oriole, Woodchat Shrike, Hawfinch.

Winter: Red-throated Diver, Balearic Shearwater, Gannet, Great Cormorant, Great White Egret, Glossy Ibis, Greylag Goose, other goose species, Shelduck, Wigeon, Teal, Pintail, Shoveler, Tufted Duck, Common Scoter, Red-breasted Merganser, Black-shouldered Kite, Hen Harrier, Sparrowhawk, Bonelli's Eagle, Osprey, Merlin, Crane, Golden Plover, Jack Snipe, Snipe, Woodcock, Wood Sandpiper, Razorbill, Kingfisher, Skylark, Richard's Pipit, Meadow Pipit, Water Pipit, Grey Wagtail, White Wagtail, Dunnock, Robin, Bluethroat, Ring Ouzel, Fieldfare, Song Thrush, Redwing, Blackcap, Common Chiffchaff, Firecrest, Penduline Tit, Common Starling, Siskin, Linnet, Bullfinch, Reed Bunting.

Passage periods: Honey Buzzard, Knot, Temminck's Stint, Curlew Sandpiper, Purple Sandpiper, Common Sandpiper, Turnstone, Little Gull, Common Tern, Scops Owl, Short-eared Owl, Alpine Swift, Roller, Crag Martin, Tawny Pipit, Tree Pipit, Common Redstart, Whinchat, Northern Wheatear, Black-eared Wheatear, Grasshopper Warbler, Sedge Warbler, Olivaceous Warbler, Subalpine Warbler, Orphean Warbler, Whitethroat, Garden Warbler, Bonelli's Warbler, Willow Warbler, Spotted Flycatcher, Pied Flycatcher, Rock Bunting, Ortolan Bunting.

SIERRA PELADA   H6

Status: Paraje Natural and ZEPA (Sierra Pelada y Rivera del Aserrador). 12,980 ha.

Site description

This is a quiet corner of northwesternmost Andalucía, near the Portuguese border, offering undulating wooded hillsides and areas of more open cistus scrub. Cork and holm oaks are characteristic as well as extensive stands of stone and maritime pines. Pleasant rocky streams cross the site. Some of the area is well preserved notwithstanding the unwelcome encroachment of *eucalyptus* plantations. However, these latter are an unmissable feature of the western and southern parts of the site. Eucalyptus has fallen from favour in recent years. However, some extensive recent reforestation has involved pines and the forestry activity has led to disturbance and displacement of some Black Vulture pairs especially.

Species

The area boasts the highest density of breeding Black Vultures in Andalucía, with some 30 pairs present. Griffon Vultures also are regularly present, probably commuting from Badajoz province given that Huelva is the only province in our area with no breeding Griffons at all. In general the variety of raptors is high and includes Golden, Short-toed and Booted Eagles. Other interesting breeding species include Black Storks, Eagle Owls and White-rumped Swifts. The woodlands and watersides support a good range of passerines, including Rock Sparrows. Otters, Spanish lynx and wild boar are present too but, as ever, elusive.

Timing

Springtime visits are most rewarding; displaying raptors are obvious and the woodland community is in song and easily located.

Access

The area is crossed by a labyrinth of minor roads and forest tracks, some of which are of very indifferent quality. Straightforward access to some of the better areas is obtained by driving southwest from Aroche; this is a broad dirt road (H-9002) which is in excellent repair. It crosses a small river and several streams before entering the eucalyptus plantations in the vicinity of the largely deserted farm of El Mustio. The raptors, which are the chief attraction of this site, can be seen by stopping and scanning frequently along the road, which has very little traffic.

The northern entry point is found by taking the westernmost (HV-1431) of the two turnings for Aroche off the N-433 road. The road bypasses Aroche to the west. Once level with the village turn right up a gravel track past a large red-brick building (a school, which accommo-

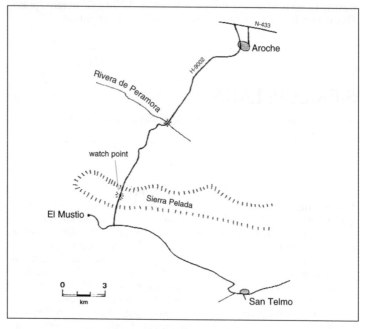

dates 150+ House Martin nests). This track ascends and then descends to a fork after 2.2 km. Take the left fork and keep straight on. This is the main road through the sierra and crosses all the main habitats. The stone bridge on the Rivera de Peramora, a few kilometres south of Aroche, is a good stopping point with Red-rumped Swallows very much in evidence and a likelihood of waterside species such as River Kingfisher and Grey Wagtail. Little Ringed Plover and White-rumped Swift also occur. The main ridge across the Sierra is reached 18.7 km from Aroche and provides points of vantage to scan for raptors. Black Vultures are often obvious and, if not, soon appear. A scattering of sheep carcases, provided for the vultures by well-wishers, give the ridge-top region a curious admixture of the heady scent of cistus and the homely aroma of (sun)roast lamb.

The same road may also be reached from the south but the access is poor; a dusty track descends to a quarry just southwest of San Telmo, heading north from the tarmacked San Telmo/Cabezas Rubias road, before turning east to follow the southern fringes of the Sierra Pelada to join the Aroche road at El Mustio. This road passes through some pleasant woodland but it also traverses the worst of the eucalyptus badlands and is perhaps best avoided.

Calendar

All year: Griffon Vulture, Black Vulture, Common Buzzard, Golden Eagle, Goshawk, Great Spotted Woodpecker, Grey Wagtail, Blue Rock Thrush, Rock Sparrow, Cirl Bunting, woodland passerines.

Breeding season: Black Stork, Short-toed Eagle, Booted Eagle, Little Ringed Plover, Kingfisher, White-rumped Swift, Red-rumped Swallow, woodland passerines.

WESTERN SIERRA MORENA   H7

Status: The area is largely comprised by a Parque Natural/ZEPA (Sierra de Aracena and Picos de Aroche), 184,000 ha.

Site Description

The western Sierra Morena offers a range of pleasant and tranquil landscapes, easily accessible by road. This is a relatively humid zone: Aracena has an annual rainfall of some 1000 mm. The mountains of the Sierra de Aracena proper, in the south of the area, are accordingly lushly wooded in parts, with extensive forests of sweet chestnut being particularly typical. Forests of cork oaks, Canarian oaks and encinas are also evident as well as extensive stands of maritime and stone pines. Riverine forest is well developed, for example along the course of the Río Múrtiga, and again includes stands of oaks and chestnut as well as white and black poplars.

The northern parts of the area include wide tracts of open grazing land and stone-walled pastures interspersed with olive groves and encinares and crossed by stony rivers. Some of the hillsides are overgrown with dense scrub, predominantly of cistus. Eucalyptus planting has devastated certain parts of the site, notably north of Aroche, but there are apparently plans to replant the affected areas with native trees in future and indeed some large new plantations of encinas have recently been established.

Species

The range of habitats and the ease of access along quiet, tarmac country roads makes this a good place for a leisurely visit in search of a representative range of Mediterranean birds. It offers a good diversity of woodland and mountain species, notably raptors, although none that cannot also be found elsewhere. White and Black Storks breed, the former on every church in every village as usual and the latter along the rocky river valleys. Vultures, including Black Vultures, are frequent overhead and other raptors include all five eagles, Red and Black Kites and numerous Common Buzzards. The woodlands, riverine forest and scrub areas have a rich passerine community which includes a good variety of warblers. Red-rumped Swallows nest under many, probably most, of the bridges and culverts. The latter's presence is undoubtedly an inducement to White-rumped Swifts which seem to be colonising the region slowly.

Timing
The breeding species are easiest to locate during springtime and early summer visits, when the flowers are also noteworthy. However, interesting species are present all year round.

Access
The area is traversed by the N-433 road, from which numerous minor roads lead to areas of some interest. The region offers plenty of scope for quiet exploration with potential for long walks on woodland tracks or across the uplands, or for just simply driving around and stopping at likely-looking places. Recommended areas include:

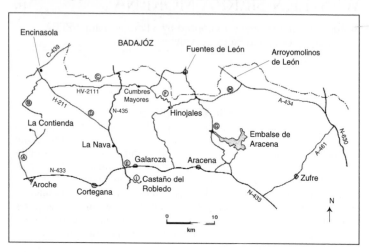

A Aroche/La Contienda
Drive north from Aroche, crossing encinares and a river before ascending through a region of barren hillsides, the results of eucalyptus plantations, to reach open meadowland, with scattered mature encinas, new plantations of encinas and large tracts of cistus heath. Rock Sparrows are common near Aroche and raptors and passerines generally in the upper reaches.

B La Contienda/Encinasola
The southern part of this road follows the contours of undulating country covered in cistus scrub alive with Dartford Warblers. Vultures and other raptors are common overhead. A short drive up a vertiginous track west of the road, about 1 km from its C-439 sector, leads to a mirador which offers panoramic views and an excellent vantage point to scan for raptors. The Río Múrtiga, southwest of Encinasola, is very scenic: a broad stony bed with clumps of oleanders. Black Storks occur here and there are many passerines in the nearby woods of cork oaks.

The old road bridge, adjacent to the new one, both at Km 22, is a good viewpoint and both Crag Martins and Red-rumped Swallows nest on the bridges themselves.

C Encinasola/Las Cumbres
The winding road (HV-2111) crosses several river valleys and also ascends to traverse open pastureland. The villages have the usual picturesque gatherings of White Stork nests. Raptors are frequent and the passerine community includes Rock Sparrows.

D Río Múrtiga valley
The H-211 road from Encinasola to the N-435 just north of La Nava follows the river valley, traversing mature woodlands of encina and also excellent areas of riverine woodland and scrub. The road is very quiet and repays frequent stopping and short walks to search for passerines and others. There are many lay-bys and some woodland tracks which facilitate exploration. Wall-to-wall Nightingales are a particular feature in spring but other characteristic species include Turtle Doves, Bee-eaters, Hoopoes, Wrynecks, Woodlarks, Red-rumped Swallows, Blackcaps, Rock Sparrows and Serins. Garden Warblers may also breed here.

E Río Múrtiga at Galaroza
Lush riverine woodland along the N-433, popular with warblers. The road through Galaroza itself suffers from heavy traffic but the short branch to the village of Las Chinas, immediately west of Galaroza, is very quiet and gives good views of the riverine habitats.

F Las Cumbres/Cañaveral de León
A picturesque transect across the north of the region, crossing open pastureland, encinares and olive groves, all enclosed by the characteristic stone walls. Rock Sparrows and Cirl Buntings are typical.

G Cañaveral de León/Aracena
Woodland habitats, with magnificent encinares in the north. Further south there is some open stony country. The road crosses the western arm of the Embalse de Aracena.

H Cañaveral de León/Arroyomolinos
This road traverses encinares near Cañaveral and a pleasant stream (Rivera de Montemayor), with associated riverine woodland, before ascending steeply to a col above Arroyomolinos. Stop south of the col to scan the panorama for raptors. Blue Rock Thrushes are present here and Thekla Larks along the wooded stretches. Cork oaks on the north side of the col support breeding Common Redstarts.

I Castaño del Robledo
Reached by driving south from the N-433 on the N-435, turning east at El Quejigo. Castaño del Robledo is a secluded village, named after the surrounding woods of sweet chestnut. The area may be explored on foot or by driving a short way up the tracks which lead east just before entering the village. Drive up the steep concrete ramp (to the local cemetery!) and continue upwards to enter the woodlands. Chestnut, cork oak and pinewoods offer a good variety of passerines.

Calendar

All year: Black-shouldered Kite, Red Kite, Griffon Vulture, Black Vulture, Goshawk, Sparrowhawk, Common Buzzard, Spanish Imperial Eagle, Golden Eagle, Bonelli's Eagle, Eagle Owl, Tawny Owl, Little Owl, Great Spotted Woodpecker, Crested Lark, Thekla Lark, Crag Martin, Blue Rock Thrush, Cetti's Warbler, Zitting Cisticola, Dartford Warbler, Sardinian Warbler, Blackcap, Nuthatch, Southern Grey Shrike, Azure-winged Magpie, Raven, Spotless Starling, Rock Sparrow, Cirl Bunting.

Breeding season: Black Stork, White Stork, Black Kite, Egyptian Vulture, Short-toed Eagle, Booted Eagle, Turtle Dove, Scops Owl, White-rumped Swift, Bee-eater, Hoopoe, Wryneck, Red-rumped Swallow, Nightingale, Common Redstart, Black-eared Wheatear, Melodious Warbler, Subalpine Warbler, Orphean Warbler, Whitethroat, Garden Warbler, Bonelli's Warbler, Golden Oriole, Woodchat Shrike.

CÁDIZ PROVINCE

Cádiz province is in itself one of the prime birding regions of southern Spain, offering as it does the great majority of the species of the region. The position in the extreme south of the region and the proximity to the African shore across the Strait of Gibraltar make Cádiz the key province in which to observe migration of raptors, storks and many other birds. The Strait itself is of major significance for seabird migration. The Cádiz coastlands have important sites for both passage and wintering seabirds, waders and other aquatic species. The province offers a range of lagoons attractive to White-headed Ducks, Purple Gallinules and the full range of marsh birds. The sierras are relatively lush, since Cádiz is

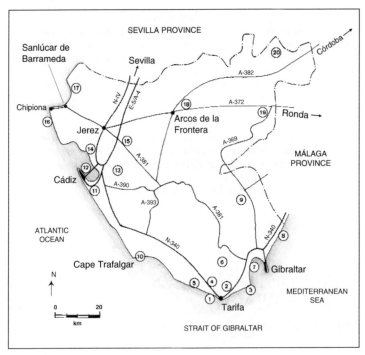

Sites in Cadíz Province

CA1 Playa de Los Lances (Tarifa beach)
CA2 Montes de Tarifa
CA3 Punta Secreta
CA4 La Janda
CA5 Bolonia, Zahara and Sierra de la Plata
CA6 Los Alcornocales and the Ojén valley
CA7 Palmones estuary
CA8 Sotogrande
CA9 Jimena and La Almoraima

CA10 Cape Trafalgar and the Barbate pinewoods and estuary
CA11 Marismas de Sancti Petri
CA12 Bahía de Cádiz
CA13 Lagunas de Puerto Real
CA14 Lagunas del Puerto de Santa María
CA15 Laguna de Medina
CA16 Chipiona coast
CA17 East bank of the Río Guadalquivir
CA18 Embalse de Arcos
CA19 Sierra de Grazalema
CA20 Peñon de Zaframagón

one of the wetter Spanish provinces, and they support a full range of raptor and passerine communities. Even steppe species, such as bustards, occur at a limited number of sites. This is probably the best province for a single-base visit; all its sites are within easy reach of Gibraltar, Jimena or other centres in the west of the region.

Maps
Mapa Provincial Cádiz, IGN, 1:200,000.
Mapa Guía Parque Natural Bahía de Cádiz, IGN, 1:50,000 (covers the Costa de la Luz, from Chipiona to south of Sancti Petri and the hinterland, including most of the wetland sites described below).
Mapa Guía Parque Natural Sierra de Grazalema, IGN, 1:50,000.
Gibraltar and the Costa del Sol, Clyde Leisure Map 15, 1:125,000. Covers the hinterland of Gibraltar, north to Jimena. Available at W.H. Smith and most United Kingdom bookshops.

Getting there
Direct access by air to the province is available at Jerez and Gibraltar is also an obvious arrival point by air. Within the province, rapid travel between the listed sites is available using the N-340 trunk road, which skirts the entire coastline. The province is well served by lesser roads; among these the A-381 Los Barrios/Jerez road is useful for reaching a number of the inland sites listed.

Where to stay
Hotels and campsites are widespread all along the coast and in most of the towns inland, notably Jimena and Grazalema. There are paradores at Arcos de la Frontera and at El Bosque, on the A-372 west of Grazalema. Gibraltar provides an excellent base for exploring the province; all sites are within day-trip distance of the Rock.

PLAYA DE LOS LANCES (TARIFA BEACH) CA1
Status: Paraje Natural and Reserva Ornitológica, 226 ha.

Site description
Los Lances is Tarifa Beach, the southernmost and one of the best of the many long sandy beaches of the Costa de la Luz. The beach itself is a broad sweep of fine sand some 3 km long, fronting on to the Strait of Gibraltar. Several rivers, notably Río de la Jara and Río de la Vega combine to form a shallow lagoon just behind the beach proper. The whole area is flooded occasionally by spring tides. The beach is flanked by low sand dunes giving onto rough pasture and plantations of young stone pines. The beach hinterland used to be a favourite and traditional site for hunters, especially finch-trappers in autumn. Happily these last

were dislodged in the mid-1990s, not without protest, and the area is now a bird reserve.

The beach is popular with tourists, especially the perennial and hardy windsurfers, and local people. However, its great size allows it to accommodate large numbers of birds even in summer.

Species

The beach is a favourite loafing ground for gulls, including Audouin's Gulls, which are present all year round but are especially numerous from mid-August to October. Tern flocks also form on the lagoon fringes especially and regularly include a few Lesser Crested Terns in May and October/November. Other seabirds are visible offshore. The lagoons attract waders, notably large flocks of Sanderlings and Dunlins. Ringed Plovers are usually present and Kentish Plovers breed. The strategic siting means that legions of raptors and other migrants cross the area and many will land and rest in the hinterland. Passerines throng the fields and pines at migration times and in winter. The beach is exceptionally well-placed to attract scarce or vagrant species, which have recently included Dotterel, Terek Sandpiper, Cream-coloured Courser and Royal Tern.

Timing

Visits are rewarding at all times of year but the largest gatherings of gulls and waders occur in winter. In summer, visits early in the morning will allow you to beat the beach-bums who might later frighten off the birds. The setting sun inhibits seawatching from late afternoon but is not otherwise a problem. The beach is very exposed and visits on days with strong winds (east or west) are likely to be unproductive and will certainly be most uncomfortable.

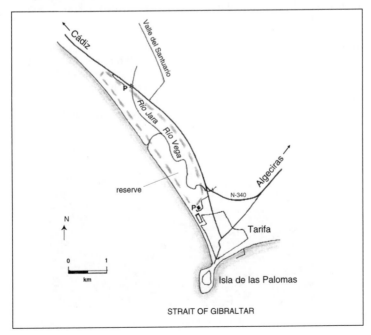

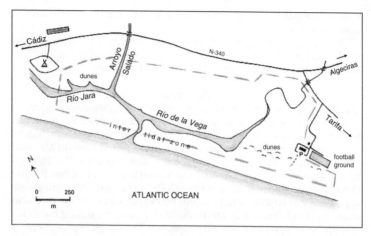

Access
Park in the car parks off the N-340 and explore on foot. Be prepared to wade across the shallow lagoons. A telescope is highly desirable.

Calendar
All year: Cory's Shearwater, Balearic Shearwater, Gannet, Cattle Egret, Little Egret, Grey Heron, Ringed Plover, Kentish Plover, Sanderling, Dunlin, Redshank, Arctic Skua, Great Skua, Audouin's Gull, Yellow-legged Gull, Thekla Lark, Zitting Cisticola, Spotless Starling, Serin, Greenfinch, Goldfinch, Linnet, Corn Bunting.

Breeding season: The above species, the non-passerines being mostly represented by non-breeders. Also: Turtle Dove, Cuckoo, Hoopoe, Short-toed Lark, Woodchat Shrike.

Winter: Oystercatcher, Golden Plover, Grey Plover, Lapwing, Knot, Snipe, Black-tailed Godwit, Bar-tailed Godwit, Whimbrel, Curlew, Common Sandpiper, Turnstone, Grey Phalarope, Mediterranean Gull, Little Gull, Black-headed Gull, Lesser Black-backed Gull, Kittiwake, Caspian Tern, Sandwich Tern, Razorbill, Puffin, Kingfisher, Calandra Lark (may breed), Skylark, Crag Martin, Meadow Pipit, White Wagtail, Black Redstart, Common Chiffchaff, Common Starling.

Cream-coloured Coursers

76

Passage periods: In addition to the above: Purple Heron, Black Stork, White Stork, Spoonbill, Greater Flamingo, raptors, Black-winged Stilt, Avocet, Stone Curlew, Collared Pratincole, Little Ringed Plover, Little Stint, Curlew Sandpiper, Ruff, Spotted Redshank, Greenshank, Green Sandpiper, Wood Sandpiper, Pomarine Skua, Gull-billed Tern, Lesser Crested Tern, Common Tern, Little Tern, Whiskered Tern, Black Tern. All the many species of landbirds crossing the Strait on migration also occur in the area: swifts, larks, swallows, pipits, wagtails, chats, warblers and finches are all well represented.

MONTES DE TARIFA   CA2

Status: Parque Natural (in part) and ZEPA; the southern portion of Los Alcornocales.

Site description

Tarifa is the southernmost point of Europe: the 36th parallel runs through the naval base of Isla Cristina situated on the island just off-shore. It lies roughly at the midpoint of the northern shore of the Strait of Gibraltar and only 16 km (10 miles) from the nearest point on the African shore (Cape Cires). The hinterland consists of rolling open hill-sides, with numerous rocky gullies and outcrops, climbing to the Sierra del Bujeo and Sierra del Cabrito. There are areas of pines and cork-woods, much favoured by resting raptors and other migrants.

Regular coordinated counts of migrating soaring birds take place in the area each autumn, from mid-July to mid-October, under the aus-pices of Programa Migres, a project funded by the regional government (Junta de Andalucía) and organised by the SEO. Volunteer observers are always in demand and should contact the organisers at Programa Migres, Centro de Vistantes Huerta Grande, El Pelayo, 11390 Algeciras, Cádiz (tel: 956-679156; email p.migres@teleline.es). Participants receive board and lodging. This is an excellent way to get acquainted with the area and to make a useful contribution to an important long-term pro-gramme. The Huerta Grande includes an information centre and is at Km 96.2 on the N-340, south side.

Over the last decade or so, the hilltops north and east of Tarifa have been grotesquely disfigured by hundreds of windmills; a European Community funded experiment in generating electricity using wind power. Some 800 are in place with an eventual total of up to 3,000 apparently under consideration. The direct impact of the windmills on birds was investigated in 1993 by the Spanish Ornithological Society (SEO). The study ran for one year during which 69 corpses were recov-ered. Most were raptors, with Griffon Vultures (30) and Common Kestrels (12) predominating. Experiments with dead kestrels on the length of time in which dead birds remained on-site suggested that the actual total mortality was of the order of 106 birds (49 of them kestrels). This is unfortunate but is a negligible fraction of the birds using the area. The visual impact is another matter: in many respects an area of outstanding, indeed world-class, natural beauty has been ruined. One looks back with nostalgic regret to the days when a wind farm was just a field of beans!

Species
The Tarifa hinterland is rich in the breeding species of rocky, wooded country, including diurnal raptors, White-rumped Swifts and Eagle Owls, and also Iberian Chiffchaffs in the denser riverine woodland. Some very large vulture colonies are here and the Griffons themselves are omnipresent, the strong winds allowing them to fly at any time independently of thermal activity. Other vultures are attracted too: Egyptian Vultures nest and are common on passage, a few Black Vultures occur in some winters, there have been several recent records of wandering Lammergeiers and Rüppell's Vultures (see Introduction) have recently begun to appear with some regularity.

The chief attraction of Tarifa is that it is overflown by the hundreds of thousands, probably millions, of birds using the Strait as the short sea-crossing between Europe and Africa. The visible flights of storks and raptors are particularly noteworthy. Important seabird movements also occur through the Strait but these are more easily observed further west, at Punta Secreta (CA3) and Gibraltar.

Timing
The area is of greatest interest during the main migration periods: February–May and August–November. However, it is probably true to say that some migration across the Strait occurs on every single day of the year. Seabird movements through the Strait are also daily events. The breeding species too warrant summer visits and populations of wintering species are also high and of interest.

Access
A number of locations in this area will repay a visit.

A Tarifa town
The seawall in Tarifa town offers a reasonably high vantage point for seawatching; a telescope is highly desirable here. The island would be better but it is off-limits as a military base. The military have similarly monopolised almost the entire shore of the Strait east of Tarifa (but see Punta Secreta, CA3). However, for watching migration there are good locations on the upper slopes.

B El Mirador/Alto del Cabrito
The public watchpoint over the Strait (Mirador del Estrecho) is actually best avoided since as often as not you will be surrounded by hordes of tourists and the litter they leave sometimes is depressing to see. In 'spring', raptors etc. arrive on a broad front but a proportion should be overhead or nearby if you watch from the various points east and west of the mirador mentioned below. The general rule is that the birds arrive mainly at the downwind end of the Strait, i.e. towards and east of Tarifa in easterly winds and towards Gibraltar in westerlies. The same applies in 'autumn' but then the birds will be much higher up, having gained altitude for the crossing over the Spanish mainland.

The best place to stop, especially if you intend to spend some time here, is the migration watch point on the rise of Alto del Cabrito. Take

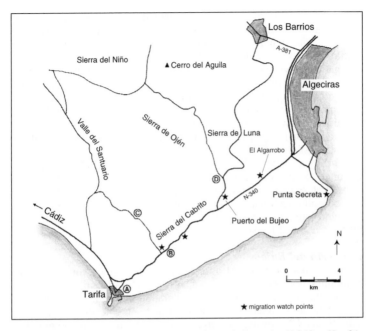

the good dirt road which branches northwards from the N-340 at Km 91, just west of El Mirador. Traffic on the main road is often busy and fast and great care is needed here; if you arrive from the south (Tarifa) it may be wiser to overshoot and turn around in the mirador car park instead of cutting across oncoming traffic. Once attained, a signpost at the top of the initial rise indicates a 700-m track, which is narrow but easily drivable. Park at the top and view the area from the concrete 'observatory', which is an open, roofed structure, with a table and seats. The site offers commanding views and is only marred by the metallic rattles and grating of the nearby windmills. On the positive side, the many access tracks to the windmills offer opportunities for searching the scrub-covered hillsides for grounded migrants and resident passerines.

A second useful watchpoint is at Km 92, just east of the mirador and safely accessible from the eastbound carriageway only. You *will* notice a large 'sculpture' of debatable significance, involving a large blue ball and a larger blue hand — a monument to the unknown bowls player perhaps — to the south of the road. It is possible to park at the entrance to the access track to this azure artefact and then to watch from its vicinity.

A third location, likely to be most useful during westerly winds in spring, is the migration watch point at El Algarrobo, accessible up a short track to the northwest of the N-340 at Km 99.1, just opposite a collection of radio transmission masts. This site, along with that at El Cabrito and another ten locations, forms part of the array of observatories which are manned during the Programa Migrés autumn campaigns.

C El Mirador/Valle del Santuario
The dirt roads leading inland from the Strait offer outstanding scenery and ample opportunities to stop and search the scrub and woodlands for migrants and breeding/wintering species. A visit is highly recom-

mended. The cork oaks here have forsaken the demands of geotropism: the powerful levanter winds have made them all lean decidedly westwards. Spectacular 'falls' of raptors occur during prolonged easterlies in 'autumn' especially; kites and others dot the hills like flocks of small, elongated brown sheep. Traffic is negligible and the roads are in quite good condition but care is needed to avoid potholes and related hazards, such as rockfalls and crumbling verges, along some stretches. The principal road connects with the N-340 at Km 91, just west of El Mirador, mentioned above. The dirt road mainly descends northwestwards from El Mirador for 16 km, joining the tarmacked road to El Santuario de la Luz at a point 10.8 km from the N-340. This tarmac/dirt junction is marked by a house with solar panels and grey chain-link fencing. The entrance to the Santuario road off the N-340 is on the northern side of the stretch which borders Tarifa beach, just east of Camping Río Jara and conspicuously flanked by tall white masonry brackets. The roads to the wind farms have recently provided extra avenues of access to the hillsides north of Tarifa.

D Puerto del Bujeo

This provides an excellent and secluded watchpoint for raptor and other migration. It is situated about halfway between Tarifa and the Bay of Gibraltar and as such sees most migration during light winds or on days of moderate westerlies. Access is from the picnic area on the north side of the N-340 exactly at Km 95 (marked by a red kilometre post). Take great care when entering/leaving the main road. Once in the picnic area follow the track upwards. The condition of the track is quite appalling: it was once tarmacked but has been allowed to deteriorate completely. With care, the track is perfectly passable nonetheless and the first 500 m are the worst. After this one soon clears the tree-line of cork oaks and eucalyptus and can enjoy stunning views of Gibraltar, the Bay, the Strait and the Moroccan shore. Migration can be observed from anywhere along here. The intrepid may wish to continue further along this road. It eventually descends through corkwoods to Los Barrios, passing several Griffon Vulture colonies en route. Again, care is urged since the road is in dangerous disrepair in parts. The descent to Los Barrios crosses a few farms; please remember to close all gates.

Calendar

All year: Cattle Egret, White Stork, Griffon Vulture, Goshawk, Sparrowhawk, Common Buzzard, Bonelli's Eagle, Lesser Kestrel, Kestrel, Peregrine, Barn Owl, Eagle Owl, Little Owl, Tawny Owl, Calandra Lark, Crested Lark, Thekla Lark, Woodlark, Crag Martin, Blue Rock Thrush, Cetti's Warbler, Zitting Cisticola, Dartford Warbler, Sardinian Warbler, Firecrest, Crested Tit, Southern Grey Shrike, Raven, Spotless Starling, Serin, Hawfinch, Cirl Bunting, Rock Bunting. (For seabirds, see Gibraltar.)

Breeding season: Black Kite, Egyptian Vulture, Short-toed Eagle, Montagu's Harrier, Booted Eagle, Hobby, Quail, Scops Owl, Red-necked Nightjar, Common Swift, Pallid Swift, Alpine Swift, White-rumped Swift, Bee-eater, Hoopoe, Short-toed Lark, Red-rumped Swallow, Tawny Pipit, Rufous Bush Chat, Black-eared Wheatear, Olivaceous Warbler, Melodious Warbler, Subalpine Warbler, Orphean Warbler, Whitethroat, Bonelli's Warbler, Iberian Chiffchaff, Golden Oriole, Woodchat Shrike, Ortolan Bunting.

Winter: Black-shouldered Kite, Red Kite, Black Vulture, Hen Harrier, Spanish Imperial Eagle, Merlin, Crane, Golden Plover, Lapwing, Woodcock, Alpine Accentor, Fieldfare, Redwing, Common Starling, Brambling, Siskin. (For seabirds, see Gibraltar.)

Passage periods: The potential list is extensive and includes 'frequent rarities'. Regular migrants include: Night Heron, Little Egret, Grey Heron, Purple Heron, Black Stork, Spoonbill, Greater Flamingo, Honey Buzzard, Marsh Harrier, Golden Eagle, Osprey, Eleonora's Falcon, Stone Curlew, Collared Pratincole, Stock Dove, Great Spotted Cuckoo, Short-eared Owl, Common Nightjar, Kingfisher, Roller, Wryneck, Sand Martin, Tree Pipit, Red-throated Pipit, Water Pipit, Yellow Wagtail, Bluethroat, Whinchat, Northern Wheatear, Rock Thrush, Ring Ouzel, Grasshopper Warbler, Savi's Warbler, Reed Warbler, Great Reed Warbler, Spectacled Warbler, Garden Warbler, Wood Warbler, Willow Warbler, Pied Flycatcher, Spanish Sparrow, Tree Sparrow, Crossbill and Bullfinch. (For seabirds, see Gibraltar.)

PUNTA SECRETA   CA3

Status: No special protection.

Site description
Punta Secreta is an accessible portion of the northern shore of the Strait; the rest of it, west to Tarifa, is controlled by the military. The headland lies just beyond the western entrance to Gibraltar Bay at Punta Carnero and offers excellent views east to the Rock and southwards to the African shore some 22 km away. The hillsides leading down to the shore are largely barren or covered with a thin scrub of spiny broom and fan palm, with oleanders along the occasional streams but the rapid expansion of villa-type developments has occupied much of the lower slopes.

Species
This is an alternative site to Gibraltar for seawatching in the Strait and for observing the northbound arrivals of raptors and storks in spring. The rocky shore attracts resting flocks of gulls, including Audouin's Gulls, as well as waders such as Whimbrels and Turnstones. Single Purple Sandpipers, rare in southern Spain, are seen here with some regularity in winter. All these birds like to sit on the numerous rocks just offshore. Falls of passerines may occur in spring and, to a lesser extent, in autumn, most frequently during periods of strong, easterly winds.

Timing
All year for seabirds. February–May for northward raptor passage; arrivals in this part of the Strait occur chiefly in westerly and calm wind conditions. The southward raptor passage passes high over the site and is seen better from Tarifa (CA2) and Gibraltar. Passage periods for migrants.

Access

The coast road from Algeciras to Getares Bay winds on to the lighthouse at Punta Carnero and then round to Punta Secreta. There are small lay-bys all along the road from which elevated views of the rocky shore and the coastal scrub may be had. This area is always worth searching during passage periods. The roads serving the scattered villas around Punta Secreta provide access to the shore there. Migration watching from Punta Secreta is best done under the small electricity pylon next to the sign Av. Punta Carnero, on the south side of the access road.

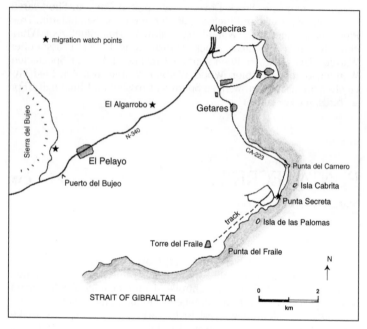

Calendar

All year: Seabirds; as Gibraltar (although the Rock's Shags rarely come here).

February–May: Storks, raptors and passerines (species as Gibraltar).

August–November: Raptors and passerines. Audouin's Gulls are often numerous in August–September on the rocks.

LA JANDA

Status: No special protection, 20,000 ha.

Site description

The plain of La Janda is a remarkable place. Most of it was formerly an extensive shallow lake, La Laguna de la Janda, which with its associated reedbeds and marshland was numbered among the finest of the Spanish wetlands. Among its claims to fame was its status as the last breeding site of the Crane in Spain. Sadly its fate was decided in less conservation-conscious times and it was drained in the early 1960s. Recently the Junta de Andalucía has commissioned hydrological studies to see whether the Laguna may be restored, at least in part. It remains to be seen whether or not anything positive will result but there are grounds for optimism.

The former lake basin is still criss-crossed by deep drainage channels, which retain permanent water and fringing reedbeds. Peripheral reservoirs hold back much of the water which formerly entered the lake. Still, in wet winters, the area floods and La Laguna temporarily re-asserts itself. The interest of the site as a wetland was of course vastly diminished once the lake was drained. Nevertheless, the recent expansion of rice cultivation has helped to sustain the attraction of the region to aquatic birds and other wildlife.

The remaining plains and pastures are attractive to open-country birds although much habitat has been lost to intensive cultivation in recent years. The area is a magnet for raptors and migrants generally. An extensive and very private estate (Las Lomas), between Vejer and Benalup, includes the large-scale rearing/shooting of pheasants among its sundry activities; the area is thus an unintentional bird table for large numbers of raptors, especially in winter. The hillsides along the northern fringe of the plain include the conspicuous triangular escarpment known as La Laja del Aciscar, home to a sizable colony of Griffon Vultures.

Species

La Janda offers a taste of the steppes of Extremadura to visitors to southern Andalucía. Little Bustards and Stone Curlews breed commonly but Great Bustards became virtually if not actually extinct in this, their last redoubt in the province, by the beginning of 2000, when just one individual was reputed to survive. In spring the area resounds to the song of abundant Thekla and Calandra Larks and Montagu's Harriers quarter the pastures. White Storks breed on most of the farms and occur in very large numbers on migration. Collared Praticoles are also characteristic in spring and summer.

In winter the calls of Cranes are frequently heard and flocks of up to several hundred are present, mainly from November to February. Golden Plovers and Lapwings are typical in winter, with other waders, gulls and waterfowl frequenting the rice fields and drainage canals and occurring more widely when the region floods. Hen Harriers replace Montagu's Harriers in winter, when other regular raptors include Black-shouldered Kites, Red Kites and Spanish Imperial Eagles. The western end (Las Lomas) is a reliable site for finding wintering Booted Eagles, as well as Black-shouldered Kites, Penduline Tits and Spanish Sparrows.

Timing

The area is rewarding at all times of year. Winter is a particularly interesting season. Visits in high summer are least productive since many
birds keep a low profile then. Windy days are also best avoided. Early
morning and late evening visits are advisable in hot weather to coincide
with peak bird activity and to avoid the heat-haze.

Access

La Janda can be accessed from minor roads and farm tracks, The central track, bordering the main drainage ditch and skirting the rice fields,
is recommended. The track is usually in good condition although it can
become impassable in very wet weather to all but 4WD vehicles. The
entrance to this track is on the north side of the N-340 at the junction
with the Zahara road, immediately opposite the Venta de Retín.

Further inland, the road from Facinas towards Benalup skirts the
northern edge of the former lake basin for some 20 km and gives good

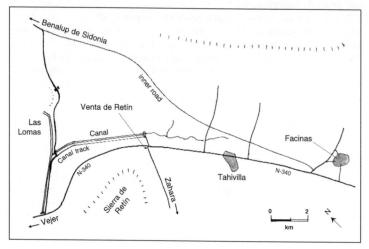

views of the pastures and open country frequented by bustards and
other 'steppe' species. The road is most easily found by taking the western turning for Facinas off the N-340 and then turning left almost at once
onto the wide sandy dirt track marked Camino Agricola Facinas-
Benalup, which is the road in question. There is little traffic, allowing frequent stops to be made to scan the fields. Entry to the pastures is not necessary and is downright dangerous wherever cattle are grazing; fighting
bulls are reared here. Distances are great and a telescope is advisable.

Calendar

All year: Cattle Egret, Little Egret, White Stork, Mallard, Griffon Vulture,
(Great Bustard), Little Bustard, Stone Curlew, Barn Owl, Eagle Owl,
Calandra Lark, Thekla Lark, Zitting Cisticola, Raven, Spotless Starling.

Breeding season: Black Kite, Egyptian Vulture, Short-toed Eagle, Marsh
Harrier, Montagu's Harrier, Booted Eagle, Lesser Kestrel, Quail, Collared
Pratincole, Scops Owl, Red-necked Nightjar, Bee-eater, Hoopoe, Short-
toed Lark, Red-rumped Swallow, Tawny Pipit, Rufous Bush Chat,
Ortolan Bunting.

Winter: Little Grebe, Grey Heron, Greylag Goose, Wigeon, Teal, Pintail, Shoveler, Black-shouldered Kite, Red Kite, Black Vulture, Hen Harrier, Spanish Imperial Eagle, Golden Eagle, Booted Eagle, Bonelli's Eagle, Merlin, Crane, Black-winged Stilt, Avocet, Kentish Plover, Golden Plover, Grey Plover, Lapwing, Dunlin, Ruff, Jack Snipe, Snipe, Whimbrel, Curlew, Redshank, Greenshank, Common Sandpiper, Great Spotted Cuckoo, Short-eared Owl, Woodlark, Red-throated Pipit, Water Pipit, Penduline Tit, Southern Grey Shrike, Common Starling, Spanish Sparrow, Tree Sparrow, Siskin, Cirl Bunting.

Passage periods: The main raptor and passerine routes leading to the Strait cross the area and almost anything can turn up here. In addition to all the species mentioned above, the regulars include Purple Heron, Black Stork, Garganey, Honey Buzzard, Sparrowhawk, Osprey, Wood Sandpiper, Green Sandpiper, Roller, Wryneck, Lesser Short-toed lark, Tree Pipit, Yellow Wagtail, Bluethroat, Common Redstart, Northern Wheatear, warblers and finches. The area has produced a number of rarities recently including Cream-coloured Courser, Little Swift, Richard's Pipit and Little Bunting.

BOLONIA, ZAHARA AND SIERRA DE LA PLATA CA5

Status: No special protection.

Site description

This is a sector of the Costa de la Luz, lying some 20–30 km northwest of Tarifa. The fine sandy beaches and brilliant light provide a cheerful setting to several interesting sites. The hinterland consists of barren hillsides and rough pastures, strikingly beautiful in spring when the rains bring out masses of wild flowers. These are the famous painted fields and they are worth a visit in their own right. The sierras shelter extensive patches of coastal scrub and there are large stone pine woods at Bolonia and along the Sierra de la Plata. Watercourses are overgrown with oleanders, which bloom pink in summer. Rocky escarpments on the hillsides support vulture colonies. Zahara offers seawatching and a small estuary.

Species

The area's chief claim to fame is as the first known breeding site in Europe of White-rumped Swift, a species not previously known to occur closer than tropical Africa. The first discoveries, in 1964 were assumed to be Little Swifts, also a white-rumped species and one which has nested for decades at Tangier, in full view of Zahara and not 30 km away. (For all that, Little Swifts are rarely seen in Spain; but see below.) Photographs published in *The Ibis* initiated a heated argument but, finally, netting the birds established their true identity. The swifts use

White-rumped Swifts and Little Swift

the old nests of the Red-rumped Swallows, which build commonly under overhangs along the slopes of the sierra. Both swallows and swifts are still here; the swifts in particular being present from May to at least September.

The small swift population (fewer than ten pairs) may mean a patient wait before you find one, but watching in the mornings and evenings from the southern flanks of the Sierra de la Plata is generally successful. Recently there have been a considerable number of sightings of Little Swifts in the area so there is an added incentive to inspect any white-rumped swifts here closely. In fact, Little Swifts have been annual here since 1995, with up to five individuals seen together. The square tails and large, wrap-around white rumps of Little Swifts make them easily distinguishable from the original colonists, with their slender forked tails and small, crescent-shaped white rumps. In spring 2000 both species could be seen visiting caves on the Sierra de la Plata, suggesting that Little Swifts may also be breeding here. Since in Africa White-rumped Swifts often use Little Swift nests the juxtaposition of the two species here may prove interesting. Since Pallid and Common Swifts are generally present over the area, and Alpine Swifts often occur on passage, this is the only place in Europe where there is any real chance of seeing five swift species at once.

The Sierra de la Plata also has a large colony of Griffon Vultures (on the Bolonia side) and Egyptian Vultures nest on the facing hillside. The watercourses at Bolonia are a reliable site for nesting Rufous Bush Chats.

Zahara offers seawatching; the species are those which occur generally in the Strait (see Gibraltar). The shallow estuary here holds waders and egrets in small numbers, as well as Garganey and other transient waterfowl on migration.

The whole area is below the flightpaths of storks, raptors and other migrants using the Strait. It is particularly busy during periods of easterly winds. Passerine migrants occur abundantly in season.

Timing
May to September for White-rumped and Little Swifts. All times of year will produce interesting birds.

Access

Main roads lead from the N-340 to Bolonia and Zahara, providing simple access to the main sites. White-rumped Swifts may be seen anywhere in the area but the best option is to drive to and past Bolonia and up the eastern side of the Sierra de la Plata to the sites shown on the map. Little Swifts are present in the same area. The military camp and pinewoods to the west of the beach are out of bounds and, strictly-speaking, it is also not permitted to drive all the way up the tarmac road onto the Sierra, but nobody seems to mind.

The coastal sites at Zahara are reached by driving southeastwards through the village. The incomplete and abandoned Hotel Atlanterra on the beach is arguably the largest nest box for Spotless Starlings ever built! The best point for seawatching is on the rocky headland below the lighthouse at Punta Camarinal. Park in the car park at the foot of the access road and walk up to the headland, which gives elevated views of the coastline. The pinewoods and scrub around the beach and the cove south of the headland are attractive to passerine migrants and are worth inspecting during passage periods.

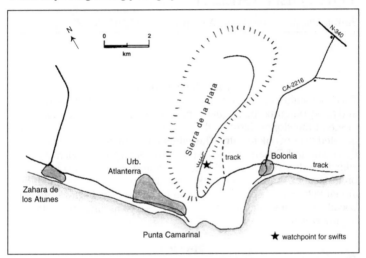

Calendar

All year: Cory's Shearwater, Balearic Shearwater, Gannet, Cattle Egret, Little Egret, White Stork, Griffon Vulture, Common Buzzard, Peregrine, Kentish Plover, Arctic Skua, Great Skua, Blue Rock Thrush, Zitting Cisticola, Dartford Warbler, Sardinian Warbler, Raven.

Breeding season: Black Kite, Egyptian Vulture, Short-toed Eagle, Montagu's Harrier, Booted Eagle, Lesser Kestrel, Hobby, Quail, Scops Owl, Red-necked Nightjar, White-rumped Swift, Little Swift, Bee-eater, Hoopoe, Short-toed Lark, Red-rumped Swallow, Tawny Pipit, Rufous Bush Chat, Black-eared Wheatear, Melodious Warbler, Whitethroat, Ortolan Bunting.

Winter: Leach's Storm-petrel, Common Scoter, Red-breasted Merganser, Red Kite, Hen Harrier, Osprey, Merlin, Oystercatcher, Ringed Plover,

Golden Plover, Grey Plover, Lapwing, Sanderling, Dunlin, Whimbrel, Redshank, Turnstone, Grey Phalarope, Mediterranean Gull, Little Gull, Audouin's Gull, Kittiwake, Caspian Tern, Sandwich Tern, Razorbill, Puffin, Crag Martin.

Passage periods: Herons, Black Stork, Spoonbill, Greater Flamingo, waterfowl including Garganey, raptors including Eleonora's Falcon, waders, Pomarine Skua, Audouin's Gull, Gull-billed Tern, Lesser Crested Tern, Roseate Tern, Common Tern, Arctic Tern, Little Tern, Black Tern, Great Spotted Cuckoo, Short-eared Owl, swifts, Kingfisher, Roller, Wryneck, passerines.

LOS ALCORNOCALES AND THE OJÉN VALLEY CA6

Status: Parque Natural (Los Alcornocales), 170,025 ha. ZEPA.

Site description

This is an attractive region of mainly low, heavily-wooded sierras. Cliffs and rocky outcrops are frequent and numerous streams and small rivers descend the slopes. Most of the area is well preserved, being largely devoted to cork oak forestry. The wilder forest tracts include Lusitanian, Pyrenean and Canarian oaks, white poplars and smooth-leaved elms, with an understorey of rhododendrons. Forests of maritime pines occur on the higher slopes. Open rocky areas have many heathers and there are large tracts of asphodel steppe in the more heavily-grazed regions. Locally there are extensive olive groves, as well as citrus plantations in the lower valleys.

Species

This is an excellent area for breeding raptors, with all five eagles present as well as several large colonies of Griffon Vultures and a substantial population of Eagle Owls. The woodlands have a rich passerine community, including a breeding population of Iberian Chiffchaffs, these last in lusher riverine tracts especially, including those in the central portion of the Ojén valley. Red-rumped Swallows are locally common and have their attendant White-rumped Swifts; the Jimena area (CA9) and the Ojén valley are reliable for the latter but they are widespread. The region is adjacent to the Strait and so holds many migrants on passage. The park is crossed by the flyways of raptors and storks and large flocks may be seen throughout the area. The corkwoods themselves are of great importance to migrant raptors, which roost there in droves. The smaller towns, notably Los Barrios and Alcalá de los Gazules, have colonies of Lesser Kestrels. In addition to birds, the region has good numbers of red and roe deer, wild boar, genet and mongoose. The Hozgarganta and other rivers have otters (rarely seen) and the ubiquitous terrapins. The Spanish lynx is also reputed to occur.

Timing

The area is rewarding throughout the year. Raptors are always obvious and there is generally a great deal of activity among the smaller birds. Visible migration is most evident from late February to early May and again from August to October. White-rumped Swifts are generally present from May to September. Iberian Chiffchaffs are summer visitors, best detected by song in April and May; they depart in August. Bird populations remain high in winter when large numbers of migrants arrive from the north.

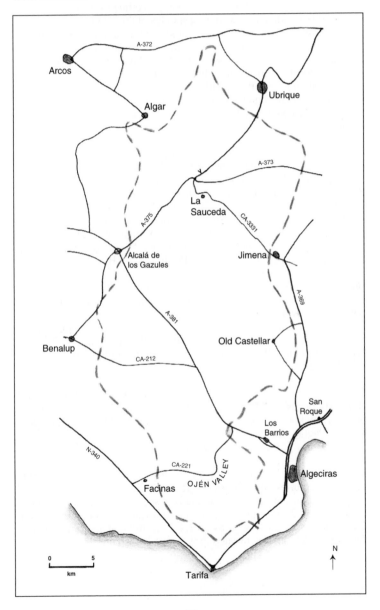

Access

Much of the area comprises large private estates, including a number of fighting-bull ranches. Minor roads provide good access to most areas, however, and numerous forest tracks permit exploration on foot. It is best to drive along slowly, with frequent stops to scan the sky and vegetation (or whenever something interesting shows itself). Areas of corkwood should be visited to see the full range of passerines.

The scenic road from Los Barrios to Facinas (Ojén valley) is particularly good, crossing corkwoods, riverine forest, open scrub and rocky hillsides. Raptors and storks pass directly overhead on migration and most of the breeding and wintering species of the region can be found here. Iberian Chiffchaffs are best located by song and are present in the lush riverside woodland where the road reaches the valley bottom; they are summer visitors and present only from April to August. The road itself was formerly in an appalling state but in 2000 the tarmac was stripped off and the surface graded, making access safe and straightforward. Traffic is negligible, so it is easy to stop anywhere, although it would increase very substantially should the road be tarmacked again in future.

Calendar

All year: Cattle Egret, White Stork, Red Kite, Griffon Vulture, Goshawk, Sparrowhawk, Common Buzzard, Spanish Imperial Eagle, Golden Eagle, Bonelli's Eagle, Common Kestrel, Peregrine, Eagle Owl, Little Owl, Tawny Owl, Great Spotted Woodpecker, Thekla Lark, Woodlark, Crag Martin, Grey Wagtail, Robin, Stonechat, Blue Rock Thrush, Cetti's Warbler, Zitting Cisticola, Dartford Warbler, Sardinian Warbler, Blackcap, Firecrest, Crested Tit, Short-toed Treecreeper, Raven, Spotless Starling, Serin, Hawfinch, Cirl Bunting, Rock Bunting, Corn Bunting.

Breeding season: Black Kite, Egyptian Vulture, Short-toed Eagle, Booted Eagle, Lesser Kestrel, Peregrine, Cuckoo, Red-necked Nightjar, Common Swift, Pallid Swift, Alpine Swift, White-rumped Swift, Bee-eater, Hoopoe, Red-rumped Swallow, Tawny Pipit, Rufous Bush Chat, Nightingale, Black-eared Wheatear, Melodious Warbler, Subalpine Warbler, Orphean Warbler, Bonelli's Warbler, Iberian Chiffchaff, Golden Oriole, Woodchat Shrike, Ortolan Bunting.

Winter: Raptors, including increased numbers of Red Kites and Buzzards, occasional Black-shouldered Kites and Black Vultures, Great Spotted Cuckoo, Skylark, large roosts of Crag Martins, Meadow Pipit, White Wagtail, Black Redstart, Song Thrush, Common Chiffchaff, Southern Grey Shrike, Common Starling.

Passage periods: Migrant raptors and storks overhead, passage of Bee-eaters, hirundines and finches. Migrant passerines of a wide range of species can turn up anywhere and falls of such migrants happen in wet overcast conditions especially. There is always a chance of encountering vagrant species as well as scarce and irregular migrants such as Eleonora's Falcon, Red-thoated Pipit, Rock Thrush and Fieldfare.

PALMONES ESTUARY

Status: Paraje Natural 'Marismas del Río Palmones', 58 ha.

Site description

The floodplain and estuary of the River Palmones lie just north of Algeciras, on the western shore of the Bay of Gibraltar. The western side of the bay has been ravaged by the construction of heavy industry, most conspicuously the large oil refinery. However, the Palmones area provides a sizeable expanse of surviving open country which often attracts migrants and other species. The upper reaches consist of grazing marsh with reedy ditches. Small patches of saltmarsh border the river as it approaches its shallow, sandy estuary. The river has suffered from pollution by the paper factory near the N-340, but this seems to have ameliorated recently.

Species

The principal interest of Palmones is as a staging point for migrant storks, herons, waders and passerines. Flocks of White Storks, sometimes many hundreds of birds, often linger here. Little and Cattle Egrets are everywhere and flocks of waders frequent the riverside and saltmarsh creeks. Wader numbers are seldom very high but a good variety of species use the site. Waders and gulls apart, interesting wintering birds include regular Ospreys, Bluethroats and Penduline Tits.

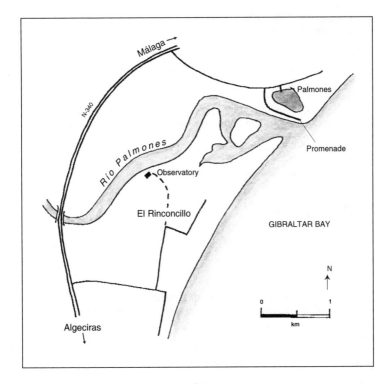

Timing
The site is most rewarding during winter and the main passage periods.

Access
The estuary and river may be viewed at leisure from Palmones village, where there is an attractive waterfront promenade, conveniently supplied with garden benches. Palmones is reached from the N-340 dual carriageway; follow the signs from exit (Km) 112 southbound or from exit (Km) 111 northbound. The marshes are best seen from El Rinconcillo on the south bank. Follow signs to the village from the N-340, south of the river bridge, or from Algeciras waterfront. Turn left on entering the village and follow the road (Calle Camino La Mediana) northwards towards the river; the tarmac gives way to sand before the road curves round to end by the local sewage works, adjacent to the saltmarshes. Park by the metal gate which gives access to a small municipal park and children's playground, from which there are elevated views across the saltmarshes. Explore on foot from here.

Local ornithologists have constructed an observatory on the south bank complete with sun-terrace for open-air viewing of raptor migration overhead. The observatory gives good views northwestwards across the river. You can hardly miss it: the yellow ochre building is even visible to the naked eye from the top of Gibraltar, 8 km away.

Calendar
All year: Cattle Egret, Little Egret, White Stork, Griffon Vulture, Kentish Plover.

Breeding season: Black Kite, Booted Eagle, Kentish Plover, Short-toed Lark, Yellow Wagtail.

Winter: Great Cormorant, Grey Heron, ducks, Osprey, waders, Mediterranean Gull, Little Gull, Sandwich Tern, Bluethroat, Penduline Tit, Reed Bunting.

Passage periods: Overhead passage of storks, raptors, hirundines and finches. Spoonbill, Greater Flamingo, wildfowl, waders, terns, chats and warblers.

SOTOGRANDE   CA8

Status: Paraje Natural (Estuario del Rio Guadiaro), 27 ha.

Site description
Sotogrande is the name of an upmarket residential area and marina built around the estuary of the River Guadiaro, on the Mediterranean coast just north of Gibraltar. Lush gardens, palm groves, golf courses and polo fields appeared 'overnight'. Nevertheless, the estuary proper is a small reserve protecting an expanse of reeds and tamarisks sheltered from the sea by a

sand bar. The area is important as one of the few remaining wetlands on the Costa del Sol and it is popular with waterbirds accordingly.

The area to the north of the estuary includes a small reed-fringed lagoon (Las Camelias) and damp scrubby fields which are also worth visiting, attracting ducks and both migrant and wintering passerines. Temporary pools and Tamarisk scrub to the south of the area are of similar interest, especially in winter when flooding occurs.

Species

Gulls and waders are always obvious. The flocks of the former often reward scanning. They usually include Audouin's Gulls, especially in late summer and autumn. Lesser Crested Terns occur with some frequency in autumn especially. The wader variety may be considerable but numbers are usually small. A range of seabirds are often visible offshore. The freshwater marsh on the south side of the estuary has resident Purple Gallinules. Migrant Ospreys often linger in the area for a few days and occasionally appear in winter. Notable passerines include wintering Bluethroats and Penduline Tits.

Timing

Of interest all year round.

Access

Sotogrande is clearly marked on the N-340 from both directions. The service roads to the complex provide easy access to both banks of the river. If you enter from the Gibraltar direction, follow the central road as far as the sea, where it loops northwards towards the river. Continue along this road until it turns inland again. Park where a large wooden gate, beside an information board, gives access to a track leading to the south bank. Explore the beach and sand spit on foot. Here a hide allows the freshwater marsh to be scanned in seclusion and there is also a boardwalk giving access to the central part of the estuary. The upper estuary may be viewed from a second boardwalk, signposted at the southern end of the bridge across the River Guadiaro. Traffic across the bridge is sometimes brisk and you should park kerbside between the palm trees by the villas to the south of it.

If you approach from the Málaga direction, turn off for Puerto Sotogrande and then right for the Guadiaro bridge. Turn left south of the bridge to reach the estuary.The lagoon at Las Camelias is on the beach

Sandwich Terns with a Lesser Crested Tern

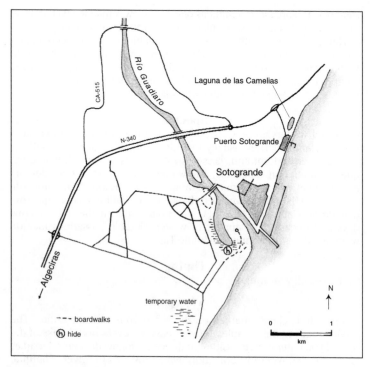

side of the N-340/Puerto Sotogrande link road. A lay-by adjacent to the south bank of the pool is convenient. From here, a track between a brick wall and a clump of giant reeds south of the lay-by provides access to the scrub areas.

Calendar

All year: Cory's Shearwater, Balearic Shearwater, Gannet, Cattle Egret, Little Egret, White Stork, Yellow-legged Gull, Water Rail, Purple Gallinule, Kentish Plover, Cetti's Warbler, Zitting Cisticola, Common Waxbill (sporadic), Reed Bunting.

Breeding season: Booted Eagle, Little Ringed Plover, Scops Owl, Red-necked Nightjar, Bee-eater, Hoopoe, Short-toed Lark, Red-rumped Swallow, Tawny Pipit, Rufous Bush Chat, Reed Warbler, Great Reed Warbler, Ortolan Bunting.

Winter: Little Grebe, Black-necked Grebe, Great Cormorant, ducks including Shelduck, Common Scoter and Red-breasted Merganser; Marsh Harrier, waders, Arctic Skua, Great Skua, Mediterranean Gull, Little Gull, Audouin's Gull, Lesser Black-backed Gull, Sandwich Tern, Razorbill, Kingfisher, Water Pipit, Bluethroat, Black Redstart, Penduline Tit.

Passage periods: Little Bittern, Night Heron, Purple Heron, Greater Flamingo, Garganey, raptors including Osprey, Spotted Crake, waders, Pomarine Skua, Audouin's Gull, Gull-billed Tern, Caspian Tern, Royal Tern (occasional), Lesser Crested Tern, Common Tern, Little Tern, Whiskered Tern, Black Tern, passerines.

JIMENA AND LA ALMORAIMA   CA9

Status: Part of the Parque Natural of Los Alcornocales. ZEPA.

Site description

La Almoraima is 'The Corkwoods', formerly much beloved of picnickers from Gibraltar. Cork oak forests dominate the area but the higher slopes have barren rocky outcrops and heathland vegetation. Small rivers, notably the Río Hozgarganta and Río Guadarranque, have boulder-strewn beds and shelter a good population of otters (seldom seen) and terrapins (unmissable) among other wildlife. The towns of Castellar de la Frontera, an abandoned hamlet on a strategic hill overlooking a reservoir, and Jimena, both provide good vantage points for watching migration.

Species

The whole area has a high density of raptors, with several important colonies of Griffon Vultures and a notable presence of Eagle Owls in the rocky valleys. The corkwood passerine community is a pleasing assembly of such species as Hoopoe, Bonelli's Warbler, Iberian Chiffchaff, Firecrest, Crested Tit, Golden Oriole and Hawfinch. Migrant raptors in their thousands descend in the evenings to roost in the cork woods. Jimena is a reliable site for seeing White-rumped Swifts. Castellar is also often a good place to find the latter. The nearby Pinar del Rey, behind San Roque, has breeding Red-necked Nightjars. Castellar, Jimena and the roadsides to Algeciras have numerous White Stork nests; at least the storks nest on top but the body of some nests is often occupied by colonies of House Sparrows.

Timing

All year but spring (February–May) produces migrant and resident raptors, the latter soaring and calling over their territories. May–September for White-rumped Swifts. August–November for southbound migration. Evening visits to La Almoraima during the raptor migration season can provide spectacular views of large numbers descending to roost; in early May and early September especially it rains Honey Buzzards here.

Access

Several sites within the area are easily visited.

A Jimena television repeater station

The road to the TV repeater station west of Jimena provides a peaceful vantage point to watch raptor migration in both seasons, although strong easterly winds will be least useful for this. The same road passes through good cork and pine woods, rock formations, spiny broom scrub and open heathland. The views south to Gibraltar and the Strait, and indeed all around, are superb on a clear day. Access to the road is via Jimena. Enter Jimena from the A-369 Gaucín road, take the first significant left turning down to the bridge across the Río Hozgarganta and continue upwards on this road. The road itself is a degraded tarmac track, drivable with due care, which climbs fairly steadily for 12 km to the TV station.

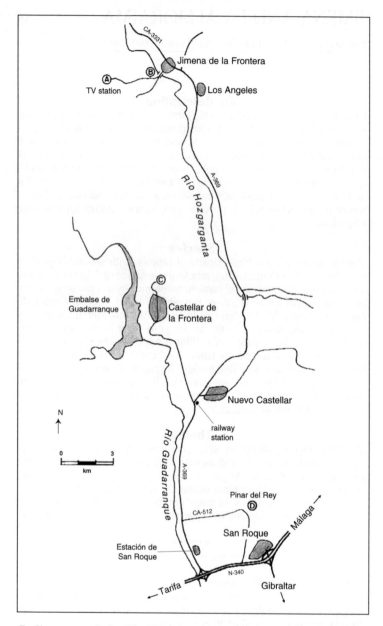

B *Jimena and the Río Hozgarganta*

The ruined castle tower at the top of Jimena village is a useful perch from which to watch the ubiquitous local Griffons, Crag Martins and Red-rumped Swallows, the latter often accompanied by their presumably-unwelcome White-rumped Swift guests. Descend on foot or by car to the river and then follow the path along the north bank; the waterside scrub and trees contain warblers and other passerines.

C Castellar de la Frontera (Old Castellar)
Castellar also provides a watchpoint for raptor migration and the nearby corkwoods have their passerines. Hirundine and swift flocks should be examined for White-rumped Swifts. Access is along the road to Castillo de Castellar, which branches west from the A-369 at La Almoraima railway station. The village of Old Castellar is renowned for its semi-resident population of 'New Wave' persons and accordingly is not always as tranquil a spot as it might be, but the itinerants seem to have declined recently. It is sometimes preferable to park below the village, near the dam, and explore the area from there. The reservoir (Embalse de Guadarranque) is not usually of interest although migrant raptors and others may be seen drinking there at times.

D El Pinar del Rey
The stone pine woods north of San Roque are disturbed by picnickers and trail-bikers but are quieter after dusk when the local Red-necked Nightjars may be seen and heard (April–September). Access is north from San Roque town or east from the A-369 at Km 86. The latter road crosses the railway line and after 3 km curves south; the entrance gate to El Pinar is here.

Calendar
All year: Cattle Egret, White Stork, Red Kite, Griffon Vulture, Goshawk, Sparrowhawk, Common Buzzard, Golden Eagle, Bonelli's Eagle, Common Kestrel, Peregrine, Eagle Owl, Little Owl, Tawny Owl, Great Spotted Woodpecker, Thekla Lark, Woodlark, Crag Martin, Grey Wagtail, Black Redstart, Stonechat, Blue Rock Thrush, Cetti's Warbler, Zitting Cisticola, Dartford Warbler, Sardinian Warbler, Firecrest, Crested Tit, Short-toed Treecreeper, Raven, Spotless Starling, Serin, Hawfinch, Cirl Bunting, Rock Bunting, Corn Bunting.

Breeding Season: Black Kite, Egyptian Vulture, Short-toed Eagle, Booted Eagle, Lesser Kestrel, Peregrine, Little Ringed Plover, Cuckoo, Red-necked Nightjar, Common Swift, Pallid Swift, Alpine Swift, White-rumped Swift, Bee-eater, Hoopoe, Red-rumped Swallow, Tawny Pipit, Rufous Bush Chat, Nightingale, Black-eared Wheatear, Olivaceous Warbler, Melodious Warbler, Subalpine Warbler, Orphean Warbler, Bonelli's Warbler, Iberian Chiffchaff, Golden Oriole, Woodchat Shrike, Ortolan Bunting.

Winter: Raptors including increased numbers of Red Kites and Buzzards. Great Spotted Cuckoo, Skylark, large roosts of Crag Martins, Meadow Pipit, White Wagtail, Robin, Song Thrush, Blackcap, Common Chiffchaff, Southern Grey Shrike, Common Starling.

Passage periods: Migrant raptors and storks overhead, passage of Bee-eaters, hirundines and finches. Migrant passerines of a wide range of species.

CAPE TRAFALGAR AND THE BARBATE PINEWOODS AND ESTUARY

Status: Partly protected by a Parque Natural (Acantilado y Pinar de Barbate — Barbate cliffs and pinewoods), 2017 ha. Also Parque Natural Marismas de Barbate.

Site description

The sandy hillsides to the west of Barbate are covered by an extensive pinewood (2000 ha) of stone pines. These are a source of edible pine kernels which are harvested annually. Large tracts of the woods are of very young trees and there is a well-developed understorey of junipers, fan palm and rosemary. Minor tracks through the pines lead southwards to precipitous sandstone cliffs giving fine views over the western approaches to the Strait and of the rocky, lighthouse-capped promontory of Cape Trafalgar, site of the famous sea battle. Sandy beaches flank the Cape, the western beach being particularly splendid and unspoilt, sweeping for some 15 km towards Conil de la Frontera. A series of low dunes separate this beach from the rough pastures inland.

Species

The pinewoods are of most interest during passage periods when they shelter a wide range of passerine and other migrants. The cliff bases are the site of a colony of Cattle Egrets (declining; a few hundred pairs in 2000 but over 2,500 pairs in the 1980s), here departing from their usual habit of nesting in trees. The nests are on clumps of oraches on the basal escarpments. The Cattle Egrets share the cliffs with some 40 pairs of Little Egrets, a colony of Yellow-legged Gulls, Common Kestrels, a pair of Peregrines, Rock Doves, Jackdaws and Ravens but no longer, alas, with Ospreys. White-tailed Eagles too are reputed to have nested here in previous centuries but they are more or less unknown in Iberia nowadays. At least the Ospreys still occur regularly on passage and not infrequently in winter.

The Cape has obvious potential as a seawatching site, during passage periods and in winter. Visible passage of Gannets and terns is often evident and Cory's Shearwaters visit tidal upwellings just offshore. It also marks the westernmost fringe of the raptor flyways across the Strait but soaring birds generally occur here only when strong easterly winds are blowing. Pools of rainwater near the Cape attract gull flocks in winter, which often include a few Audouin's Gulls.

The estuary and abandoned salt pans immediately east of Barbate attract waders, gulls and terns, especially on passage and in winter. Rubbish dumps inland from the estuary encourage spectacular aggregations of thousands of Black-headed, Lesser Black-backed and Yellow-legged Gulls in winter when the flocks are worth scrutinising for rarer species.

Timing

Seawatching from the Cape is recommended in winter and during migration periods. Days with onshore (southwesterly) winds are likely to be most productive. Late afternoons and evenings can be difficult on bright days as one faces the setting sun. The migrants occur in the pinewoods from March–May and from August–November mainly. Nesting activity on the cliff faces can be seen from March–May. The Barbate estuary is most interesting in winter and during passage periods.

Access

A Tajo de Barbate (Barbate cliffs)
Minor roads and tracks lead off through the pinewoods from the coast road connecting Barbate with the resort of Los Caños de Meca. The cliffs may be approached on foot through the woods. The best starting point is the small carpark on the south side of the road, 2.5 km above Barbate. Care should be taken when approaching the cliff edges: there is a brisk drop of over 100 m to the rocky shore below.

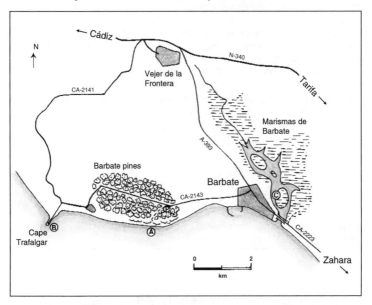

B Cabo Trafalgar (Cape Trafalgar)
A branch road leads from the Caños/Vejer road to the Cape itself. This is tarmacked and in good repair although drivers run an excellent risk of getting stuck in the sand if they veer or park off it. Fortunately, numerous hefty windsurfers are reliably available to help extricate bogged-down motorists. The road can be busy in summer when the beaches are quite popular but access is easy at other times. Park at the seaward end and walk up past the barrier to the lighthouse and beyond. The area is well supplied with small hotels and campsites.

C Barbate estuary
The estuary may be viewed from the bridge where the Barbate/Zahara road crosses the river. Parking on the bridge itself is not allowed but is possible nearby. At Km 1, just southeast of the town and opposite a white-fenced cluster of buildings, a blue Parque Natural sign marks a

drivable sandy track, giving access to an area of disused salt pans, worth exploring for waders and passerines. Further south still there are tracks along the fringes of the saltmarsh north of the road, used by lorries visiting the rubbish dumps. These can serve to give closer access to the gull flocks in winter too.

Calendar

All year: Cory's Shearwater, Balearic Shearwater, Gannet, Cattle Egret, Little Egret, White Stork, Griffon Vulture, Peregrine, Kentish Plover, Arctic Skua, Great Skua, Rock Dove, Blue Rock Thrush, Raven.

Breeding season: European Storm-petrel, Black Kite, Egyptian Vulture, Short-toed Eagle, Montagu's Harrier, Booted Eagle, Lesser Kestrel, Hobby, Quail, Scops Owl, Red-necked Nightjar, Bee-eater, Hoopoe, Short-toed Lark, Red-rumped Swallow, Tawny Pipit, Rufous Bush Chat, Black-eared Wheatear, Melodious Warbler, Spectacled Warbler, Bonelli's Warbler, Ortolan Bunting.

Winter: Leach's Storm-petrel, Common Scoter, Red-breasted Merganser, Red Kite, Hen Harrier, Osprey, Merlin, waders including Grey Phalarope, Mediterranean Gull, Audouin's Gull, Kittiwake, Caspian Tern, Sandwich Tern, auks, Crag Martin.

Passage periods: Great Shearwater, Sooty Shearwater, herons, waterfowl, raptors, waders, Pomarine Skua, Audouin's Gull, Gull-billed Tern, Common Tern, Little Tern, Black Tern, passerines.

MARISMAS DE SANCTI PETRI   CA11

Status: In part, Paraje Natural, 170 ha, forming part of the Parque Natural de la Bahía de Cádiz. ZEPA.

Site description

A sand bar across the tidal inlet at Sancti Petri shelters an extensive area of saltmarsh. Just offshore, a ruined castle is picturesquely placed on the islet of Farallón Grande. Sancti Petri itelf is essentially a ghost-town: an abandoned fishing village, but there is an active yacht club and other developments too. Pinewoods and dune scrub south of the town along the splendid Playa de la Barrosa often shelter migrants although most of this area has been heavily developed with golf courses, hotels and chalets (Nuevo Sancti Petri), which are continuing to proliferate. Some of the chalet-owners could assemble impressive garden lists if they were so inclined.

Species

Waterfowl, waders and seabirds, especially in winter. Passerine migrants.

Timing

Visits may be rewarding at any time of year. The very good beach is very busy in summer and in warm weather generally so visits at other times are advisable.

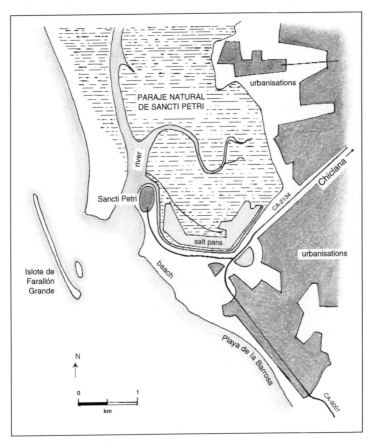

Access

From Chiclana, a tarmac road leads to Sancti Petri village. The sea, beach and saltmarsh are viewed from the road. Boat trips — Cadiz Park Safari boats — depart from the jetty in Sancti Petri, where tickets are available from a kiosk. These boats provide an opportunity for closer views of the saltmarshes; trips during intermediate states of the tide may be best since the waders then frequent the mudbanks. The main creeks of the saltmarsh should also be inspected from the waterfront road which follows the village perimeter. If migrants are in evidence it is worth following the coast road south from Sancti Petri and visiting the woodlands and dunes there.

Calendar

All year: Cattle Egret, Little Egret, Grey Heron, White Stork, Spoonbill, Greater Flamingo, Black-winged Stilt, Avocet, Kentish Plover, Sanderling, Dunlin, Redshank.

Breeding season: Little Tern.

Winter: Red-throated Diver, Little Grebe, Great-crested Grebe, Black-necked Grebe, Gannet, Great Cormorant, waterfowl; including Greylag Goose, Shelduck, Wigeon, Common Scoter and Red-breasted Merganser; Hen Harrier, Osprey, Peregrine, Water Rail, Oystercatcher, Ringed Plover, Golden Plover, Grey Plover, Lapwing, Knot, Little Stint, Ruff, Jack Snipe, Snipe, Black-tailed Godwit, Bar-tailed Godwit, Whimbrel, Curlew, Spotted Redshank, Greenshank, Turnstone, Grey Phalarope, Arctic Skua, Great Skua, Mediterranean Gull, Little Gull, Kittiwake, Caspian Tern, Sandwich Tern, Razorbill.

Passage periods: Seabirds, waders and passerines.

BAHÍA DE CÁDIZ   CA12

Status: Parque Natural, 10,000 ha. ZEPA

Site description
Cádiz Bay is a natural harbour sheltered behind the rocky spit which bears the provincial capital. The bay is bordered by extensive salt-marshes and much of the hinterland comprises salt pans. The natural park also takes in large areas of sand dunes and copses of stone pines. The estuary of the Río Guadalete empties into the northwestern portion of the Bay. Cádiz Bay is principally a wetland, and of great ornithological interest and although much of it is difficult to access there are a number of sites which often repay visitors.

Species
The bay attracts waterfowl and seabirds, including grebes and divers, especially in winter and on passage. At these times too, many thousands of waders frequent the immense expanses of salt pans and salt-marshes. There are significant breeding colonies of Black-winged Stilts, Avocets and Little Terns. Wintering Ospreys are regular and Great Northern Divers have also been reported with some frequency in recent winters.

Timing
The largest concentrations of waders and wildfowl occur between October and May but the area holds interesting birds all year round.

Access
The N-340 motorway and the N-IV intersect in the centre of the bay area and both provide rapid access to the region. Both cross interesting expanses of salt pans but, needless to say, stopping along them is impossible or illegal (but see below). Much of the protected region is inaccessible. The salt pans in particular are privately owned and entry

is generally forbidden (although it is always worth asking). Nevertheless, the following sites offer ample opportunities to sample the avifauna of this vast area.

A San Fernando

A bridge on the N-IV crosses the central creek of the southern saltmarshes, immediately east of San Fernando. Leave the motorway at San Fernando and drive south along any of the various possible roads through the town until you reach the waterfront (Paseo Maritimo), which overlooks the creek. Scan the creek and the saltmarshes for waders and others; a telescope is all but essential. Waders frequent the muddy fringes of the creek at low tide, affording closer views. It is worth following the waterfront westwards and then onwards through a residential area until signs on the left indicate the Puerto de Gallineras, where a short jetty also provides excellent views, again especially at low tide.

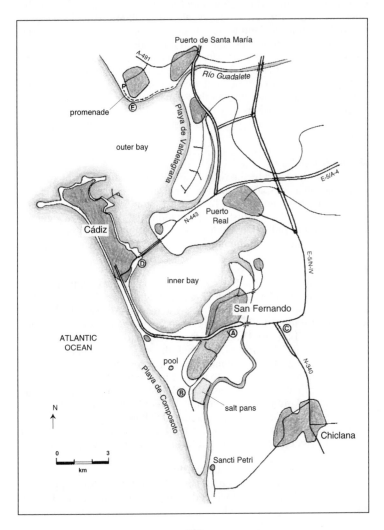

B Playa de Composoto

This is the beach extending southwards from San Fernando to the creek entrance at Sancti Petri (CA11). The beach is on a long sand bar which encloses an excellent expanse of salt pans. Access is straightforward: drive along the San Fernando waterfront (as above) or skirt the town to the north (see map), to reach a long straight road which separates the beach from the saltmarshes and salt pans. The road is a dead end and provides ideal opportunities to view the salt pans along their entire length, about 1 km. The beach and sand dunes are also worth visiting, especially during passage periods, when migrants may rest on the latter. A small, reed-fringed freshwater lake to the north of the site is liable to hold interesting species.

C The central salt pans (salinas)

The N-IV and N-340 cross large tracts of the salt pans. The N-340 Chiclana/San Fernando stretch is motorway and stopping is out of the question. However, an overpass at the southern (Chiclana) end, marked 'Cambio de Sentido' (change of direction) gives access to service roads which fringe the salinas on both sides of the motorway. It is also obviously possible to transfer between carriageways here. The N-IV loops northwards towards Puerto Real from its junction with the N-340. Again, stopping is not advised but there are some obvious lay-bys where you can park and then inspect the salinas on foot. Large numbers of waders are often obvious very close to the main road. A good lay-by is on the northbound carriageway (on the right!) shortly after the N-IV/N-340 junction.

D The inner bay

Cádiz Bay is bisected by the N-443 Cádiz/Puerto Real road, which crosses the bay on a conspicuous bridge. Good views of the bay are available from the southwestern corner. Take the N-IV from San Fernando towards Cádiz and pull off at the first (Poligono Industrial) exit. Follow signs for Puerto Real but pull off just before joining the dual carriageway which crosses the bridge. Scan the inner bay for seabirds and waterfowl.

E The outer bay

Views eastwards over the bay can be had from Cádiz city, from where the sea wall also offers seawatching possibilities over the Atlantic. The bay is also easily inspected from the western side. Access is from the A-491 Rota/El Puerto de Santa María road. Follow signs for Costa Oeste just north of El Puerto. Drive straight through the new residential area (Urbanicación Vistahermosa) to reach the coastal promenades along the bay entrance. The promenade gives elevated views (20m) over the bay and continues right round to the marina (Puerto Deportivo). A series of waterfront cafés have the usual outdoor tables so that seawatching can be carried out in unusual comfort. A telescope is essential.

The Playa de Valdelagrana, just south of El Puerto de Santa María and on the northwestern shore of the outer bay, attracts waders in winter especially. Access is indicated southwards from the N-IV.

Calendar

All year: Cattle Egret, Little Egret, Grey Heron, White Stork, Spoonbill, Greater Flamingo, Black-winged Stilt, Avocet, Kentish Plover, Sanderling, Dunlin, Redshank.

Breeding season: Little Tern.

Winter: Red-throated Diver, Great Northern Diver, Little Grebe, Great-crested Grebe, Black-necked Grebe, Gannet, Great Cormorant, water-fowl including Greylag Goose, Shelduck, Wigeon, Common Scoter and Red-breasted Merganser; Hen Harrier, Osprey, Peregrine, Water Rail, Oystercatcher, Ringed Plover, Golden Plover, Grey Plover, Lapwing, Knot, Little Stint, Ruff, Jack Snipe, Snipe, Black-tailed Godwit, Bar-tailed Godwit, Whimbrel, Curlew, Spotted Redshank, Greenshank, Turnstone, Grey Phalarope, Arctic Skua, Great Skua, Mediterranean Gull, Little Gull, Kittiwake, Caspian Tern, Sandwich Tern, Razorbill.

Passage periods: Seabirds and waders. Also passerines.

LAGUNAS DE PUERTO REAL CA13

Status: Reserva Natural, 104 ha, plus 735 ha of peripheral protection. ZEPA.

Site description
This secluded site comprises three lagoons: Lagunas del Taraje, de San Antonio and del Comisario, surrounded by agricultural land but fringed with reedbeds and fan palm scrub. Tamarisks (tarajes) are not particularly prominent. The Laguna de San Antonio, which is largely an excellent reedbed, is fed by water from a nearby waterworks. It drains along a reedy dyke into the Laguna del Taraje, which has extensive open water as well as fringing reedbeds and muddy areas popular with passage waders. Both these lagoons generally enjoy permanent water, thanks to the waterworks, unlike the Laguna del Comisario which is prone to drying up in some years.

Species
This site has received relatively little attention but it has first-class potential and is well worth a visit. The reedbeds support nesting Little Bitterns, Purple Herons and Purple Gallinules, as well as Red-knobbed Coots in some years. Raptors are frequent and include all three harriers. Waterfowl and waders occur in winter and on passage especially.

Timing
The site is of interest all year round and especially if the Laguna de Medina is dry. Midday visits in hot weather are not advisable because of the haze.

Access
The site lies to the north of the Puerto Real/Paterna de Rivera road (CA-2012), west of the A-381. Immediately west of Km 9 (marked by a white stone) there is a gap in the pines and an entrance to a broad dirt road, also flanked by two white stones. Follow this road north for 1.5 km.

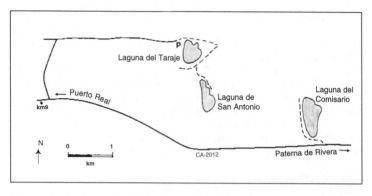

Then take the right fork and continue for 2.6 km to park by the Laguna del Taraje. Explore the lake margin and the surrounding scrub on foot. A north-facing hide overlooks the lake. A 500-m path south of the drainage dyke gives access to the Laguna de San Antonio from the margins of La Laguna del Taraje. La Laguna del Comisario is reached separately by a footpath from the main road at Km 15.8.

Calendar

All year: Little Egret, Marbled Duck, White-headed Duck, Marsh Harrier, Purple Gallinule, Coot, Calandra Lark.

Breeding season: Little Bittern, Purple Heron, Red-knobbed Coot, Montagu's Harrier, Reed Warbler, Great Reed Warbler,

Winter: Grey Heron, waterfowl including Gadwall, Teal, Mallard, Shoveler, Marbled Duck, Red-crested Pochard and Pochard; Hen Harrier, Osprey.

Passage periods: Waterfowl, waders, Gull-billed Tern, Whiskered Tern, passerines.

Purple Gallinule

LAGUNAS DEL PUERTO DE SANTA MARÍA

CA14

Status: Reserva Natural, 63 ha, plus 228 ha of protected zone. ZEPA.

Site description

This site, also known as the Lagunas de Terry, is one of the most accessible of the several freshwater-lagoon complexes in the Cádiz Bay area. There are three lagoons: Laguna Salada, Laguna Chica and Laguna Juncosa. The first of these is the largest and best and the least prone to drying up completely in summer, although it still happens in some years. The three lakes and their surrounding reedbeds and scrub comprise a reserve of 228 ha.

Species

This is a site of great interest on account of the species which breed and winter there. Regular nesters include Little Bitterns, White-headed Ducks, probably Baillon's Crakes, Purple Gallinules and Red-knobbed Coots. Collared Pratincoles breed nearby and flocks of up to several hundred may be seen in the area in summer.

In winter the hundreds of wildfowl regularly include flocks of Marbled Ducks and Red-crested Pochards, as well as good numbers of White-headed Ducks. The thin bordering scrub of tamarisks can hold a good variety of passerines during migration periods. Waders are also attracted to the muddy lakeshores at most times of the year.

Timing

The site is rewarding throughout the year except when the lakes dry up completely in dry summers.

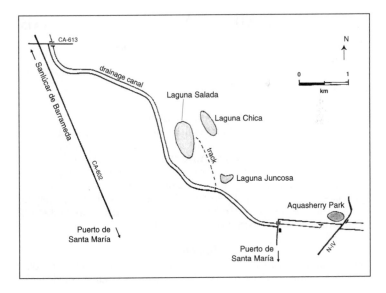

Access

The site is easiest to locate from Aquasherry Park, which lies west of the N-IV south of Jerez. Drive west past the park and follow the roadside drainage canal for about 3 km until it is bridged on the right by a short sandy track, which leads through the vineyards to the lakes. Laguna Juncosa is a sedge-filled hollow which may hold the occasional Snipe but not much else. Laguna Chica is also undistinguished. Laguna Salada is accessible on foot; a track leads right around the lake but entry is sometimes prohibited by wardens. In any event, the lake can be inspected from the banks bordering the vineyards nearby.

Calendar

All year (water permitting): Little Grebe, Black-necked Grebe, Greater Flamingo, White-headed Duck, Water Rail, Purple Gallinule, Red-knobbed Coot.

Breeding season: Little Bittern, Montagu's Harrier, Baillon's Crake, Black-winged Stilt, Collared Pratincole, Bee-eater, Hoopoe, Reed Warbler, Great Reed Warbler.

Winter: Grey Heron, ducks including Marbled Duck and Red-crested Pochard; Hen Harrier, Golden Plover, Lapwing, Snipe, Mediterranean Gull, Wryneck, Water Pipit, Bluethroat, Penduline Tit, Southern Grey Shrike.

Passage periods: Purple Heron, storks, waterfowl, raptors, waders including Little Ringed Plover, Little Stint, Curlew Sandpiper, Ruff, Black-tailed Godwit, Spotted Redshank, Redshank, Greenshank, Green Sandpiper, Wood Sandpiper, Common Sandpiper, Common Tern, Little Tern, Whiskered Tern, Black Tern, hirundines and other passerines.

LAGUNA DE MEDINA   CA15

Status: Reserva Natural, 121 ha, plus 254 ha peripheral protection. ZEPA.

Site description

The rolling hillsides of the sherry country near Jerez produce a superb product but they make for a monotonous landscape. The whitish soil is largely covered in vines with extensive areas of cereals and pasture. The Laguna de Medina is a veritable oasis in this agricultural steppe, a shallow lagoon of some 120 ha, surrounded by an extensive protected zone. The lagoon is fed by a small stream but it still dries up completely in some summers. The extensive fringing reedbeds and a peripheral scrub of tamarisks and buckthorn hold many birds.

Species

The lagoon is a key site for waterfowl, especially in winter. The comprehensive range of duck species always includes White-headed Duck, whose small breeding population is greatly increased in winter when over 350 birds may be present. Marbled Ducks (100+) are regular in autumn and winter. Ferruginous Ducks are sometimes present and recent scarcer species have included Ruddy Duck, Scaup and Goldeneye. Garganey occur on passage. The ducks share the water with Little, Great-crested and Black-necked Grebes, Greylag Geese, Greater Flamingos and, most obviously, large flocks of Coots. The Coot flocks are largest in late summer and autumn, when many arrive from the Guadalquivir marismas and gatherings of over 25,000 birds form. One or two pairs of Red Knobbed Coots breed but they can be elusive among the Coot hordes. Whiskered and Black Terns occur on passage and flocks of up to 350 Mediterranean Gulls occur occasionally in winter.

The lake margins are attractive to waders, especially in dry years when the lake partly dries up. Passage waders include Spotted Redshanks, Little Stints, Curlew Sandpipers and occasional rarer species, such as Temminck's Stints and Marsh Sandpipers. The reedbeds have a good population of Purple Gallinules and a few Little Bitterns. Great Reed Warblers and Reed Warblers both breed and Sedge Warblers occur on passage. A spectacular roost of hundreds of thousands of transient Swallows and other hirundines develops in the reedbeds in autumn. The peripheral scrub holds a range of maquis species and Quail and Red-legged Partridges frequent the farmland nearby. Wrynecks, Bluethroats and Penduline Tits occur in winter, the latter being very common.

The gathering of so many prey species attracts predators: Montagu's Harriers breed nearby and Marsh Harriers are sometimes present. Common Buzzards and Red Kites are frequent, the latter mainly in winter.

Timing

The lake is always worth visiting, except when it dries up completely, which it may do in August or even earlier if the winter rains have been poor. Winter holds the greatest variety of waterfowl but passage periods are also excellent for waterfowl, waders and passerines. Late spring and early summer are best to see the breeding species, notably Redknobbed Coots. The largest numbers of waders occur between late July and September in those dry years when a broad muddy margin is exposed as the lake levels fall. As usual, morning and evening visits are essential in hot weather when the heat haze is prevalent.

Access

The lake is clearly visible from the A-381 Jerez/Los Barrios road at Km 10, south of Jerez. Follow the signs to the car park. Access is on foot along a track which follows the southern shore and which gives good views over the reedbeds. The other parts of the reserve are out of bounds. Good viewing conditions can be had at any time of day given the north-facing viewpoints. The lake is large and a telescope is recommended although not essential.

A short distance (1 km) north of the lake there is a marshy area of sedges and some reeds just south of the A-381 at Km 8, behind the Venta on the west side of the road. This site (known optimistically as La Laguna de las Pachecas) holds Savi's Warblers in some years, as well as other warblers, Little Bitterns and Purple Gallinules. Park at the Venta and explore on foot.

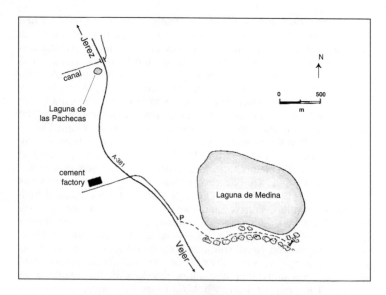

Calendar

All year (water permitting): Black-necked Grebe, Cattle Egret, Little Egret, Greater Flamingo, White-headed Duck, Marsh Harrier, Purple Gallinule, Red-knobbed Coot, Barn Owl, Cetti's Warbler, Zitting Cisticola, Dartford Warbler.

Winter: Greylag Goose, Shelduck, Wigeon, Gadwall, Teal, Mallard, Pintail, Shoveler, Marbled Duck, Red-crested Pochard, Pochard, Tufted Duck, Red Kite, Mediterranean Gull, Wryneck, Bluethroat, Penduline Tit, Southern Grey Shrike.

Spring: Little Bittern, Purple Heron, waterfowl including Greylag Goose (stragglers to early April), Garganey, Marbled Duck, Red-crested Pochard, Ferruginous Duck; Red Kite, Montagu's Harrier, Quail, Baillon's Crake, Black-winged Stilt, Collared Pratincole, Little Ringed Plover, Whiskered Tern, Black Tern, Bee-eater, Hoopoe, Wryneck, Rufous Bush Chat, Sedge Warbler, Reed Warbler, Great Reed Warbler, Orphean Warbler, Wood Warbler, Penduline Tit, Woodchat Shrike, Southern Grey Shrike.

Breeding season: Little Bittern, Purple Heron, Red-crested Pochard, Ferruginous Duck, Montagu's Harrier, Quail, Baillon's Crake, Black-winged Stilt, Collared Pratincole, Little Ringed Plover, Kentish Plover, Whiskered Tern, Rufous Bush Chat, Black-eared Wheatear, Reed Warbler, Great Reed Warbler, Woodchat Shrike.

Autumn: Little Bittern, Purple Heron, waterfowl including Marbled Duck, Red-crested Pochard and Ferruginous Duck, Red Kite, Quail, Baillon's Crake, Black-winged Stilt, Avocet, Collared Pratincole, waders including Little Ringed Plover, Ringed Plover, Kentish Plover, Little Stint, Curlew Sandpiper, Dunlin, Ruff, Jack Snipe, Snipe, Black-tailed Godwit, Spotted Redshank, Redshank, Greenshank, Green Sandpiper, Wood Sandpiper, Common Sandpiper, Whiskered Tern, Black Tern, hirundines especially Barn Swallow, Penduline Tit, Southern Grey Shrike.

Status: No special protection.

Site description

The town of Chipiona guards the southern approaches to the Guadalquivir estuary; the tall lighthouse (El Faro de Punta del Perro) can be seen for miles around. The rocky foreshore at Chipiona is soon replaced by a sandy coast, running southwards to the Bay of Cádiz at Rota. The beaches give onto sand dunes, these being better developed at the southern end of the area where dune vegetation and pinewoods often shelter migrants. There are also good stretches of dunes behind the public beaches just south of Chipiona. Much of this coastline has recently been submerged under holiday homes and other touristic developments.

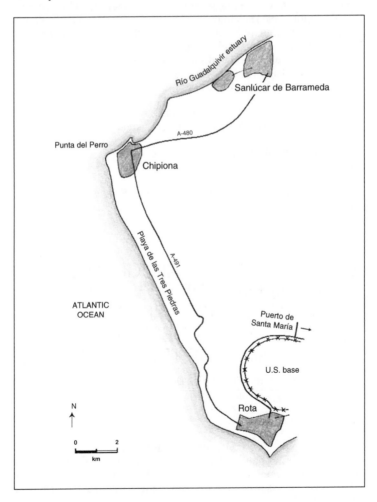

Species

Seawatching from the lighthouse reveals shearwaters, scoters and other seabirds, notably terns, feeding off the river mouth. The dunes often harbour large numbers of migrants during passage periods.

Timing

Summer is best avoided since the beaches are then busy although seabirds may still be watched for. Seawatching is promising in south-westerlies from autumn through winter to spring. The dunes are most interesting in spring, especially when strong easterlies affect the region.

Access

From the Chipiona/Rota coastal road. A number of minor roads give access to the shore. The lighthouse at Chipiona has a large car park and terrace at its foot, ideal for seawatching. Telescope advisable. Rota town is interesting to anyone wanting to experience the southern USA without crossing the Atlantic: the massive air and sea base has its attendant American town, complete with wide avenues cruised by vast, rectangular limousines. The atmosphere may be transatlantic but the birds are definitely Iberian. At the northern end of the area, the waterfront at Sanlúcar de Barrameda is ideally placed to allow birder-hedonists to consume the local seafood and sherry in some comfort whilst scanning across the Guadalquivir estuary for Spanish Imperial Eagles and such-like over the Doñana pinewoods opposite.

Calendar

All year: Seabirds, notably shearwaters, gulls and terns. Kentish Plover.

Passage periods: Waders, skuas, Hoopoe, Wryneck and passerines; Woodchat Shrikes are often particularly abundant.

Winter: Common Scoter, waders, Caspian Tern, Sandwich Tern.

EAST BANK OF THE RÍO GUADAL-QUIVIR, SALINAS DE BONANZA AND DE MONTE ALGAIDA, PINAR DE LA ALGAIDA, LAGUNA DE TARELO AND MARISMAS DE TREBUJENA CA17

Status: Parque Natural (Entorno de Doñana) — in part. ZEPA.

Site description

This region forms part of the protected periphery of the Doñana National Park. Its position on the east bank of the river means easier and quicker access from the Costa del Sol and Gibraltar than Doñana proper (the drive from Gibraltar takes about 2 hours each way); yet most if not all of the species to be seen in Doñana also occur here.

The Bonanza and Algaida Salinas comprise a great expanse of active salt pans and *Salicornia* flats. The latter continue into the Trebujena marismas, seasonally-flooded expanses of salt flats and saltmarshes following the riverbank northwards from Bonanza. Inland the country becomes gently undulating rough pastureland. Plastic greenhouses are a fairly recent and disturbing intrusion into the salt flats, especially near Bonanza, but their initial expansion seems to have been checked. The town boasts the extensive stone pine woods of La Algaida, similar in character to the much larger forests of Doñana just across the river. The freshwater Laguna de Tarelo, adjacent to La Algaida, is also often of interest.

Species
The salt pans are of the greatest interest for migrant and wintering waders and waterfowl, which are often very numerous. Scarce species such as Red-necked Phalarope turn up occasionally and here a patient observer stands a very good chance of finding vagrant species. Slender-billed Gulls are reliably present for most of the year. Gull-billed Terns breed and Caspian Terns winter. Western Reef Egrets and Great White Egrets occur occasionally among the many Little Egrets, individuals often staying for many weeks. Raptors include Marsh Harriers and great numbers of Black Kites. Spanish Imperial Eagles from the Coto also include the salinas in their beat occasionally.

The Trebujena area is notable for its views across the river, with its egrets, waders, gulls and terns. Enormous flocks of Lapwings and Golden Plovers occur in winter, when numbers of Stone Curlews and Pin-tailed Sandgrouse are also typical. Lesser Short-toed Larks and Spectacled Warblers breed and are present for all or most of the year. Harriers and other raptors are obvious and include numbers of Red Kites in winter especially.

La Algaida is the only place in Cádiz province which regularly holds Azure-winged Magpies. A search through the woods usually meets with success; flocks of up to 40 occur. Black Kites breed in numbers and flocks of over 100 form regularly. Red-necked Nightjars also breed locally.

The Laguna de Tarelo offers Purple Gallinules and waterfowl. It is particularly noted as a refuge for White-headed Ducks, which may accumulate here in years when favourite sites, such as the Laguna de Medina (CA15) dry up.

Timing
All times of year are productive but the largest numbers of birds are present in winter. Wader numbers during migration are also considerable. Heat-haze is a problem and midday visits to the salt pans during hot weather will prove frustrating. The Laguna de Tarelo has proved its worth during particularly arid years, when other lakes may dry up in summer.

Access
From the A-471 Sanlúcar de Barrameda/Lebrija road.

A Salinas de Bonanza
The Bonanza salinas are reached by driving up a short dirt track from the bend where the Sanlúcar/Bonanza road turns inland. A large

'Entorno de Doñana' sign is to the left of the entrance. The salinas are private but the owners are sympathetic to conservation and allow bird-watchers to enter. Access used to be restricted to the winter months and required prior permission from the company's (Apromasa) offices. Recently access has been freely available at all times, perhaps indicating a decline in the company's fortunes following the infamous 'Doñana incident' (see H5). (It is hard to envisage a worse eventuality for an industry relying on extracting salt from water by evaporation than to have the water supply contaminated with cadmium, zinc and other toxic residues.) Site D below is an excellent, perhaps superior, altern-ative should access to the Bonanza site become difficult in future.

B Pinar de la Algaida
Access to La Algaida is unrestricted. The main road into the pinewood is broad, tarmacked and impressive but soon peters out into a stony/sandy track which is still passable with care. Numerous tracks allow easy exploration of the woods.

C Laguna de Tarelo
This is a freshwater lake situated immediately adjacent to the Algaida pinewoods, at the Bonanza end. A short track leads westwards from just inside the southern entrance to the woods to a watchpoint overlooking the lake. This is not a hide but more of a screen. Unfortunately the birds can see you and will not approach closely. Purple Gallinules are often visible, together with waterfowl such as both Common and Red-crested Pochards, and White-headed Ducks.

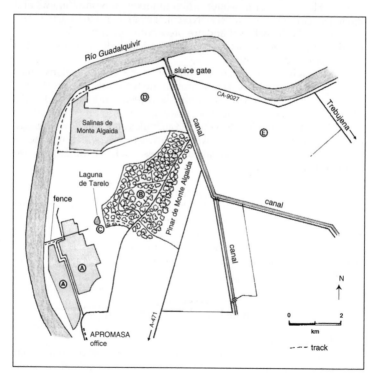

D Salinas de Monte Algaida

These salt pans have become easily accessible since February 2000, when the site was inaugurated as a wildlife observation area. It is a wonderful place to visit and we strongly recommend it; it is far larger than the Bonanza salinas, offering vast open vistas of sky and water and with often very large numbers of a wide range of species. The entrance is a broad sandy track which leads towards the river on the west side of the Trebujena canal sluice gate (see map). Two short stone columns flank the entrance. The access track leads westwards parallel to the river for 2.2 km, passing salt flats and shallow, sandy pools. These last often attract wader flocks. Park at the end of the track and explore further on foot along the numerous dyke banks flanking the immense complex of salt pans. Waterfowl and waders frequent these, together with Greater Flamingos, herons and Spoonbills. The salt flats are covered with glassworts (*Salicornia*) and other halophytic flora. They accommodate both Short-toed and Lesser Short-toed Larks, the former only as summer visitors. Spectacled Warblers and Yellow Wagtails breed here too. The site allows access to the riverbank where waders feed along the muddy fringes at low tide and assorted herons lurk in the reeds. Small, scattered trees and bushes should be inspected for passerines, especially during passage periods.

E Marismas de Trebujena

The Trebujena area is traversed by long, straight, tarmacked roads which give good views over the river and salt flats. Stop and scan frequently. There are many points where fishermen's paths allow access to the riverbank itself. The northern roads, within the Provincia de Sevilla, are poor and pot-holes are a hazard. The other roads are in reasonable condition.

Calendar

All the species which occur in Doñana are liable to turn up. The principal species of the region are as follows:

All year: Little Grebe, Great Crested Grebe, Black-necked Grebe, Cattle Egret, Squacco Heron, Little Egret, Grey Heron, White Stork, Spoonbill, Greater Flamingo, Gadwall, Mallard, Marbled Duck, Red-crested Pochard, Pochard, White-headed Duck, Red Kite, Egyptian Vulture, Griffon Vulture, Marsh Harrier, Spanish Imperial Eagle, Booted Eagle, Lesser Kestrel, Common Kestrel, Peregrine, Red-legged Partridge, Quail, Moorhen, Purple Gallinule, Coot, Little Bustard, Oystercatcher, Black-winged Stilt, Avocet, Stone Curlew, Little Ringed Plover, Ringed Plover, Kentish Plover, Grey Plover, Lapwing, Sanderling, Little Stint, Dunlin, Ruff, Black-tailed Godwit, Bar-tailed Godwit, Whimbrel, Curlew, Spotted Redshank, Redshank, Marsh Sandpiper, Greenshank, Green Sandpiper, Black-headed Gull, Slender-billed Gull, Lesser Black-backed Gull, Yellow-legged Gull, Caspian Tern, Sandwich Tern, Pin-tailed Sandgrouse, Barn Owl, Little Owl, Tawny Owl, Long-eared Owl, Hoopoe, Calandra Lark, Lesser Short-toed lark, Crested Lark, Thekla Lark, Woodlark, Spectacled Warbler, Short-toed Treecreeper, Southern Grey Shrike, Azure-winged Magpie, Magpie, Jackdaw, Raven, Spotless Starling, Tree Sparrow, Cirl Bunting.

Breeding season: Little Bittern, Night Heron, Purple Heron, Garganey, Black Kite, Short-toed Eagle, Montagu's Harrier, Hobby, Collared Pratincole, Gull-billed Tern, Little Tern, Whiskered Tern, Black Tern, Turtle Dove, Great Spotted Cuckoo, Cuckoo, Red-necked Nightjar, Bee-eater, Short-toed Lark, Rufous Bush Chat, Nightingale, Savi's Warbler, Reed Warbler, Great Reed Warbler, Melodious Warbler.

Winter: Great Cormorant, Great White Egret, Glossy Ibis, Greylag Goose, Shelduck, Wigeon, Teal, Pintail, Shoveler, Tufted Duck, Black-shouldered Kite, Hen Harrier, Sparrowhawk, Bonelli's Eagle, Osprey, Merlin, Crane, Golden Plover, Jack Snipe, Snipe, Woodcock, Wood Sandpiper, Kingfisher, Skylark, Meadow Pipit, Water Pipit, Bluethroat, Common Chiffchaff, Penduline Tit, Starling, Spanish Sparrow, Siskin, Reed Bunting.

Passage periods: Knot, Temminck's Stint, Curlew Sandpiper, Common Sandpiper, Turnstone, Little Gull, Common Tern, Scops Owl, Short-eared Owl, Alpine Swift, Roller, Crag Martin, Tawny Pipit, Tree Pipit, Common Redstart, Whinchat, Northern Wheatear, Black-eared Wheatear, Grasshopper Warbler, Sedge Warbler, Olivaceous Warbler, Subalpine Warbler, Orphean Warbler, Whitethroat, Garden Warbler, Bonelli's Warbler, Willow Warbler, Spotted Flycatcher, Pied Flycatcher, Rock Bunting, Ortolan Bunting.

EMBALSE DE ARCOS CA18

Status: Paraje Natural (Cola del Embalse de Arcos), 120 ha.

Site description

The reservoir at Arcos de la Frontera has a considerable area of reedbeds along its northern flanks. These, and the adjacent portion of the reservoir, comprise the protected zone.

Species

This site attracts numbers of waterfowl, specifically grebes, coots and ducks, especially in winter. Ospreys also occur regularly at this season.

Timing

This is chiefly a site for wintering species (October–March), but waterfowl also occur on passage.

Access

The site can be viewed from the road which skirts the western side of the reservoir and particularly, from the village of El Santiscal on the southern bank of the western arm. A waterfront road (Avenida Principe de España) gives good elevated views northwards across the western arm from El Santiscal. Reedbeds and sandy islets in the reservoir and open water can be surveyed easily from this position. A dead tree directly opposite this watchpoint is a favoured perch of wintering and transient Ospreys. Purple Gallinules, which probably breed here, are also often visible from the same place. A telescope is desirable.

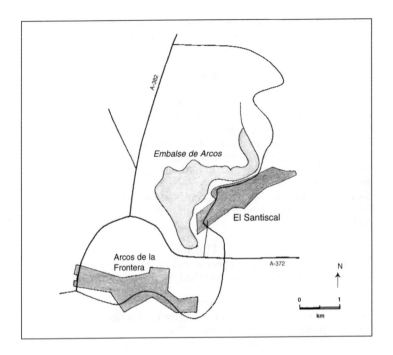

Calendar

All year: Great Crested Grebe, Cattle Egret, Little Egret, Mallard, Purple Gallinule, Coot, Cetti's Warbler.

Breeding season: Bee-eater, Nightingale, Savi's Warbler, Reed Warbler, Great Reed Warbler.

Winter: Little Grebe, Grey Heron, ducks including Gadwall, Mallard, Shoveler, Red-crested Pochard and Pochard; Osprey.

SIERRA DE GRAZALEMA   CA19

Status: Parque Natural (Sierra de Grazalema), 51,695 ha. ZEPA.

Site description

This extensive natural park includes the western portion of the Serranía de Ronda, the limestone mountains of the Baetic Cordillera. These are rugged slopes, with bare rocky summits reaching to over 1600 metres. The valleys are heavily forested with cork, holm and Lusitanian oaks and stands of maritime pine. Locally there are residual woods of the endemic Spanish fir (Pinsapo). Sheer cliff faces are typical, flanking rocky gorges in which seasonal streams flow briskly and sometimes torrentially; the park boasts the highest rainfall in the entire Iberian Peninsula! The flora is correspondingly lush and exceptionally attractive in spring and early summer.

Species
The rocky terrain is attractive to raptors and most sierras of the region have nesting eagles: Short-toed, Booted and either Bonelli's or Golden; the last two are mutually exclusive in their territories. Griffon and Egyptian Vultures nest commonly accompanied by other cliff-nesting birds, notably Eagle Owls and Red-billed Choughs. The typical breeding species also include Northern, Black-eared and Black Wheatears, Rock Thrushes, Rock Sparrows and Rock Buntings. Red-rumped Swallows are common and so, unsurprisingly, are the White-rumped Swifts which they accommodate. The crags are also shared by herds of Spanish ibexes. The montane flora is of great interest and includes a number of endemic species.

Timing
The area is worth visiting all year round but is especially rewarding in spring and summer when the breeding species are most evident.

Access
The area is well served by good (if narrow) roads which offer opportunities for parking and exploring the hillsides on foot. Grazalema itself is a centre for 'fell' walkers and numerous footpaths ascend the sur-

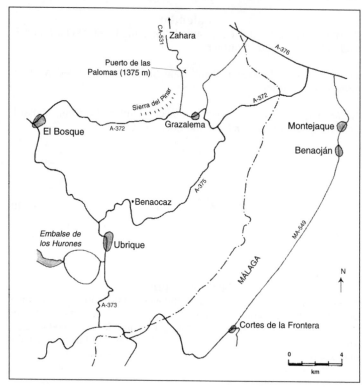

rounding slopes. Good local maps of the area are available in Grazalema and are a must if you plan to spend some time here and intend to
explore widely on foot. It isn't necessary to go far from the main roads
to see the typical bird species however. The roads between Cortes de la
Frontera and Benaocaz, between Ubrique and Grazalema, and
between Grazalema and Zahara are potentially rewarding. The Graza-
lema/Zahara road rises from Grazalema northwards to a col at Puerto
de las Palomas (1357 m). A footpath leads east from the col to the top
of the adjacent sierra, offering spectacular views in all directions and a
good spot to sit and wait for raptors; Black Wheatears are also regularly
present here as well as Rock Thrushes and Alpine Accentors in season.

Bonelli's Eagles

Calendar

All year: Griffon Vulture, Goshawk, Golden Eagle, Bonelli's Eagle,
Peregrine, Eagle Owl, Green Woodpecker, Thekla Lark, Woodlark, Crag
Martin, Black Redstart, Blue Rock Thrush, Crested Tit, Coal Tit, Nut-
hatch, Short-toed Treecreeper, Southern Grey Shrike, Red-billed Chough,
Raven, Rock Sparrow, Hawfinch, Cirl Bunting, Rock Bunting.

Breeding season: Black Kite, Egyptian Vulture, Short-toed Eagle, Booted
Eagle, Lesser Kestrel, Hobby, Scops Owl, Common Nightjar, Alpine
Swift, White-rumped Swift, Bee-eater, Hoopoe, Red-rumped Swallow,
Northern Wheatear, Black-eared Wheatear, Melodious Warbler, Sub-
alpine Warbler, Orphean Warbler, Bonelli's Warbler, Golden Oriole.

Passage periods: Raptors, passerines.

Winter: Alpine Accentor.

PEÑON DE ZAFRAMAGÓN CA20

Status: Reserva Natural (Peñon de Zaframagón), 135 ha within a protected zone of 311 ha.

Site description

The Peñon de Zaframagón is a conspicuous limestone outcrop, fringed with sheer limestone cliffs, which rises to the north of the Sierra de Lijar and the town of Algodonales. The surrounding pastures on the lower slopes are interrupted by small olive groves and patchy woodland and scrub, of encinas, hawthorn, myrtle and strawberry tree.

Species

This is the site of a noteworthy colony of Griffon Vultures (120+ pairs), on the western scarps, with attendant Egyptian Vultures and other raptors and cliff-nesting species.

Timing

Springtime coincides with periods of maximum activity in the vulture colony and other raptors are then at their most visible.

Access

El Peñon lies to the north of the minor road (CA-448) linking Olvera and the village of La Muela, very near the Cadiz/Sevilla provincial boundary. Turn off this road at Km 8, which is about 10 km from the junction of the road and the CA-339 to the west. The turning coincides with a cluster of white chalets to the south of the road. The entrance is opposite these; pass under the stone arch beneath the disused railway line, ignoring the alternative right turn. The dirt road heads north for 4.1 km to the farm (Cortijo de Zaframagón) at the foot of El Peñon. The going is very bumpy but is otherwise good. Drive through the farm and park immediately to the west of it. El Peñon may be inspected from here. Alternatively, follow the obvious footpaths up the olive groves to the

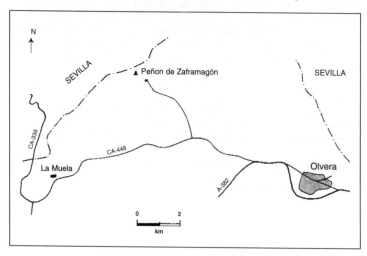

base of the cliffs, from where tracks skirt the fringes of the rock. The gritty soil makes for a devastating climb, not recommended in hot weather. The compensation is close views of the vultures and other inhabitants of the cliffs, and fine vistas across the barren hills to the town of Olvera, with its commanding Arab castle on a distant summit.

Calendar

All year: Griffon Vulture, Bonelli's Eagle, Eagle Owl, Little Owl, Red-billed Chough.

Breeding season: Egyptian Vulture, Lesser Kestrel, Alpine Swift, warblers and other passerines.

SEVILLA PROVINCE

Sevilla province is dominated by the valley of the Río Guadalquivir, most of which is an intensively agricultural region. The northern sierras (SE4), a section of the Sierra Morena, are worthy of note, however. Undoubtedly the greatest ornithological interest in the province is the southwestern portion, which includes the eastern sectors of Doñana national park. Sites SE1 and SE2, which fall within this region, are without doubt two of the very best places in Spain for finding and watching birds and you are strongly urged to include them in any itinerary. (The major part of Doñana National Park is in Huelva Province; site H5.) The agricultural regions of the Guadalquivir valley (SE3) are noteworthy for their thriving populations of Rufous Bush Chats and Olivaceous Warblers, which are often difficult to find elsewhere.The interesting reservoirs in the east of Sevilla province, bordering on Córdoba, are described in chapter 9 (sites CO6 and CO7).

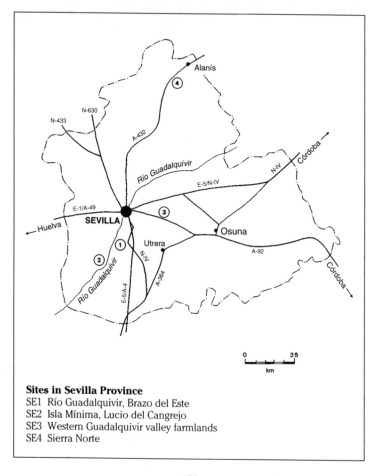

Sites in Sevilla Province
SE1 Río Guadalquivir, Brazo del Este
SE2 Isla Mínima, Lucio del Cangrejo
SE3 Western Guadalquivir valley farmlands
SE4 Sierra Norte

Maps

Mapa Provincial Sevilla, IGN, 1:200,000.
Mapa Guía Parque Nacional de Doñana, IGN, 1:50,000.

Getting there

Sevilla itself is highly accessible via its international airport and the new high-speed 'bullet train' from Madrid. The city is the hub of a number of motorways connecting it with Extremadura, the rest of Andalucía and Portugal. Access to the sites mentioned here is via the E5/A4 Sevilla/Cádiz toll motorway (SE1, SE2 and SE3) and from the N-630 Sevilla/Extremadura trunk road for the north of the province (SE4).

Where to stay

Sevilla city has numerous hotels including motels along the access roads. Hotels and/or pensiones are also available in the Sierra Norte, at Cazalla de la Sierra, Constantina and San Nicolás del Puerto. With the exception of SE4, the sites described here are easily accessible from a base in Cádiz province, however, and they are (just) within a return day's journey of Gibraltar.

RÍO GUADALQUIVIR, BRAZO DEL ESTE   SE1

Status: Paraje Natural (Brazo del Este), 1336 ha.

Site description

The delta of the Guadalquivir includes a number of subsidiary channels to the main river which delimit several large 'islands'. The Isla Menor, on the east bank, is crossed by a former branch of the river which in parts now comprises a winding lagoon with extensive fringing reedbeds, surrounded by farmland, rice fields and a veritable labyrinth of drainage ditches. Dirt roads criss-cross the entire area and skirt the main marshes.

The Brazo del Este is a superb site which we cannot recommend too strongly. We would go so far as to say that for many species of aquatic birds it is often better than Doñana proper, and it is certainly a much more peaceful site to visit than the national park itself since traffic and tourists are absent.

Species

As might be expected, the avifauna resembles that of the marismas in Doñana nearby. However, the numbers of certain species are noteworthy and make visits here so memorable. This is one of those places where 100 species or more may be encountered in a single visit within a fairly limited area.

Bitterns, as well as Little Bitterns, are seen here fairly frequently and may breed. Squacco Herons breed and so do large numbers of Purple

123

Herons. Night Herons are common, especially along the river, and appear in numbers at dusk when they leave their daytime roosts. Spoonbills and egrets are often prominent; the latter include occasional Great White Egrets. Glossy Ibises are locally abundant, especially in winter when flocks of 100+ occur.

Waterfowl occur in numbers on passage and in winter especially, with Marbled Ducks being regularly found here and breeding in some years at least. This is a prime site for Purple Gallinules; they are simply unmissable and records of 30 or more in view at once are quite normal, especially in spring, when territorial squabbles are being noisily resolved with much splashing and chasing, and when the birds are feeding in the adjacent rice fields. The total size of the gallinule population may only be guessed at but there are certainly many hundreds present. A conservative estimate put the gallinule population of the lower Guadalquivir region at about 3,000 birds in (year) 2000.

It is worth inspecting the marsh margins carefully: Spotted Crakes, Little Crakes and Baillon's Crakes occur, as well as Water Rails; all these crakes may breed locally. Collared Pratincoles breed and waders are common, again especially on passage and in winter. The latter regularly include otherwise elusive species such as Temminck's Stints and Marsh Sandpipers.

Passerines include breeding Savi's Warblers. A particular feature is the considerable variety of African finches which have been recorded here, some of which have bred. In recent years the species have included Yellow-crowned Bishop, Red Bishop, Common Waxbill, Black-rumped Waxbill and Orange-cheeked Waxbill (nearby). Most or all of these birds are of escape origin but the Guadalquivir wetlands clearly provide them with an excellent approximation to their native habitats.

Timing

This is an excellent site to visit all year round, although it is important to avoid the hottest part of the day in summer especially. Visits in the mornings and evenings are most productive. Springtime visits will coincide with maximum activity. Passage periods and winter also produce a large variety of interesting species.

Access

The area may be approached from the north (Sevilla), from the south (Lebrija/Trebujena; see CA17) or from the east, leaving the Sevilla/Cádiz motorway (E-5/A-4) at exits 1 (Dos Hermanas), 2 (Los Palacios) or 3 (Lebrija–Las Cabezas) — see map. Arriving via the motorway exits 1 and 2 allows relatively quick access but the approach route from exit 3 is often itself of interest since it crosses extensive rice paddies, attractive to waders especially. To visit these leave the motorway at exit 3, turn left immediately after passing through the toll gate and drive through the town of Las Cabezas de San Juan. Turn left at the roundabout at the foot of the hill and then drive straight on through the rest of the town. The road approaches the motorway again and crosses over it, descending towards a very visible white silo, where there is a T-junction. Turn left here and cross the railway line. From here keep straight on until the tarmac road turns right at a rice depot. Drive straight on here, off the tarmac, and on to either of the two broad, dead-straight, parallel, sandy tracks which continue northwest for 7.6 km. Rice paddies may be inspected on the right all along this drive. Bear right where

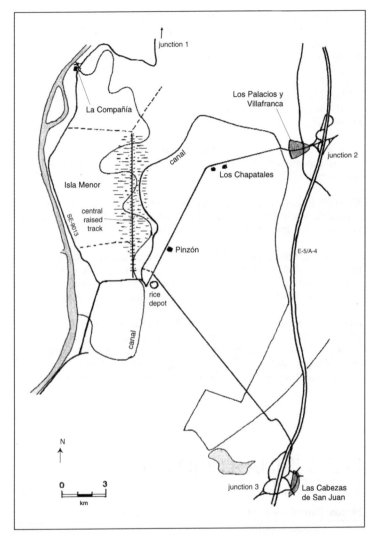

the dirt tracks rejoin poor quality tarmac until you reach a shiny grey and blue rice depot. The entrance to the Brazo del Este forks left from here.

The central winding marshland will be the main attraction and it is easily seen from the adjacent dirt roads. Road traffic is extremely light and you can stop anywhere. The main road through the area is on a raised dyke which crosses the main marshes and gives good views over the pools and reedbeds.The network of dirt roads in the area is a total maze but the river provides a point of reference. It is worth exploring the smaller tracks on foot but care should be taken not to disturb nesting birds by approaching too closely. Waders and crakes are most readily seen by employing the car as a hide.

It is often worth driving alongside the river, with frequent stops to scan for herons, waders, gulls and terns. The riverside road is good apart from the section to the south of the site, linking it with the Trebujena area. This part is pothole-ridden tarmac and demands careful driving. The river here is extensively obscured by a fringe of eucalyptus and so is much less accessible. The broad straight 'river' which joins the main channel to the north of the site is the main drainage sewer of Sevilla — avoid it!

The village of Pinzón, just east of the site, is strategically placed, the usual bar providing drinks and also excellent food at amazingly low prices.

Calendar

Most of the species of Doñana (H5) are liable to occur but the following are especially typical.

All year: Bittern, Cattle Egret, Little Egret, Grey Heron, White Stork, Spoonbill, Marsh Harrier, Water Rail, Spotted Crake, Little Crake, Purple Gallinule, Black-winged Stilt, Tree Sparrow.

Breeding season: Little Bittern, Night Heron, Squacco Heron, Purple Heron, Marbled Duck, Black Kite, Montagu's Harrier, Baillon's Crake, Collared Pratincole, Gull-billed Tern, Whiskered Tern, Lesser Short-toed Lark, Yellow Wagtail, Savi's Warbler, Reed Warbler, Great Reed Warbler.

Passage periods and winter: Great White Egret, Glossy Ibis, Greater Flamingo, waterfowl including Greylag Goose, Garganey and Marbled Duck; waders including Ruff, Spotted Redshank, Redshank, Temminck's Stint, Marsh Sandpiper, Green Sandpiper and Wood Sandpiper; Gull-billed Tern, Whiskered Tern, Black Tern, vagrants and exotics.

ISLA MÍNIMA, LUCIO DEL CANGREJO
SE2

Status: Part of the Parque Natural, Entorno de Doñana.

Site description

The Isla Mínima is an island in the Guadalquivir delta. It lies to the west of the main channel and is otherwise skirted, to the west, by a subsidiary channel — often dry in parts — El Brazo de la Torre. The island itself is almost entirely devoted to agriculture; the rice fields and other cultivation have a ready source of irrigation. It provides access to the west bank of a large tract of the river, however.

The western part of the site, fringing Doñana national park, is of the greatest interest. Here various drainage ditches and accompanying dykes enclose small pools and larger areas of marshland and salt flats. The appearance of the whole area depends on water levels, and when these are high the place resembles an inland sea. This is the Zona de

Purple Heron

Entremuros (between-walls zone) which was badly affected by the diversion through it of the polluted effluent from the Aznalcollár mine disaster in 1998 (See Doñana — H5) but there were no visible signs of ill-effects by spring 2000, when large numbers of birds were present (although insidious effects of the spillage may yet have to be felt). The southern part is a shallow lagoon, El Lucio del Cangrejo, which tends to dry up in summer but which is highly attractive to birds at other times. The whole area offers the characteristic habitats of the marismas of the Guadalquivir and, as with the Brazo del Este (SE1), is many respects more rewarding to visit for birding purposes than is most of Doñana national park itself.

Species
All or most of the characteristic waterfowl and waders of Doñana occur here. In particular, El Lucio del Cangrejo and the adjacent wetlands attract Spoonbills, Greater Flamingos, dabbling ducks including Marbled Ducks and Red-crested Pochards, and numerous waders, notably Ruffs and Black-tailed Godwits. Marsh Harriers are locally numerous. Gull-billed, Whiskered and Black Terns are abundant on passage especially. Lesser Short-toed Larks are typical and may be seen alongside Short-toed Larks; both breed here. Yellow Wagtails are abundant. Spectacled Warblers breed.

Timing
Visits in springtime are particularly productive. Winter and passage periods generally are also very good. Summer visits should be avoided; much of the wetland dries up completely then.

Access
The Isla Mínima is reached by driving south from Sevilla to Puebla del Río, via Coria del Río and continuing south to Villafranco and beyond. Access to and from Doñana is possible via El Rocío, crossing the northern marismas (See H5-E). The key habitats on the western part of the Isla Minima are easily viewed from the good roads along the parallel

fringing dykes. There are a couple of concrete fords linking the dykes but these may be impassable when water levels are very high (relatively infrequently), when a long detour to the north is necessary to reach the opposite side. A gate across the western dyke south of the Lucio marks the boundary of the national park. Access to Doñana through here is not permitted but the right turn shortly before the gate leads on to El Rocío (although 4WD may be necessary to complete the journey in all but the driest conditions).

A visit to this site can usefully be combined with one to the Brazo del Este (SE1) on the east bank. The river can be crossed at three points by ferries (barcas). The convenient one (see map), which links the Isla Mínima with the Isla Menor, operates during daylight hours all year round except during January (when you may still cross at Coria). La Barca is a rickety-looking, diesel-powered raft, which chugs across the river carrying at best a couple of cars. Crossing is on demand: shout/wave across if the ferry is on the opposite side. There is a modest charge for the service. The crossing itself provides an opportunity to see Night Herons, Gull-billed Terns and other birds on the river, and there is access to the west bank for the same purpose.

The Zona de Entremuros is reached from La Barca by driving to Villafranco del Guadalquivir. Drive through the town and turn right opposite No. 34 ('Ferretería García' — no known relation of EG and, incidentally, a Ferretería is an ironmonger; ferret-fanciers will be turned away), just before reaching an avenue of scraggy palm trees. Drive 4 km from the turn-off to reach the dykes.

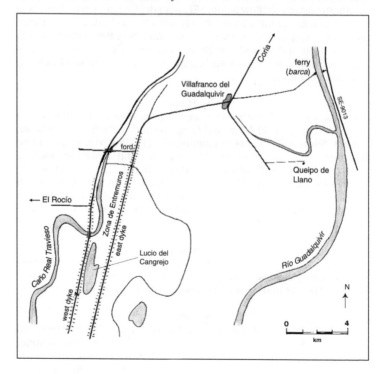

128

Calendar

Many of the species of Doñana (H5) are liable to occur but the following are especially typical.

All year: Cattle Egret, Little Egret, Grey Heron, White Stork, Spoonbill, Purple Gallinule, Red Kite, Marsh Harrier, Black-winged Stilt, Crested Lark, House Sparrow, Tree Sparrow.

Breeding season: Little Bittern, Night Heron, Squacco Heron, Purple Heron, Black Kite, Montagu's Harrier, Collared Pratincole, Whiskered Tern, Short-toed Lark, Lesser Short-toed Lark, Yellow Wagtail, Savi's Warbler, Reed Warbler, Great Reed Warbler, Spectacled Warbler.

Passage periods and winter: Greater Flamingo, waterfowl including Greylag Goose, Garganey, Marbled Duck and Red-crested Pochard; waders including Lapwing, Little Stint, Curlew Sandpiper, Dunlin, Ruff, Snipe, Spotted Redshank, Redshank, Green Sandpiper, Wood Sandpiper and Common Sandpiper; Gull-billed Tern, Whiskered Tern, Black Tern.

WESTERN GUADALQUIVIR VALLEY FARMLANDS

SE3

Status: No special protection.

Site description

The Guadalquivir valley is intensively farmed and the vast tracts of monoculture in some parts are not encouraging on first acquaintance. Nevertheless there is abundant ornithological interest and we are very much indebted to the advice of local birder, Francisco Chiclana, whose expertise has helped us in identifying the most productive areas. The western sector of the valley included here, in the vicinity of the city of Sevilla, has immense, flat wheat fields stretching for miles across the floodplain. Small rivers cross the plain and feed into the Río Guadalquivir. Their courses, and that of the main river, are marked by extensive olive and citrus groves, as well as vineyards. These orchards are also characteristic of the valley fringes and the surroundings of the numerous towns and villages. The riverbeds have useful stretches of riverine vegetation, including stands of willows and poplars and, most significantly, large clumps of tamarisks.

Species

This a regional stronghold of both Rufous Bush Chats and Olivaceous Warblers, two of the most sought-after but often most elusive species of our area. Both occur in numbers in late spring and summer. The chats are characteristic of citrus and olive groves whereas the warblers favour tamarisks along riverbeds and lake margins. They are easily located in

season, particularly once you know their songs. Species of open country may be encountered in the wheatfields. Small numbers of both Great
and Little Bustards occur but are elusive. Montagu's Harriers, Stone Curlews and Short-toed Larks are characteristic and rather more common.
Flocks of Lapwings, larks and pipits occur in winter.

Timing
Both Rufous Bush Chats and Olivaceous Warblers are summer visitors
and both are among the tardiest in arriving in Spain. They begin to turn
up in May but some do not appear until early June. They are most easily
located from late May through June and into July. By late August most
have already returned to Africa. Their stay coincides with the hottest time
of year in the hottest part of southern Spain, where shade temperatures
(not that there is any shade) regularly exceed 40°C by a good margin. It
goes without saying that the mornings and evenings are the most pleasant times in which to locate both species (and most others) and of course
these are the times when both are most vocal. Adequate protection
against the ferocious sun and regular fluid replacement are essential.

Many of the open-country species are resident and they are more easily located in winter and after crops have been cut.

Access
The region is fringed by the E-5/A-4 Sevilla/Cádiz motorway in the west
and by the E-5/N-IV Sevilla/Córdoba motorway in the north. A network
of minor road and farm tracks link the towns and villages and provide
good access to the interesting areas, which are spread over a very wide
area. Rufous Bush Chats are readily located around the Laguna de la
Mejorada, which lies a couple of kilometres north of the town of Los
Palacios y Villafranca, which is immediately west of the E5/A4 at junction 3 (Los Palacios). The easiest way to locate the lagoon is to ask for
directions within the town of Los Palacios: ask for the 'Lago de Diego

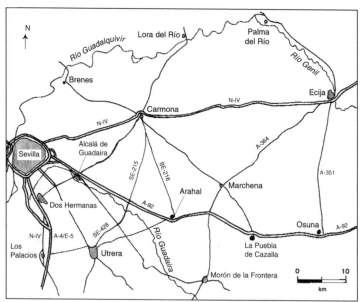

Puerta', which is the local name for the site. Otherwise, follow the canal which is adjacent to the N-IV road, from Los Palacios, which will lead to the lake. The lagoon is a hollow which resulted when material for the motorway construction was excavated. The fringing olive groves and vineyards have a good population of the chats and the tamarisks around the lagoon support Olivaceous Warblers. There is also a major Cattle Egret roost here.

Elsewhere, Rufous Bush Chats are characteristic of the olive groves around the towns of Arahal, Morón and Puebla de Cazalla. The tamarisks along the watercourses of the Ribera del Genil, between Herrera and Ecija, and the Ribera del Guadaira, and along the Guadalquivir itself, all support good populations of Olivaceous Warblers. Stop at suitable bridges and inspect the riverine scrub.

Open-country species may be searched for in the wheatfields between Carmona and Utrera (SE-215 & SE-428) and between Carmona and Arahal (SE-216) and also between Ecija and Osuna (A-351). The open expanses may be scanned with a telescope. It is also worth exploring these regions more closely along the numerous dirt roads and farm tracks which present themselves.

Calendar

All year: Cattle Egret, White Stork, Common Kestrel, Red-legged Partridge, Great Bustard, Little Bustard, Stone Curlew, Little Owl, Calandra Lark, Crested Lark, Barn Swallow, Zitting Cisticola, Cetti's Warbler, Southern Grey Shrike, Raven, Corn Bunting.

Breeding season: Short-toed Eagle, Montagu's Harrier, Lesser Kestrel, Quail, Collared Pratincole, Short-toed Lark, Yellow Wagtail, Rufous Bush Chat, Nightingale, Olivaceous Warbler, Golden Oriole,

Winter: Merlin, Lapwing, Pin-tailed Sandgrouse, Skylark, Meadow Pipit, White Wagtail, Song Thrush, Blackcap.

SIERRA NORTE   SE4

Status: Parque Natural, 164,840 ha. ZEPA.

Site description

This region forms the central portion of the Sierra Morena. It lies between the natural parks of the Sierra de Aracena y Picos de Aroche in Huelva province (H7) and the Sierra de Hornachuelos in Córdoba province (CO9). Like those sites, the region is not ornithologically outstanding but it offers many good birds and lends itself to gentle exploration if your priority is getting away from the tourist-beaten track.

These are smooth rounded hills rather than the jagged sierras so common in Spain. There are extensive woods of stone pines, encinas, cork oaks and Lusitanian oaks. Numerous small rivers cross the region, in places fringed by woods of sweet chestnuts, smooth-leaved elms and poplars. Extensive meadows and tracts of gum cistus scrub are also characteristic.

Species

The region offers a good variety of raptors and other species typical of the Mediterranean woodlands. All five eagles breed as do Black and White Storks and Eagle Owls. Characteristic passerines include Woodlarks, Red-rumped Swallows, Azure-winged Magpies and Rock Sparrows.

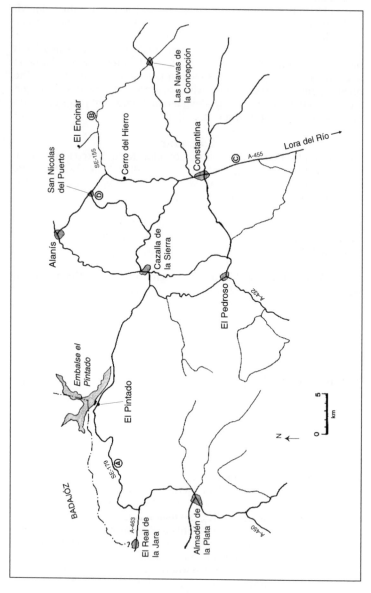

Timing
Springtime visits are most productive.

Access
The region is crossed by a network of minor roads and well-marked footpaths, permitting exploration at leisure. The SE-179 road between El Real de la Jara and El Pintado (A) ascends cistus-covered slopes to cross several high passes, with good views over the region. Very large open pastures are characteristic between San Nicholas and Las Navas (SE-155, B) and southwards from Constantina towards Lora del Río (A-455; C). Riverside habitats can be visited, for example, from the village of San Nicholás del Puerto, on the Río Huéznar (D). An information centre in Constantina provides information on recommended footpaths and other amenities of the park.

Calendar
All year: Great-crested Grebe, Black-shouldered Kite, Red Kite, Griffon Vulture, Black Vulture, Common Buzzard, Golden Eagle, Bonelli's Eagle, Eagle Owl, Woodlark, Crag Martin, Blue Rock Thrush, Mistle Thrush, Southern Grey Shrike, Nuthatch, Azure-winged Magpie, Raven, Rock Sparrow, Hawfinch.

Breeding Season: Black Stork, White Stork, Black Kite, Egyptian Vulture, Short-toed Eagle, Booted Eagle, Turtle Dove, Alpine Swift, Hoopoe, Golden Oriole, Woodchat Shrike.

CÓRDOBA PROVINCE

There is a considerable amount of very interesting birding in this province which, even now, receives much less attention than those further south and west. Basically, the birding areas of Córdoba can be split into five. In the extreme north and northwest there is the region known as Los Pedroches, which is an extension of the steppe habitats of adjacent Badajoz. It is included as one huge site, Northwest Córdoba (CO11). Here are nearly all the steppe species which you might expect to find in Extremadura, with the general exception of Great Bustards, which do occur but are very scarce and localised.

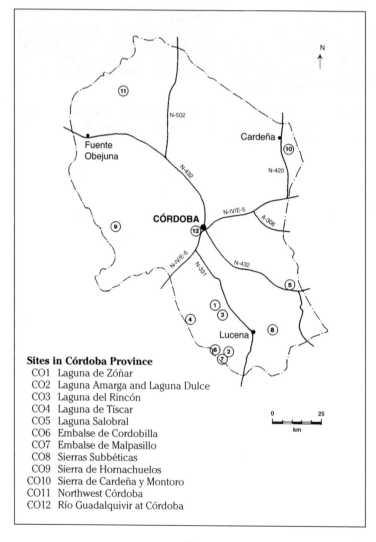

Sites in Córdoba Province
CO1 Laguna de Zóñar
CO2 Laguna Amarga and Laguna Dulce
CO3 Laguna del Rincón
CO4 Laguna de Tíscar
CO5 Laguna Salobral
CO6 Embalse de Cordobilla
CO7 Embalse de Malpasillo
CO8 Sierras Subbéticas
CO9 Sierra de Hornachuelos
CO10 Sierra de Cardeña y Montoro
CO11 Northwest Córdoba
CO12 Río Guadalquivir at Córdoba

The sierras are represented by the Sierra Morena, which includes the Parques Naturales of the Sierra de Hornachuelos (CO9) and Sierras de Cardeña y Montoro (CO10). These hold a large number of raptors and other species and rather complement each other, although if you need to choose between them then the best choice would be in favour of Hornachuelos. Hornachuelos is at the eastern extreme of the Sierra Norte (SE4).

The third area is in the southeast where there is the Sierra Subbética (CO8), another interesting region but one which holds nothing which cannot be seen elsewhere.

In fourth place there are the lagoons and reservoirs, which are mostly in the southwest sector of the province (CO1–7). All these wetland sites are important for waterfowl and, in particular, for White-headed Ducks and Purple Gallinules. The distances between the various wetland sites are considerable. However, the three most interesting are undoubtedly the Lagunas Amarga and Dulce (CO2), Laguna del Rincón (CO3) and Laguna de Tíscar (CO4).

Finally there is the Río Guadalquivir in Córdoba city itself (CO12), which is well worth a visit for the egrets and other species.

Maps

Mapa Provincial Córdoba, IGN, 1:200.000.
Plaza & Janes Euromapa, Andalucía Occidental, 1:300,000.

Getting there

Córdoba is linked with other provincial capitals by major trunk roads. Rapid movement within the province is possible using the Autovía de Andalucía (N-IV/E-5) which follows the Guadalquivir valley and links Córdoba with Sevilla. The southerly link to the Costa del Sol from Córdoba is by the N-331 towards Antequera. An autovía between Córdoba and the A-92 near Antequera (Málaga province) is planned but it is difficult to imagine that this will be completed before 2004. To go north from Córdoba, the N-432 gives access to the northwest of the province and on to Zafra in Extremadura. By branching off the N-432 on to the N-502 you eventually enter western Ciudad Real province.

Where to stay

There are ample tourist facilities throughout the province, especially in Córdoba itself.

LAGUNA DE ZÓNAR   CO1

Status: Reserva Natural, 385 ha. ZEPA.

Information

There is an information centre, El Lagar, for the Laguna de Zónar at Km 80.5 on the A-309 road between Puente Genil and Aguilar, some 4 km from Aguilar, where it is possible to obtain information on the current state of the lagoons of south Córdoba. However, this centre is not always open. At Km 82 there is a large, well built centre, complete with car park and hide. The opening hours here differ between winter and summer but it never opens before 10 am.

Site description
The Laguna de Zóñar is surrounded by tamarisk and a wide fringe of *Phragmites* reeds. It is set in a basin, as are all the south Córdoba lagoons.

Species
This lagoon was the last redoubt of White-headed Duck, whose entire Spanish population reputedly diminished to just 22 birds in 1977. Fortunately, since then, the protection given to this and other sites, plus the captive-breeding programme carried out in Doñana, has resulted in a current population of well over 4,000 birds (in 2000). You will be aware that this much healthier population has recently been threatened from a most unlikely source: hybridisation with the congeneric Ruddy Duck, a North American species with a thriving population in Britain and elsewhere in northern Europe. Itinerant Ruddy Ducks turn up in Spain from time to time and are prone to interbreeding with White-headed Ducks. Hence, wherever possible, and much to the annoyance of some, these intruders are sent to meet their maker in order that the White-headed Ducks (which, compared with the sparky Ruddy Ducks, look somewhat dim) may retain their specific identity.

As it happens, White-headed Ducks are no longer to be found at Zóñar. Introduced carp eliminated the subaquatic vegetation to the detriment of the ducks. Attempts to remove the carp by netting have failed, although such a programme has been carried out successfully at the Laguna del Rincón, where the ducks may be seen easily.

There are both Great Crested and Little Grebes on the lagoon. Cormorants occur sparingly in winter. The winter months are undoubtedly best and ducks to be seen include Shelduck, Wigeon, Gadwall, Teal, Pintail, Shoveler, both Common and Red-crested Pochards, Ferruginous Ducks and Tufted Ducks. Garganey move through in March during the spring migration. There are a few Marsh Harriers in the area which may be seen virtually throughout the year. Purple Gallinules occur although they take some finding. Coots are common (literally) although there have been occasional reports of Red-knobbed Coots here. There is the possibility of occasional migrant Gull-billed or Black Terns during passage periods. The reedbeds and the lake fringes hold hordes of Nightingales in the spring. The former also have colonies of Great Reed Warblers and Reed Warblers, with Melodious Warblers on the outermost fringes where there are tamarisks. In the winter months there are sometimes roosts of several thousand starlings, chiefly Common Starlings. Bluethroats also winter in the same area.

Timing
The species diversity is probably highest in winter although spring is good for warblers.

Access
Access is from the A-309 road between Aguilar de la Frontera and Puente Genil. The information centre is approximately 4 km south of

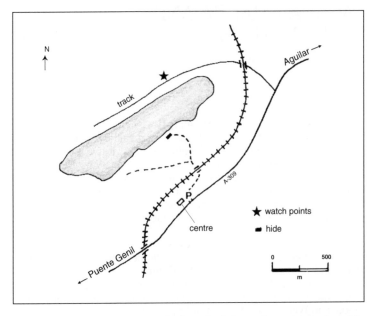

Aguilar. The obvious access point is at the information centre when this is open. It is then worth going down to the hide and walking the trail, after signing for and receiving a returnable visitors badge from the information desk at the centre. When the centre is closed it is best to go in to the far side of the laguna by returning towards Aguilar for about 1 km and turning off along a track on the left side of the road. The turn-off is just on the curve so caution is needed. Negotiating the track needs some care as it gets rather rough and very muddy after rain and it is unsuitable for low-slung vehicles. Pass under the railway line, take the left fork and continue until you can park near the embankment, where there is an unofficial view point. A telescope is essential here.

Calendar

All year: Little Grebe, Great Crested Grebe, Mallard, Pochard, Red-crested Pochard, Purple Gallinule.

Breeding season: Garganey, Gull-billed Tern, Black Tern, swifts and hirundines, Nightingale, Great Reed Warbler, Reed Warbler, Melodious Warbler.

Winter: Great Cormorant, Black-necked Grebe, Shelduck, Wigeon, Gadwall, Teal, Shoveler, Ferruginous Duck, Tufted Duck, Bluethroat.

LAGUNA AMARGA AND LAGUNA DULCE

Status: Reserva Natural, 250 ha. ZEPA.

Site description

This interesting site has lakes of contrasting salinity. The freshwater Laguna Dulce is to the left of the entrance track. It has recently been reclaimed and has relatively little fringing vegetation. The Laguna Amarga (bitter lake) is to the right of the track. It is virtually circular and is surrounded by tamarisks with a few canes, reeds and bulrushes. These lagoons are among the few to benefit from permanent standing water, although levels are somewhat variable in the Laguna Dulce.

Species

Both White-headed Ducks and Purple Gallinules are to be found where water and reed conditions are right. Common species include Little, Great Crested and Black-necked Grebes and the ubiquitous Moorhens, Coots and Mallards. There are also Red-crested Pochards, which may breed, and Wigeon and Tufted Ducks in winter.

Bonelli's Eagles and Montagu's Harriers hunt over the general area and Ravens frequently overfly. Hoopoes are common along the access track and Nightingales sing loudly at all hours in the spring. Short-toed Treecreepers are common and Goldfinches are everywhere.

Access

The site is just off the CO-753 Jauja/Moriles road. The reserve is well sign-posted but ignore the large sign and go in by the small one on the south-east side of the road. Here there is a parking area with a closed gate

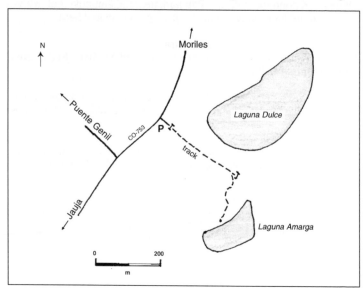

denying further vehicular access. Walk along the track and view the Laguna Dulce to the left. The track to the Laguna Amarga rises off on the right by a little whitish building and then climbs up for less than a kilometre to the observatory which overlooks the lake.

Calendar
All year: Little Grebe, Mallard, Red-crested Pochard, White-headed Duck, Bonelli's Eagle, Moorhen, Coot, Purple Gallinule, Wren, Dartford Warbler, Sardinian Warbler, Short-toed Treecreeper, Chaffinch.

Breeding season: Marsh Harrier, Montagu's Harrier, Little Ringed Plover, Hoopoe, Nightingale.

Winter: Wigeon, Pochard, Tufted Duck.

LAGUNA DEL RINCÓN   CO3
Status: Reserva Natural, 150 ha. ZEPA.

Site description
This is also a lagoon with permanent water. It is set in a virtually circular depression and has a wide fringe of canes, reeds, tamarisks and bulrushes. Vineyards surround the lake.

Species
This is an excellent site for White-headed Ducks. Other species include Little, Great Crested and Black-necked Grebes, the ubiquitous Mallard in large numbers and both Red-crested and Common Pochards. Wintering species include occasional Greylag Geese as well as Teal, Shovelers and Tufted Ducks. Coots and Moorhens are common and there are resident Water Rails and occasional Purple Gallinules. Marsh Harriers hunt over the area from time to time. Waders occur occasionally, especially during

White-headed Duck

139

migration periods. Large numbers of swifts and hirundines feed over the area at times. The reedbeds and surrounding vegetation hold Reed Warblers and Great Reed Warblers, as well as Melodious Warblers and Nightingales. In the fields around there is a chance of seeing Rufous Bush Chats and Short-toed Larks, and there are good numbers of Corn Buntings.

Timing
The best time is spring for an abundance of species, followed by winter if you are particularly interested in ducks.

Access
Access from the CO-760 Aguilar de la Frontera/Moriles road. The rather inconspicuous Consejería de Medio Ambiente signs on the west side of the road at Km 5 mark the entrance. The access track, some 750 m long, is very rough and may only be accessible to 4WD vehicles when wet. Park at the disused information centre at the end. The public hide at the far end of the lake is usually closed, in which event it is best to walk around the outside of the fenced perimeter of the lake and watch from suitable points. A telescope is useful, although the lagoon is not large.

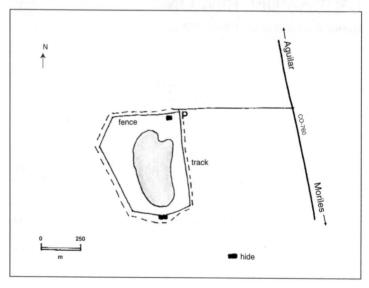

Calendar
All year: Little Grebe, Great Crested Grebe, Mallard, Red-crested Pochard, Pochard, White-headed Duck, Water Rail, Moorhen, Purple Gallinule, Coot, Corn Bunting.

Breeding season: Marsh Harrier, Black-winged Stilt, Rufous Bush Chat, Nightingale, Cetti's Warbler, Reed Warbler, Great Reed Warbler, Melodious Warbler.

Winter: Greylag Goose, Wigeon, Teal, Shoveler, Tufted Duck.

Passage periods: Waders, swifts and hirundines.

LAGUNA DE TÍSCAR

Status: Reserva Natural, 185 ha. ZEPA.

Site description

The laguna is one of the seasonal lakes and so it lacks the abundant fringe of vegetation of those with permanent water. As a compensation it does have more open shore space. The saline nature of the water means that there is some glasswort, as well as reeds and some scattered tamarisks. A wonderful selection of thistles extends between the road and the hide.

Species

The salinity attracts small numbers of Greater Flamingos from time to time. Breeding ducks include Mallard, in the usual large quantities, and one or two pairs of Red-crested Pochards. It holds a greater population of ducks, including Wigeon, Pintail and Shoveler, in winter. The open habitat attracts a variety of migrant and breeding waders, the latter including plenty of Black-winged Stilts and a few pairs of Avocets and Little Ringed Plovers. A few Gull-billed Terns use the lagoon during the migration periods and there are often some non-breeding birds to be seen here.

The thistles attract large numbers of Goldfinches and Greenfinches, and provide excellent cover for Melodious Warblers, which can be easily seen in front of the hide and along the approach path.

Timing

Spring for migrant waders and the winter months for ducks and the possibility of a few wintering waders.

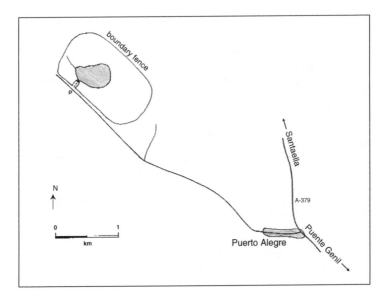

Access

This site is easily missed as the provincial map does not show an easy access point. Take the A-379 north from the A-340 immediately north of Puente Genil. The junction is marked by a furniture store 'Muebles Manuel Espejo'. Continue for nearly 2 km before turning left by the small village of Puerto Alegre. Thereafter continue for 3.5 km along the track marked on the maps. The track is normally in good condition and should not present any problems. Continue a few hundred metres past the large sign and the usually locked gates at the lake entrance and park by the roadside. The 200 m path to the hide is on the right on top of a hillock. The hide overlooks the lagoon and you can see everything from here. Please remain on the marked track.

Calendar

All year: Greater Flamingo, Mallard, Red-crested Pochard, Moorhen, Coot.

Breeding season: Black-winged Stilt, Avocet, Little Ringed Plover, Gull-billed Tern, Melodious Warbler.

Winter: Wigeon, Pintail, Shoveler, waders.

Passage periods: A large variety of waders in small numbers.

LAGUNA SALOBRAL (LAGUNA DEL CONDE) CO5

Status: Reserva Natural, 345 ha. ZEPA.

Site description

This seasonal lagoon has no surrounding fringe of tall permanent vegetation, although there are some tamarisks and glassworts on the fringes. The lagoon is prone to drying out by late summer, although in dry years it may be empty by late spring.

Species

The lagoon attracts occasional Flamingos and some Greylag Geese in the winter months. Wintering ducks include Shelducks, Shoveler, Wigeon, Red-crested Pochards and Common Pochards. Occasional migrant waders, such as Redshanks and Common Sandpipers, occur, especially in spring. The fields around the lagoon harbour some Little Bustards as well as Crested Larks.

Timing

The winter months are best, provided that there has been sufficient rainfall to make the place attractive to ducks.

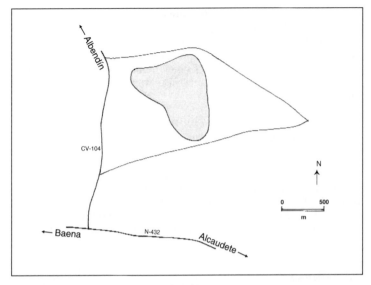

Access
The Laguna Salobral lies to the north of the N-432 between Baena and Alcaudete (Jaén province), some 7 km west of the A-333 turn-off to the south for Priego de Córdoba. The entrance track is marked Cortijo de Juncar and gives access to both the northern and southern sides of the lake.

Calendar
All year: Little Bustard, Crested Lark.

Winter: Greater Flamingo, Greylag Goose, Shelduck, Wigeon, Shoveler, Mallard, Red-crested Pochard, Pochard.

Passage periods: Redshank, Common Sandpiper, waders.

EMBALSE DE CORDOBILLA   CO6
Status: Paraje Natural, 1,460 ha.

Site description
This is a reservoir on the Río Genil and is the furthest downstream of a series of three on this river. The southern part of the site is within Sevilla province. The banks are covered with abundant tamarisks, willows and reedbeds and they provide a good nesting site for waterbirds, as there are no major fluctuations of water levels.

Species
This is yet another site where patience and luck may be rewarded with views of White-headed Ducks and Purple Gallinules. Grey Herons are always present together with Purple Herons and White Storks in the breeding season. Wintering ducks include Mallard, Gadwall, Wigeon and Red-crested Pochards. Cranes also winter in the area in small numbers.

Timing
Winter and spring visits, between November and June, are most productive.

Access
Access is not easy and large areas are difficult to reach. The best route is to take the CV-179 southwest from Puente Genil to the village of Cordobilla and to continue along this road to the northwestern corner of the reservoir, which is the only part which is easily accessible.

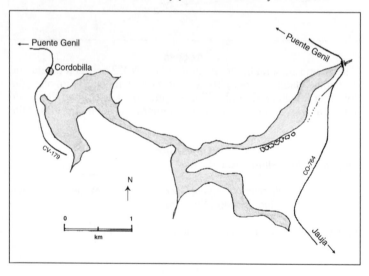

Calendar
All year: Grey Heron, White-headed Duck, Purple Gallinule.

Breeding season: Purple Heron, White Stork.

Winter: Wigeon, Gadwall, Mallard, Red-crested Pochard, Crane.

EMBALSE DE MALPASILLO

Status: Paraje Natural, 512 ha.

Site description
It is convenient to consider this area within the context of the Córdoba wetlands, although the entry point, the village of Badolatosa, is in Sevilla province and the provincial boundary more or less follows the centre line of the reservoir. This reservoir on the Río Genil is relatively steep-sided but there are flat areas along its course where there are reedbeds and occasional stands of willow and tamarisk.

Species
The reservoir attracts some wintering Cormorants, which usually congregate near the sluice gates. The area is best for ducks in winter, when apart from the resident Mallards and a few Common Pochards there are sometimes Wigeon and Teal. Marsh Harriers breed and are often to be seen quartering the reedbeds. Cetti's Warblers are resident and in the spring the song of Nightingales wafts upwards from the valley.

Timing
This reservoir may be visited at any time of year although it is most interesting for wintering waterfowl.

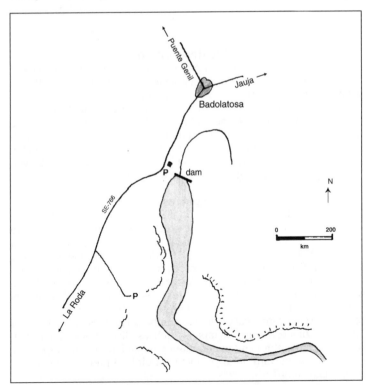

Access

Take the SE-766 southwest from the village of Badolatosa towards La Roda. The first stop is just outside Badolatosa, on the bank above the sluice gates, just by the Sevillana electricity company building. This part of the reservoir is generally less productive, apart for the Cormorants in winter. A better viewpoint is reached about 1 km further south where a track turns off on the east side of the road, just on a bend. Follow this track for 400 m and take the left fork. Park just before the hillock which rises up on the left side. A short walk then brings you to a steep slope overlooking the reedbeds.

Calendar

All year: Grey Heron, Mallard, Pochard, Peregrine, Common Kestrel, Coot, Cetti's Warbler, Jackdaw, Raven.

Breeding season: Purple Heron, Marsh Harrier, Nightingale.

Winter: Great Cormorant, Wigeon, Teal.

SIERRAS SUBBÉTICAS   CO8

Status: Parque Natural, 31, 568 ha.

Site description

The sierras are in the southern part of Córdoba between Lucena and Priego de Cordoba. There are four significant ranges of over 1000 m within the park. In the north are the sierras of Zuheros (1217 m at Virgen de la Sierra) and Luque (1380 m at Lobatejo). To the south there are the sierras of Rute and Horconera (1570 m at Tiñosa), separated by the lower Sierra de Gaena. The geomorphology is limestone with sharp escarpments and narrow valleys. The vegetation is typically Mediterranean with encinas and cork oaks at lower levels and thick scrub, with willows and some poplars, around the watercourses.

Species

There is a small colony of Griffon Vultures on the cliff face of Albuchite, off the Carcabuey–Luque track. The accumulated whitewash of vulture droppings is visible from afar. Bonelli's Eagles nest nearby. Egyptian Vultures bred in the same area until 1992. There is also at least one pair of Golden Eagles in the whole area, these being more frequently seen between the peak at Virgen de la Sierra and Carcabuey. Short-toed Eagles are present in summer. Peregrines breed in small numbers despite the unwelcome depredations of nest-robbers, which have caused a significant local decline in numbers. Hobbies occur in spring and may breed. Parties of raptors such as Black Kites and Honey Buzzards move through the area during migration periods, especially during the southward passage. Nocturnal birds of prey include Scops, Eagle, Little and Tawny Owls.

Red-necked Nightjars occur at lower levels in suitable areas. Common Nightjars also occur, mainly in the spring migration period, but have not been proved to breed. Alpine Swifts, Bee-eaters and Hoopoes are common and Wrynecks occur in small numbers. It is worth noting that they are reputed to have bred in the rather pleasant park in the centre of Cabra, just outside the area. Other characteristic breeding species include Green Woodpeckers, Crested Larks, Thekla Larks, Woodlarks, Red-rumped Swallows and Crag Martins. Alpine Accentors frequent the tops in winter, when Dunnocks occur at lower levels in suitable habitat.

The thrushes are amply represented. Nightingales, Black Redstarts, Black-eared Wheatears, Black Wheatears, Blue Rock Thrushes and Mistle Thrushes are widespread and Rock Thrushes breed at the highest levels of the sierras. Ring Ouzels and Song Thrushes occur on migration and in winter, together with occasional Redwings and Fieldfares. Breeding warblers include Blackcaps, the omnipresent Sardinian and

Red-rumped Swallows

Dartford Warblers, Melodious Warblers, Bonelli's Warblers in the more wooded areas and Subalpine Warblers. Orphean Warblers do not appear to breed within the park but do so just to the north in the region of Nueva Carteya.

Spotted Flycatchers breed and Pied Flycatchers occur on passage. In spring, the fluting song of Golden Orioles is characteristic of some areas, especially where there are poplars. Both Southern Grey and Woodchat Shrikes are to be found. The corvids are represented by Jays, Red-billed Choughs, Jackdaws and Ravens. Rock Sparrows occur locally within the area. Breeding finches include Crossbills, and both Hawfinches and Siskins are frequent winter visitors. Cirl Buntings and Rock Buntings breed.

Timing
This site is interesting at any time of year, although it can get very cold, with snow in the winter months. Species diversity is highest in spring.

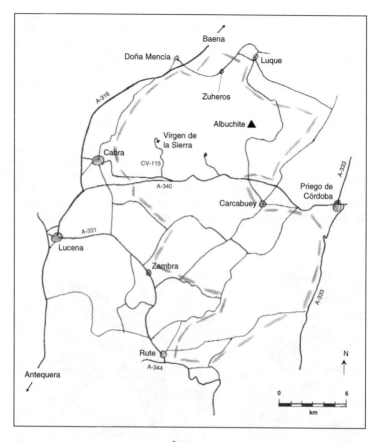

Access

Access from the west is easy via the Málaga/Córdoba road (N-331), either via Rute on the A-344 or turning off eastwards at Lucena. From the east (Jaén) access is via the A-340 Priego de Córdoba/Lucena road, which bisects the area east-west. A variety of minor roads around and through the area connect with the A-340. The better area is the part north of the A-340.

The road (CV-115) up the sierra to the Ermita de la Virgen de la Sierra is of interest. The entrance is off a minor road linking the A-340 and Cabra, 1 km from the A-340 junction. Drive up slowly, stopping at appropriate points and particularly near the top by a quarry on the right. The views from the summit (1217 m) are terrific on a clear day.

Calendar

All year: Griffon Vulture, Egyptian Vulture, Goshawk, Common Buzzard, Golden Eagle, Common Kestrel, Peregrine, Woodpigeon, Eagle Owl, Little Owl, Tawny Owl, Green Woodpecker, Crested Lark, Thekla Lark, Woodlark, Crag Martin, Dunnock, Black Redstart, Black Wheatear, Blue Rock Thrush, Mistle Thrush, Dartford Warbler, Sardinian Warbler, Blackcap, Southern Grey Shrike, Jay, Red-billed Chough, Jackdaw, Raven, Rock Sparrow, Crossbill, Cirl Bunting.

Breeding season: Short-toed Eagle, Turtle Dove, Scops Owl, Red-necked Nightjar, Common Swift, Pallid Swift, Alpine Swift, Bee-eater, Roller, Hoopoe, Wryneck, Barn Swallow, Red-rumped Swallow, House Martin, Grey Wagtail, Nightingale, Black-eared Wheatear, Rock Thrush, Melodious Warbler, Subalpine Warbler, Orphean Warbler, Bonelli's Warbler, Spotted Flycatcher, Golden Oriole, Woodchat Shrike.

Winter: Meadow Pipit, White Wagtail, Alpine Accentor, Ring Ouzel, Song Thrush, Redwing, Fieldfare, Common Chiffchaff, Siskin, Bullfinch, Hawfinch.

Passage periods: Honey Buzzard, Black Kite, Hobby, Common Nightjar, Tree Pipit, Common Redstart, Northern Wheatear, Willow Warbler, Pied Flycatcher.

SIERRA DE HORNACHUELOS   CO9

Status: Parque Natural, 67,202 ha. ZEPA.

Information

There is an information centre, 'Huerta del Rey', at Km 1.5 on the CO-142, Hornachuelos/San Calixto road.

Site description

This park is another protected sector of the Sierra Morena and is contiguous with the Sierra Norte (SE4) in Sevilla province. The vegetation is varied and boasts four species of oak and two species of pine, as well as the typical garrigue scrub with cistus, fan palm and holly. There are some deep ravines. Water is plentiful. The Río Bembézar drains a large part of the park and there are three reservoirs, the Embalse del Retortillo in the west, the Pantano de Bembézar in the centre, and the Pantano de Breña in the southeast. Another reservoir, Breña 2, is planned.

Species

The species of the park are typical of the sierras and raptors are prominent. All three species of vultures breed including a few pairs of Egyptian Vultures and over 50 pairs of Black Vultures. Griffon Vultures are common. Other breeding raptors include Spanish Imperial, Golden, Bonelli's, Booted and Short-toed Eagles, Common Buzzards, Goshawks and Common Kestrels. Sparrowhawks may breed but are more frequently seen during migration periods. Merlins occur as rare winter visitors in the more open areas. Nocturnal raptors are represented by Scops, Eagle, Tawny and Little Owls, with a few Barn Owls.

One or two pairs of Black Storks nest within the park and they may be seen particularly in the region of the Pantano de Bembézar. The reservoirs attract considerable numbers of Great Cormorants in winter. Other breeding species include Red-necked Nightjars, Hoopoes, Bee-eaters Alpine Swifts and Pallid Swifts. White-rumped Swifts also occur and have been suspected of breeding. There are some Rufous Bush Chats, although this species is generally scarce. Black Redstarts, Black Wheatears, Black-eared Wheatears, Mistle Thrushes and Blue Rock Thrushes breed. Small numbers of Redwings and Song Thrushes, with occasional Fieldfares, occur in winter.

Melodious Warblers nest but are generally scarce. Spectacled and Subalpine Warblers both breed commonly in suitable habitats. Crested Tits are scarce and localised in the region but may be found in the pinewoods especially. Golden Orioles occur locally; as so often is the case the best places to find them are near water where there are poplars.

Both Southern Grey and Woodchat Shrikes occur commonly. Azure-winged Magpies are abundant here and there are also Jays, Magpies, Red-billed Choughs, Jackdaws and Ravens. Wintering finches include Bramblings. Rock Sparrows are local; the best place to find these is at Mina de la Plata, southeast of Bembézar, where they breed.

Mammals are well represented in the park. There are very small populations of Iberian lynx and perhaps the occasional wolf still survives. Mongooses occur in small numbers and genets are relatively much more common. Otters frequent the reservoirs and rivers. Red deer and wild boars are common.

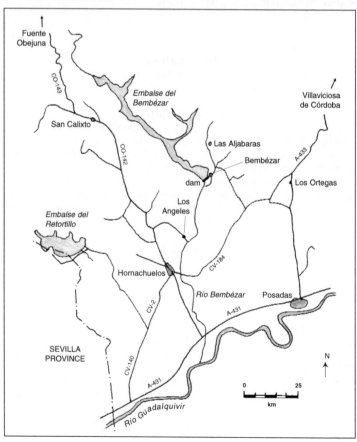

Timing

The best time is undoubtedly spring and early summer, between April and the end of June or even mid-July. However, the wide variety of species to be seen makes a visit to this area attractive at nearly any time of year, although it does get jolly cold in winter.

Access

The natural entry point is from the village of Hornachuelos itself. From there you can traverse the park to the northwest, heading for San Calixto and Fuente Obejuna on the CO-142 and then the CO-143. Alternatively, just south of Hornachuelos, turn northeast for Villaviciosa de Córdoba on the CV-184, which joins the A-433.

There are several tracks to either side of the San Calixto route which are worth visiting, notably that to Los Angeles, 5 km north of Hornachuelos, and another, just under 2 km further north, to El Romano. This region, on the western side of the Embalse del Bembézar, is generally productive. Another recommended sector is north of the CV-184, where a minor road 12 km northeast of Hornachuelos leads to Poblado del Embalse and Las Aljabaras; this region is good for vultures especially.

It is worth parking in Hornachuelos village and walking north along the west bank of the river. Here you stand a good chance of seeing foraging Black Storks and also both White-rumped Swifts and Red-rumped Swallows. The CV-2 road, southwest from Hornachuelos to the Embalse del Retortillo, is also of interest and not to be missed.

Calendar

All year: Egyptian Vulture, Black Vulture, Griffon Vulture, Goshawk, Spanish Imperial Eagle, Golden Eagle, Common Buzzard, Common Kestrel, Red-legged Partridge, Woodpigeon, Barn Owl, Eagle Owl, Little Owl, Tawny Owl, Crag Martin, Wren, Robin, Black Wheatear, Blue Rock Thrush, Mistle Thrush, Dartford Warbler, Sardinian Warbler, Crested Tit, Coal Tit, Blue Tit, Great Tit, Nuthatch, Short-toed Treecreeper, Southern Grey Shrike, Jay, Azure-winged Magpie, Magpie, Red-billed Chough, Jackdaw, Raven, Spotless Starling, Rock Sparrow, Chaffinch, Serin, Greenfinch, Goldfinch, Linnet, Crossbill, Rock Bunting, Corn Bunting.

Breeding season: Black Stork, White Stork, Short-toed Eagle, Booted Eagle, Quail, Turtle Dove, Cuckoo, Scops Owl, Red-necked Nightjar, Common Swift, Pallid Swift, Alpine Swift, White-rumped Swift, Bee-eater, Roller, Hoopoe, Crested Lark, Thekla Lark, Woodlark, Barn Swallow, Red-rumped Swallow, House Martin, Nightingale, Rufous Bush Chat, Black-eared Wheatear, Melodious Warbler, Spectacled Warbler, Subalpine Warbler, Spotted Flycatcher, Golden Oriole, Woodchat Shrike.

Winter: Hen Harrier, Skylark, Meadow Pipit, Song Thrush, Redwing, Fieldfare, Common Chiffchaff, Brambling, Siskin.

Passage periods: Black Kite, Sparrowhawk, Merlin, Sand Martin, Northern Wheatear, Common Redstart, Whitethroat, Willow Warbler, Pied Flycatcher.

SIERRA DE CARDEÑA Y MONTORO

Status: Parque Natural, 41,212 ha. ZEPA.

Site description

This is another of the protected areas within the general ambit of the Sierra Morena. It is adjacent to the Parque Natural de las Sierras de Andújar (J4). The western part of the park is rather rolling terrain with a considerable amount of cereal farming, not to mention herds of malodorous goats. The landscape becomes rougher in the east along the course of the Río de las Yeguas, with high points of no more than 820 m. There are areas of open oakland, intermixed with plantations of pines and lower vegetation of typical Mediterranean species.

Species

The area is good for birds of prey, with Black and Griffon Vultures straying into the area from the northern side of the Sierra Morena. All five species of eagles are present, as well as Common Buzzards, Goshawks and Peregrines. Nocturnal raptors are represented by Scops, Eagle, Little, Tawny and Long-eared Owls. Rollers, Bee-eaters and Hoopoes all occur, although Rollers are scarce. Green and Great Spotted Woodpeckers are typical of the woodland areas. The relative lack of open spaces means few larks, pipits or wagtails in general, the most frequently seen species being Crested and Thekla Larks, Meadow Pipits and both White and Grey Wagtails. The chats are represented by Nightingales, Robins and Black Redstarts whilst in the winter there are considerable arrivals of thrushes including the scarce Redwings. There are the usual warblers: Dartford Warblers, Sardinian Warblers, Subalpine Warblers and Blackcaps, with Firecrests in the pines. The wooded areas also hold Spotted Flycatchers and various species of tits, as well as Nuthatches and Short-toed Treecreepers. Golden Orioles are not infrequent in the breeding season in suitable areas. Both the common shrikes occur. Magpies are abundant and Azure-winged Magpies and Ravens are always present.

Together with the Sierra de Andújar (J4), the area is important for its mammal populations. The elusive Iberian lynx occurs at high density and there is a relict population of wolves. Mongooses, otters, genets, wild cats and foxes are relatively numerous as are wild boars. There is an excellent range of ungulates; Spanish ibex, mouflon, red deer, roe deer and fallow deer.

Timing

Although this area could be visited at any time of year, wild boar, deer and other species are hunted on the big estates, and it is always possible that in the autumn and winter you could coincide with one of these hunts (*cacerías*) which would not do much to encourage successful birding. For widest variety, the period April–mid July is best.

Access

The park is of easy access from both north and south. From the north,

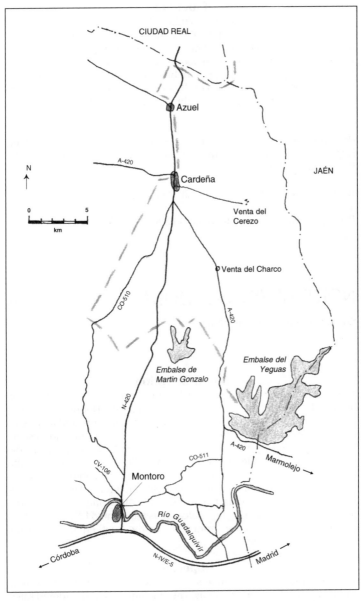

you may drive down to Cardeña from Ciudad Real on the N-420. Access from the south is from the N-IV Autovía de Andalucía. From the Jaén direction it is best to turn off at Marmolejo and take the A-420 road for Cardeña, or, failing that, turn off at Villa del Río on to the N-420 for Cardeña. From the Córdoba direction you turn north on to the N-420 at Montoro for Cardeña. Three north–south roads within the park converge on Cardeña. It also worth taking the track east from Cardeña to Venta del Cerezo from where you can follow a track to the Río de las Yeguas, which gives good representative birding.

Calendar

All year: Black Vulture, Griffon Vulture, Goshawk, Common Buzzard, Spanish Imperial Eagle, Golden Eagle, Bonelli's Eagle, Peregrine, Common Kestrel, Eagle Owl, Little Owl, Tawny Owl, Long-eared Owl, Green Woodpecker, Great Spotted Woodpecker, Crested Lark, Thekla Lark, Meadow Pipit, Grey Wagtail, Robin, Black Redstart, Mistle Thrush, Dartford Warbler, Sardinian Warbler, Blackcap, Firecrest, Nuthatch, Short-toed Treecreeper, Southern Grey Shrike, Azure-winged Magpie, Magpie, Raven.

Breeding season: Short-toed Eagle, Roller, Hoopoe, Bee-eater, Nightingale, Subalpine Warbler, Spotted Flycatcher, Golden Oriole, Woodchat Shrike.

Winter: White Wagtail, Song Thrush, Redwing.

Passage periods: Black Kite, Booted Eagle, Pied Flycatcher.

NORTHWEST CORDOBA   CO11

Status: No special protection.

Site description

This is the extreme northwest of Córdoba province within the area bounded in the south by the villages of Hinojosa del Duque and El Viso, to the west of Belalcázar by the border with Extremadura and in the east by El Viso and Santa Eufemia along the N-502. To the north and west the area is bounded by the provincial borders with Badajoz and in the northeast by Ciudad Real. It is generally rolling steppe grassland with open oak woodland and some olives, some rather rougher areas of hillside with low scrub, and also some cereal agriculture. There are areas with standing water along the Río Guadamatilla and Río Zújar. The northern part, at Estación de Belalcázar, is adjacent to La Serena (BA9) and one can look across from here to the southern fringe of the Embalse de La Serena.

Species

The area houses good numbers of a considerable variety of resident, summering and wintering raptors. They include Black-shouldered Kites, which are more likely to be met with in winter but which may breed. Other characteristic nesting raptors include Spanish Imperial, Golden, Bonelli's and Short-toed Eagles, Montagu's Harriers, Common Buzzards, Common Kestrels and Lesser Kestrels. Hen Harriers and occasional Merlins occur in winter.

Several thousand Cranes winter within the region, especially in the more westerly part. Their numbers build up during the late winter/early spring before they depart north. White Storks are common and nest on the church in Hinojosa. Black Storks are much scarcer but there is

Black Storks

always a good chance of encountering them around Estación de Belalcázar and around the Embalse de la Serena.

The steppe species are well represented. Little Bustards and Stone Curlews are common but Great Bustards are distinctly scarce. Black-bellied Sandgrouse are abundant in the north and west. Pin-tailed Sandgrouse are also present but are much scarcer. Considerable numbers of Golden Plovers winter in the region. Large numbers of Skylarks and Meadow Pipits join the resident Calandra Larks in winter.

There are breeding Little Ringed Plovers along the Río Guadamatilla and the Río Zújar where you may also find summering waders such as Wood and Green Sandpipers. White-headed Ducks, as well as the ubiquitous Mallards, sometimes occur on a small lake to the west of the CO-451.

Other breeding species include Rollers, Bee-eaters, Hoopoes, Woodchat Shrikes and Southern Grey Shrikes. Azure-winged Magpies and Ravens are not uncommon. Spanish Sparrows are abundant in some areas and totally replace House Sparrows. Ortolan Buntings occur during migration periods and may have bred recently.

Timing
The winter is good for many of the steppe species, as well as the Cranes and for the possibility of encountering Black-shouldered Kites and other wintering raptors. Otherwise, spring is the best time, between March and early July.

Access
You should be able to achieve a good list by travelling all the roads within the area Fuente Obejuna–Blázquez–Belalcázar–Estación de Belalcázar–Santa Eufemia–Peñarroya-Pueblonuevo. The northern part may be reached from Córdoba by turning off the N-432 at Espiel on to the N-502 for El Viso and then turning off left on to the A-420 at Alcaracejos for Hinojosa and going on to Belalcázar from there.

The triangular route Belalcázar–Estación de Belalcázar–Santa Eufemia is recommended. This is a total drive of some 60 km, visiting all the main habitats. To work the region properly could take a full day. The road to the Estación de Belalcázar turns east off the Belalcázar–Cabeza del Buey (ox-head) road at about Km 4. It is worth stopping

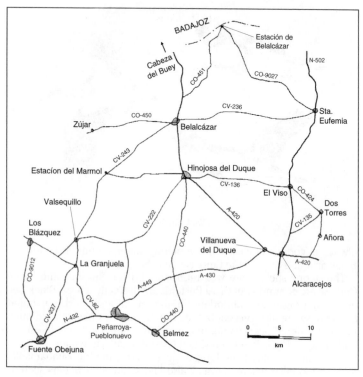

along the course of the Río Guadamatilla, particularly where this road (CO-451) crosses the river between Belalcázar and Estación de Belalcázar, and exploring both upstream and downstream for a kilometre or so in each direction. The river attracts a good variety of birds and sandgrouse come to drink at the pools in the summer. It is also worth stopping between Km 11 and 12 where there is a small lake on the left which is worth a look.

The Río Guadamatilla runs more or less parallel with the CO-451 road for a while and later joins the Río Zújar. Another recommended stop is just north of Estación de Belalcázar, in the area of the bridge which leads to Badajoz province and which is signposted 'Embalse de la Serena'. Here you stand a good chance of finding Black Storks. After this, the CO-9027 road southeast to Santa Eufemia becomes a track which is perfectly passable, although with roughish parts which require some attention.

Steppe species should be sought in the Fuente Obejuna–La Granjuela–Blázquez triangle, in the southwest of the area. Here too the roads are quite passable but of indifferent quality.

Calendar

All year: White Stork, Mallard, Spanish Imperial Eagle, Golden Eagle, Bonelli's Eagle, Common Buzzard, Common Kestrel, Red-legged Partridge, Moorhen, Little Bustard, Great Bustard, Stone Curlew, Black-bellied Sandgrouse, Pin-tailed Sandgrouse, Rock Dove, Woodpigeon, Little Owl, Calandra Lark, Black Wheatear, Cetti's Warbler, Southern Grey Shrike, Azure-winged Magpie, Raven, Jackdaw, Spanish Sparrow.

Breeding season: Black Stork, White-headed Duck, Black Kite, Short-toed Eagle, Montagu's Harrier, Booted Eagle, Lesser Kestrel, Little Ringed Plover, Common Sandpiper, Turtle Dove, Cuckoo, Red-necked Nightjar, Bee-eater, Roller, Hoopoe, Short-toed Lark, Crested Lark, Woodlark, Nightingale, Black-eared Wheatear, Reed Warbler, Great Reed Warbler, Spectacled Warbler, Sardinian Warbler, Orphean Warbler, Spotted Fly-catcher, Woodchat Shrike.

Winter: Black-shouldered Kite, Red Kite, Hen Harrier, Merlin, Crane, Golden Plover, Skylark, Meadow Pipit.

Passage periods: Raptors, waders, Ortolan Bunting.

RÍO GUADALQUIVIR AT CÓRDOBA

CO12

Status: No special protection.

Site description

The River Guadalquivir (the 'big river' of the Moors) is some 250 m wide as it flows through the ancient city of Córdoba. There are small shingle and sandy beaches along the riverbed as well as large reedbeds and a stand of small trees. The interesting sector of some 500 m lies between two of the main bridges, the Puente de San Rafael (to the west) and the Puente Romano (to the east). Regrettably, there is still no protection for this site and, during the Córdoba festivals, rockets and other fireworks are launched into the night skies from very near the egret colony here. However, the birds are stoic in the face of this periodic cacophony, probably since they first encountered it when they were just eggs. The birding site is immediately adjacent to the massive and ancient mosque, with its integrated Catholic cathedral. This magnificent edifice will amply reward inspection by all but the most single-minded of birding visitors.

Species

There are several attractions amongst a quite amazing list of species of birds to have been recorded in the area between the bridges but the main one must be the mixed heronry in the trees near the Puente de San Rafael. There are nesting Cattle Egrets, Night Herons, Little Egrets, Squacco Herons and Little Bitterns. Purple Gallinules also breed. Grey and Purple Herons, as well as White Storks, feed along the pool edges and in the vegetation. The same site houses a very large winter roost of Cattle Egrets, with smaller numbers of Little Egrets. Observation, prefer-ably in the early morning, from the Puente de San Rafael or from the south bank nearby can reveal all the above species.

A variety of raptors have been recorded, mainly on passage. There is a small Lesser Kestrel colony on the mosque/cathedral and birds from there often overfly this area. Apart from these, there are annual records of Ospreys, not to mention Short-toed Eagles, many Black Kites and also the less frequent Red Kites.

As with all major rivers, many birds follow the Guadalquivir during migration, and several species of waders and gulls have been recorded. Great Cormorants are to be found commonly during the winter months. Migrant waders regularly include Redshanks, Green, Wood and Common Sandpipers, Dunlin and occasionally Ruff. Snipe are frequent in winter. Several thousand gulls Black-headed and Lesser Black-backed Gulls roost in the area in winter. Slender-billed Gulls have also been recorded. Common, Whiskered and Black Terns are seen annually during migration periods.

There are often several thousand swifts and hirundines feeding over the river, especially during migration periods. Large numbers of White Wagtails winter and roost in the area. Several species of passerines, including Rufous Bush Chats, Whinchats and Olivaceous Warblers have been recorded during migration periods. Penduline Tits are believed to have nested close to the site.

Timing

This is a particularly accommodating site. The light is nearly always right at any time of day, distances are optimal, the birds are highly visible and there is a very good list of species of egrets and herons to be had. A visit is worthwhile at any time of year, but the best time is between February and July, especially in the evening and early in the morning, when the birds are most active.

Access

The N-IV Autovía de Andalucía skirts Córdoba city to the south. Follow signs to the city centre. If you arrive from the east, from the Madrid

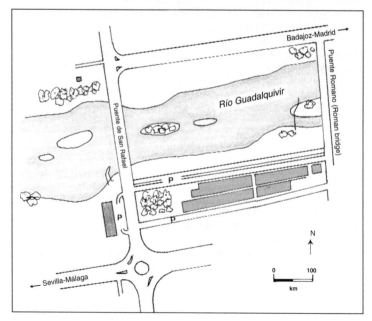

direction, divert right for the city centre and then follow signs for Sevilla and Málaga. The road borders the river in places and as soon as you have turned left and crossed the bridge (Puente de San Rafael) to the south bank there is space for parking on the right and as indicated on our map. If you arrive from the west, from the Sevilla direction, again follow signs to the town centre until you come to the roundabout near the south bank. Park in either the first or second street on the right. Parking is also available on the north bank, near the mosque/cathedral, but competition for spaces with orthodox tourists is often acute here.

Once parked, observation of the egret colony and reedbeds is a simple matter. The best views are from the promenade on the south side of the river or from the bridges. Do not forget to inspect the reedbeds on the downstream side of the west bridge. You can scramble down to the path on the south bank by the ruins, or go over the small gate on the upstream side, and walk upstream or downstream from there.

Calendar

All year: Little Bittern, Night Heron, Cattle Egret, Little Egret, Grey Heron, Purple Gallinule.

Breeding season: Squacco Heron, Purple Heron, Lesser Kestrel, Little Ringed Plover.

Winter: Great Cormorant, Snipe, Black-headed Gull, Slender-billed Gull, Lesser Black-backed Gull, Yellow-legged Gull, White Wagtail, Penduline Tit (may breed).

Passage periods: Black Kite, Red Kite, Short-toed Eagle, Osprey, Dunlin, Redshank, Green Sandpiper, Wood Sandpiper, Common Sandpiper, Common Tern, Whiskered Tern, Black Tern, passerines.

MÁLAGA PROVINCE

Málaga is the most densely populated of the provinces of the Costa del Sol, with a huge tourist industry upon which depend, directly or indirectly, over 60% of the provincial jobs. Vast numbers of tourists descend on the coastal zone, especially between July and mid-September. Away from the coastal conurbations there still remain unspoilt sites, of which Fuente de Piedra (MA1) and the ponds at the mouth of the Río Guadalhorce (MA8) are of major importance on a national scale, although the latter has been undergoing great structural changes which were still happening at the time of writing (summer 2000). There are also plenty of other very attractive sites in the province for the birder. Most of these are sierras, some being of great beauty. In this respect, we particularly recommend the Sierra de Camarolos (MA6), Sierra de las Nieves (MA10) and parts of the Sierra Bermeja and Serranía de Ronda (MA12), not forgetting the weird eroded rock formations at El Torcal (MA5). Some sites suffer considerable tourist pressure, notably El Chorro (MA4) and the Montes de Málaga (MA7), but this can be avoided in the summer months by going early in the morning and studiously

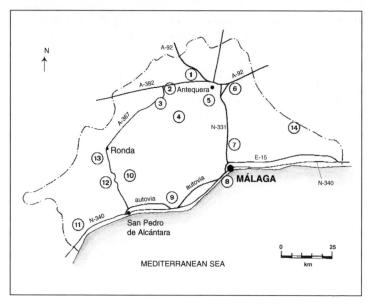

Sites in Málaga Province

MA1 Laguna de Fuente de Piedra
MA2 Lagunas de Campillos
MA3 Teba: sierra and gorge
MA4 El Chorro and Valle de Abdalajís
MA5 El Torcal
MA6 Sierra de Camarolo
MA7 Montes de Málaga
MA8 Río Guadalhorce

MA9 Juanar (Sierra Blanca)
MA10 Sierras de las Nieves, Tolox and Blanquilla
MA11 Sierra Crestellina
MA12 Sierra Bermeja and Serranía de Ronda
MA13 Upper Río Guadiaro valley
MA14 Zafarraya and Sierra Tejeda

avoiding Saturdays and Sundays. All sites have species of particular interest to birders from northern Europe.

AP has been asked on several occasions why the undoubtedly interesting site at the mouth of the Río Vélez has not been included. The answer is simple: this is a very dangerous site because of the presence of drug users and suppliers, as well as being a venue for male prostitution, both of these pastimes attracting persons of undesirable reputation and recognised aggressiveness. Members of SEO-Málaga only visit there in groups. We have no desire to land our readers in tricky situations.

Maps

Mapa Provincial Málaga, IGN, 1:200.000.
Gibraltar and the Costa del Sol. Clyde Leisure Map 15, 1:125,000. A very clear map which includes most of the above sites and which is readily available from newsagents and bookshops in Britain.

Getting there

Málaga airport is an obvious point of arrival in southern Spain. It is adjacent to the E-103/N-340 coastal highway, which provides ready access east/west to other provinces. Virtually all parts of Málaga province are within two hours drive of the N-340. The major trunk roads linking Málaga and other provincial capitals also provide speedy access to all parts of the province.

It should be noted that driving along the coast road, the infamous N-340, can be difficult at times, especially in summer, when it is often heavily congested. Fortunately, the former bottlenecks of Marbella and Estepona were eliminated, when their respective bypasses opened in summer 1993 and there is also a toll motorway (not very visibly signalled by the word 'peaje' on a white ground inside a red circle) in two sections between Fuengirola and Marbella and then again between Marbella and the west side of Estepona. Toll prices vary according to the day and time: peak charges in 2000 were about 1,100 pesetas ($4) one way for the two sections. This is not particularly cheap for the distance involved but the motorway certainly does hasten progress considerably and permits you to reduce the stress of driving in the often very dense traffic of the coastal N-340.

Take care not to enter Marbella or Estepona in error any afternoon after 17.00 hrs, particularly if you are in a hurry to catch a flight from either Gibraltar or Málaga airports. The gap in the motorway between Estepona and the Río Guadiaro is bridged by the N-340 and traffic here is often down to a crawl at peak times. A motorway link is planned but seems unlikely to appear before 2005 at the earliest. So if you are going towards Gibraltar from the east or Málaga from the west you should allow plenty of time.

Traffic is also very heavy entering Málaga from either west or east on Sunday evenings after 18.00 hrs. at any time of year, when tailbacks of several kilometres may occur. Again, allow plenty of time if heading to catch a flight. Work on the autovía to the east of Málaga towards Almería proceeds at a snail's pace and there the N-340 remains narrow and winding in places. The *autovía* was scheduled to be open as far as eastern Nerja by the end of 2000 but eastwards from there the habitual crawl through Granada province as far as Adra (Almería), where the motorway resumes, is set to continue.

Where to stay

This area is one of the major tour destinations from the UK. The tourist industry provides an enormous range of facilities along the coastal strip between Nerja in the east and Estepona in the west, the greatest concentration being between Torremolinos and Marbella. There are prices to suit nearly all pockets. For general tourist information, as well as listings of hotels, hostals, apartments, camping, etc., write to: Oficina de Turismo, Pasaje de Chinitas 4, 29015 Málaga (tel and fax: 952-229421). There is also a tourist office at 'Arrivals' at Málaga airport and very many of the towns and areas have their own municipal tourist offices.

Away from the coast, there is a reasonable hotel selection within most of the Serranía de Ronda and the Sierra Bermeja (MA12), much of it centred on Ronda itself. There is also accommodation in other towns such as Ubrique and Gaucín. Within this area, we have no hesitation in recommending the Hotel Molino del Santo in Benaoján, to the northwest of Ronda, as an ideal base for those wishing to explore this region and further west into Cádiz province. The proprietor, Andy Chapell, is a birder and a ready source of up to the minute advice: Hotel Molino del Santo, 29370 Benaoján, Málaga (tel: 952-167151; fax: 952-167327; email: molino@logiccontrol.es).

Nearer the coast, for those who have the money and who want peace, tranquillity, good food and some reasonable birding as well, there is the lovely but rather expensive hotel of the Refugio de Juanar at Ojén (MA9) in the Sierra Blanca. We have again no hesitation in recommending this hotel although it is by no means cheap. It was formerly a hunting lodge and it was here that the late General de Gaulle finished writing his memoirs and complaining of his treatment by the Allies in World War II: Refugio de Juanar, Coto de Serranía de Ronda s/n., Ojén, Málaga (tel: 952-881000).

At Fuente de Piedra there is a campsite on the south side of the village which seems quite reasonable from the exterior. For a modicum of comfort in the Fuente de Piedra area the Hotel Restaurante 'La Laguna' is recommended. It is handily situated just off the A-92 at very few metres from the exit for Fuente de Piedra: Hotel Restaurante 'La Laguna', Carretera Sevilla-Málaga, Km 135.4, Fuente de Piedra, Málaga (tel: 952-735292).

LAGUNA DE FUENTE DE PIEDRA
MA1

Status: Reserva Natural, 1364 ha, with surrounding protection area. ZEPA.

Information

There is an information and display centre just outside the village on the road to Sierra de Yeguas (closed Mondays).

Site description

The Laguna de Fuente de Piedra is a large, natural, saline lake, some 6.5 km long by 2.5 km wide, which lies just off the A-92 main Granada–Sevilla road, close to the village of the same name. The lake is set in a basin of surrounding sierras from which small streams provide its only direct water supply. It is a seasonal lagoon, only 140 cm deep at its maximum, which dries out in heat of summer and refills with the autumn rains from early October onwards. However, in dry years the lake may be effectively dry as early as March. Cultivation of sunflowers, wheat and olives takes place around the lake.

The sheltered site, in the basin of the sierras, means that it can be remarkably cold in the winter months, with temperatures near or even below freezing in the mornings. Night-time temperatures may remain very cool even as late as early June. However, daytime summer temperatures can easily exceed 40°C, with very high evaporation rates as the result. This means that the lake is often dry by June or, at the latest July, except for an area to which water is pumped if the Greater Flamingos have bred and there are still chicks in the crèche. It is uncommon for the lake to remain flooded all year and then only after exceptional winter rains.

A commercial salinera, an enterprise using evaporation for salt-extraction, operated at the lake until the early 1950s. The salt pans then fell into disuse but the lake's potential as a site for birds was not discovered until the early to mid-1960s when Greater Flamingos were found to be breeding, along with Gull-billed Terns, Slender-billed Gulls and some other notable species. It was taken over as a Reserva Natural by the then Agencia (now Consejería) de Medio Ambiente in the mid-1980s and since then has prospered very considerably.

Species

The lake is renowned for its breeding population of Greater Flamingos, the only regular colony in Spain, whose size and output has often surpassed that of the more famous Camargue population in southern France. The breeding population has frequently been in excess of 8,000 pairs in recent years and has reached over 16,000 pairs exceptionally. Large numbers of young are produced in good years, the record output being 15,000+ in 1998. Breeding is regular but not annual; it requires a minimum depth of 30 cm of water at the end of February. If there is less water, as occurs in drought years, the birds do not breed. In years when the birds are successful, there is a large-scale ringing session in late July or early August, during which about 10% of the chicks are ringed using standard metal rings and large, easily-read, coloured DARVIC rings with a number/letter code. Sightings and readings of these rings anywhere outside the immediate area of the laguna should be sent to: Dr. Manuel Rendón, Director, Reserva Integral de Fuente de Piedra, Aptdo. de Correos 1, Fuente de Piedra, Málaga. Occasional Lesser Flamingos appear in the colony. These are presumably escapes and indeed one caught in 1998 was bearing a waterfowl-collection ring.

Breeding populations of ducks and grebes vary according to water availability but White-headed Ducks and Red-crested Pochards both breed when levels permit. Kentish Plovers, Avocets and Black-winged Stilts also breed within the boundaries of the lake. Stone Curlews are reasonably common but these tend to stay well outside the boundaries of the lake itself and are often difficult to see, although the fields around

Greater Flamingos with Garganey

Cortijo de la Plata on the south side of the lake harbour them in winter. There is a small colony of Black-headed Gulls which has gradually increased to over 200 pairs since 1987. There is normally also a colony of 250 to 400 or more pairs of Gull-billed Terns. Slender-billed Gulls are only very occasional breeders; a pair bred in 1980, 15 pairs bred in 1992 and there were 7–8 pairs in 2000. More recent additions to the breeding list since 1997 include Shelduck and Collared Pratincole but it remains to be seen if these will manage to establish themselves permanently.

The lake is very attractive to numbers of waders, especially around the few freshwater inlets, particularly during the spring migration. At times waders can be seen to drop out of the sky to the water, which they have spotted whilst flying over at great altitude. There are variable, but usually small, numbers of migrant Common, Little, Whiskered and Black Terns.

Regrettably, the small lake and marshy area on the village side of the information centre, generally known as the laguneta, suffered heavy accidental contamination from a sewage spillage in 1999. This killed off nearly all the reed cover and thus evicted the Purple Gallinules, Squacco Herons and Great Reed Warblers which used to frequent it. The reeds should regrow eventually.

Some 20 pairs of Montagu's Harriers nest in the surroundings of the lake. Common Kestrels are widespread, Griffon Vultures occasionally wander over from the colony at Valle de Abdalajís, and Peregrines sometimes flash through, causing consternation. Hen Harriers and occasional Merlins occur in winter. A diversity of other raptors occur, especially during passage periods when species such as Short-toed Eagles and Black Kites are frequent. There is always the chance too of encountering something more exciting, such as an immature Spanish Imperial Eagle.

Other characteristic species in the nearby fields and around the lake side include Bee-eaters, Hoopoes, Short-toed Larks, Crested Larks, occasionally large numbers of swifts and hirundines, (Iberian) Yellow Wagtails, Black-eared Wheatears, Zitting Cisticolas, Spectacled Warblers, Southern Grey Shrikes and Woodchat Shrikes.

Wintering species, mainly ducks, include Shelducks, Pochards, Red-crested Pochards, Teal and the ubiquitous Mallards. Marbled Ducks occur occasionally. Both Black-necked Grebes and Great Crested

Grebes occur. Some waders winter, including several hundred Stone Curlews both within the reserve and in the surrounding fields and also Little Stints, which also occur in quite large numbers during the migration periods. Little Bustards are also present in the cultivated land in winter. Up to 400 Cranes winter along the western edge of the lake. Hoopoes are often present in small numbers during the winter months. Several thousand Greater Flamingos are often present by the end of December if the autumn rainfall has been adequate to provide sufficiently high water levels.

Timing

The best time is normally between December and June or early July, Greater Flamingos occurring throughout this period if there is sufficient water. From late May onwards it is best to visit the lake before 11.00 hrs; heat haze can be a problem later. Wintering species occur from mid-October onwards and spring migration is evident from early March through to the end of May.

The dry period, July to October, or even as late as early November, depending upon the rains, is usually very unproductive and the lake is not really worth visiting then. The lake usually re-floods from November onwards and most wintering species may be easily seen.

Access

The lake is approachable from either the Sevilla or Granada directions by following signs to the village of Fuente de Piedra from the A-92 autovía. Map 1 shows the whole lake and the perimeter roads. Map 2

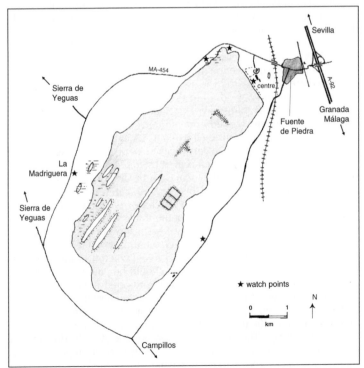

165

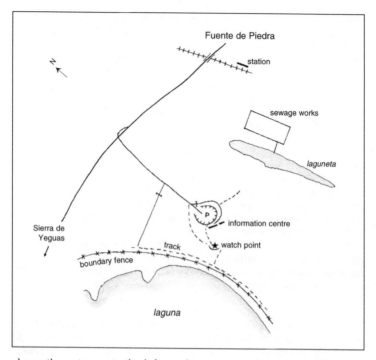

shows the entrance to the information centre and its surrounding area. Enter Fuente de Piedra from the A-92 and pass straight down through the village. Continue downhill and across the bridge over the railway line. The entrance to the information and display centre is 100 m beyond on the left. It is easily seen as it is set on a hillock on the left-hand side of the road overlooking the lake. Parking is below the information centre in the quarry. The marshy pond area mentioned above is down on the left as you go up to the information centre. There is an excellent audio-visual display (in Spanish but easily understood visually) in the centre, and information leaflets in English and Spanish.

It is not permitted to go inside the chain-link fencing which surrounds the lake and if you do you are very likely to be prosecuted. Regrettably, occasionally the fence has been scaled by foreign birders intent upon getting better views. Neither the local Guardia Civil or wardens are sympathetic to such behaviour. However, all can easily be seen by approaching the fence carefully and watching from there, both near the information centre and by following the track around to the left. It is impossible to approach most of the few freshwater inlets within the reserve boundary, where the greatest concentrations of migrant waders occur, although one of these is quite visible if you follow the fence left from the information centre. Attention should be paid to the laguneta for waders. When water is abundant, the flooded area just after the entrance on the way to Sierra de Yeguas is worth inspecting.

It is possible to go all around the lake (Map 1), taking the road to the Sierra de Yeguas. Keep left all the way around, which will bring you back to the village. The best observation point is at La Madriguera on the west side of the lake, where a seasonally-flooded area can be of interest for ducks and waders and where there are also Spectacled

Warblers. Here there are also some hundreds of wintering Cranes in most winters. You are requested not to go in through the cultivation near Cortijo de la Plata as access is through private farmland and the owner is not sympathetic to birders. However, further on there there is a derelict building with a track down to the lakeside and the car may be parked here and the perimeter fence approached on foot.

Calendar

All year: Stone Curlew, Kentish Plover, Black-headed Gull, Hoopoe, Crested Lark, Zitting Cisticola, Cetti's Warbler, Southern Grey Shrike.

Breeding season: Black-necked Grebe, Greater Flamingo, Little Bittern, Red-crested Pochard, White-headed Duck, Montagu's Harrier, Black-winged Stilt, Avocet, Slender-billed Gull (sporadic), Gull-billed Tern, Bee-eater, Short-toed Lark, Crested Lark, Yellow Wagtail, Reed Warbler, Great Reed Warbler, Melodious Warbler, Spectacled Warbler.

Winter: Black-necked Grebe, Great Crested Grebe, Grey Heron, Greater Flamingo, Shelduck, Wigeon, Teal, Mallard, Pintail, Shoveler, Red-crested Pochard, Pochard, Marbled Duck, White-headed Duck, Crane, Little Bustard, Black-headed Gull, Lesser Black-backed Gull, Yellow-legged Gull, Meadow Pipit, Common Chiffchaff.

Passage periods: In spring, waders, overflying raptors, Little Tern, Whiskered Tern, Black Tern. Little to see in autumn (lake dry) except occasional raptors and White Storks.

LAGUNAS DE CAMPILLOS   MA2

Status: Reservas Naturales, 1342 ha.

Site description

These are a series of seasonal lagoons to the east and southeast of Campillos. They comprise, in descending order of size, the Lagunas Dulce, Salada, Capacete and Cerero (this last on private land and inaccessible). A fifth, the Laguna Redonda is in a poor state but is scheduled for the cleaning out of the builders' rubble and other rubbish which has been dumped there. All these lagoons are reed-fringed.

The water levels in all these lagoons fluctuate considerably with the rainfall. The Laguna Salada nearly always has water but the Lagunas Dulce and Capacete may dry out in drought periods. The information given in the Calendar section applies to normal years.

Species

White-headed Duck is to be found irregularly at all the lakes, its presence and breeding depending totally on water levels. All the lakes hold varying numbers of wintering ducks, notably Shovelers, but with a fair variety of other species. Garganey occur, mainly during spring migration, and there are occasional reports of rarer species such as Ferruginous and Marbled Ducks. Greater Flamingos from Fuente de Piedra nearby also visit in small numbers on a regular basis and indeed there is frequent interchange of waterfowl between Fuente de Piedra and these lakes. There have been occasional records of Red-knobbed Coots at the Laguna Dulce. This lake in particular may hold an interesting variety of waders when water levels are low, including the ubiquitous Black-winged Stilts, a few Avocets, parties of Black-tailed Godwits, occasional Wood, Green and Curlew Sandpipers, and good numbers of Little Stints, including one autumn record of 500 birds.

Timing
All year, but summer and autumn visits are less productive in drought years when the Lagunas Dulce and Capacete especially may dry out.

Access
The Laguna Dulce is to the north of the A-382, some 3 km east of Campillos. This is normally the most attractive and the most accessible lagoon; an observation point over the lake was under development in 2000. The Lagunas Salada and Capacete are also easily accessible. For these it is necessary to enter Campillos and take the MA-452 exit southbound at the roundabout through the town. For the Laguna Salada, the only sign from the road is a dirt track, occasionally very muddy after rains, on the left at about 1 km south of Campillos. Do not drive in but park instead by the road side and walk the brief distance up over the hill, to view the lake. The Laguna Redonda is a km or so further along this road on the left and further still, beyond the railway bridge, the Laguna Capacete is on the right.

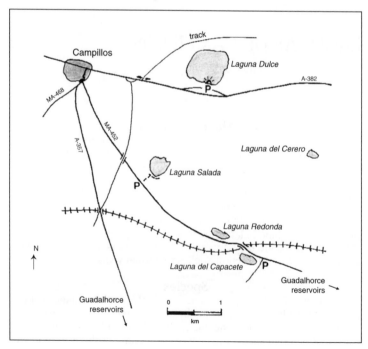

Calendar

All year: Greater Flamingo, Mallard, Shoveler, Pochard, White-headed Duck, Coot, Moorhen, Little Bustard, Lapwing, Crested Lark, Cetti's Warbler, Raven.

Breeding season: Garganey, Great Reed Warbler, Reed Warbler.

Winter: Pintail, Red-crested Pochard.

Passage periods: Waders when water levels are low.

TEBA: SIERRA AND GORGE   MA3

Status: No special protection.

Site description

The sierra is set back from the northwest side of the road and consists of angled strata with holes and overhangs. Olive groves occur on the sloping ground between the rocks at the cliff base and the road. Downhill of the road there is a small stream edged with trees. The sheer-sided gorge is a superbly scenic site, although the Río La Venta which flows through it is rather unpleasantly contaminated. The walls of the gorge have numerous cavities and scattered bushes are tenuously implanted in the walls.

Species

Obviously there are major differences between the two areas. The sierra, although somewhat distant from the road, is good for Egyptian Vultures (one pair breeds in the area), wandering Griffon Vultures, Common Buzzards, Peregrines, Hobbies and both kestrel species. The gorge is a traditional nesting site for both Bonelli's Eagles and Eagle Owls but disturbance from climbers and children playing may have displaced them. However, breeding of both species is possible in the sierra, particularly on the more secluded northern side. Alpine Swifts, Ravens, Red-billed Choughs, Blue Rock Thrushes, occasional Rock Thrushes, Black Wheatears, Black-eared Wheatears, Melodious Warblers, Rock Sparrows and Rock Buntings all occur in the area around the sierra. Several of these species also occur in the gorge, as well as Rock Doves, Crag Martins, Wrens, Jackdaws, Grey Wagtails and Cetti's Warblers. Black Wheatears and Blackcaps are highly visible in the gorge. Do not neglect the track and river area downstream from the gorge as there are numbers of Nightingales in the spring and also Rufous Bush Chats around the orchards. Woodchat Shrikes occur throughout the area.

Timing

Both areas can be profitably visited at any time of year, but undoubtedly for variety the area is best in the spring. Note that the gorge, which faces due south, can get unbearably hot at midday on windless days.

Access

Access is on the MA-468 Ronda road, between Campillos and El Chorro, north of the village of Teba. The direction from which you come will decide which you encounter first, the sierra or the gorge. The sierra is easily recognisable on the western side of the road. It is set back from the road somewhat, with scrub and olives on the sloping ground before the diagonally layered strata of the sierra rise up from the rocks at the base. It is possible to walk from the road up to the base of the cliff face.

Further west, the gorge is easily visible where the road crosses the Río La Venta. Entering involves a scramble down to the riverbed, water volumes permitting, the easiest route being on the downstream side of the bridge. Once in the gorge, care should be taken as the rocks are somewhat slippery in places and the going becomes more difficult about halfway along. Access is definitely more practicable for the agile than for the calcified.

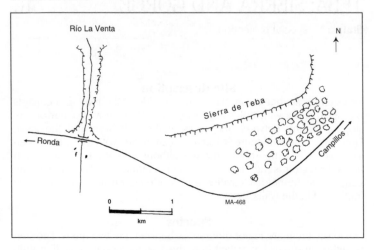

Calendar

All year: Griffon Vulture, Common Buzzard, Bonelli's Eagle, Peregrine, Common Kestrel, Lesser Kestrel, Rock Dove, Eagle Owl, Little Owl, Crested Lark, Thekla Lark, Crag Martin, Grey Wagtail, Wren, Black Redstart, Blue Rock Thrush, Blackcap, Cetti's Warbler, Southern Grey Shrike, Red-billed Chough, Jackdaw, Raven, Rock Sparrow, Rock Bunting.

Breeding season: Egyptian Vulture, Hobby, Alpine Swift, Bee-eater, Hoopoe, Rufous Bush Chat, Nightingale, Black-eared Wheatear, Rock Thrush, Melodious Warbler.

Passage periods: Migrant raptors.

EL CHORRO AND VALLE DE ABDALAJÍS

MA4

Status: Paraje Natural (Desfiladero de los Gaitanes) in part, 2016 ha.

Site description

This region of some 50 km^2 consists of some quite high sierras running about 12 km from the village of Abdalajís to the area of El Chorro. The Río Guadalhorce flows through the Chorro and there are reservoirs near the latter. The area therefore offers habitats ranging from mountains to chasms, steep slopes wooded with pines, reservoirs and the river itself.

Species

The whole area offers a good variety of species and details of what might be seen in each of the habitats are given below. Griffon Vultures as well as both Bonelli's Eagles and Golden Eagles are regularly present and there are occasional Black Vultures and Egyptian Vultures. The attractions include Crested Tits and Crossbills in the pinewoods, Bonelli's Warblers in both pines and deciduous growth and Alpine Swifts wheeling high overhead.

Timing

The whole area is interesting at virtually any time of year, but it is undoubtedly at its best in spring because of the breeding species. Weekday visits are usually more productive since there are large numbers of visitors at weekends and the roads become congested then. July and August also see a considerable presence of holidaying humans.

Access

There are several access routes to El Chorro and Abdalajís. The first, and probably the most used, is from the coast, where you go inland from Málaga for Pizarra and Alora on the MA-402 (or A-357). The road separates just before Alora itself. Signs indicate a left turn for El Chorro and straight on for Valle de Abdalajís. If you take the left option, the distance to the Chorro from Alora is 12 km. When you arrive at the first of the water-control gates, with the electricity sub-station, you can turn off to the right to arrive eventually at Abdalajís. Otherwise, keep straight on for 1 km to the Desfiladero de los Gaitanes. If you are approaching from Abdalajís, turn right to enter El Chorro.

Alternatively, you can arrive from the north either on the A-357 via Teba and Ardales, if coming from Fuente de Piedra and Campillos, or on the A-343 from the Antequera direction through Abdalajís.

There are several sites worth looking at within the whole area. The Desfiladero (A) and Las Ruinas de Bobastro (B) are probably the most attractive of these although there are many access roads, usually narrowish but generally well paved, which allow further exploration. Off road, the terrain is often extremely rough and is covered with pines of all sizes.

A Desfiladero de Los Gaitanes

This spectacular gorge marks the southern point of entry into the whole area. If you arrive from the Abdalajís direction you pass over the river

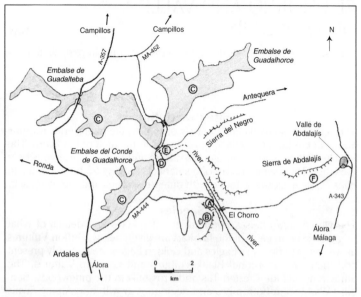

and turn right (north). From the Alora direction you pass the electricity substation. Half a kilometre after this there is a bar, El Pilar, on the left which faces out over the river. This is usually a good site for the first stop, offering views of steep pine-covered cliffs and across to the gorge itself, the Desfiladero de los Gaitanes or Garganta del Chorro, a narrow chasm which has featured in several films.

From the bar it is possible to watch Griffon Vultures, occasional Egyptian and Black Vultures (the latter usually in winter) and Bonelli's and Golden Eagles, as well as Peregrines, Lesser Kestrels and occasional Goshawks. In spring and summer there are often large numbers of Alpine Swifts flying at all altitudes, sometimes whipping through the area at eye-level. Red-billed Choughs are common, as are Jackdaws, although the former usually remain at high levels. Alpine Choughs have also been reported in the past. The pines beside the bar often provide Crested Tits. Wallcreepers have been recorded very occasionally in winter.

Next you can drive (for the lazy, but parking can be difficult) or walk further in along the road for less than a kilometre. Here the pine-clad slopes rise high on the left of the road whilst on the right there is a ravine with cliffs rising up beyond it. This area can provide excellent views of Alpine Swifts and Crag Martins. The trees in the ravine often hold Golden Orioles, whilst in the pines there are Crested Tits, Bonelli's Warblers, Firecrests and Spotted Flycatchers. There is an August record of an Olivaceous Warbler in the reeds in the stream bed and this species may well be regular here given the riparian growth. Opposite the road, the rock face should be able to provide good views of Blue Rock Thrushes, Black Redstarts, Black Wheatears and Black-eared Wheatears.

B Ruinas de Bobastro

Continuing on westwards through the winding road of the Chorro, after about 3 km there is a signposted left turn to the Ruinas de Bobastro, a further distance of about 5 winding km. It is not really worth driving up there although there is a slim chance of close views of Golden or Bonelli's Eagles and Rock Buntings and Red-billed Choughs also occur. On the other hand, and it can be a definite compensation if there are few birds, the view on a clear winter's day to as far east as the Sierra Nevada is absolutely fantastic.

C The Reservoirs
On maps the reservoirs are usually shown as the Embalses del Guadalhorce. If you are coming from the direction of the Chorro itself, in the last kilometre or so, just before the T junction where you would turn off to the right for sites D and E, there is an area of more open land dotted with tamarisks. Red-necked Nightjars occur here, as also in other open areas within the general vicinity of the reservoirs. The reservoirs themselves are usually pretty sterile birdwise and hold little of attraction at any time of year, although you should always give them a swift look, just in case. The unexpected does happen; one memorable January census produced two Great Northern Divers. Generally, they hold very few waterbirds even in winter, with the exception of some Mallards, occasional Grey Herons and small wintering populations of Great Crested Grebes and Great Cormorants. Small numbers of Black-headed, Lesser Black-backed and a few Yellow-legged Gulls occur, again mainly in winter.

D The Tunnel
Heaven knows what the real name of this area is, but this is good enough. To get to it, continue on westwards from the Chorro itself, past the turn off for the Ruinas de Bobastro, and turn right at the T junction. Eventually, after passing campsites on the left of the road and a bar or two, you come to a large bar on the right hand side of the road, directly across from the largest of the lakes. Park here and go through the tunnel to the right of the bar as you face it. Alternatively go down by the steps some 100 m to the left of it, and you come to a track, easily negotiable to start with, rougher later. Follow this down under the canopy of trees and watch from here to the stream below, where there are often Kingfishers. Scops Owls, Golden Orioles, Nightingales and Bonelli's Warblers are also present in the breeding season.

This site can also be reached from the other side by continuing northwards along the road, over the head of the reservoir and, 500 m past some houses, taking the first track off to the right. This is bordered by pines on each side which hold Crossbills occasionally and also various tits, including Crested Tits. Walk on down until coming to a barred entrance just over the same stream seen earlier. From here you can see just as much but from a different level.

E The Three Pines
Again, a site with a name of our own (until somebody cuts or burns them down!). There are three tracks which you can follow, one down to the river which is an extension from site D, with more water from the outfall of the reservoir. The track which overlooks the deep valley with the river in the bottom is the best for variety of bird species and a wide range of butterflies also. The birds are the same as in the other areas, with the addition of wagtails and also Olivaceous Warblers and Great Reed Warblers down by the river.

F Valle de Abdalajís

This is the eastern fringe of El Chorro and it is the home base of the Griffon Vultures and Bonelli's Eagles which overfly the whole area. The interesting features of the site are the cliff face on the northern side of the road and, to a lesser extent, the track through to the Chorro itself. The best time to visit this area is February–June and preferably in the first two or three hours after sunrise.

Access involves either entering Abdalajís and then trying to find your way through the labyrinthine village to the asphalted road towards the west for El Chorro or the eastwards approach from El Chorro. If you are foolhardy enough to come in through the village the easiest way is simply to ask, in a questioning tone, for El Chorro, and some kind soul usually points the way. The other access, much easier, is by coming in from the Chorro direction and, frankly, it is almost easier to leave by the same route. We strongly suspect there may be long-lost birders in the village trying to find their way out!

Black-eared Wheatear

The best site is the cliff face, which is just off from the road about 2 km west from Abdalajís, and impossible to miss as it looms over you. This is where the Griffon Vultures nest and it is best visited in the early morning, before the Griffons and other raptors begin to disperse from the cliffs for the day's foraging. At the same time it is easy to watch for other large raptors, such as Bonelli's Eagles and Golden Eagles, which sail along the cliff face amongst the Jackdaws and Red-billed Choughs, while the Alpine Swifts fly higher still. Peregrines are also frequent in this area. The rocks and fields at the foot of the cliff and the valley side of the road are good for at least hearing Quail. Black-eared Wheatears, Bee-eaters and Woodchat Shrikes occur commonly along the track all the way to El Chorro in the summer months.

Calendar

All year: Mallard, Griffon Vulture, Goshawk, Golden Eagle, Bonelli's Eagle, Common Kestrel, Peregrine, Eagle Owl, Little Owl, Kingfisher, Crested Lark, Woodlark, Crag Martin, Grey Wagtail, Wren, Black Redstart, Black Wheatear, Blue Rock Thrush, Zitting Cisticola, Dartford

Warbler, Sardinian Warbler, Southern Grey Shrike, Jay, Red-billed Chough, Jackdaw, Raven, Crested Tit, Coal Tit, Chaffinch, Serin, Linnet, Rock Bunting.

Breeding season: Egyptian Vulture, Lesser Kestrel, Scops Owl, Quail, Red-necked Nightjar, Common Swift, Pallid Swift, Alpine Swift, Bee-eater, Hoopoe, Barn Swallow, Red-rumped Swallow, Yellow Wagtail, Nightingale, Black-eared Wheatear, Melodious Warbler, Olivaceous Warbler, Bonelli's Warbler, Spotted Flycatcher, Golden Oriole, Wood-chat Shrike.

Winter: Great Cormorant, Grey Heron, Black Vulture, Shelduck, Shoveler, White Wagtail, Alpine Accentor, Robin, Common Chiffchaff, Wallcreeper, Southern Grey Shrike, Brambling, Redwing, Siskin, Crossbill.

Passage periods: White Stork, raptors including Osprey.

EL TORCAL   MA5

Status: Paraje Natural, 1171 ha. ZEPA.

Site description
This is a strikingly attractive expanse of highly-eroded, surreal, karstic rock formations to the southwest of Antequera. The whole area forms a tortuous labyrinth of gullies and passages. The vegetation, which consists of twisted and stunted trees and bushes such as maple, elder, and hawthorn, grows out of the cracks and crevices between rocks.

Species
Bird numbers are not high but there are several interesting resident species such as Bonelli's Eagles, Sparrowhawks, Peregrines, Ravens, Red-billed Choughs, Blue Rock Thrushes, Rock Buntings and Cirl Buntings, along with a remarkably high concentration of Wrens. Migrants and summering species are generally rare, although Short-toed Eagles do occur occasionally. Subalpine Warblers also occur sparingly in the area. There are regular autumn and winter records of Ring Ouzels, Redwings and Fieldfares and also Dunnocks and Alpine Accentors. Cirl and Rock Buntings occur near the car park, although the former seem to be declining.

Timing
The area receives a large number of visitors during the summer months and, especially, many school parties in the period April–June. Early mornings are best then to avoid the disturbance later. The views are tremendous on clear days, extending all the way down to the coast between Málaga and Torremolinos.

Access

The easiest access is south from Antequera, taking the road (A-343) signposted for Valle de Abdalajís, Villanueva de la Concepción and El Torcal from the centre of the town. Two kilometres out of the town take the left fork for El Torcal and Villanueva. From then on it is simply a matter of following the road some 12 km until it forks up to the right for El Torcal itself, where there is a good-sized car park with a seasonal bar and information centre. However, there have been recent rumblings from the administration about putting in a car park at the bottom of the access road with a shuttle service up and down by bus and this may yet materialise.

Signposted walks, indicated by not overly visible colour markers, traverse the area. Care should be taken not to twist an ankle, as the rock is slippery in some parts. It is also possible to take a good walk by going uphill to the right just before the car park and this can often be quite fruitful.

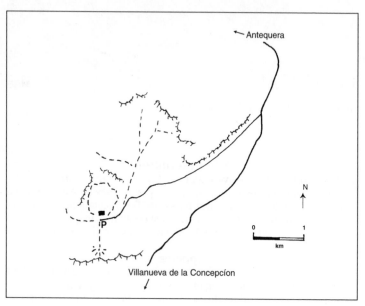

Calendar

All year: Bonelli's Eagle, Common Kestrel, Wren, Black Redstart, Blue Rock Thrush, Red-billed Chough, Jackdaw, Raven, Cirl Bunting, Rock Bunting.

Breeding season: Short-toed Eagle, Melodious Warbler, Subalpine Warbler, Woodchat Shrike.

Winter: Common Buzzard, Hen Harrier, Meadow Pipit, White Wagtail, Common Chiffchaff, Redwing, Fieldfare, Southern Grey Shrike, Alpine Accentor, Dunnock.

Passage periods: Raptors including Black Kite and Short-toed Eagle, Rock Thrush.

SIERRA DE CAMAROLO

Status: No special protection.

Site description

This is, in fact, two sierras joined by a saddle, although the ensemble is usually known by this name. It is a beautiful place to visit, especially early on sunny, late spring mornings, with the higher crags of the sierra around to the south and a fantastic view away to the northwest. At the first stop (A), you are initially in well-vegetated terrain before climbing to more open land. The second stop (B) is higher up and less wooded, with the sierra much closer.

Species

This is a good site for seeing Golden Eagles and, less frequently, Bonelli's Eagles, as well as Peregrine Falcons. Booted Eagles and a variety of other raptors are likely to be observed during migration periods.

The site is most noteworthy for the passerine community. The diversity of thrushes is high. The resident Black Wheatears, Blue Rock Thrushes and Blackbirds are joined for the breeding season by Black-eared Wheatears and Nightingales at the lower levels and Rock Thrushes higher up. Northern Wheatears may also breed at the highest elevations. There are records of quite large flocks of migrant Ring Ouzels in autumn and a few overwinter in the area. Song Thrushes are common in winter when there also also a few Fieldfares and Redwings, these last both at the southern limit of their wintering range. There is a also good variety of warblers. Bonelli's and Dartford Warblers are common and there is a reasonable chance of finding both Orphean Warblers and Melodious Warblers in suitable territory on the lower slopes, with Subalpine Warblers occurring somewhat higher up. Iberian Chiffchaffs may also breed locally.

Azure-winged Magpies occur in small numbers in the lower areas. There is a variety of tits: Great, Blue, Coal and Crested Tits are resident and Long-tailed Tits may well breed too; a family party of the latter was seen in May 2000. This is one of the few areas in the province where seeing Rock Sparrows is virtually guaranteed. Both Rock and Cirl Buntings are very common.

Timing

Any time of year is interesting but spring (April–May) is undoubtedly the most attractive, followed by autumn for migrant raptors and thrushes. Be warned that in midsummer it can get extremely hot and in the middle of winter full cold weather birding gear (gloves, scarf and little woolly hat!) is desirable.

Access

This is from the section of autovía A-359 which joins the N-331 from Málaga to the eastbound (Granada direction) A-92. Come off the autovía for Villanueva del Rosario. The road into the village has several narrow bridges with traffic priority signs and at the last one, just where the village name sign is located, you cross the bridge to see two roads more or less ahead. Ignore these and turn sharp back to the right by the

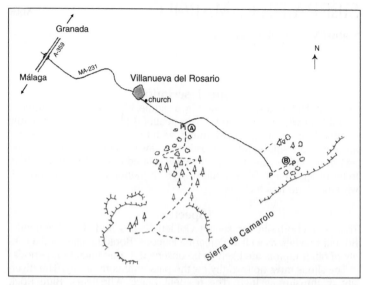

wide garage doors and then go up through the village, maintaining a general heading towards the right (this will be to the left coming down). Eventually the tarmac road ends by a little church (ermita) on the left. The track from then on is more or less good going although slippery when wet.

Continue as far as a track on the right leading up to some pines. This is the first stop (A). Park on the corner, or just along the track on the left, and walk up through the pines and mixed woodland (and it is quite a stiffish pull in places). The land opens out beyond the pines and is flatter, allowing exploration across to the right through rocks and low scrub.

For the second stop (B), continue 2 km along the track as far as the sharp left-hand bend, where it deteriorates quite notably, although it is still passable when dry. If further progress is deemed unwise, there is space to park on the bend and the walk can be continued for another 400 m to the normal parking spot. From here, you may explore up to the base of the cliffs, for as far and as long as the weather or your personal fitness will permit.

Calendar

All year: Golden Eagle, Bonelli's Eagle, Peregrine, Thekla Lark, Blue Tit, Great Tit, Coal Tit, Crested Tit, Long-tailed Tit, Wren, Blue Rock Thrush, Black Redstart, Black Wheatear, Azure-winged Magpie, Red-billed Chough, Jackdaw, Cirl Bunting, Rock Sparrow, Rock Bunting.

Summer: Alpine Swift, Nightingale, Black-eared Wheatear, Rock Thrush, Subalpine Warbler, Orphean Warbler, Bonelli's Warbler, Iberian Chiffchaff.

Winter: Redwing, Fieldfare, Song Thrush, Ring Ouzel, Bullfinch.

Passage periods: Raptors, Water Pipit, thrushes, Common Redstart, warblers, Ortolan Bunting.

MONTES DE MÁLAGA

Status: Parque Natural, 4956 ha.

Site description

This is a large area of medium-sized mountains, due north of Málaga city. The slopes are steep and well vegetated with scrub and mixed forests of pines, cork oaks, Kermes oaks and encinas. The summits rise to 1030 m. The site falls between the old Madrid road, the C-345, on the eastern side and the N-331 Autovía de Málaga on the western side.

Species

Breeding raptors include Common Buzzards, Short-toed Eagles, Booted Eagles (which also occur in winter) and one or two pairs of Goshawks. Considerable numbers of other raptors, notably Black Kites, Honey Buzzards and Short-toed Eagles overfly and often roost here during the autumn migration. Large flocks of migrant Griffon Vultures are also recorded in October and November. There are also records too of small numbers of both Black and White Storks on passage. Nocturnal raptors are represented by Eagle, Scops, Little, Barn and Tawny Owls.

The woods accommodate a considerable variety of passerines, including wintering thrushes, considerable numbers of Jays, the ever-attractive Azure-winged Magpies, Golden Orioles, several species of warblers including Orphean Warblers, and tits, Crossbills, Serins, Siskins and Rock Buntings.

The Montes are a redoubt of the Mediterranean chameleon, part of a wide variety of reptiles and amphibians present. The site is also well known for the large variety of medium-sized mammals it supports. Foxes, badgers, mongooses, weasels, polecats, red squirrels, beech martens and genets all occur, together with numerous smaller mammals, although seeing most of these is pure luck.

Timing

The area is very pleasant and worth visiting at any time of year. However, *malagueños* in their thousands invade the area, which is on the very doorstep of Málaga city, during weekends and public holidays year round. Weekday visits are therefore recommended, especially early mornings from March to early June.

Access

It is possible to reach the area from Málaga itself but the easiest way in is from the autovía (N-331), some 20 km north of Málaga. Take the A-356 east from the motorway at Casabermeja towards Colmenar and then south just before that village at the intersection, heading towards Málaga on the C-345. There are various entry points into the woods on the west side of the road. These are not particularly well marked and are often chained-off. The main access point is at Fuente de la Reina, some 14 km south of Colmenar. From here there is a series of tracks and paths, all colour coded, which can be followed. These are bumpy, and somewhat sticky after heavy rains, but perfectly drivable. Select a promising looking spot and explore on foot.

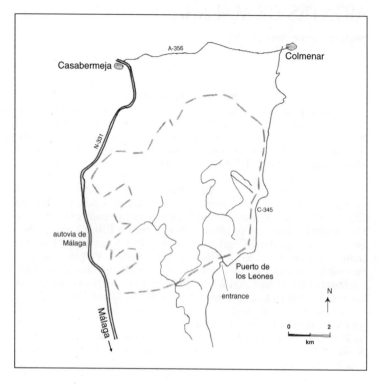

Calendar

All year: Booted Eagle, Common Buzzard, Goshawk, Eagle Owl, Jay, Crested Tit, Great Tit, Coal Tit, Blue Tit, Crossbill, Azure-winged Magpie, Rock Bunting.

Breeding season: Short-toed Eagle, Scops Owl, Nightingale, Melodious Warbler, Bonelli's Warbler.

Winter: Song Thrush, Redwing, Common Chiffchaff, tits, Siskin.

Passage periods: Raptors and storks.

RÍO GUADALHORCE
MA8

Status: Paraje Natural, *c.*130 ha.

Site description

This site is the mouth of the Río Guadalhorce and the complex of ponds and low scrub between the two arms of the river. The ponds on the eastern side of the estuary were the remains of gravel extraction workings around which copious amounts of solid fill had been dumped, much of which has been partially covered by grasses and bushes. The area has been subjected to partial or total inundation by the river on several occasions in recent years and the widening of the river into two arms has been carried out to alleviate flooding further upstream and hasten the evacuation of flood waters. The portion nearest to the beach is also flooded occasionally by the sea.

There are cane brakes and a certain amount of reed cover along the banks of ponds. The ponds themselves experience great fluctuations of water levels according to season and rainfall. Some, especially that nearest the sea, are shallow and dry out during the summer months. They are separated from each other by banks from the original gravel workings which are rather overgrown for the most part.

There is a constant human presence and disturbance is a nuisance in spite of wardening by the C.M.A. The problem is greatest in summer as the site gives the public access to the beach.

The whole site has undergone massive topographical changes since the first edition of this book and works to widen the river were still in progress at the time of writing (summer 2000). Parts of our map lack detail for this reason. There has been widespread felling of the eucalyptus trees along the riverbanks and as yet no replanting by native species has taken place, although this is planned both for the banks and elsewhere within the reserve.

In spite of all these problems, this is still one of the best sites within eastern Andalucía and over 250 species have been recorded here. Indeed, even while the works have been in progress there have been records of Western Reef Heron, Lesser Yellowlegs and Terek Sandpiper. The attraction is probably due to the privileged coastal location and the presence of fresh water and mud in a region which has next to no wetlands.

Species

The list of species recorded, including rarities, gives some idea of the variety, which it is impractical to list in full. Suffice to say that this area can be attractive at any time of year for a wide diversity of species. This range has included several Nearctic vagrants: Blue-winged Teal, dowitcher sp., Lesser Yellowlegs, Spotted Sandpiper, Laughing Gull, Franklin's Gull, Ring-billed Gull and also Sooty Tern.

Little Grebes, Mallard and Coots breed at the ponds, while Pochard and Gadwall have tried to do so in recent years. One or two pairs of Purple Gallinules have colonised the area, especially along the eastern arm of the river near the cowsheds. The numbers and variety of water-birds increases during autumn and winter, when the above are joined by Great Crested Grebes, Black-necked Grebes, and a good variety of ducks. These latter regularly include Shoveler, Teal, Wigeon, Pochard, Gadwall and Pintail, with less frequent records of Red-crested Pochards, Ferruginous Ducks and Marbled Ducks.

There are considerable numbers of wintering Grey Herons, migrant and wintering Cattle and Little Egrets, and migrant Squacco Herons, as well as breeding Little Bitterns. Purple Herons have bred. Night Herons also used to breed along the river and wandered into the area before the felling of the eucalyptus took place but they are still to be seen. There have been annual records of what are believed to be Western Reef Herons.

The most common raptor, Common Kestrels apart, is the Marsh Harrier, with up to five birds regularly present during migration and in winter. One or two Common Buzzards and several Booted Eagles over-winter in the area. Peregrines are not infrequent (they breed on the cathedral in the centre of Málaga) and terrify the waders as they flash over the ponds.

The works have resulted in a welcome increase in wintering and pas-sage waders, which should become a major attraction of the site if the planned modifications are fully implemented. The wintering species usually comprise Lapwings, Kentish Plovers, Ringed Plovers, Redshanks and Common Snipe. Breeding waders, or rather ones which have att-empted to breed, include Kentish Plovers and Black-winged Stilts.

Migrant waders are abundant at times. Up to 15 species have been recorded on good days in spring. Collared Pratincoles are quite com-mon along the shore in spring and Common Sandpipers are everywhere during this season. There are often small numbers of Little Ringed Plov-ers, Wood and Green Sandpipers, Black-tailed Godwits, Redshanks and Greenshanks during both passage periods, and occasional records of Marsh Sandpipers, Terek Sandpipers, Temminck's Stints and Grey Phal-aropes.

♂ *Bluethroat*

Large numbers of Yellow-legged, Lesser Black-backed and Audouin's Gulls congregate on the beach, around the ponds and on the levelled overflow surfaces along the eastern arm of the river (and presumably they will also do so on the western arm when the work there is com-pleted). Mediterranean Gulls are less numerous although some are pre-sent all year round. Sandwich Terns also occur throughout the year. Little, Common, Black and Whiskered Terns are commonly recorded during migration periods, with less frequent records of Caspian Terns, White-winged Black Terns and Lesser Crested Terns. There have been single records of Royal and Sooty Terns.

Hoopoes occur all year round but Rollers are only occasionally seen on migration. Little Swift has been seen here in addition to all the com-mon swifts and hirundines. Zitting Cisticolas and Cetti's Warblers are always present and often highly visible. In winter they are joined by hordes of Meadow Pipits and Common Chiffchaffs. Other wintering

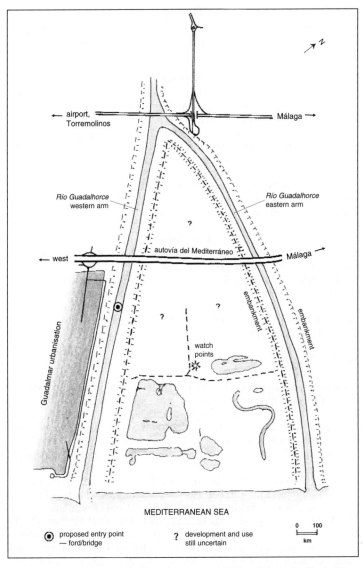

airport, Torremolinos ←

Málaga →

Río Guadalhorce western arm

Río Guadalhorce eastern arm

?

autovía del Mediterráneo

← west

Málaga →

embankment

embankment

Guadalmar urbanisation

?

?

watch points

MEDITERRANEAN SEA

⊙ proposed entry point — ford/bridge

? development and use still uncertain

0   100
km

species of interest include Bluethroats and Yellow Wagtails. Both Barn Swallows and House Martins may be seen here in January alongside Crag Martins. In general, anything and everything may turn up and this excellent site often produces surprises.

The position also makes it a popular place for escaped and naturalised species, notably Monk Parakeets and also Rose-ringed Parakeets, which in turn are likely to attract any other escaped parrots. There are small populations of Common Waxbills and Red Avadavats, both which are seen reasonably frequently. In recent years there have been sightings of up to five Black-collared Starlings in the area and these have almost certainly bred on at least one occasion. A pair of Village Weavers was present in 2000.

Timing

A walk through the area, or even a fleeting visit, is nearly always productive at any time of year, even in winter or mid summer. A telescope is useful.

Access

The ongoing works, and the lack of consensus between the Consejería de Medio Ambiente on the one hand and the waterboard and works contractors on the other, mean that it is not possible to advise on points of access at the time of writing (summer 2000). Similarly, although the plans for the reserve include building an information and ringing centre, the doubling of water surface, the construction of areas for waders and the demolition of the old cowsheds, it is not yet possible to know when and where these changes might occur. Potential visitors are welcome to write to AP for information at least six weeks before a visit, enclosing an international reply coupon.

Calendar

All year: Little Grebe, Greater Flamingo, Mallard, Pochard, Shoveler, Coot, Little Egret, Night Heron, Common Kestrel, Purple Gallinule, Kentish Plover, Common Sandpiper, Sandwich Tern, Little Owl, Hoopoe, Stonechat, Cetti's Warbler, Dartford Warbler, Zitting Cisticola.

Breeding season: Little Bittern, Squacco Heron, Avocet, Black-winged Stilt, Little Ringed Plover, non-breeding gulls including Mediterranean and Audouin's Gulls, Pallid Swift, Common Swift, Barn Swallow, Yellow Wagtail, Nightingale, Great Reed Warbler, Reed Warbler.

Winter: Great Crested Grebe, Black-necked Grebe, Great Cormorant, Cattle Egret, Grey Heron, Common Buzzard, Booted Eagle, Wigeon, Gadwall, Teal, Pintail, Shoveler, Marbled Duck, Red-crested Pochard, Ferruginous Duck, Tufted Duck, Common Scoter, Lapwing, waders, Arctic Skua, large numbers of gulls, Short-eared Owl, Meadow Pipit, Yellow Wagtail, Bluethroat, Common Chiffchaff, Southern Grey Shrike.

Passage periods: Purple Heron, Grey Heron, Garganey, Common Buzzard, Black Kite, Marsh Harrier, Montagu's Harrier, Osprey, Peregrine, Collared Pratincole, Grey Plover, Knot, Redshank, Greenshank, Green Sandpiper, Wood Sandpiper, Bar-tailed Godwit, Black-tailed Godwit, Pomarine Skua, Arctic Skua, Great Skua, Mediterranean Gull, Little Gull, Audouin's Gull, Gull-billed Tern, Caspian Tern, Royal Tern, Common Tern, Little Tern, Black Tern, White-winged Black Tern, swifts including White-rumped Swift, Roller, Bee-eater, hirundines, pipits, White Wagtail, races of *flava* wagtails including Yellow, Blue-headed and Iberian, Grey Wagtail, Whinchat, Northern Wheatear, Black-eared Wheatear, warblers including Orphean and Spectacled, and a wide variety of other passerines.

JUANAR (SIERRA BLANCA)

Status: No special protection.

Site description

This is another section of the southeastern end of the Serranía de Ronda, part of the Sierra Blanca, the mountain which looms conspicuously behind Marbella.

Species

This site is not renowned for raptors, although there are usually some to see, including breeding Golden, Bonelli's and Booted Eagles and the local Peregrines. Griffon Vultures often overfly. In the migration periods, and more so in the autumn, it is not uncommon to come across small parties of Black Kites and Short-toed Eagles moving along the sierra, as well as occasional Common Buzzards. Eagle Owls breed in the area of the mirador and there are also resident Little Owls.

In spring, which is the most productive period, Woodlarks are highly audible and somewhat less visible as they circle high in songflight. Blue Rock Thrushes are to be found on the rocky outcrops along the access road, at about Km 4, as well as just past the Refugio, and in this latter area there are often Rock Buntings. You must go high to stand any chance of finding the elusive Rock Thrushes. The wooded area around the Refugio de Juanar, and the first half-kilometre of track as it winds up from there to the mirador, should be inspected for Melodious and Bonelli's Warblers in spring and summer, Firecrests, Short-toed Tree-creepers and Crossbills at any season, and the occasional Hawfinches in winter alongside the resident Chaffinches and Greenfinches. Dartford Warblers frequent the more open, scrub habitat. Orphean Warblers should be looked for with care in areas of taller woodland. A variety of tits is to be found generally, although the Crested Tits prefer the pines and, like the Bonelli's Warblers, they seem to have a particular preference for the first bend on the walk up through to the pines to the mirador. Southern Grey Shrikes and Woodchat Shrikes are present.

Timing

The Refugio de Juanar area is ideal for a half-day excursion, preferably a weekday morning, at any time of year. Spring visits, between April and June, provide the maximum variety of species. If visiting on a Sunday at any time of year, then it is best done early before the picnickers arrive.

Access

This is from the A-355 Marbella/Coín road. Much of this road is new. From the south (Marbella) it climbs up past the white village of Ojén and over the pass (Puerto de Ojén). The road to the hotel of the Refugio de Juanar is on the left approximately 1 km over the top of the pass, just beyond the eyesore of the quarry. From the north (Coín) the turn-off is some 7 km past Monda. The distance from the turnoff to the Refugio itself is approximately 5 km. It is difficult to stop anywhere along this narrow, winding road and care should be exercised.

It is worth looking at the pines on the way in, immediately after the turn-off, as well as the area around Km 4, where there are rocky out-

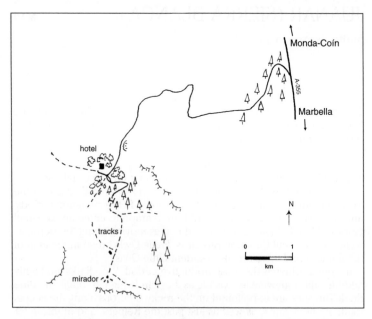

crops on the left above the road. The hotel is on the right and it is also worth looking in the trees around it. We also suggest that you go on another 150 m and park in the open area just beyond where the road splits round a clump of trees. Sitting and watching in this area, where it opens out, and in the scrub down to the right of the track can be quite productive. You can then walk or drive on a bit further as far as the gates, then continue on foot up the track to the mirador. The track passes through pines initially, then opens out with olives on each side of the road and passes the ruins of an old farm on the right before arriving at the mirador. The views down to the Mediterranean and Marbella are wonderful.

There are various paths off the track between the hotel and the mirador, some of which are worth exploring. The first is behind the hotel itself and is a stiff walk upwards from the tennis court. The fit (or foolhardy) will find that this route eventually reaches Istán, some 13 km and quite a few hours later. It can also be worth walking off to the left as soon as you come out of the pines on the way up to the mirador, exploring the woodland edge for a short distance. You can also take the path off to the right at the ruined farmhouse which leads through the olives to more pines and doubles back to the hotel.

Calendar

All year: Griffon Vulture, Golden Eagle, Bonelli's Eagle, Peregrine, Red-legged Partridge, Eagle Owl, Little Owl, Green Woodpecker, Woodlark, Crag Martin, Blue Rock Thrush, Great Tit, Blue Tit, Crested Tit, Firecrest, Short-toed Treecreeper, Jay, Red-billed Chough, Raven, Crossbill, Rock Bunting.

Breeding season: Booted Eagle, Alpine Swift, Hoopoe, Rock Thrush, Melodious Warbler, Subalpine Warbler, Orphean Warbler, Bonelli's Warbler.

Winter: Hawfinch, Serin.

Passage periods: Black Kite, Short-toed Eagle, Common Buzzard, swifts and hirundines.

SIERRAS DE LAS NIEVES, TOLOX AND BLANQUILLA   MA10

Status: Parque Natural (Sierra de las Nieves), 18,530 ha.

Site description

This large area consists of three sierras within the eastern Serranía de Ronda on the eastern side of the A-376 San Pedro de Alcantara/Ronda road. Of these, the Sierra de las Nieves is a parque natural which includes the Sierra de Tolox at its eastern end. The Sierra Blanquilla is to the north of the Sierra de las Nieves. The terrain is generally high with a mean altitude of 1100 m in the Sierra de las Nieves. The highest point is Torrecilla (1919 m) in the Sierra de Tolox. In large part the ground is very broken with outcrops of limestone and steep slopes and cliffs. The vegetation varies according to altitude. Low down there are areas of impenetrably thick scrub with some more open areas. Maritime pines occur higher up with scrub in between stands. The summits are relatively barren above about 1500 m. There are also significant stands of Spanish firs (pinsapos) in the Sierra de las Nieves. Large areas have also been planted with pines.

Species

The area offers a good diversity of species, especially in the Los Quejigales area, and most of those referred to here are from this area. Many species are found all year round, although some move down to lower levels in winter, when the climate can be relatively harsh. As ever, the raptors claim attention, although these are not particularly numerous. There are a few Egyptian Vultures and rather more Griffon Vultures, as well as Golden Eagles and Booted Eagles in small numbers. Bonelli's Eagles occur but seem to be getting scarcer, as in some other parts of their range. Goshawks, Peregrines and Common Kestrels breed. Merlins have been recorded in winter. Numbers of Honey Buzzards and Black Kites are among the abundant raptors which overfly the area on passage, especially during the southbound migration towards the Strait. Nocturnal raptors include Eagle Owls.

The area is also interesting for smaller species and spring is the best season for finding the greatest range of these. Quail occur, as do Red-legged Partridges. Alpine Swifts breed and White-rumped Swifts are colonising the area. Woodlarks and Thekla Larks are common. This is one of the few areas in southernmost Spain where Skylarks breed, although only at higher altitudes. Tawny Pipits breed here too. Alpine Accentors have been recorded in winter. Black Wheatears, Black-eared

Wheatears, Blue Rock Thrushes, Black Redstarts and (possibly) Common Redstarts breed, as do Northern Wheatears and Rock Thrushes at the highest levels. There is a good variety of warblers which includes nesting Melodious, Dartford, Subalpine, Orphean and Bonelli's Warblers, with Common Chiffchaffs in winter and occasional Willow Warblers on passage. The woodland community also includes Crested Tits, Firecrests and Crossbills. Both Southern Grey and Woodchat Shrikes breed. Corvids are represented by Ravens, Red-billed Choughs and Jackdaws. Rock Sparrows occur, most often near the cliff up the track from Los Quejigales (A) and also in the small valley to the east of Ronda in the Sierra de Blanquilla (C) and in the gorge at Jorox (F). Rock Buntings are widespread and common.

The whole area is outstanding for spring flowers and so, unsurprisingly, for butterflies as well.

Timing

The best time is spring, which at these altitudes means from late April until mid-July. This is not to say that the area is devoid of ornithological interest at other seasons but it can get very hot in summer, over 40°C, and temperatures may fall below −5°C in winter. The name Sierra de las Nieves, 'sierra of the snows', is not without significance. Also, it does get rather crowded anywhere in the region at weekends in spring and autumn, especially in July and August in the Tolox area when the balneario (curative mineral water spa) is open.

Access

A Sierra de las Nieves (Los Quejigales)

The entrance is from the A-376 San Pedro–Ronda road and is remarkably easy to overshoot as it is on a bend, even though it is marked by a C.M.A. sign. Coming from the Ronda direction, the entrance is on the left of the road exactly 1 km past a restaurant, 'El Navasillo'. Coming from the south, from San Pedro, the entrance is on the right 1.4 km after the 'Cruz Roja' (Red Cross) first aid post. The road is perfectly passable under normal conditions but is accessible only to 4WD vehicles in periods of heavy rain or snow.

The first place to stop is 2.1 km from the entrance, where there is a little stream bed on the left. Park here and take the track off up to the left for about 1.5 km. The track passes through dense scrub at first, then widens, before entering a natural rocky basin in which there is an uninhabited house. This site is excellent for Black and Black-eared Wheatears, Subalpine Warblers, Dartford Warblers and Rock Buntings, amongst other species.

Return to the fork and then continue onwards. The area is fenced off for the first few kilometres and there are not many stopping places along this road. Continue past the farm (Cortijo de la Nava) at 4.5 km from the entrance, after which the road starts to rise. Turn left here and continue to a fork in the road at 9.1 km where you bear left for the foresters' houses, the campsite and car park at Los Quejigales, 10 km from the entrance.

A number of walking tracks are available at Los Quejigales. The entrance road continues northwards and is accessible on foot (it is chained off, so don't attempt to drive further). You can walk up towards the cliff to the right, or up through the pines on either side. The track up

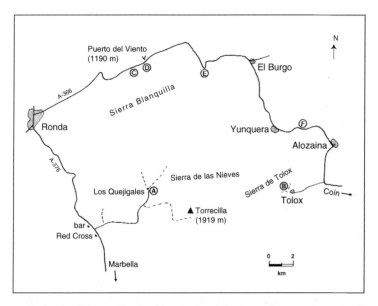

to the peak of Torrecilla provides the best chances of seeing the upland species, notably Rock Thrushes, Northern Wheatears and Skylarks. You can also return to the fork at 9.2 km (800 m from the Los Quejigales car park) and take the track up to the left which follows a circuitous course through the woodlands back to the campsite and car park.

B Sierra de Tolox

The Sierra de Tolox is at the eastern end of the Sierra de las Nieves. Take the A-366 Ronda/Coín road and turn off for Tolox. Bypass the village at the lower level where the road overlooks the river. Park on the bluff by the balneario (a mineral water spa with reputedly curative properties for asthmatics and others), and follow the rather precarious track upwards along the cliff and river. This area is somewhat less attractive than the Sierra de las Nieves but there is usually something of interest. Raptors often overfly and there are wagtails, pipits and warblers. You can follow the stream upwards for as far as you can manage. Alternatively, you drive up along the forest track by car, stopping to scan on the way. Finding a place to turn on this track can be difficult and it is not always open.

C Sierra Blanquilla – the valley

This is a small, unnamed valley to the south of the A-366 Ronda/El Burgo road on the northern edge of the Sierra Blanquilla. Access is easy from Ronda and a trip to this area could easily be combined with one to Jorox and Ronda itself. Take the A-366 northeastwards from Ronda and, past Km 8, look for a quarry set back on the left of the road. Where the fencing ends there is a drivable track on the right of the road which angles back in. Park about 1 km from the entrance and explore further up the valley on foot. Bonelli's, Booted and Golden Eagles occur. Black Wheatears, Black-eared Wheatears, Rock Sparrows and Rock Buntings are often around the rocks in the lower part of the valley. Both Wood-chat and Southern Grey Shrikes are also present. Further up the valley, follow the track which goes up through the trees, where you are likely to find Bonelli's and Subalpine Warblers.

D Puerto del Viento
The Puerto del Viento (Windy Pass), which usually lives up to its name, is on the A-366. Parking is difficult but a stop can produce Red-billed Choughs, Ravens and Rock Buntings, as well as occasional raptors.

E Mirador del Guardia Forestal
This a monument to the forest guards, a relic of the Franco regime. The stop and car park are signposted from both directions on the A-366 and a brief visit is worthwhile, if only for the fantastic views over the Río Burgo and to the Sierra de las Nieves. Crested Tits occur in the pines nearby and Rock Buntings often feed around the monument and on the rock face below.

F Jorox Gorge
This small gorge lies off the A-366 Coín/Ronda road between Alozaina (4.1 km) and Yunquera (3.8 km). The entrance is signposted and there is parking about 50 m east of the bridge (the Alozaina side). The gorge is difficult going and passable only on foot for little more than 150 m. However, in spite of its small accessible area, it holds several interesting and highly visible species such as Crag Martins, a few Dunnocks, a pair of Black Wheatears, Blue Rock Thrushes, some Rock Sparrows and Rock Buntings in abundance.

Calendar

All year: Griffon Vulture, Golden Eagle, Bonelli's Eagle, Common Kestrel, Peregrine, Goshawk, Woodpigeon, Eagle Owl, Little Owl, Tawny Owl, Thekla Lark, Woodlark, Skylark, Crag Martin, Wren, Robin, Black Redstart, Stonechat, Black Wheatear, Blue Rock Thrush, Dartford Warbler, Sardinian Warbler, Blackcap, Firecrest, Crested Tit, Coal Tit, Blue Tit, Great Tit, Nuthatch, Short-toed Treecreeper, Southern Grey Shrike, Red-billed Chough, Jackdaw, Raven, Hawfinch, Rock Sparrow, Rock Bunting.

Breeding season: Egyptian Vulture, Booted Eagle, Quail, Cuckoo, Scops Owl, Red-necked Nightjar, Alpine Swift, White-rumped Swift, Bee-eater, Hoopoe, Tawny Pipit, Nightingale, Common Redstart, Northern Wheatear, Black-eared Wheatear, Rock Thrush, Melodious Warbler, Subalpine Warbler, Orphean Warbler, Bonelli's Warbler, Spotted Flycatcher, Woodchat Shrike.

Winter: Merlin, Meadow Pipit, Alpine Accentor, Ring Ouzel, Redwing, Common Chiffchaff, Siskin.

Passage periods: Short-toed Eagle, Black Kite, swifts and hirundines, Willow Warbler, Pied Flycatcher.

SIERRA CRESTELLINA MA11

Status: Paraje Natural, 478 ha.

Site description
The Sierra Crestellina is at the southwestern end of the Sierra Bermeja.
It is a limestone ridge which runs for some 4 km in an approximately
north-south line between the picturesque towns of Casares and Gaucín
near the Mediterranean coast. The highest point is 926 m. The ridge
forms the eastern scarp of the Río Genal. Much of the hillsides are open
pasture, intensively grazed by goats and cattle, but there are extensive
tracts of hawthorn, buckthorn and cistus scrub, together with woods of
encina. The sierra proper has cliffs and scree slopes. Near Casares there
are areas of limestone pavement in what is otherwise a sandstone
region. The aspect of the southern approaches to the site is marred by
a wind farm, whose giant white windmills are visible from a great
distance.

Species
This is one of the easiest sites to reach from the Costa del Sol and it
offers a good range of the mountain species typical of the Serranía de
Ronda. The colony of Griffon Vultures is obvious at the northern end of
the ridge. Bonelli's Eagles also breed and are frequently visible, as are
the Lesser Kestrels around the castle at the top of Casares itself. There is
the usual range of swifts, the most notable being the White-rumped
Swifts, which are regularly present in small numbers. The road between
Manilva and the turn-off for Casares is also good for Tawny Pipits.
Warblers include Dartford Warblers, Spectacled Warblers, Subalpine
Warblers, Sardinian Warblers and Blackcaps. Other characteristic
breeding species are Stonechats, Black Wheatears, Red-billed Choughs
and Ravens. Rock Sparrows are frequent on the roadside on the way
down towards the Río Genal, at the north end of the site. Rock Buntings
also occur.

Timing
Morning visits are usually recommended, especially in summer, but
afternoon visits allow the sierra to be viewed with the sun behind you.
All times of year are rewarding; raptors are always present flying up and
down the ridge. The scrub and woodlands show a great deal of passerine activity and may hold significant numbers of a wide range of
species during migration periods.

Access
There are two points of access from the N-340 coast road. The most
straightforward is to take the A-377 Manilva/Gaucín road. Alternatively
follow signs to Casares, at the southern foot of the sierra, and continue
west to the A-377. The sierra is viewed from the A-377 which closely
skirts the western side of the sierra before descending to the Río Genal.
Footpaths and goat tracks allow access to the lower slopes where these
are unfenced. The valley of the Río Genal is a popular and pleasant
picnic spot and there is easy access to the river on the north side of the
bridge. Explore on foot for passerines.

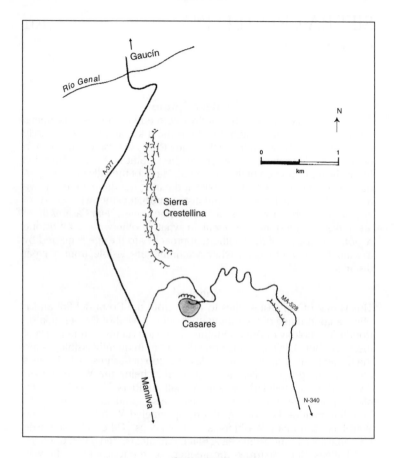

Calendar

All year: Griffon Vulture, Sparrowhawk, Bonelli's Eagle, Common Kestrel, Peregrine, Red-legged Partridge, Little Owl, Thekla Lark, Crag Martin, Stonechat, Black Wheatear, Blue Rock Thrush, Mistle Thrush, Dartford Warbler, Sardinian Warbler, Blackcap, Firecrest, Short-toed Treecreeper, Red-billed Chough, Jackdaw, Raven, Spotless Starling, Chaffinch, Rock Sparrow, Cirl Bunting, Rock Bunting.

Breeding season: Black Kite, Egyptian Vulture, Short-toed Eagle, Booted Eagle, Turtle Dove, Cuckoo, Common Swift, Pallid Swift, Alpine Swift, White-rumped Swift, Bee-eater, Red-rumped Swallow, Tawny Pipit, Nightingale, Black-eared Wheatear, Melodious Warbler, Spectacled Warbler, Subalpine Warbler, Woodchat Shrike, Ortolan Bunting.

Winter: Red Kite, Common Buzzard, Meadow Pipit, White Wagtail, Robin, Song Thrush, Common Chiffchaff, Southern Grey Shrike, Common Starling, Siskin.

Passage periods: A wide range of raptors overfly the area, especially on their approach to the Strait during the southward migration. Grounded migrant passerines are sometimes prominent.

SIERRA BERMEJA AND CENTRAL SERRANÍA DE RONDA

MA12

Status: Partly protected. Paraje Natural (Los Reales de Sierra Bermeja), 1236 ha.

Site description

This is a very large region consisting of two mountain ranges. The Sierra Bermeja is to the south, just inland from the coast at Estepona, to which it provides a rugged and largely unspoilt backdrop. The Serranía de Ronda lies further inland. The two are separated by the valley of the Río Genal. The area described here is bounded at its western end by the A-377 Manilva/Gaucín road and the Sierra Crestellina, which is considered separately (MA11). The eastern boundary is the A-376 San Pedro de Alcantara–Ronda road. The eastern sectors of the Serranía de Ronda, including the Sierra de las Nieves, are described above (site MA10). The northern boundary is the A-369 Gaucín–Ronda road. Further west the Serranía de Ronda merges with the Sierra de Grazalema (CA19).

This is a limestone region with a distinctive and interesting flora, boasting a good range of endemic species including Spanish fir (pinsapo), which is a feature of the Sierra Bermeja especially. Areas of open mountain pasture alternate with woods of pine, cork oak and encina. Sheer cliffs provide ideal nest sites for raptors and other species. There are also extensive areas of barren, stony uplands around the summits. Fast-flowing streams provide abundant water all year round. It is unhelpful to emphasise any particular site within this very large region, as what might be seen at one spot could be seen at any other, but we give general pointers to certain areas. The choice is considerable and birding is usually based on the 'stop at a suitable-looking site and watch' method.

Species

The region is of interest for its resident and migrant raptors as well as for its mountain, woodland and scrub passerines. Breeding raptors include Griffon Vultures, Golden, Bonelli's, Booted and Short-toed Eagles and Goshawks. Peregrines are relatively common throughout the area and especially around Ronda. Large flocks of Black Kites and Honey Buzzards, and the full range of migrant raptors, use the lines of the sierras as flyways during migration, especially in the autumn.

Alpine Swifts are characteristic of the high tops and are easily seen at Ronda. White-rumped Swifts range widely throughout the region and should be looked for among feeding parties of other swifts in late summer especially. Tawny Pipits are present in suitable habitat. Golden Orioles are common along the wooded valleys in the breeding season. Both the pine and broadleaf woodlands hold a wide variety of species. Characteristic species of the open terrain include Black Wheatears and Black Redstarts, with Northern Wheatears and Rock Thrushes at the upper levels. Ring Ouzels, Redwings and Bramblings occur infrequently in winter and there have been reports of Fieldfares and Trumpeter Finches in the same season. Rock Sparrows and Rock Buntings are both locally common in areas of suitable habitat.

Timing

This area offers such a wide range of species that a visit anywhere at any time is likely to produce something of interest. Spring and early summer will give maximum variety.

General access

The region is readily accessed from the N-340 to the south, and also from the north, along any of the major roads leading to Ronda (see map). The Sierra Bermeja is reached via the tortuous and locally rough MA-557 local road, which joins the N-340 at Estepona.

A Ronda

This ancient town has been inhabited since long before the Romans, who settled here, as did the Moors much later. The town bestrides the Tajo, a giant cleft in the rock which is spanned by a bridge. There are cliffs on the northwestern side of the gorge and a steep slope and fields beyond on the southwest side. The heavily polluted Río Guadalevín runs through the gorge.

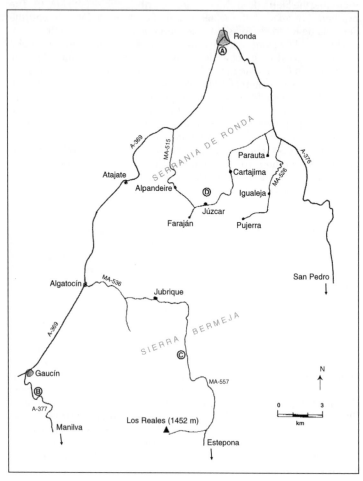

The vertiginous views from the bridge and the nearby viewpoint (mirador) are renowned. A variety of species may be seen from either of these. Peregrines often flash through the chasm looking for errant Rock Doves. They pose a lesser threat to the Alpine Swifts which also whistle through. Common Kestrels and Lesser Kestrels are also present in this area. Black Redstarts and Blue Rock Thrushes frequent the walls of the gorge. White and Grey Wagtails are common in the bottom of the Tajo itself and in summer there are Nightingales all the way along the course of the river. If you venture down into the bottom of the gorge, keep an eye open for Melodious Warblers and Rock Sparrows, both of which occur by the river and in the surrounding fields.

Park in the town centre, from where there is ready access to the mirador and bridge. If you are feeling energetic and want to visit the bottom of the gorge, cross the bridge southwards and keep right past the Palacio de Mondragón, until you reach the top of the fairly steep downward path. The descent is a stiffish walk but the return journey is slow going for all but the super-fit.

Nightingale

B Manilva-Gaucín
This is the most westerly of the entry points into the region. Take the A-377 Manilva–Gaucín road up from the coast, which first passes the Sierra Crestellina (MA11) before joining the A-369 just to the west of Gaucín. The vicinity of the Río Genal, between Gaucín and the Sierra Crestellina, provides ample opportunities to explore the scrub and riverine vegetation for passerines, especially on the north bank of the river.

C Sierra Bermeja
Estepona and Algatocín are joined by a rather narrow and twisting mountain road, which passes through a variety of woodland habitats. Goshawks, Sparrowhawks and Booted Eagles breed locally. Stop frequently. The ascent of the Sierra Bermeja proper is along a rather rough tarmac road signposted for Los Reales. The views are absolutely stunning on a clear day and migrant raptors are often evident in autumn especially.

D Cartajima–Júzcar–Alpandeire

A circular tour on the MA-515 through these villages to the south of Ronda gives access to a range of habitats as you pass through broadleaf woodland between Cartajima and Alpandeire and also more open areas between Alpandeire and junction with the Gaucín/Ronda road. A cliff face close to the road about 1.5 km north of Cartajima is likely to produce Blue Rock Thrushes and numbers of Rock Sparrows.

Calendar

All year: Griffon Vulture, Goshawk, Sparrowhawk, Bonelli's Eagle, Common Kestrel, Peregrine, Red-legged Partridge, Little Owl, Thekla Lark, Crag Martin, Dipper, Stonechat, Black Wheatear, Blue Rock Thrush, Mistle Thrush, Dartford Warbler, Sardinian Warbler, Blackcap, Firecrest, Short-toed Treecreeper, Red-billed Chough, Jackdaw, Raven, Spotless Starling, Chaffinch, Crossbill, Cirl Bunting, Rock Bunting.

Breeding season: Egyptian Vulture, Short-toed Eagle, Booted Eagle, Scops Owl, Turtle Dove, Cuckoo, Bee-eater, Alpine Swift, White-rumped Swift, Red-rumped Swallow, Nightingale, Black-eared Wheatear, Melodious Warbler, Whitethroat, Woodchat Shrike, Ortolan Bunting.

Winter: Red Kite, Common Buzzard, Meadow Pipit, White Wagtail, Robin, Song Thrush, Ring Ouzel, Fieldfare, Redwing, Common Chiffchaff, Southern Grey Shrike, Common Starling, Brambling, Siskin, Trumpeter Finch (exceptional).

Passage periods: A wide range of raptor species overfly the area. Passerines are also prominent.

UPPER RÍO GUADIARO VALLEY   MA13

Status: Parque Natural (Sierra de Grazelema) in part. ZEPA.

Site description

This is the area between Montejaque and Jimera de Líbar, west of Ronda, where the upper reaches of the Río Guadiaro run down a beautiful, quite steep-sided and well-wooded valley in a southwest direction. The valley is bounded on the western side by the Sierra del Palo and, immediately behind Montejaque and Benaoján, by the Sierra de Libar. To the east there is a minor sierra of the Serranía de Ronda.

Species

The course of the Río Guadiaro attracts a number of waterbirds, including Grey Herons and occasional Squacco Herons, Water Rails, Moorhens and Common Sandpipers. Dippers are a possibility. The sierras have nesting Griffon and Egyptian Vultures, Short-toed, Golden, Booted and Bonelli's Eagles and Sparrowhawks. All four swifts, including White-rumped Swifts, occur and this is a reliable site for the latter species, especially in late summer. Golden Orioles are common along the valley in the breeding season. Rock Sparrows and Rock Buntings are locally common in suitable habitat around Montejaque and Benaoján.

Timing

This is a lovely area at any time of year. Undoubtedly the best season is spring, especially between late April and the end of May or first week of June. Visit in summer to find White-rumped Swifts.

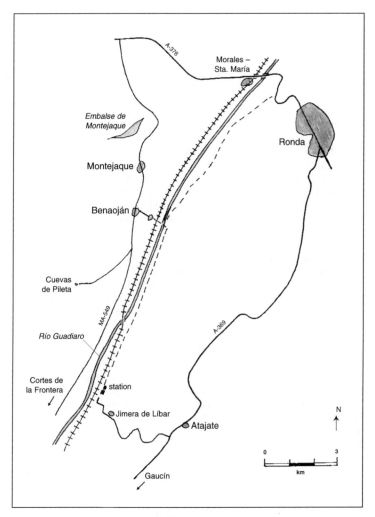

Access

Enter the valley from the north, turning off from the A-376 Ronda–Algodonales road for Montejaque and Benaoján. Access from the south is via Jimera de Líbar, off the A-369 Gaucín–Ronda road.

This is excellent walking country and a comprehensive range of species may be located within rambling distance of Benaoján. Andy Chapell, of the Hotel Molino del Santo at Benaoján, provides maps of the many and various walks around the region for those staying at the hotel. These are available to non-resident visiting birders who call in at Molino del Santo, for a nominal fee per route description and map. Telephone Andy at least a couple of days before visiting. The phone number and address are in the introduction to this province chapter. The four routes outlined below are recommended by Andy, to whom we are much indebted, as best for birding. A visit to the Embalse de Montejaque is another of the many additional possible routes to take.

A Benaoján–Jimera de Líbar
This is a riverside stroll along the path following the east bank of the Río Guadiaro from Benaoján towards Jimera de Líbar (or vice-versa).

B El Hacho
El Hacho is the mountain behind Montejaque and there is a walk, or even a scramble, to the top where vultures may be seen at close quarters. The route takes in two small valleys, one cultivated, the other wild and rocky, which offer a wide range of species.

C Valley between El Hacho and Tabizna
This beautiful valley, with a very good birdlist, is to the northeast of Montejaque and is well worth a visit. A brief visit should provide some good birding. There is a dirt track off to the northeast by the farmhouse, some 400 m north of the roundabout at Montejaque. There are some 10 km of tracks within the valley, most of which are passable under normal circumstances.

D Sierra de Líbar
This a longish walk, of some three hours excluding stops for birding, on a circuitous route from Montejaque to Benaoján. The entry point is a track by the Bar La Cabaña in Montejaque. A shorter walk along the same track is also worthwhile if you don't wish to embark on a major expedition.

Calendar
All year: Squacco Heron, Grey Heron, Griffon Vulture, Goshawk, Sparrowhawk, Golden Eagle, Bonelli's Eagle, Common Kestrel, Peregrine, Red-legged Partridge, Water Rail, Moorhen, Common Sandpiper, Little Owl, Eagle Owl, Kingfisher, Green Woodpecker, Great Spotted Woodpecker, Crested Lark, Thekla Lark, Woodlark, Crag Martin, Grey Wagtail, Dipper, Wren, Stonechat, Black Redstart, Black Wheatear, Blue Rock Thrush, Mistle Thrush, Dartford Warbler, Sardinian Warbler, Blackcap, Firecrest, Short-toed Treecreeper, Southern Grey Shrike, Jay, Red-billed Chough, Jackdaw, Raven, Spotless Starling, Chaffinch, Crossbill, Rock Sparrow, Cirl Bunting, Rock Bunting.

Breeding season: Egyptian Vulture, Short-toed Eagle, Booted Eagle, Lesser Kestrel, Turtle Dove, Cuckoo, Scops Owl, Red-necked Nightjar, Common Swift, Pallid Swift, Alpine Swift, White-rumped Swift, Bee-eater, Hoopoe, Wryneck, Sand Martin, Red-rumped Swallow, Rufous Bush Chat, Nightingale, Black-eared Wheatear, Melodious Warbler, Subalpine Warbler, Bonelli's Warbler, Spotted Flycatcher, Golden Oriole, Woodchat Shrike.

Winter: Common Buzzard, Meadow Pipit, White Wagtail, Robin, Song Thrush, Ring Ouzel, Fieldfare, Redwing, Common Chiffchaff, Long-tailed Tit, Southern Grey Shrike, Common Starling, Siskin.

Passage periods: A wide range of raptor species overfly the area. Passerines are also prominent.

ZAFARRAYA AND SIERRA TEJEDA   MA14

Status: Reserva de Caza.

Site description

The Sierra Tejeda is a superbly rugged mountain range with scree slopes which straddles the borders of Málaga and Granada provinces. In fact, most of it lies within Granada province but the two routes given are accessed from Málaga province. The A-335 between Málaga and Granada runs past the western end of the Sierra Tejeda at Venta de Zafarraya. On the western side of the road the land is relatively more open and less rugged generally, while to the east it is strikingly abrupt.

Species

Typical sierra species, particularly Crag Martins, Thekla Larks, Black Redstarts and Rock Buntings are evident. Stonechats, Linnets and Goldfinches are everywhere. There are a few Red-billed Choughs at the highest levels and also occasional Ravens. The area is good for raptors with a selection that includes resident Golden and Bonelli's Eagles, Peregrines, and Common Kestrels, as well as summering Black Kites, Short-toed Eagles and Booted Eagles. The cliffs hold resident Eagle Owls and in the summer months Scops Owls are found at the lower levels. The thrushes are well represented; the resident Blue Rock Thrushes and Black Wheatears are joined in summer by Black-eared Wheatears, Northern Wheatears and Rock Thrushes, the latter two occurring only at higher levels. Ring Ouzels and Song Thrushes are often present in winter. There are a few Rock Sparrows at the foot of the cliffs beyond the tunnel. High into the sierra, the magnificent Wallcreeper has been recorded as a regular but very scarce winter visitor in recent years, while Alpine Accentors are rather more common there then.

Timing

Interesting species are present all year but spring visits tend to be most productive.

Access

There is ready access from the A-335, via Ventas de Zafarraya or Vélez Málaga in the south. Two areas are recommended. The first (A) is immediately south of Ventas de Zafarraya, where you should park on the eastern side of the road just outside the village. From here follow

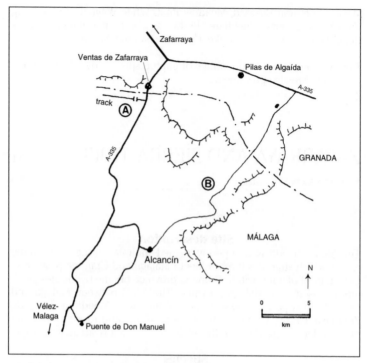

what is no more than a goat track running eastwards, or head west, through the tunnel, and onwards for about 2 km until you arrive at the first cultivated land on the right-hand side. This latter track tends to produce a greater species diversity.

The second area is the Sierra Tejeda itself (B), which is best approached from Alcaucín in Málaga province, just east of the A-335. In Alcaucín turn left along the track known as 'el carríl del Alcázar' up into the sierra. This takes you past a campsite and freshwater spring. This is a narrow and winding road of some 12 km. It is passable by ordinary cars but a 4WD vehicle is necessary in adverse conditions. The views are fantastic, especially in the winter when there is often snow on the tops, and the birding isn't at all bad either.

Calendar

All year: Common Buzzard, Golden Eagle, Bonelli's Eagle, Goshawk, Sparrowhawk, Peregrine, Common Kestrel, Eagle Owl, Crag Martin, Thekla Lark, Stonechat, Blue Rock Thrush, Black Redstart, Black Wheatear, Dipper, Southern Grey Shrike, Raven, Red-billed Chough, Goldfinch, Linnet, Rock Sparrow, Rock Bunting.

Breeding season: Black Kite, Short-toed Eagle, Booted Eagle, Scops Owl, Red-necked Nightjar, Alpine Swift, Tawny Pipit, Northern Wheatear, Black-eared Wheatear, Rock Thrush, Subalpine Warbler, Spectacled Warbler, Bonelli's Warbler, Woodchat Shrike.

Winter: Alpine Accentor, Ring Ouzel, Wallcreeper.

GRANADA PROVINCE

Granada province lacks a diversity of birding sites. It is dominated by mountains, large tracts of which are inaccessible. Most significant is the lofty Sierra Nevada (GR1), notable for its isolated breeding population of Alpine Accentors. The remaining selected sites comprise more sierras (GR2, GR4, GR5), and two steppe areas (GR3, GR6), all of which hold some interesting species in small numbers. The species diversity of the steppe areas compares poorly with similar sites in Almería, Córdoba or Extremadura however.

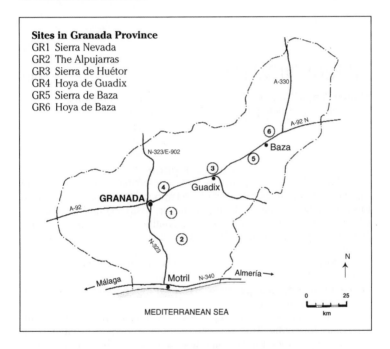

Sites in Granada Province
GR1 Sierra Nevada
GR2 The Alpujarras
GR3 Sierra de Huétor
GR4 Hoya de Guadix
GR5 Sierra de Baza
GR6 Hoya de Baza

Maps
Mapa Provincial Granada, IGN, 1:200,000.
Sierra Nevada, IGN Serie Turística, 1:50,000 (also includes the Alpujarras).
Plaza & Llanes Euromapa, Andalucía Oriental, 1:300,000.

Getting there
Nearly all the sites are within a three-hour drive from the N-340, which follows the coastal region of the province, or from Málaga city. The A-92 and A92-N provide rapid transit east/west across the centre of the province and to/from Sevilla.

Where to stay
All sites are within easy reach of Granada city, which has a considerable range of hotels, including motels along the approach roads. For

201

those who would like to sample staying up high, there is the tourist accommodation in the Solynieve complex on the top of Sierra Nevada. This is geared towards the skiing fraternity and so generally is open only between November and the end of April. A few hotels near the ski complex remain open all year round, one being the Parador Nacional, which is lovely but relatively expensive. Fortunately, there is cheaper, year-round accommodation lower down towards Granada. There is also accommodation in Guadix and Baza.

For more information on where to stay, write to either of the following: Oficina de Turismo, Edificio Ayuntamiento, Libreros, 2, 18001 Granada (tel: 958-221022 and 958-225990; fax: 958-228918); Patronato Provincial de Turismo, Plaza Mariana Pineda, 10 bajo, 18009 Granada (tel: 958-226688).

SIERRA NEVADA GR1

Status: Parque Natural, 171,646 ha. The central peak region is in the process of being designated a national park.

Site description

The Parque Natural de Sierra Nevada covers the imposing range of mountains to the south and east of the famous city of Granada. It boasts the two highest peaks in Spain: Mulhacén (3481 m) and Pico Veleta (3392 m), both over 11,000 feet. The southern foothills of the Sierra Nevada are the Alpujarras (GR2). At its eastern end the range extends into the province of Almería.

The lower slopes were once wooded with forests of oak with pines higher up. Much of the forest cover has been lost and the range has a characteristic barren appearance. The high tops have extensive alpine moorland and stony scree.

The area suffers considerable pressures from tourist development, especially for skiing. This is in spite of being a zone of major international importance for its alpine flora and fauna. The flora is special and of the greatest interest; the 200 species of the alpine zone include 40 endemics. The butterfly community is also distinguished. The Sierra Nevada was declared a Biosphere Reserve by UNESCO in 1986. Regrettably that declaration did not prevent considerable degradation of the alpine terrain in some areas. The large monetary interests attached to the ski industry result in powerful economic pressures which often run counter to conservation interests. Nevertheless, the designation of the central peaks as a national park, the highest level of protection available, was underway in 2000.

Species

On the way up from Granada you pass through wooded and scrub areas where there are good chances of encountering species such as Subalpine Warblers, Melodious Warblers and Black-eared Wheatears, as well as occasional Rollers. Nightingales sing loudly in the moist vegetated gullies where Golden Orioles may also be heard. The pines hold Fire-crests and occasional Crossbills. Siskins are present in winter. Great and Coal Tits are common; the latter will even leave the trees and fly several hundred metres to feed at the edge of the snow on fine winter days.

Somewhat higher, at the upper limit of the tree-line, there are Black Wheatears and Rock Buntings. These move to lower levels during the winter months, although this depends on the extent of snow cover. Both Rock Buntings and Alpine Accentors are often absent in winter, even at lower levels, when both descend to less severe conditions in other sierras, even as far as Gibraltar. House Sparrows remain at the top all year round to scavenge the leavings of visitors.

Ortolan Buntings occur in very small numbers, nesting on north-facing slopes particularly. There are also isolated winter records of Wallcreepers, although you would be immensely lucky to find one in so huge an area. Once up high, around the Estación Invernal ski complex and the parador (the latter is rather better), you can be virtually certain of seeing Alpine Accentors in late spring and summer, as well as Red-billed Choughs and Ravens. Birds of prey are very scarce in the general area with usually only occasional Common Kestrels or Peregrines to be seen. Golden Eagles occur regularly but other large raptors, such as Griffon Vultures, are generally unusual. Water Pipits sometimes occur around the little lake — Laguna de las Yeguas — to the south of the through road, but have not been proved to breed. Similarly there are occasional records of Citril Finches from the high tops but they have not been proved to nest in the Sierra Nevada. Tawny Pipits and Northern Wheatears nest on the tops in the summer months.

Spanish ibex occur amongst a variety of other mammals. The latter are generally on the lower slopes and include wild cats, wild boars, beech martens and dormice.

Timing

Homo sapiens skiensis is present in huge numbers between the start of the winter snow, at any time after early November, and its official end in late April, although there can be large numbers of this abundant species until late May. Outside this season there are far fewer of them, although there are always some summering stragglers out for a day with the immature members of the family. Late spring and the summer months are the best times to visit the higher areas, which become essentially birdless in winter.

Warning: A few words of warning are necessary about going high in the Sierra Nevada and also in parts of the Alpujarras (GR2), from Capileira upwards. Warm, waterproof and windproof clothing is an essential precaution even in summer and is absolutely indispensable at any other time of year. In normal years there is snow in some of the corries even in July, and it is possible to experience a 30°C difference between the tops and the coast in July and August. A high-factor suntan cream and a lipsalve of some sort are always advisable. Good sunglasses will also be needed if you are contemplating going into the snow.

Access

There are only two routes on to the tops, one from the north and one from the south. The approach from the north side is from the city of Granada, from where you take the road (A-395) signposted for Sierra

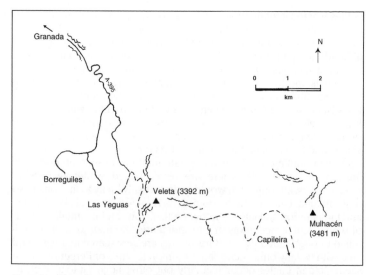

Nevada. The distance from Granada to the complex of hotels at the Estación Invernal is approximately 45 km, ascending through a variety of habitats. This route, like many in Spain, is not only winding and with the usual lack of good areas in which to stop, but also climbs all the time until it reaches an altitude of 2500 m at the Estación Invernal and parador. In order to get right on to the top, in the summer months, follow the signs for Veleta.

The second approach is from the south side, from Capileira in the Alpujarras (GR2). Continue through that village on the road, soon to be a track, which takes you right over the top to come out eventually near the parador and Estación Invernal on the north side. This track is shown as a faintly marked line on the Firestone map and also on the Mapa Provincial, but not in the Guía Práctica. It is more or less passable with care in summer in a standard car with a reasonably high ground clearance and better still in a 4WD vehicle, but is out of the question in winter. An alternative, but which takes you up only on to the western slopes, is to come out from Granada on the road (GR-410) signposted for La Zubia and then continue up from there. However, you do not get much above 1500 m.

At the eastern end of the range there are two roads which traverse the sierra from north to south, as well as a network of mountain tracks. There is little information available on this region, although Wallcreepers possibly occur in winter and you can be certain of the presence of Alpine Accentors, as well as Rock Buntings, at the higher levels. Carrion Crows are likely at intermediate levels, in open wooded terrain. This is a region which may well repay closer attention.

Calendar

All year: Goshawk, Golden Eagle, Common Kestrel, Peregrine, Eagle Owl, Thekla Lark, Dipper, Alpine Accentor, Black Redstart, Stonechat, Black Wheatear, Blue Rock Thrush, Dartford Warbler, Blackcap, Firecrest, Crested Tit, Coal Tit, Great Tit, Short-toed Treecreeper, Jay, Azure-winged Magpie, Red-billed Chough, Jackdaw, Carrion Crow, Raven, Crossbill, Rock Bunting.

Breeding season: Lesser Kestrel, Common Sandpiper, Alpine Swift, Roller, Hoopoe, Skylark, Woodlark, Water Pipit, Tawny Pipit, Nightingale, Northern Wheatear, Black-eared Wheatear, Rock Thrush, Melodious Warbler, Spectacled Warbler, Subalpine Warbler, Spotted Flycatcher, Pied Flycatcher, Golden Oriole, Woodchat Shrike.

Winter: Ring Ouzel, Common Chiffchaff, Wallcreeper, Siskin.

THE ALPUJARRAS   GR2

Status: The higher levels fall partly within the Parque Natural of Sierra Nevada. The rest of the area has no special protection.

General description
This is not one particular site but a whole region on the south side of the Sierra Nevada. It is the long valley area which runs east-west between Padules and Lanjarón. The region overlaps into the province of Almería to the east of Ugíjar. The valley is separated from the sea by another sierra range. Along the bottom in the western section runs the Río Guadalfeo ('ugly river'), which is fed by other smaller rivers and streams which run down from the Sierra Nevada after the autumn rains and during the snow-melt in spring. The three sites given are fairly representative of the northern side of the Alpujarras. They offer considerable opportunities for exploration of interesting habitats in a region of great scenic merit.

Timing
The best time is undoubtedly the spring and early summer, between late March and early July, although it can be interesting in some areas throughout the year.

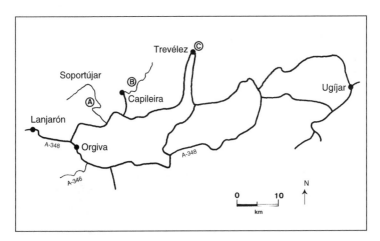

General access

Some words of warning to visitors seem advisable. Straight stretches of road are rare. They are extremely winding throughout and this one of only two areas in which we have come across the road sign *Peligros Diversos* — 'several dangers' — so take your pick! Some of the tracks, particularly that up to the Cortijo Dar al Habibi, are really not for the nervous or weak of heart, although that road improves thereafter up to the Parque Forestal de Soportújar.

The Alpujarras tourist offices provide a reasonable map of the whole area with all roads and tracks shown, but note that some of the latter are either very difficult to locate or difficult to travel — or both!

Enter the Alpujarras either from the west, by coming off the N-323/E-902 Granada/Motril road for Lanjarón on the A-348, or from the Almería direction by coming off the N-340 just east of Puente del Río, on the A-347, for Ugíjar.

A Cortijo Dar al Habibi and Parque Forestal de Soportújar

Site description

As far up as the Cortijo you overlook steep slopes covered with scrub, before entering the pine belt. The pines continue to border the track up past the Cortijo and also westwards towards Prado Grande. The terrain is more open along the easterly track to Soportújar.

Species

Golden Eagles overfly the area with some frequency. On the slopes below the Cortijo there are Hoopoes, Thekla Larks, Blue Rock Thrushes and Black Redstarts, with Common Redstarts during migration periods. Dartford Warblers and Melodious Warblers both occur as well as the ubiquitous Sardinian Warblers. All the tits, including some Crested Tits, occur in the pines, as well as Short-toed Treecreepers. Higher up you

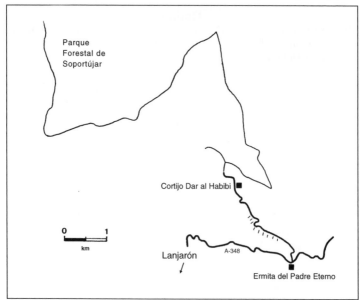

can expect to come into contact with occasional Tawny Pipits and Northern Wheatears, as well as Rock Buntings.

Access

Access is off the main road between Lanjarón and Orgiva, opposite the local crafts and ceramics building notably named 'El Padre Eterno' ('The Eternal Father'; you may well need His help to negotiate the road), from where the road then winds up towards the Cortijo. This road is narrow, with a steep drop on one side, and is definitely not for those of a nervous disposition. The first really practicable stopping points are just before and just after the Cortijo, or by continuing on to the round-about at the end and stopping there.

The left-hand road is marked as going to Prado Grande but is not usu-ally open to cars and it is easy to imagine being locked in. If it is open, it seems sensible to ask if you can enter if there is anyone around the building on the left. However, foot access is certainly permitted and the walk can be worth it. The right-hand road goes on for about 16 km to the Parque Forestal de Soportújar. Take care here in winter, when there is a risk of ice and the very real possibility of bouncing downwards a large number of metres.

B Capileira to Sierra Nevada

Site description

The region is similar to site A. Once through the village there are planted pines, with open stretches of rough grassland between. Higher up are open mountain slopes.

Species

Birds of prey are represented by Common Buzzards, Golden Eagles, Common Kestrels and Lesser Kestrels. Alpine Swifts are often in the area and occasionally you may find Red-rumped Swallows just up from

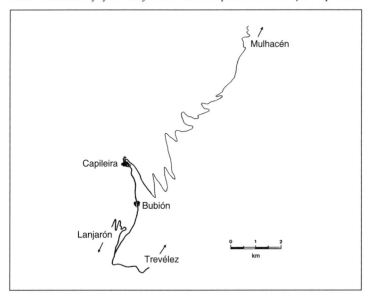

Capileira itself. Thekla Larks are the only common larks although Skylarks do occur. Tawny Pipits are scarce but are to be found in the higher areas. There is a small chance of finding Alpine Accentors here; these are more frequent around the Estación Invernal on the north side of the Sierra Nevada (GR1) and up from there.

Chats are represented by Black Redstarts and Blue Rock Thrushes in craggy areas, and Northern Wheatears occur on the more open higher levels. Warblers are generally scarce although at the lower levels Sardinian Warblers and Bonelli's Warblers may be found with some effort. There are Firecrests too in the pines, as well as Spotted Flycatchers, but Pied Flycatchers only appear to occur on migration. Coal and Great Tits occur up to the tree limit, as do Short-toed Treecreepers. Red-billed Choughs, Jackdaws and Ravens are the normal corvids to be found. The common finches are all present: Linnets range remarkably high above the tree-line at times. Rock Buntings occur along the track in the more open rocky spaces, but these again are much more easily found on the Granada side around the Estación Invernal (GR1).

Access
Continue through the village of Capileira and upwards along the track. In summer, if you continue far enough, the track will bring you over the summit ridge to the Parador Nacional and Estación Invernal (GR1) on the north side of the Sierra Nevada.

C Trevélez

Site description
This is the highest village in Spain (1560 m above sea level), positioned at the end of a long, pleasant valley which produces some of the finest *jamón serrano* (sierra air-dried ham). Above it rises the Sierra Nevada, down from which cascades the Río Trevélez. It is the area above the bridge which is interesting. The sides of the valley rise up steeply on each side from the floor, which has open grassy areas and trees.

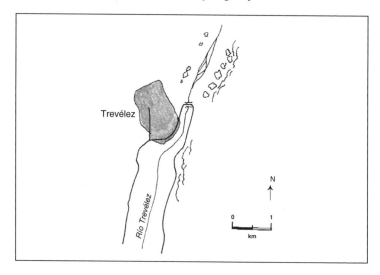

Species

The area holds a pleasing variety of passerines including Grey Wagtails, Melodious Warblers, Sardinian Warblers, Bonelli's Warblers and Black-caps. Watch for overflying raptors and corvids: Golden Eagles, Ravens and Jackdaws.

Access

Access to the village is easy from either west or east. The western approach is more attractive as you look up and across the valley. Park in the village or near the bridge. Access upstream depends very largely on how much water is coming down. It is somewhat difficult overall as the river uses a variety of courses at different levels, depending upon season. When the river is in full flood in spring the upstream area is virtually impassable but wet feet are a natural result of a visit at just about any time of year.

Calendar

All year: Common Buzzard, Golden Eagle, Bonelli's Eagle, Common Kestrel, Peregrine, Eagle Owl, Little Owl, Crested Lark, Thekla Lark, Crag Martin, Dipper, Wren, Alpine Accentor, Robin, Black Redstart, Black Wheatear, Blue Rock Thrush, Mistle Thrush, Dartford Warbler, Sardinian Warbler, Blackcap, Crested Tit, Blue Tit, Great Tit, Short-toed Treecreeper, Jay, Red-billed Chough, Jackdaw, Raven, Chaffinch, Serin, Greenfinch, Linnet, Crossbill, Rock Bunting.

Breeding season: Short-toed Eagle, Lesser Kestrel, Cuckoo, Scops Owl, Alpine Swift, Bee-eater, Hoopoe, Barn Swallow, Red-rumped Swallow, Skylark, Grey Wagtail, Tawny Pipit, Northern Wheatear, Black-eared Wheatear, Melodious Warbler, Subalpine Warbler, Bonelli's Warbler, Spotted Flycatcher, Golden Oriole, Woodchat Shrike.

Winter: Common Chiffchaff, Siskin, Citril Finch.

Passage periods: Raptors, larks, wagtails, pipits, Common Redstart, warblers.

SIERRA DE HUÉTOR   GR3

Status: Parque Natural, 12,168 ha.

Information

There is a visitors' centre 'Puerto Lobo' in the village of Iznar. For further information, contact the regional office in Granada.

Site description

This is a large area of medium-sized mountains to the northeast of Granada. The altitude ranges between 1100 and 1675 m above sea level. The whole zone has large expanses of natural and planted vegetation, or rather it had until August 1993 when over 5000 ha of the site were devastated by an enormous forest fire. A replanting programme has taken place since then. The flora includes a large number of endemic species and subspecies.

Species

Various raptors, most frequently Common Buzzards and Golden Eagles, are to be found in the area. The woodlands hold a wide variety of coniferous forest passerines such as Crested Tits, Coal Tits, Great Tits, Firecrests, Robins, Short-toed Treecreepers, Crossbills and Chaffinches. At higher altitudes, where the pines thin out, there are Subalpine Warblers, as well as the resident Dartford and Sardinian Warblers, Red-billed Choughs, Ravens and Rock Buntings.

Apart from the birdlife, the Sierra de Huétor also holds important populations of mammals such as genets, badgers, beech martens, wild cats, wild boars and Spanish ibex.

Timing

This area is normally worth a visit at any time of year. The most productive season is the spring between March and June, although it can be good as late as August. It is a useful site to visit and explore if stopping for lunch when in transit along the A-92.

Access

Exit Granada eastwards on the A-92 for Huétor, El Molinillo, Diezma and Guadix. The main turn-off is well signposted and you can go in on the north side of the road at exit 26. You can then cross over to the south side of the A-92 and follow the track up several kilometres. This is not recommended during weekdays as it ends at a quarry and you are likely to meet heavily loaded trucks, although there are ample passing places

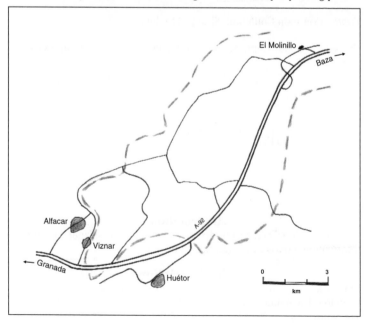

on the otherwise narrow road. It is far better to go in to the north side where, after a kilometre, you come to an information board, displaying a map giving various routes which you can follow. Follow this track on for another 5 km, past the picnic area (which is heavily used at weekends), until you come to a fork. Here there is a sign which gives distances for left and right tracks. To the left, you come out eventually after 9 km at Alfacar. To the right the maximum distance before coming out at the main road is 10 km. Either track is worth following, although the right-hand one offers a wider choice of habitats and, therefore, more birds.

Little Bustards

Calendar
All year: Common Buzzard, Golden Eagle, Common Kestrel, Crested Tit, Coal Tit, Great Tit, Dartford Warbler, Firecrest, Short-toed Treecreeper, Red-billed Chough, Jackdaw, Raven, Chaffinch, Crossbill.

Breeding season: Subalpine Warbler, Bonelli's Warbler, Spotted Flycatcher, Golden Oriole.

HOYA DE GUADIX   GR4
Status: No special protection.

Site description
This is a large, flat, semi-arid depression which runs roughly north/south to the west of Guadix on the northern side of the Sierra Nevada, at an altitude of between 900 and 1100 m above sea level. The ground is chalky with many gullies and ravines in its eastern part, but somewhat less broken in the west. Agriculture in this steppe area is limited to cereals, with interspersed areas of false esparto grass, encinares and some olives, through which flocks of sheep and goats wander with their attendant herders. There is little human presence except for isolated farms, and along the course of the Río Gor.

Species

There are some birds of prey, many of which visit the area from the surrounding sierras. These include Egyptian and Griffon Vultures, Goshawks, Montagu's Harriers, Golden Eagles, Bonelli's Eagles, Peregrines and Hobbies. There are populations of Eagle Owls and Long-eared Owls as well as the common Little Owls. This is one of the better areas in Andalucía for steppe birds, although in such a large expanse they take some finding. A telescope is highly desirable, as is an element of luck. There are small populations of Little Bustards, Stone Curlews and Black-bellied Sandgrouse.

All three 'exotic' species — Roller, Hoopoe and Bee-eater breed. Great Spotted Cuckoos occur sparingly. Both Thekla and Crested Larks occur, as do Calandra Larks of which there is a large population. Both Short-toed and Lesser Short-toed Larks are abundant and there are small populations of both Dupont's and Lesser Short-toed Larks. Tawny Pipits breed in small numbers. Large numbers of Meadow Pipits occur in winter. Both Black-eared and Black Wheatears are common. Golden Orioles breed in the isolated stands of trees, especially in the poplars along the course of the Río Gor, and in the same areas there are also Melodious and Spectacled Warblers. Southern Grey Shrikes are to be

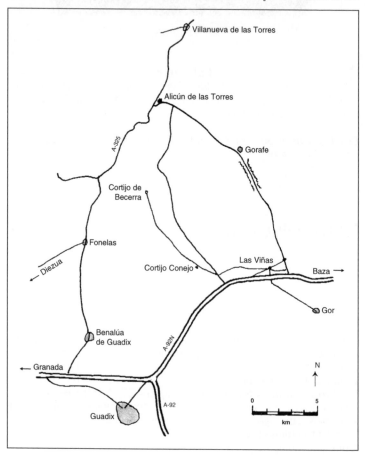

seen, perched ominously in wait for the unwary, and there are also Woodchat Shrikes. There are also a considerable number of Red-billed Choughs which breed in the surrounding sierras and along the cliffs of the Río Gor, as well as the ubiquitous Ravens and some Magpies. Both Tree Sparrows and Rock Sparrows are also found in the right habitats.

Timing

Although the area may be visited at any time of year with some success, the best time is undoubtedly spring between late February and late May. Early morning visits and evenings are best for locating the steppe species.

Access

There are a variety of minor roads and tracks to the north of the A-92N Granada/Guadix road. Once in this region, it is simply a matter of stopping and scanning in likely areas.

A useful route is to drive north from the A-92N towards Gorafe and the village variously marked on maps as Baños de Alicún or Alicún de las Torres or a mixture of both. This road drops down through the scenically beautiful course of the Río Gor after about 5 km, and can be followed round to the A-325 and Fonelas. Near Alicún there is an intermediate turn-off to the left, not marked on most maps and which comes out near the main road at the entrance signposted Cortijo Conejo (rabbit farm). The track to the cortijo can also be covered for a few kilometres. Alternatively you can continue south towards Guadix and the A-92N via the A-325 through Fonelas and Benalúa de Guadix. This road runs through the centre of the area.

Calendar

All year: Egyptian Vulture, Griffon Vulture, Golden Eagle, Bonelli's Eagle, Goshawk, Peregrine, Little Bustard, Stone Curlew, Eagle Owl, Little Owl, Long-eared Owl, Black-bellied Sandgrouse, Crested Lark, Thekla Lark, Calandra Lark, Dupont's Lark, Black Redstart, Black Wheatear, Dartford Warbler, Sardinian Warbler, Southern Grey Shrike, Magpie, Red-billed Chough, Jackdaw, Raven, Tree Sparrow, Rock Sparrow.

Breeding season: Montagu's Harrier, Hobby, Red-necked Nightjar, Great Spotted Cuckoo, Roller, Hoopoe, Bee-eater, Red-rumped Swallow, Lesser Short-toed Lark, Tawny Pipit, Nightingale, Black-eared Wheatear, Melodious Warbler, Spectacled Warbler, Woodchat Shrike.

Winter: Skylark, Meadow Pipit, White Wagtail.

SIERRA DE BAZA

Status: Parque Natural, 53,844 ha.

Information

There is an information centre along the local road which comes out of Gor going up to Las Juntas.

Site description

This is another very large area of sierra, forming part of the central Penibetic system. It consists of a series of elongated anticlines with a calcine soil in the western part, whilst on the eastern flanks there are some agricultural areas. There are also some agricultural areas at the lowest levels, near the main road, with strips of scrub and pines in between. Further up into the sierra there are oaks, and pines of various species, with open mountainsides at the highest levels.

Species

The birds of prey are represented by Egyptian Vultures, Golden Eagles, Peregrines and Common Kestrels, with nocturnal raptors including Scops, Eagle and Tawny Owls. The common species of woodland and open country are present, although Rock Sparrows do not appear to occur. The lower fringes of the sierra, with open agricultural land, scrub, bushes and pines hold a good mixture of typical species. Red-legged Partridges and Hoopoes are common on the farmland and in the most open scrub. Crested Larks are common at low level in the farmland areas but are replaced higher up by Thekla Larks. Turtle Doves are common in the more wooded areas and coo monotonously, being interrupted at times by the 'machine-gunning' of the Green Woodpeckers and the loud song of the occasional Wrens.

Black-eared Wheatears are other obvious inhabitants of the more open areas. Warblers include Dartford Warblers in the scrub, a few Melodious Warblers in thicker bushy areas and Bonelli's Warblers and Firecrests in the mature woodland. Spotted Flycatchers are common in the woodland. Both Southern Grey and Woodchat Shrikes hunt in the more open patches. There is a small population of Carrion Crows in the oak woods, part of the southern outpost population of what is generally a northern species in Spain.There is a good mixture of finches, including Chaffinches, Serins, Greenfinches, Goldfinches, Linnets and Crossbills.

The local mammals include genets, beech martens, foxes and badgers.

Access

There are various points of access (see map), but the easiest are the two off the A-92N Guadix–Baza road. The entry points are well signposted; the more northerly of the two is better and a complete circle can be made back to Baza. There are a variety of roads, which then degenerate into tracks, running through the area and which are worth following. The passability of these without a 4WD vehicle and the necessary ground clearance cannot always be guaranteed however. In particular, it is worth trying the local road GR-800 which runs from Caniles to the

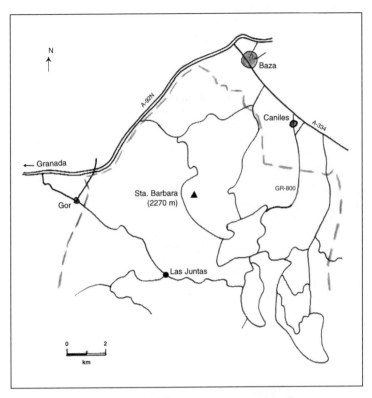

A-92 near Abla and right through the centre of the area. Another area to try is the road up from Gor to Las Juntas, which also leads to the information centre.

Calendar

All year: Golden Eagle, Peregrine, Common Kestrel, Red-legged Partridge, Eagle Owl, Little Owl, Tawny Owl, Green Woodpecker, Crested Lark, Thekla Lark, Wren, Black Redstart, Robin, Stonechat, Dartford Warbler, Firecrest, Southern Grey Shrike, Carrion Crow, Chaffinch, Serin, Greenfinch, Goldfinch, Linnet, Crossbill.

Breeding season: Egyptian Vulture, Cuckoo, Turtle Dove, Scops Owl, Hoopoe, Bee-eater, Black-eared Wheatear, Melodious Warbler, Bonelli's Warbler, Spotted Flycatcher.

HOYA DE BAZA

Status: No special protection.

Site description

This is a very large, flat, semi-arid depression of over 80,000 ha to the north of Baza. The area can be split into two parts. West of the road between Baza and Benamaurel there is greater agricultural activity and a larger number of trees. East of the road there is a much wilder and drier part, with less agriculture, much more low scrub and tamarisks, and with occasional watercourses with some trees, mostly poplars and higher tamarisks. There are plans to irrigate this latter area but, given the scarcity of rainfall recently, these irrigation plans may be a long time in coming to fruition, which is good news for the birds there.

Species

This site is not as good as the Guadix depression (GR4), which means that you have to work harder for the desired species. However, the Hoya de Baza does hold an interesting variety and it is regarded as one of the best areas in Spain for Lesser Short-toed Larks. The site can be split into three habitats.

Calandra Larks

The steppe and arid areas hold such typical open-country species as Little Bustards, a small population of Black-bellied Sandgrouse in the driest areas, and Stone Curlews, which should be searched for on the edges of the more open agricultural areas given over to cereals. Tawny Pipits also occur in small numbers in this area. Calandra Larks are abundant and two other larks, Lesser Short-toed and Dupont's, are the major attractions. Lesser Short-toed Larks are abundant but Dupont's Lark has only a small population. These two larks should be searched for in the driest areas. The typical raptor is Montagu's Harrier, although there are few pairs.

The tamarisks and areas with few trees, such as olives, offer Great Spotted Cuckoos, Hoopoes, Rollers, Bee-eater, Nightingales and Melodious Warblers, while in the more open areas there are numerous Black Wheatears, Black-eared Wheatears and Corn Buntings.

The paucity of water means that the course of the Río Baza, with greater vegetation and trees, also holds Golden Orioles, more Nightingales and Melodious Warblers. Red-rumped Swallows occur, there are some Iberian-race Yellow Wagtails, and Ravens and Magpies are generally common, the latter attracting small numbers of the Great Spotted Cuckoos which parasitise them.

Timing
The best time is undoubtedly spring, before the end of April, when the cereals are not yet sufficiently high to conceal the bustards, the larks are highly vocal and the heat does not strike so hard before mid-morning. Visit preferably in the first three hours after dawn.

Access
Turn northwards off the main road (A92N) in the town of Baza following signs for Benamaurel and Castilléjar. There is a crossroads after about 5 km where there are signs marked 'Canal de Jabalcón — camino de servicio'. Here you can turn left for Baños de Zújar or right to follow the track along the side of the irrigation channel. This right-hand track is more interesting and makes a full loop of some 11.5 km, eventually coming back onto the main road. The first stop is after less than 2 km when the land rises slightly to the right of the track where there are some scattered tamarisks. These can be investigated as they

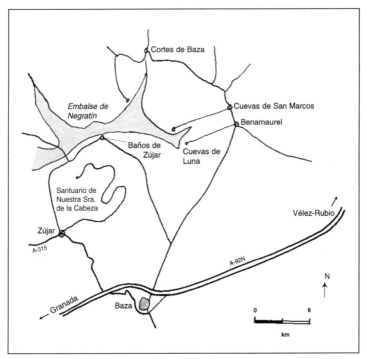

often hold some species of interest, and the opportunity can be taken to scan across the area to the north from a slightly higher vantage point.

Further on the track rises and the land becomes positively arid, with only low scrub by way of vegetation. There are a whole series of disused troglodyte dwellings hacked out of the rock which has a partial 'badlands' aspect, with low dry areas between. It is worth exploring these tracts on foot for some distance, stopping and listening from time to time.

After about 10 km you come to the Río Baza, the road dropping down to cross it at a ford. The river course is lined with willows and some poplars, as well as much more abundant vegetation in general, and this too is worth a look. After another kilometre the track drops down sharply to another watercourse, often dry, with a ford. From here you can turn left to regain the road, or continue on further. The left-hand road, to the Baños de Zújar, crosses a more agricultural region and is less interesting.

Calendar

All year: Little Bustard, Stone Curlew, Black-bellied Sandgrouse, Dupont's Lark, Calandra Lark, Lesser Short-toed Lark, Crested Lark, Black Wheatear, Magpie, Raven, Corn Bunting.

Breeding season: Montagu's Harrier, Great Spotted Cuckoo, Roller, Hoopoe, Bee-eater, Red-rumped Swallow, Yellow Wagtail, Tawny Pipit, Nightingale, Black-eared Wheatear, Northern Wheatear.

JAÉN PROVINCE

Jaén has been overlooked to some extent by birders, probably because it lacks the habitat diversity of other provinces. The avifaunal interest is centred on the birds of the sierras and woodlands, chiefly raptors and passerines. Nevertheless, the species lists show that some of the sites have much to recommend them.

Cazorla (J1) is a lovely site scenically and well worth a visit, although it gets very busy with tourists at certain times of year. The three reservoirs of the upper Guadalquivir (J6) may also be visited if you are visiting Cazorla, although they offer nothing which cannot be found elsewhere. A couple of days may be spent profitably visiting Aldeaquemada (J2), Despeñaperros (J3) and the Sierra de Andújar (J4), especially if you are travelling on the N-IV in this province. The Sierra Mágina (J5) is a pleasant site and worth a detour if you are in the vicinity but it does not otherwise warrant special attention.

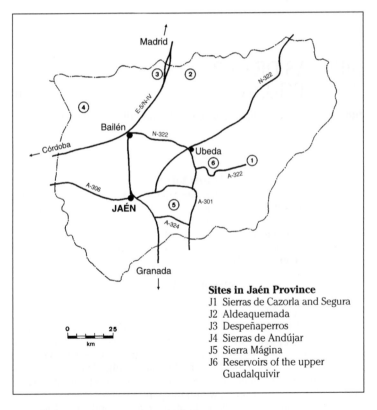

Sites in Jaén Province
J1 Sierras de Cazorla and Segura
J2 Aldeaquemada
J3 Despeñaperros
J4 Sierras de Andújar
J5 Sierra Mágina
J6 Reservoirs of the upper
      Guadalquivir

Maps
Mapa Provincial Jaén, IGN, 1:200,000.
Plaza & Janes Euromapa, Andalucía Oriental, 1:300,000.

Getting there

The E-5/N-IV, Autovía de Andalucía, connects the province with Madrid to the north and Córdoba, Sevilla and Cádiz to the west. At Bailén this road is linked by another motorway, the E-902/N-323, to Granada, where it connects with the A-92, which runs east/west across lower Andalucía. The N-322 gives access from Bailén to the northeast of the province and thence to Albacete and beyond.

Where to stay

There are reasonably good hotel, lodging and camping facilities, mainly centred on the Cazorla region. There are often small hotels or pensiones in some of the smaller towns, such as Andújar. In Cazorla itself (J1) there is a wide range of accommodation from which to select, ranging from the expensive Parador Nacional in Cazorla village to reasonably adequate pensiones. These latter are often noisy with school children on springtime excursions. There are controlled campsites within the park. Much of the accommodation is full between April and September and so should be booked well in advance. The campsites in particular are usually packed in July and August.

SIERRAS DE CAZORLA AND SEGURA   J1

Status: Parque natural, 214,300 ha. ZEPA and Biosphere reserve.

Information

There is a local tourist office in the village of Cazorla (www.cazorla. com.turismo) which supplies the Guía Práctica, a very useful combined information sheet and road map. There are also two interpretation and information centres, in the south at 'Torre del Vinagre', at Km 18 on the road from Cazorla to the El Tranco reservoir, and in the north at Río Borosa near Torres de Albánchez.

Site description

This is where the Río Guadalquivir is born. It first flows northeast from the Sierra de Cazorla but is diverted westwards by the Sierra de Segura, to meander through Córdoba and Sevilla provinces to the Atlantic. The nascent Guadalquivir is fed by innumerable rivulets and streams which descend steep-sided, forested valleys and ravines on the flanks of four sierras; Cazorla, Segura, del Pozo and de la Cabrilla. The highest summits of these reach altitudes of over 2000 m (6500 feet). This is a reservoir, the Embalse de Tranco, within the park.

The limestone terrain includes numerous gorges and cliffs. There are extensive forests of black, Aleppo and maritime pines as well as mixed woodlands, of encinas, olives and junipers. The varied and diverse flora includes at least 26 endemics including the Cazorla violet. There is also an endemic reptile, Valverde's lizard.

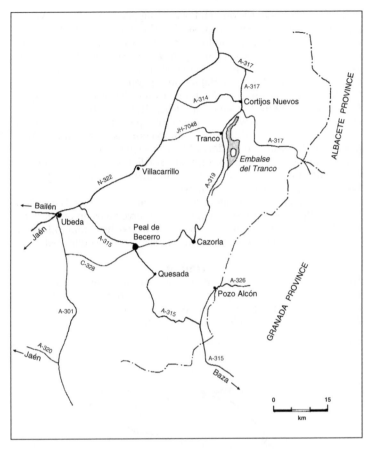

The climate is very variable. It rains frequently in spring and into early summer. Frosts are common in winter and even as late as early May. Snow is not infrequent and indeed may block the roads in the upper reaches as late as the end of April. By contrast, it is extremely hot and dry in summer, the heat sometimes triggering violent storms, with accompanying thunder and lightning, which often cause forest fires.

Species

The area is good for birds of prey. The star among these used to be the Lammergeier, the famous *Quebrantahuesos* or 'bone-breaker', but regrettably these have not bred since the late 1980s, although there are occasional records of immature birds. A Lammergeier reintroduction project, involving captive rearing, has been initiated, although this had not yet met with much success by 2000. A second captive-breeding project, for Spanish Imperial Eagles, was started locally in 2000, using birds rescued from illegal captivity. Fortunately most of the raptors of Cazorla are not under lock-and-key. The regulars include nesting Red Kites, Egyptian Vultures, Griffon Vultures, Short-toed Eagles, Golden Eagles, Booted Eagles, Bonelli's Eagles, Goshawks, Sparrowhawks, Peregrines, Lesser Kestrels and Common Kestrels. Black Vultures are seen occasionally.

The forests of both Cazorla and Segura support Turtle Doves, Wood-pigeons, Firecrests, Great Tits, Coal Tits, Crested Tits, Nuthatches and Crossbills. Lesser Spotted Woodpeckers occur with some regularity here; this is a very local species in our region. Various species of warblers are to be found at the lower levels including Melodious, Spectacled, Orphean and Bonelli's Warblers. Higher up, the open pastures hold Quail and Red-legged Partridges, Cirl Buntings and Rock Buntings. Alpine Accentors, Northern Wheatears and Rock Thrushes also breed on the high tops. Carrion Crows, an uncommon species in southern Spain, occur occasionally as well as the common corvids. Azure-winged Magpies are at the eastern boundary of their Iberian range here.

The Embalse del Tranco supports small numbers of waterfowl, chiefly Mallard, Black-necked Grebes and Little Grebes. Great Crested Grebes also occur occasionally in winter.

The local mammals include Spanish ibex and (introduced) mouflon, both usually difficult to see except in the reserve areas. In contrast, fallow deer (introduced) and red deer are everywhere and wild boar flourish to the point of being a positive nuisance in the cultivated areas.

Timing

The area attracts huge numbers of visitors from Easter onwards every weekend. In July and (especially) August the park is saturated with humans and their vehicles. Therefore, it is best to visit between mid-April and early June and from September to early November.

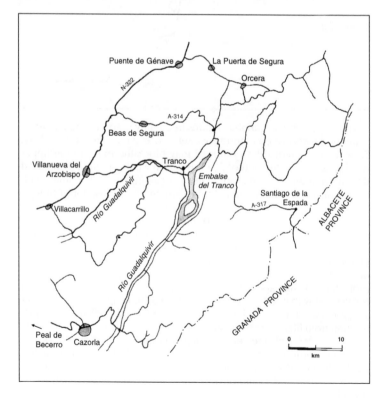

Access

Map 1 is schematic and shows the main points of access into this very large area. Map 2 shows the principal area of the park in greater detail. The most useful entry point of entry is through the village of Cazorla itself, although this is subject to considerable traffic jams at weekends and during holiday periods.

Calendar

All year: Little Grebe, Black-necked Grebe, Mallard, Griffon Vulture, Common Buzzard, Golden Eagle, Bonelli's Eagle, Goshawk, Sparrowhawk, Peregrine, Common Kestrel, Red-legged Partridge, Rock Dove, Woodpigeon, Eagle Owl, Little Owl, Tawny Owl, Green Woodpecker, Great Spotted Woodpecker, Lesser Spotted Woodpecker, Crag Martin, Woodlark, Grey Wagtail, Dipper, Wren, Alpine Accentor, Black Redstart, Black Wheatear, Stonechat, Blue Rock Thrush, Mistle Thrush, Dartford Warbler, Blackcap, Firecrest, Crested Tit, Coal Tit, Great Tit, Nuthatch, Short-toed Treecreeper, Jay, Magpie, Red-billed Chough, Jackdaw, Carrion Crow, Raven, Chaffinch, Serin, Linnet, Crossbill, Cirl Bunting, Rock Bunting.

Breeding season: Red Kite, Black Kite, Egyptian Vulture, Booted Eagle, Quail, Turtle Dove, Cuckoo, Scops Owl, Pallid Swift, Alpine Swift, Bee-eater, Hoopoe, Wryneck, Barn Swallow, Red-rumped Swallow, Nightingale, Rock Thrush, Melodious Warbler, Spectacled Warbler, Subalpine Warbler, Orphean Warbler, Bonelli's Warbler, Spotted Flycatcher, Golden Oriole, Woodchat Shrike.

Winter: Great Crested Grebe, Grey Heron, Teal, Black Vulture, Redwing, Common Chiffchaff.

ALDEAQUEMADA   J2

Status: Includes the Paraje Natural, Cascada de Cimbarra, 534 ha. ZEPA.

Site description

This is a part of the Sierra Morena, to the east of Despeñaperros. The landscape is quite deeply eroded within the general area of Aldeaquemada ('burnt village'), with ravines and waterfalls along the course of the Río Guarrizas, but it is rather more gentle elsewhere. The most spectacular of the waterfalls is the Cascada de Cimbarra, which tumbles from a great height into a deep pool. There is a variety of vegetation with mixed woodlands of encinas and cork oaks, pine plantations and expanses of Mediterranean scrub.

Species

This area has a wide variety of species. Nesting raptors include Griffon Vultures and one or two pairs of Black Vultures, all five eagles, Common Buzzards, Peregrines and Common Kestrels. Other raptors, such as Black Kites, occur on passage. Black Storks also nest within the area and there are breeding populations of Eagle, Little and Scops Owls. Alpine Swifts are commonly around the higher, more rugged areas, as well as both Pallid and Common Swifts. Blue Rock Thrushes are widespread and the more elusive Rock Thrushes also breed at the higher levels. The clear waters of the rivers host Dippers, Kingfishers and Grey Wagtails. Nightingales are common along any watercourses in spring and sing at all hours.

The diverse woodlands support a considerable variety of species. Short-toed Treecreepers and Nuthatches are common. There is an abundance of tits and warblers, these last including Spectacled and Subalpine Warblers. Southern Grey and Woodchat Shrikes are not uncommon. There is a variety of corvids including Azure-winged Magpies. Crossbills breed and both Siskins and a few Bullfinches occur in winter. Rock Buntings are common.

Timing

The climate can be relatively harsh in winter when the minor roads are occasionally closed by snow, although this is much less frequent now than hitherto. The best time to visit the area for maximum variety of species is in spring and early summer, between late April and July. It is at its best in the first hours of the day, especially after mid-June when it can get very hot later.

Access

The area is easily accessed from the E-5/N-IV, the Autovía de Andalucía. Leave the motorway eastwards, either at Santa Elena on the J-6120 or

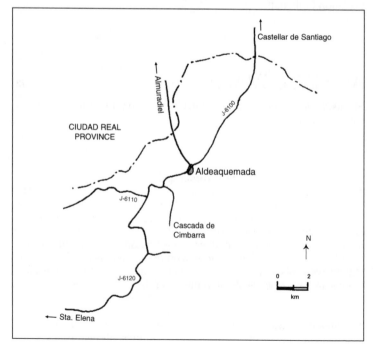

from within the Despeñaperros pass itself, at Estación de las Correderas. (This second road is only accessible from the northbound carriageway and also gives only northbound access to the motorway). Whichever entry point you choose, head for Aldeaquemada. If you enter from the south it is worth stopping in the area between the Arroyo de Lora and the impressively named Arroyo de la Hoz de las Gargantas. The Cascada de Cimbarra is reached by driving south from the J-6110, just west of Aldeaquemada.

Calendar

All year: Black Vulture, Griffon Vulture, Common Buzzard, Spanish Imperial Eagle, Golden Eagle, Bonelli's Eagle, Goshawk, Sparrowhawk, Peregrine, Eagle Owl, Little Owl, Tawny Owl, Kingfisher, Crag Martin, Green Woodpecker, Great Spotted Woodpecker, Thekla Lark, Crested Lark, Grey Wagtail, Dipper, Wren, Dunnock, Robin, Black Redstart, Stonechat, Black Wheatear, Blue Rock Thrush, Mistle Thrush, Dartford Warbler, Blackcap, Firecrest, Crested Tit, Coal Tit, Blue Tit, Great Tit, Short-toed Treecreeper, Southern Grey Shrike, Jay, Azure-winged Magpie, Magpie, Red-billed Chough, Raven, Chaffinch, Serin, Greenfinch, Goldfinch, Linnet, Crossbill, Rock Bunting.

Breeding season: Short-toed Eagle, Booted Eagle, Black Stork, Cuckoo, Scops Owl, Common Swift, Pallid Swift, Alpine Swift, Bee-eater, Roller, Hoopoe, Woodlark, Nightingale, Rock Thrush, Melodious Warbler, Spectacled Warbler, Subalpine Warbler, Bonelli's Warbler, Golden Oriole, Woodchat Shrike.

Winter: Ring Ouzel, Redwing, Fieldfare, Siskin, Bullfinch.

Passage Periods: Raptors, including Black Kite.

DESPEÑAPERROS   J3

Status: Parque Natural, 7502 ha. ZEPA.

Information

The information centre for this area is at Casa Forestal Valdeazores, ctra. N-IV, Km 243, Santa Elena.

Site description

This is the point in the central sector of the Sierra Morena where the E-5/N-IV Autovía de Andalucía, which runs from Madrid to Cádiz, joins La Mancha, the land of Don Quijote, to Andalucía. The rugged terrain offers a considerable diversity of habitat. There are woodlands of cork oaks, encinas and Lusitanian oaks, as well as stone pines, and also some areas with riverine vegetation and large tracts of cistus scrub.

Species

Breeding raptors include Griffon Vultures, all five eagles, Common Buzzards, Goshawks, Peregrines and Common Kestrels. Other raptors, such as Black Kites, may be seen during migration periods. Scops Owls, Eagle Owls and Little Owls breed within the park. Alpine Swifts are to be found commonly around the higher, more rugged areas, as well as both Pallid Swifts and Common Swifts, along with Blue Rock Thrushes in the ravines and Rock Thrushes on the peaks. Dippers and Kingfishers occur along the rivers and Grey Wagtails and Nightingales are common.

There is a considerable variety of woodland species. Green Woodpeckers, Great Spotted Woodpeckers, Short-toed Treecreepers and Nuthatches all occur. There is an abundance of tits, warblers and finches. Southern Grey and Woodchat Shrikes are not uncommon. The

Azure-winged Magpie

various corvids include Ravens, Red-billed Choughs, Jackdaws and Azure-winged Magpies, these last often being seen from the road when you drive through the pass. Rock Buntings occur in some numbers and are to be found scavenging in the car parks in winter.

Apart from the birds, there is a variety of interesting mammals, although seeing species such as wolf, lynx or mongoose would be a very large stroke of luck. On the other hand, the chances of encountering wild boar or red deer are much greater.

Timing

The climate in this area can be harsh in winter and it is not unknown for the pass to be snowbound on occasion. The area offers a maximum variety of species in spring and early summer, between late April and July. It is at its best in the first five hours of the day, especially after mid-June when the heat strikes hard later.

Access

The E-5/N-IV divides as it goes through Despeñaperros. There are regrettably few tracks within the area and none from the eastern (northbound) carriageway, although the first few kilometres of the J-6110 towards Aldeaquemada cross the easterly section of the park. There are one or two stopping places northbound but these are frequently occu-

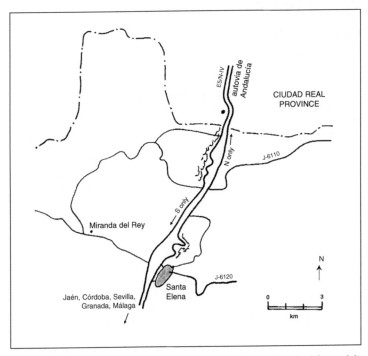

pied by other vehicles. In fact, if you are northbound and wish to visit the area it will unfortunately be necessary to enter Ciudad Real province first and do a U-turn on to the southbound carriageway there. The southbound carriageway offers more opportunities for stopping and gives access to westward tracks. The most westerly part of the park is accessible via two tracks from Miranda del Rey.

Calendar

All year: Griffon Vulture, Goshawk, Sparrowhawk, Common Buzzard, Spanish Imperial Eagle, Golden Eagle, Bonelli's Eagle, Common Kestrel, Peregrine, Eagle Owl, Little Owl, Tawny Owl, Kingfisher, Crag Martin, Green Woodpecker, Great Spotted Woodpecker, Thekla Lark, Crested Lark, Grey Wagtail, Dipper, Wren, Dunnock, Robin, Black Redstart, Stonechat, Black Wheatear, Blue Rock Thrush, Mistle Thrush, Cetti's Warbler, Dartford Warbler, Blackcap, Firecrest, Crested Tit, Coal Tit, Blue Tit, Great Tit, Short-toed Treecreeper, Southern Grey Shrike, Jay, Azure-winged Magpie, Magpie, Red-billed Chough, Raven, Chaffinch, Serin, Greenfinch, Goldfinch, Linnet, Crossbill, Rock Bunting.

Breeding season: Short-toed Eagle, Booted Eagle, Cuckoo, Scops Owl, Common Swift, Pallid Swift, Alpine Swift, Bee-eater, Roller, Hoopoe, Woodlark, Red-rumped Swallow, Nightingale, Rock Thrush, Melodious Warbler, Subalpine Warbler, Bonelli's Warbler, Golden Oriole, Woodchat Shrike.

Winter: Ring Ouzel, Redwing, Fieldfare, Siskin, Brambling, Bullfinch.

Passage periods: Raptors.

SIERRAS DE ANDÚJAR

Status: Parque Natural, 68,000 ha. ZEPA.

Site description

This area includes a large sector of the central Sierra Morena, the extensive east/west line of mountains, of modest altitude, which divides Andalucía from the rest of Spain. The Sierra de Andújar, which is adjacent to the Parque Natural de Cardeña y Montoro (CO11), covers a 70-km stretch of the range. The highest point is about 1290 m above sea level. The park boasts some of the most heavily wooded areas of the whole of the Sierra Morena, dominated by cork oaks, Lusitanian oaks, encinas and stone pines, as well as well-developed Mediterranean scrub. This is in fact one of the best preserved surviving expanses of Mediterranean forest in Spain.

Species

This area is of great importance for its diversity of breeding raptors which includes Black Vultures, Griffon Vultures, very probably Egyptian Vultures, all five eagles, Common Buzzards and both Red and Black Kites. Owls are represented by Scops, Eagle, Little and Tawny Owls.

The species list for the woodlands is very similar to that of the adjacent Sierras de Cardeña y Montoro (CO11). However, the relative lack of open spaces means fewer larks, pipits and wagtails. The common chats and thrushes are all present They are joined in winter by consid-

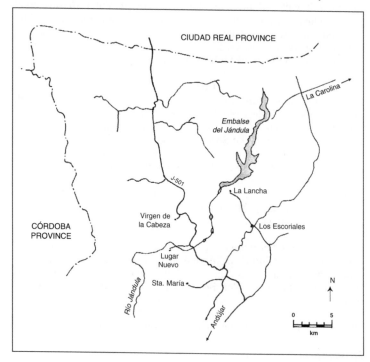

228

erable numbers of Song Thrushes and the much scarcer Redwings. There is a full range of warblers in the woodlands. Golden Orioles are not infrequent in spring and summer in suitable areas. Both the common shrikes occur. Corvids are represented by Azure-winged Magpies and Magpies, together with the ever-present Ravens.

Timing
The area is worth visiting year-round but is at its best in spring and early summer, between early March and July. It can get very cold in winter and considerable snowfalls are not unknown. A full day is necessary to do justice to this extensive area.

Access
The J-501 traverses the park north/south. It is easiest to access from the south, at Andujar on the E-5/N-IV. There are plenty of tracks off this road from which to explore the area. The surroundings of the Santuario de la Virgen de la Cabeza are also worth visiting. A turn off eastwards from the J-501, about 15 km north of Andújar, and then northwest for 10 km from Los Escoriales, gives access to the very isolated Embalse del Jándula.

Calendar
All year: Black Vulture, Griffon Vulture, Red Kite, Goshawk, Common Buzzard, Spanish Imperial Eagle, Golden Eagle, Bonelli's Eagle, Peregrine, Common Kestrel, Eagle Owl, Tawny Owl, Green Woodpecker, Great Spotted Woodpecker, Crested Lark, Thekla Lark, Meadow Pipit, Grey Wagtail, Robin, Black Redstart, Mistle Thrush, Dartford Warbler, Sardinian Warbler, Blackcap, Firecrest, Nuthatch, Short-toed Treecreeper, Southern Grey Shrike, Azure-winged Magpie, Magpie, Raven, Crossbill.

Breeding season: Egyptian Vulture, Black Kite, Short-toed Eagle, Booted Eagle, Roller, Hoopoe, Bee-eater, Nightingale, Subalpine Warbler, Spotted Flycatcher, Golden Oriole, Woodchat Shrike.

Winter: White Wagtail, Song Thrush, Redwing.

Passage periods: Black Kite, Pied Flycatcher.

SIERRA MÁGINA
J5

Status: Parque Natural, 19,995 ha.

Information
There is a visitors centre, 'Castillo de Jódar', in calle Alhori, in the village of Jódar.

Site description
This is one of the typical sierras of southern Jaén, distinguished by the highest peak in the province, Pico Mágina (2167 m). The limestone terrain includes numerous cliffs. The lower reaches, up to about 1300 m, have woods of encinas and Lusitanian oaks, with a diverse shrub understorey. Higher up, there are coniferous woodlands, interspersed with open grassy areas. The whole area is of botanical interest and supports several endemic species.

Species
This site is worth a visit if you wish to sample as many of the Andalucian sierras as possible. As ever, the raptors claim attention and the region is a stronghold of Bonelli's Eagles. A further 17 raptor species have been recorded, including Griffon Vultures, Golden Eagles, Short-toed Eagles, Peregrines and both kestrel species. The resident Eagle, Barn, Tawny and Little Owls are joined by Scops Owls in the breeding season.

Other characteristic species, at the lower and intermediate levels, include both Southern Grey Shrikes, which are reasonably frequent, and Woodchat Shrikes, which are common. Bee-eaters wheel noisily overhead. Golden Orioles occur along the wooded valleys where there are poplars. The ravine and cliff areas support Black Redstarts, Black Wheatears, Blue Rock Thrushes and Red-billed Choughs, with Northern Wheatears and Rock Thrushes at the higher elevations. Ring Ouzels occur regularly in winter. Rock Sparrows and Rock Buntings are common.

Access
The park is immediately southeast of Jaén city. The E-902/N-323 motorway skirts the western side of the park. The northern sector may be reached by taking the A-316 eastwards from Jaén to Mancha Real and then continuing towards Torres and Albánchez de Ubeda on the local

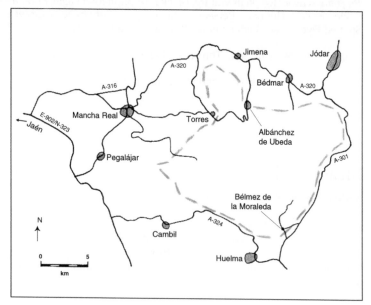

roads. The region may be viewed from the lookout point at Albánchez. It is possible to continue eastwards through Bédmar and then to head south on the A-301 to the southern sector. The A-324, which also connects with the E-902/N-323, gives access to the southern parts of the park. The minor roads around Bélmez and south from Bédmar are worth visiting.

Timing
Spring visits are recommended but the area can be rewarding at any time of year. Winters may be cold, with snow.

Calendar
All year: Griffon Vulture, Common Buzzard, Golden Eagle, Bonelli's Eagle, Common Kestrel, Lesser Kestrel, Peregrine, Woodpigeon, Barn Owl, Eagle Owl, Little Owl, Tawny Owl, Crag Martin, Crested Lark, Thekla Lark, Black Redstart, Black Wheatear, Blue Rock Thrush, Mistle Thrush, Blackcap, Short-toed Treecreeper, Jay, Magpie, Red-billed Chough, Jackdaw, Raven, Chaffinch, Serin, Greenfinch, Goldfinch, Linnet, Rock Bunting.

Breeding season: Short-toed Eagle, Booted Eagle, Turtle Dove, Scops Owl, Alpine Swift, Bee-eater, Hoopoe, Nightingale, Rock Thrush, Subalpine Warbler, Spotted Flycatcher, Golden Oriole, Woodchat Shrike.

Winter: Ring Ouzel, Redwing.

RESERVOIRS OF THE UPPER GUADALQUIVIR   J6
Status: Paraje Natural, Alto Guadalquivir, 663 ha.

Site description
These three reservoirs are spread out along about 20 km of the upper reaches of the Río Guadalquivir. Their importance is due to the general lack of wetlands in Jaén province and they attract a range of breeding, passage and wintering waterfowl. The largest is Puente de la Cerrada (A, with a surface area of 359 ha), followed by Doña Aldonza (B, 320 ha) and Pedro Marín (C, 297 ha). Water levels are relatively stable and so all three are amply fringed with reeds, bulrushes and tamarisks.

Species
The main attraction of these reservoirs is the presence of breeding Purple Herons at Pedro Marin and Doña Aldonza, Purple Gallinules at Pedro Marín and Ferruginous Ducks and Marsh Harriers at Pedro Marin and Doña Aldonza. Other breeding species include Grey Herons, Little Egrets, Shovelers, Pochards and Black-winged Stilts, as well as more

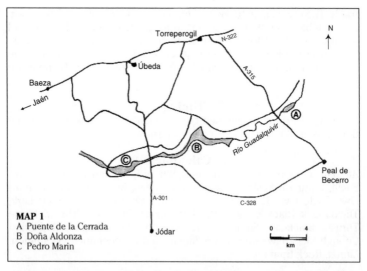

MAP 1
A Puente de la Cerrada
B Doña Aldonza
C Pedro Marin

widespread species such as Coots and Moorhens. The reedbeds have breeding populations of Savi's, Reed and Great Reed Warblers. Red-crested Pochards and waders are frequent in winter, although the latter are declining since their feeding areas are becoming progressively more overgrown. Scarcer species turn up occasionally and there are isolated records of both Ruddy Shelducks and Slender-billed Gulls. Penduline Tits occur in the fringing vegetation, especially in winter, and may breed.

Timing
The area is worth visiting at any time of year. A telescope is most useful.

Access
The three reservoirs are in the centre of the province, between Jódar and Becerro to the south and Úbeda to the north. The A-301 local road between Úbeda and Jódar, gives access to both the northern and southern sides of the complex. Map 1 shows the overall position of the reservoirs. Map 2 shows access to the individual reservoirs. This is somewhat limited but all three may be viewed from their respective dams.

Calendar
All year: Little Egret, Grey Heron, Mallard, Ferruginous Duck, Shoveler, Pochard, Coot, Moorhen, Purple Gallinule, Penduline Tit.

Breeding season: Little Bittern, Purple Heron, Marsh Harrier, Black-winged Stilt, Savi's Warbler, Reed Warbler, Great Reed Warbler, Melodious Warbler.

Winter: Gadwall, Teal, Wigeon, Pintail, Red-crested Pochard, Avocet, Lapwing, Dunlin, Common Snipe, Jack Snipe, Black-tailed Godwit, Common Redshank, gulls, Bluethroat, Penduline Tit.

Passage periods: Osprey, Black Kite, waders.

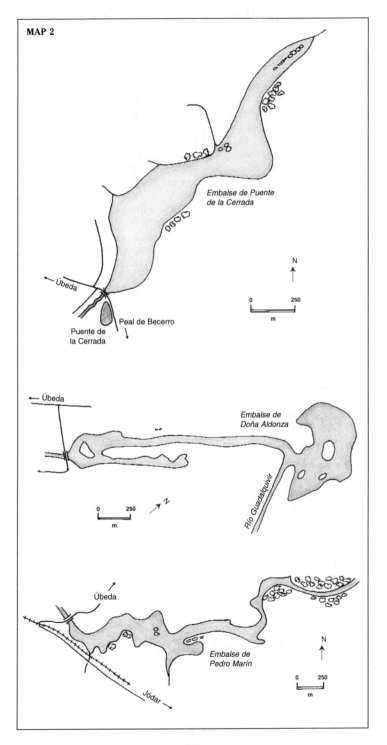

MAP 2

Embalse de Puente
de la Cerrada

N

Úbeda

0   250
m

Peal de Becerro

Puente de
la Cerrada

Úbeda

Embalse de
Doña Aldonza

Río Guadalquivir

0   250
m

N

Úbeda

Embalse de
Pedro Marín

Jódar

N

0   250
m

ALMERÍA PROVINCE

Almería province has been largely neglected by birders, although it has a great deal to offer, including sierras (AL1, AL6, AL7), dunes (AL2), some wetlands (AL3, AL4) and the excellent birding at the salinas (AL1, AL2). This is Europe at its most arid: Almería has expanses of true steppe and semi-desert (AL5, AL6), the home of Trumpeter Finch and several other elusive species. The shortage of water thwarted agricultural efforts until the introduction of the ubiquitous and unsightly plastic greenhouses. These now cover hundreds of hectares and allow crops to be raised on otherwise unsuitable terrain, but to the huge detriment of the original flora and fauna. Some interesting sites are under threat from building and indeed the salinas of Guardias Viejas have now disappeared under a huge development.

A stay in the province will undoubtedly be very worthwhile although, in the steppe areas especially, you may well have to work hard to locate some of the species.

Sites in Almería Province
AL1 Cabo de Gata
AL2 Punta Entinas–Roquetas de Mar
AL3 Cañada de las Norias
AL4 Albufera de Adra
AL5 Desierto de Tabernas
AL6 Sierra Alhamilla
AL7 Sierra de María
AL8 Río Antas
AL9 Río Almanzora

Maps
Mapa Provincial Almería, IGN, 1:200,000.
Plaza & Janes Euromapa of Andalucía oriental (1:300.000).
A 1:50,000 map of Cabo de Gata is available.

Getting there
The E-15 *autovía*, which unites with the N-340 in some sections, allows excellent transit across the south and east of the province and gives access to the network of minor roads serving the Cabo de Gata region and the inland sites. The A-92N runs across the northern section of the province between Murcia and Granada. Almería airport is an increasingly popular destination in southern Spain and is the obvious arrival point for visitors to the region.

Where to stay
There are ample tourist facilities at Roquetas de Mar, which is the centre for coastal tourism and which has the excellent saltpans of Salinas Viejas and Salinas de Cerrillo (AL2-B) right on its doorstep. Roquetas is also fairly well placed to allow you to reach nearly all the sites in the province within two hours at the most. There are other places to stay inland, and on the eastern coast in the San José, Mojácar and Carboneras areas, but these resorts are well away from the main sites.

Note that between July and early September the Roquetas/Almerimar areas, as well as Cabo de Gata, are packed with holiday-makers and that it can be very hot. However, as this is a fairly slack time, ornithologically speaking, it is not too important.

CABO DE GATA   AL1

Status: Parque Natural (land and sea), 49,696 ha. ZEPA. Biosphere Reserve of UNESCO.

General description
This is a very large area which extends from the western side of Cabo de Gata around to the eastern coast as far north as Carboneras. The three best sites are the sierra of Cabo de Gata, the salinas of Cabo de Gata, and a series of steppe areas, of which Las Amoladeras (B) is recommended as being the most productive ornithologically as well as reasonably accessible. This should not deter you from trying some of the eastern areas of the park, especially between San José and Las Negras in which 'surprise' species, such as Trumpeter Finch, are often encountered. The protected area has some 40 km of coastline and also includes the sub-littoral zone to a mile offshore. The extreme aridity of the area is reflected in the diverse community of xerophytic plants, which includes a number of endemics.

Timing

The whole area can be visited profitably at any time of year. However, the very high temperatures and crowds of tourists in July and August combine to make these two months the least attractive.

The sierra and steppe areas are best visited in spring and early summer. The salinas are most productive from March to mid- or even late May, and again from late August to October, and also in winter, although they are far from empty in midsummer. In summer the best birding is to be had in the early mornings and late evenings, especially in the steppes and sierra. The middle of the day is very unproductive as birds also shelter from the daunting heat. Heat-haze must also be taken into account at the salinas: the shimmering makes optical instruments useless at any distance.

One should definitely remember Mr Coward's dictum about mad dogs and Englishmen going out in the midday sun. Take along a good supply of water as dehydration is insidious, especially as it can be very windy as well in this region and you can lose liquid very rapidly.

A Sierra de Cabo de Gata

Site description

The sierra, which is mostly of volcanic origin, comes right down to the coast and, birds apart, is scenically most attractive. It is an intensely arid area as rainfall averages only some 120 mm per year, the lowest in Europe.

Species

The coastal region holds small colonies of Yellow-legged Gulls. Shags may breed along the coast between the lighthouse and northwards beyond San José. There are very small and isolated colonies of European Storm-petrels. Seawatching from the tip of Cabo de Gata often produces Cory's Shearwaters and Balearic Shearwaters, as well as a variety of gulls and terns and occasional skuas during the migration periods. The only sea duck to occur is the Common Scoter and then only in small numbers. Wintering auks are represented mainly by Razorbills but Puffins are seen occasionally.

It is a good area for raptors, with a few breeding pairs of Bonelli's Eagles and Booted Eagles, as well as Lesser Kestrels and Peregrines. Eleonora's Falcons occur as scarce migrants, chiefly in the autumn. Eagle Owls also breed in the area. The sierra holds a considerable population of Trumpeter Finches. There is also a small population of Dupont's Larks, principally on the western side in the steppe area, although they have been recorded in the Las Negras area outside the breeding season. Thekla and Crested Larks are also present.

Access

The visitors centre (centro de visitantes) is at Las Almoladeras on the Almería/Cabo de Gata road at Km 7. The main access is from the east of Almería town off the autovía E-15/N-340, doubling back slightly on the N-344 and turning right at any one of the marked junctions for San José or for Cabo de Gata itself. The road to Cabo de Gata takes you past the salinas to the lighthouse and southern tip of the cape. There is a footpath northwards from the lighthouse which eventually arrives at the village of San José. To visit the more northerly and easterly side of the

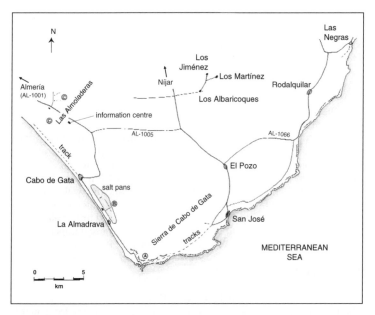

Sierra de Cabo de Gata, follow signs for San José or, further north still, for Las Negras, and explore the various minor roads and tracks throughout the area, such as that up to El Romeral.

B Las Almoladeras

Site description
This is a typical, arid, shore and steppe area, administered as a 'no hunting' area and zoological station by the Consejeria de Medio Ambiente and the S.E.O. It is contiguous with the large steppe area of the Campo de Níjar. The shore and dunes are followed further inland by steppe with low Mediterranean scrub. The scrub growth is typical of arid dune and steppe areas, with no trees, although plantations of agaves from past decades make walking through those areas nearly impossible without risking being spiked to death.

Species
In order to find the birds, stop, look and listen. As the area is very dry, very often, the parts where there is some water are best.

Little Bustards are scarce residents within the reserve but there are significant populations of Stone Curlews and Black-bellied Sandgrouse. Red-necked Nightjars breed but are scarce. Rollers are not uncommon and Bee-eaters and Hoopoes also occur. There is a good variety of larks, one of the site's main attractions. The prize species is the quite elusive Dupont's Lark which is found mainly in the northern section of the reserve in areas of thyme and false esparto grass. Lesser Short-toed Larks are abundant and Short-toed Larks are reasonably common. Both Crested and Thekla Larks also occur, the latter being much more common. Skylarks are winter visitors.

Ring Ouzels are not uncommon in winter, as are Black Redstarts and Robins. Rufous Bush Chats occur with some regularity. Sardinian Warb-

237

lers and Dartford Warblers are moderately common at all seasons, as are Spectacled Warblers in summer and Common Chiffchaffs in winter. Southern Grey Shrikes occur in the few areas with trees or bushes. Trumpeter Finches are mainly winter visitors in moderate numbers, but at least some are present in summer.

Access

This site is highly attractive for the presence of many of the steppe species, although they do take some searching for. Take the local road off the N-344 for Cabo de Gata and San José from the Retamar round-about. At Km 6, after the Retamar roundabout, prepare to turn north onto an asphalted track on the right side of the road. This track goes to the approach radio beacon for Almería airport, 1.4 km from the main road, but you do not need to go all the way up. Park and walk along the tracks off to the right at 300 m and 1000 m, both of which cut through all this area, which includes the best steppe habitat. Further along, on the right side of the road at Km 7, there are some very imposing gates which lead to the information and interpretation centre.

C Salinas de Cabo de Gata

Site description

There is an important area of dunes and steppe some 15 km long on the western side of the park, along the eastern side of Almería bay. Within this area there are some 350 ha of salinas (salt pans). They are a com-mercial operation but, thanks to an agreement between the C.M.A and the owners, Salinera USESA, they also form an ornithological wetland reserve of major importance.

Species

Virtually anything may occur. There are regularly several hundred Greater Flamingos here and these attempt to breed at times. There are Grey Herons, Purple Herons and egrets, as well as migrant White Storks and, occasionally, Black Storks and Cranes. Ospreys occur on migration and some may winter. A variety of ducks winter in the salinas, these including up to several hundred Shelducks. Waders use the salinas as a staging point and virtually any species may be found, this being one of the better sites to find rare waders. Avocets and Black-winged Stilts breed. Wintering and passage waders include Collared Pratincoles, Golden Plovers, Grey Plovers, Lapwings, Curlews, Whimbrels, Oystercatchers and various species of sandpipers and stints. There are usually large numbers of gulls and terns at the appropriate seasons, including large numbers of Audouin's Gulls and occasional Slender-billed Gulls, as well as Black-headed, Yellow-legged and Lesser Black-backed Gulls. Little Terns breed and Sandwich Terns are always pre-sent, while marsh terns occur during the migration periods. Southern Grey Shrikes, Black Redstarts and Thekla Larks are also to be expected in the general area.

Timing

Any time of year is productive, but early morning visits are advised in summer and early autumn as heat shimmer makes viewing difficult later.

Access

The salinas are easily seen from the road after passing the village of Cabo de Gata, where you skirt their northern edge but where stopping is inadvisable. Instead, take the first left turn in the village, to head southwards along the road towards the village of La Almadrava and the cape. The salinas are on the left along this road. There is parking off the road for the easily visible hide which overlooks the salinas. Both pools are visible from the hide.

Do not forget to go on to the village of La Almadrava, at the south end of the salinas. Stop immediately past the last bar on the left and look at the last of the salt pans. This is often very good, sometimes attracting considerable quantities of gulls, especially Audouin's Gulls.

Calendar

All year: Shag, Greater Flamingo, Bonelli's Eagle, Common Kestrel, Peregrine, Red-legged Partridge, Little Bustard, Kentish Plover, Stone Curlew, Black-headed Gull, Yellow-legged Gull, Sandwich Tern, Black-bellied Sandgrouse, Eagle Owl, Little Owl, Dupont's Lark, Crested Lark, Thekla Lark, Crag Martin, Black Redstart, Stonechat, Black Wheatear, Blue Rock Thrush, Cetti's Warbler, Dartford Warbler, Sardinian Warbler, Zitting Cisticola, Southern Grey Shrike, Spanish Sparrow, Linnet, Trumpeter Finch, Rock Bunting, Corn Bunting.

Black Terns and a White-winged Black Tern

Breeding season: Cory's Shearwater, Booted Eagle, Lesser Kestrel, Avocet, Black-winged Stilt, Little Tern, Turtle Dove, Red-necked Nightjar, Common Swift, Pallid Swift, Alpine Swift, Bee-eater, Roller, Hoopoe, Calandra Lark, Red-rumped Swallow, Short-toed Lark, Lesser Short-toed Lark, Black-eared Wheatear, Spectacled Warbler, Spotted Flycatcher, Woodchat Shrike, Cirl Bunting.

Winter: Little Egret, Cattle Egret, Grey Heron, Shelduck, Crane, Grey Plover, Lapwing, Curlew, Whimbrel, waders, Arctic Skua, Mediterranean Gull, Audouin's Gull, Lesser Black-backed Gull, Razorbill, Puffin, Skylark, Meadow Pipit, White Wagtail, Whinchat, Ring Ouzel, Common Chiffchaff.

Passage periods: Cory's Shearwater, Balearic Shearwater, European Storm-petrel, Purple Heron, White Stork, Black Stork, raptors including Osprey and Eleonora's Falcon; Oystercatcher, Collared Pratincole (may breed), waders, Great Skua, Mediterranean Gull, Little Gull, Slender-billed Gull, Audouin's Gull, Gull-billed Tern, Caspian Tern, Common Tern, Whiskered Tern, Black Tern, White-winged Black Tern, swifts and hirundines, Common Redstart, Willow Warbler.

PUNTA ENTINAS–ROQUETAS DE MAR   AL2

Status: The whole 15-km coastal strip is a Paraje Natural, 1949 ha.

Site description

This site consists of the 15-km coastal strip between Punta Sabinar and the salt pans just to the west of Roquetas de Mar. The west of the area comprises expanses of scrub and dunes as well as ponds and areas of saltmarsh. The eastern section has scrub, dunes and salt pans. Regrettably, the disused salt pans at Guardias Viejas have now been built over. This is a major area which should not be missed by anyone visiting eastern Andalucía. It is a superb site which needs at least two days to cover even halfway comprehensively. It also offers several species which can be difficult to find elsewhere but which make themselves visible here relatively readily.

General access

There are two ways of access into the whole area. However, it does not matter from which direction you enter. It is impossible to go along the whole coastal strip and an inland detour is always necessary to get from Punta Entinas to Punta del Sabinar and from there to the salinas near Roquetas (or vice-versa).

From either the Málaga or Almería directions, take the turn off the autovía (E-15) for Almerimar. Park at the the eastern end of Almerimar and go in through the scrub or along the beach to the first ponds. Be aware that this is rather arduous when the heat strikes hard. Alternatively, take the Roquetas road just before Almerimar and continue east. The Roquetas road runs alongside the salinas from Punta del Sabinar onwards and there are places where you can pull off the road and scan the salt pans of Salinas de Cerrillo and Salinas Viejas

If you arrive from the east, head through Roquetas and follow signs for Almerimar and Guardias Viejas, keeping as far to the south as possible. This will also mean that you pass the Salinas Viejas and Salinas de Cerrillos first.

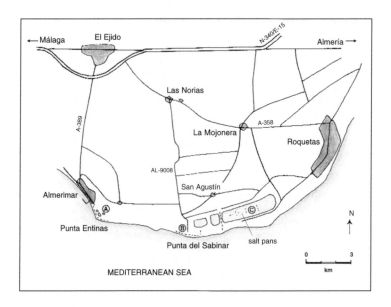

A *Punta Entinas*

Site description
This is the largest natural, seasonal wetland in Almería, consisting of four lagoons set within a littoral steppe zone of dunes fixed by scrub.

Access
There is no specific site access. Park at the extreme western end of Almerimar, after the last hotel, from where the first of the lagoons is visible eastwards. To the best of our knowledge, there are no tracks except a barred and locked one for Medio Ambiente vehicle access only. The two available choices are both likely to require a fair amount of sweat. Go through to the shore and plod along until about level with the first lagoon and then penetrate the scrub. Alternatively you can approach directly following whatever paths you can find.

B *Punta del Sabinar*

Site description
The site features stabilised coastal dunes, with low sandy scrub and the remains of salt pans to the east.

Access
Access to Punta del Sabinar is by heading southwards from Las Norias, Roquetas or San Agustín, until you reach the lighthouse at the point. From here it is simply a matter of walking the area, taking care to cast a look at the dunes and, especially, at the saltmarsh and the area to the north of the lighthouse. It is possible to walk the whole way westwards to Punta Entinas or to the Salinas Viejas and Salinas de Cerrillos along the shore and dunes but this is extremely arduous and will not, normally, produce much more than occurs within a 1-km radius of the lighthouse.

C Salinas Viejas — Salinas de Cerrillo

Site description

This site is the eastern part of the coastal strip between Roquetas de Mar in the east and the saline ponds of Punta Entinas-Punta Sabinar near Almerimar in the west. Apart from the shore and dunes, the main attraction is the two sets of disused salinas (salt pans) in different states of disrepair and of varying salinity. These are the contiguous Salinas Viejas and Salinas de Cerrillos to the west of Roquetas. There is also an interesting coastal zone of small dunes and ponds between these two salinas and the sea.

Access

If coming from the Almerimar direction, access is as described above. If coming from Roquetas, take the coastal track. If coming from Las Norias, cut through by the eastern edge of the football field to the main central track. This track, which is very dusty when dry and very muddy when wet, runs southwest for about 3 km before it comes to a dead end. The salinas are on the inland side. Between the track and the beach there is a sandy area with some bushes and reeds around the flooded gravel pits. It is impossible to exit westwards from the end of the track as it is closed off to vehicles before it reaches the end of these salinas, although you may walk onwards. The track which is shown on various maps as cutting through the salinas is also closed, which means that to go westwards you must go back and around inland. This is no hardship as it means looking over the site again and, very probably, finding something more of interest. The habitat to both sides of the track deserves to be be studied with great care as this is one of the prime areas for birding locally.

Species

The list of breeding species is interesting although not large. A surreal feature is the thriving colony of introduced Mute Swans in the salinas where they have increased from five birds in 1993 to a minimum of 27 in spring 2000. The Salinas de Cerrillos harbour breeding White-headed Ducks when water conditions permit, as well as the less choosy Mallards and, very probably, Pochards. One or two pairs of Marsh Harriers may breed and they certainly occur on migration. Bonelli's Eagles occasionally overfly the sea of plastic greenhouses to hunt in the area. Water Rails probably breed and are certainly present at Salinas Viejas, although seeing one is a matter of luck. Stone Curlews breed in the dunes and sandy areas, especially in the strip between Punta Entinas and Punta del Sabinar, as do Kentish Plovers. Little Ringed Plovers occur and may also breed occasionally. A few pairs of Avocets breed in suitable areas of the salinas, and so do Black-winged Stilts, which are much more common. Some pairs of Little Terns are present each year and may breed in small numbers.

The Iberian race of Yellow Wagtail is common virtually everywhere along this coastal strip. This same area attracts Lesser Short-toed Larks which are common at Punta Entinas and abundant along the track from Roquetas westwards past the Salinas Viejas and Salinas de Cerrillos, making this one of the easiest sites to find this species. There are some resident Stonechats. Cetti's, Reed and Great Reed Warblers all breed in suitable reedy areas.

The salinas also attract numbers of Greater Flamingos, Little Egrets and Grey Herons, plus occasional migrant Purple Herons, Coots and some migrant and wintering ducks, such as Garganey, Teal, the inevitable Mallards and occasional Red-crested Pochards. There are sometimes Common Scoters offshore in winter when there are also often significant numbers of Black-necked Grebes.

The remains of the Salinas Viejas and Salinas de Cerrillos, as well as the lagoons near Almerimar, are of major importance for waders, gulls and terns, with large numbers present at any time of year. The list of migrant and wintering waders is a large one. Cream-coloured Courser has been recorded here. Collared Pratincoles are easily seen in spring as they are common migrants. Ringed Plovers are also common both as migrants and in winter, as are Grey Plovers, which occur in small numbers. Lapwings are frequent in the winter months. A considerable number of sandpipers migrate through the area, including large numbers of Dunlins, Little Stints, Curlew Sandpipers and Redshanks, and lesser numbers of Greenshanks, Green Sandpipers and Wood Sandpipers. There are records of rarer waders such as Temminck's Stints and, infrequently, of Terek Sandpipers and Marsh Sandpipers.

Occasional Great Skuas and Arctic Skuas can be seen from the shore, as can Gannets, Balearic Shearwaters and Cory's Shearwaters in the appropriate seasons. There are thousands of gulls in the migration periods and in winter, as well as considerable numbers of non-breeding immature birds in summer. Mediterranean Gulls are common migrants and winter visitors. Audouin's Gulls occur nearly all year, but especially between April and October, with a few possibly staying all winter. The peak season for Audouin's Gulls is the period July–October. Terns too are common, notably Sandwich Terns which are present all year round. Both Little Terns and Common Terns are regular on migration, as are Gull-billed Terns. Caspian Terns occur occasionally. All three species of marsh terns are to be seen; White-winged Black Terns are most likely in the autumn after easterlies.

As to other species, anything can occur in 'falls' in spring and, to a much lesser extent, in autumn. A few Rollers and, more commonly, Bee-eaters and Hoopoes occur. Crested Larks occur but are outnumbered by the Lesser Short-toed Larks. There are also Short-toed Larks during migration times. Subspecies of Yellow Wagtail, other than of the Iberian race, are frequent in spring, especially after easterly winds. Virtually any species of migrant warbler may turn up during a 'fall'.

Timing

The whole area is of interest at any time of year but it is probably at its best in middle and late spring, from April to mid-May, when there are breeding summer visitors to add to those species which are still migrating north. After that, the next best time is definitely autumn for migration. In winter there are considerable numbers of ducks, waders, gulls and terns. The area is least attractive between early June and early August.

Calendar

All year: Little Egret, Mute Swan, Greater Flamingo, Water Rail, Coot, Avocet, Stone Curlew, Kentish Plover, Dunlin, Redshank, Black-headed Gull, Audouin's Gull, Lesser Black-backed Gull, Yellow-legged Gull, Sandwich Tern, Crested Lark, Stonechat, Cetti's Warbler, Zitting Cisticola, Southern Grey Shrike.

Breeding season: White-headed Duck, Marsh Harrier, Black-winged Stilt, Little Ringed Plover, Little Tern, Bee-eater, Roller, Hoopoe, Lesser Short-toed Lark, Yellow Wagtail, Reed Warbler, Great Reed Warbler, Wood-chat Shrike.

Winter: Gannet, Cattle Egret, Mallard, Red-crested Pochard, Pochard, Shoveler, Common Scoter, Ringed Plover, Grey Plover, Golden Plover, Lapwing, Sanderling, Snipe, Whimbrel, Curlew, Turnstone, Arctic Skua, Mediterranean Gull, Lesser Black-backed Gull, Razorbill, Puffin, Meadow Pipit.

Passage periods: Garganey, Marsh Harrier, Collared Pratincole, Ringed Plover, Knot, Little Stint, Temminck's Stint, Curlew Sandpiper, Ruff, Black-tailed Godwit, Bar-tailed Godwit, Spotted Redshank, Marsh Sandpiper, Greenshank, Green Sandpiper, Wood Sandpiper, Marsh Sandpiper, Common Sandpiper, Great Skua, Little Gull, Slender-billed Gull, Kittiwake, Gull-billed Tern, Caspian Tern, Common Tern, Whiskered Tern, Black Tern, White-winged Black Tern, swifts, Short-toed Lark, hirundines, Northern Wheatear, Black-eared Wheatear, Pied Flycatcher.

CAÑADA DE LAS NORIAS　　　　AL3

Status: Local reserve,130 ha.

Site description

Originally this site was used for soil extraction for the surrounding plastic greenhouses and there is still small scale excavation in the general area. Extraction in the now flooded and overgrown area has ceased. Some of the flooding is because of the high level of the water table and there is naturally more after rains. The extent of flooding heavily governs wintering by ducks and breeding by grebes and waders.

There are two parts to the pit when water levels are low, although it is one unified mass after rains. The shallower western part has emergent reedbeds and tamarisks, and also a considerable beach area attractive to waders during at least some periods of the year. The eastern section has deeper water, generally more reedbeds, and is more suitable for ducks. On the northern side there is dumping of agricultural waste and plastic.

Species

Numbers of Little Grebes and some Black-necked Grebes breed when water levels permit. The most interesting breeding species are White-headed Ducks and Marbled Ducks. These latter are best seen in early spring, when occasional Ferruginous Ducks also occur. This is one of a very few sites in our area where there is a reasonable chance of finding both the latter species. Other breeding ducks include Red-crested Pochards, Pochards and Mallards. Coots breed, as do Moorhens and, very possibly, Purple Gallinules. There are breeding populations of Black-winged Stilts and Avocets, Stone Curlews, Little Ringed Plovers and Kentish Plovers. Rollers and Hoopoes breed in the area as well as a few pairs of Bee-eaters. Breeding larks are represented by Calandra, Crested, Short-toed and Lesser Short-toed Larks. The considerable variety of breeding warblers includes Great Reed and Melodious Warblers.

Ducks and waders are commonest on passage. Passage ducks have included Ruddy Shelducks, Wigeon, Teal, Garganey, Pintail, Shovelers and Ferruginous Ducks, in addition to the breeding species. Wader variety is low during the spring migration but greater during the post-breeding migration when water levels are more favourable for them. The many wader species recorded have included both Little and Temminck's Stints and both Great and Jack Snipe.

Timing
This site is attractive at any time of year. Spring and early summer are best for breeding species and migrant waders. Autumn offers migrant waders and there are interesting ducks, waders and passerines.

Access
The site is just to the east of the village of Las Norias on the A-358 road for La Mojonera. The flooded area is easily visible on the left of the road just outside the village opposite an area of plastic greenhouses. Park on the south side of the road by the plastic greenhouses. Observation of the area is best carried out from the roadside, especially when water-levels are high. Visitors are requested not to go down on foot into the area when it is drier. Even without a telescope, the ducks can be easily seen and give good views.

Please treat this important and sensitive site with care and respect in the interests of conservation.

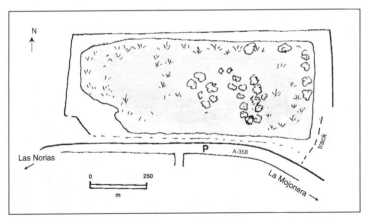

Calendar
All year: Black-necked Grebe, Little Grebe, Mallard, Marbled Duck, Red-crested Pochard, Pochard, White-headed Duck, Bonelli's Eagle, Water Rail, Moorhen, Coot, Purple Gallinule, Kentish Plover, Stone Curlew, Lesser Short-toed Lark, Crested Lark, Zitting Cisticola, Southern Grey Shrike.

Breeding season: Little Bittern, Black-winged Stilt, Avocet, Little Ringed Plover, Turtle Dove, Bee-eater, Roller, Hoopoe, Calandra Lark, Short-toed Lark, Black-eared Wheatear, Reed Warbler, Great Reed Warbler, Melodious Warbler, Woodchat Shrike.

Passage periods: Night Heron, Squacco Heron, Little Egret, Purple Heron, White Stork, Ruddy Shelduck, Garganey, Ferruginous Duck, Black Kite, Marsh Harrier, Sparrowhawk, Osprey, Collared Pratincole, Ringed Plover, Golden Plover, Knot, Little Stint, Temminck's Stint, Curlew Sandpiper, Ruff, Spotted Redshank, Redshank, Greenshank, Green Sandpiper, Gull-billed Tern, Sandwich Tern, Common Tern, Little Tern, Whiskered Tern, Black Tern, swifts, hirundines, Yellow Wagtail (various races), warblers.

Winter: Cattle Egret, Grey Heron, Teal, Wigeon, Shoveler, Pintail, Common Buzzard, Marsh Harrier, Grey Plover, Shelduck, Gadwall, Grey Plover, Lapwing, Dunlin, Common Snipe, Jack Snipe, Black-tailed Godwit, Turnstone, gulls, Bluethroat, Black Redstart, Penduline Tit.

ALBUFERA DE ADRA   AL4

Status: Reserva natural, 132 ha.

Site description
This wetland zone consists of two lakes, the Albufera Honda (Deep Lake) and the Albufera Nueva (New Lake). Both are fringed by reeds, sedges, bulrushes and tamarisks and sit surrounded by a sea of agricultural plastic on the south side of the N-340 Málaga/Almería road, close to the sea. The waters are slightly saline because of infiltration.

♂ Little Bittern

Species

The number of species which frequent the area is relatively small. The most important is White-headed Duck, which now breeds in some numbers, this site holding the principal population of eastern Andalucía. Other breeding wetland species include Little and Great Crested Grebes, Little Bitterns, Red-crested Pochards and Pochards, as well as Marsh Harriers and various species of warblers. Tree Sparrows are to be found in the area.

The winter sees a notable increase in numbers and variety of waterbirds with the arrival of Black-necked Grebes, Great Cormorants, Little Egrets and Cattle Egrets. Scaup have been recorded and Tufted Ducks are quite frequent. During winter the area also attracts Bluethroats and Penduline Tits. The presence of fresh water is attractive during migration periods when Purple Herons may drop in, as do Ferruginous Ducks, Water Rails and possibly other rails also. Occasional waders, such as Common Sandpipers, occur, although the area is not suitable for them as there is very little shore space. Marsh Terns occur, especially Black Terns but also Whiskered Terns occasionally and rarely White-winged Black Terns. Very large numbers of hirundines feed over the area and roost in the reedbeds during migration periods.

Apart from the avifauna, there is a notable population of fish and amphibians in the protected region, although one wonders how long this will last, given the widespread use of herbicides and pesticides in the immediate vicinity.

Timing

The area can be visited at any time of year if you want to see Red-crested Pochards and White-headed Ducks, although these are most in evidence in winter and spring. The most productive period is between November and June.

Access

Although this site is an important one, the physical difficulties of observation are such that it is not worth stopping unless you are desperate to

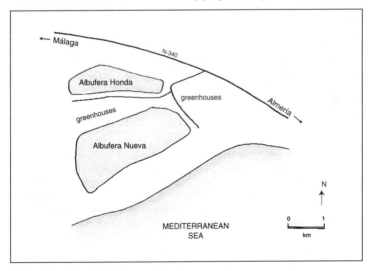

see White-headed Ducks. There are other, much easier sites, such as Las Norias (AL3) and in other provinces, where this species can be seen far more easily.

Leave the N-340 Málaga/Almería road at Km 66, some 6 km east of Adra. The turn off is marked by a Consejería de Medio Ambiente sign, but is easily missed, so beware. Having successfully entered the track, follow the tarmac for about 200 m before stopping and trying to see the smaller lake through the fence and reeds. Go straight on along the rough track for about 200 m before stopping near the locked gate and try to look at the larger lake, again through the same screen of fence and tall reeds.

Calendar

All year: Little Grebe, Black-necked Grebe, White-headed Duck, Pochard, Red-crested Pochard, Tree Sparrow.

Breeding season: Great Reed Warbler, Reed Warbler.

Winter: Great Crested Grebe, Shoveler, Wigeon, Gadwall, Pintail, Marsh Harrier.

Passage periods: Marsh terns and hirundines.

DESIERTO DE TABERNAS   AL5

Status: Paraje Natural (11,625 ha). ZEPA.

Site description

This area is the depression to the northwest of the Sierra Alhamilla (AL6). It is semi-arid, receiving less than 250 mm of rain per year, and is the only true sub-desert area in Europe. The landscape is deeply eroded with cuttings and ravines, in the bottom of which there are the ramblas, the dry riverbeds which abound in this part of Andalucía. Vegetation is scarce, low and scrubby, except in the bottom of the ravines where there are tamarisks and oleanders. The northern part of the area is higher, where you can enter the southern ramparts of the Sierra de los Filabres.

Species

Diurnal raptors are represented by Bonelli's Eagles, Peregrines, Lesser Kestrels and Common Kestrels, whilst nocturnal ones are Little Owls, Eagle Owls and Scops Owls. There is always the chance of encountering other migrant or stray raptors during passage periods. There are several interesting steppe species within or on the edges of this area, including Little Bustards, Stone Curlews and Black-bellied Sandgrouse, as well as Red-necked Nightjars, Rollers and Trumpeter Finches. Other representative species include Great Spotted Cuckoos in the sparsely wooded areas or orchards around the fringes, Bee-eaters, Red-rumped Swallows and both Thekla Larks (which are common) and Dupont's Larks (which are not). Meadow Pipits and White Wagtails occur in winter.

The chats are well represented by Black Redstarts, Black Wheatears, Black-eared Wheatears, Rufous Bush Chats and Blue Rock Thrushes. There is a wide variety of breeding warblers, which includes Sardinian Warblers, Spectacled Warblers, Subalpine Warblers at higher levels, Orphean Warblers in the semi-wooded areas around the edges, and Melodious Warblers. Common Chiffchaffs are abundant in winter. Ravens and Jackdaws are common. Rock Sparrows also occur locally in the area and Rock Buntings are to be found at higher levels.

Timing
This is a good area with a wide variety of species, many of which are particularly attractive to birders from northern Europe, although you may have to work very hard to find some of them. Given the desert nature of the region, one of the best methods of finding birds is to go down into a rambla, preferably one which still retains some of the precious liquid, and walk along or wait and sit in the shade and watch.

Although the area may be visited profitably at any time of year, even in December and January, the best period is March–May. Early mornings, when temperatures are not at their peak, are best. It can become unbearably hot in the ramblas in the middle of the day after mid-May and an ample supply of drinking water is vital in order to prevent dehydration.

Access
The A-92 passes through the area. Turn off northwards on the road to Gérgal. You can turn also turn north from the A-370 just east of Tabernas, on the road to Castro de Filabres. It is also possible to go to Olula de Castro from the A-339 Gérgal-Serón road, which involves enter-

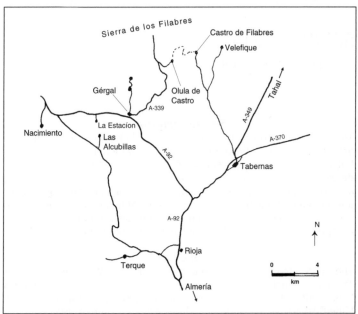

ing the lower part of the Sierra de los Filabres. The road is steep and rough in places and may be slippery on the rare occasions when it rains. A worthwhile stopping place is about 2 km south of Olula, where the road crosses a 'stream', the Arroyo de Verdelecho. The southern section of the A-349 Tabernas/Tahal road is also worth inspecting. In addition, there are two local roads south of the A-92, along the western fringe of the desert between Terque in the south and Nacimiento in the north which may repay exploration.

There are several tracks off the A-92/A-370 between Rioja and Tabernas which lead down into the Rambla del Barranco, many of which can be profitably followed on foot. Heavy storms in the hills can and do produce flash flooding so it would be unwise to linger within the rambla in the event of rain.

Calendar

All Year: Bonelli's Eagle, Peregrine, Common Kestrel, Stone Curlew, Black-bellied Sandgrouse, Eagle Owl, Little Owl, Crested Lark, Thekla Lark, Crag Martin, Black Redstart, Black Wheatear, Blue Rock Thrush, Sardinian Warbler, Jackdaw, Raven, Rock Sparrow, Trumpeter Finch, Rock Bunting.

Breeding season: Lesser Kestrel, Scops Owl, Great Spotted Cuckoo, Bee-eater, Roller, Hoopoe, Red-rumped Swallow, Tawny Pipit, Nightingale, Black-eared Wheatear, Olivaceous Warbler, Melodious Warbler, Spectacled Warbler, Subalpine Warbler, Orphean Warbler, Spotted Flycatcher, Woodchat Shrike.

Winter: Meadow Pipit, White Wagtail, Common Chiffchaff, Firecrest.

SIERRA ALHAMILLA   AL6

Status: Paraje Natural, 8392 ha.

Site description

This is a small sierra and steppe site, about 25 km long, with some flat-tish sections below the mountain proper, which rises to a peak at Calativí (1387 m). It is extremely dry, bordered as it is by the Tabernas desert region (AL5) in the north and the Campo de Níjar in the south, and is cut by deep ravines on its flanks. There is a relict forest of encinas, a sort of green lung in this semi-desert area. At higher levels most of the vegetation is low scrub. Parts of the southern side, running up from the Campo de Níjar, are deeply eroded and care should be exercised.

Species

The main attraction of this area is that it is a most important site for Trumpeter Finches and there is also a good population of Dupont's Larks. Other steppe or semi-arid country species here include a few Little Bustards, Stone Curlews and Black-bellied Sandgrouse.

The higher levels of the sierra hold a variety of raptors, including Bonelli's Eagles, Booted Eagles, Common Buzzards, Goshawks, Lesser Kestrels and Common Kestrels, as well as Little Owls and Eagle Owls. Great Spotted Cuckoos occur in the olive groves, orchards and sparsely wooded scrub areas. Bee-eaters, Thekla Larks, Alpine Swifts, Pallid Swifts, Common Swifts, Crag Martins, Red-rumped Swallows, Golden Orioles, Black Wheatears and Blue Rock Thrushes breed. There are winter records of Whinchats, which are probably exceptional. Southern Grey and Woodchat Shrikes occur. There are a few Rock Sparrows in suitable areas. At Cuevas de los Ubedas there is a population of untypical House Sparrows, some males of which appear to show characters of both this species and Spanish Sparrow. Rock Buntings occur at higher altitudes in the sierra.

Timing
Visits can be profitable at any season but, as in other dry areas, the best time is in the early part of the day between March and early June when the summer visitors are present and breeding. It does get extremely hot and dry in the summer and temperatures well in excess of 40°C are not uncommon.

Access
The site is only 15 km northeast of Almería city and skirted south/north by the road from Níjar to Lucainena at its eastern end, and by tracks which run west/east more or less across the top. Another fairly satisfactory access point is along the western flank of the sierra, taking the local

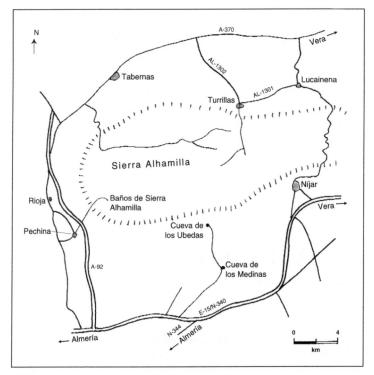

road AL-1101 from Pechina up to Baños de Sierra Alhamilla. Also, about 2 km further north from here, towards Tabernas, there is a track on the southeast side of the road which may be investigated on foot.

The approaches to the village of Cuevas de los Ubedas, in the south of the area, are worth exploring. Turn north off the N-340 following signs for Cuevas de los Medinas and Cuevas de los Ubedas. Take the left fork, at Cuevas de los Medinas. There are several recommended stopping points before Cuevas de los Medinas. The first is some 4.1 km from the N-340 where there is a low, wide flat area, semi-circular in form with a few olive trees, to the right side of the road. On the left, there is a high, lattice electric pylon near a ruined house up on the hillside. It is worth walking across the flat area here and up the track past the ruined house. Dupont's Larks occur in this area and there are the more mundane Black-eared Wheatears also to be seen.

The second stop worth making is past Cuevas de los Medinas, 6.6 km from the main road, where there are deserted dwellings and trees on the right of the road. In fact, all the habitat for the next 3 km is worth exploring carefully for the often-elusive Trumpeter Finches. Beware the danger of falling into the deep gullies. It could really ruin your holiday and there are no vultures here to clear up after you!

The final stop is at Cuevas de los Ubedas itself. Park where the road ends by a house and where an earthen track leads up to the left. The track overlooks a little citrus orchard, with some poplars. There are usually Red-rumped Swallows feeding in the area as well as the previously mentioned hybrid-type House x Spanish Sparrows. It is worth descending into the gorge and exploring within in either direction.

Calendar

All year: Bonelli's Eagle, Common Buzzard, Peregrine, Goshawk, Little Bustard, Stone Curlew, Little Owl, Eagle Owl, Black-bellied Sandgrouse, Thekla Lark, Dupont's Lark, Black Wheatear, Blue Rock Thrush, Dartford Warbler, Sardinian Warbler, Blackcap, Southern Grey Shrike, Jackdaw, Raven, Rock Sparrow, Rock Bunting, Trumpeter Finch.

Breeding season: Booted Eagle, Lesser Kestrel, Great Spotted Cuckoo, Bee-eater, Hoopoe, Alpine Swift, Red-rumped Swallow, Black-eared Wheatear, Golden Oriole, Woodchat Shrike.

Winter: Whinchat.

SIERRA DE MARÍA   AL7

Status: Parque Natural, 18,962 ha.

Site description

This sierra is of dolomitic chalk and forms part of the Betic Cordillera. The vegetation is typically Mediterranean, with zones of evergreen scrub, followed by pines and oaks at the highest levels. This variety of vegetational zones accommodates a considerable number of species.

Species

This sierra is good for raptors, including Common Buzzards, Golden Eagles, Goshawks, Sparrowhawks and Peregrines. Short-toed Eagles, Booted Eagles, Hobbies and Scops Owls are also present in summer. The more open spaces of semi-steppe attract small numbers of Little Bustards and Stone Curlews. In the pines and oaks there are Wrens, Short-toed Treecreepers, Coal Tits, Great Tits and Crested Tits with Long-tailed Tits, Robins, Mistle Thrushes and sometimes Redwings in winter. There are Nightingales in the denser cover. The more open areas have Bee-eaters, Rollers and Hoopoes, three species of breeding wheatears; Northern, Black and Black-eared, and also Southern Grey and Woodchat Shrikes. Winter visitors include Lapwings, Ring Ouzels, Dunnocks and Alpine Accentors.

Timing

This sierra is worth visiting at any time of year, even in winter, when the mild climate attracts species which descend from the higher and harsher Sierra Nevada to the west.

Access

Take the A-317 northwards off the A92-N at Vélez Rubio to the village of María. Just west of María there is a road southwards to the Ermita de la Virgen de la Cabeza, in an area known as Umbría de la Virgen. There is a visitors centre (centro de vistantes) at Km 2.7 on the María–Orce road with the unforgettable name: El Mirador de la Umbría de María (once seen, never forgotten!). Once you reach the Ermita (hermitage) there is a track which climbs to the high point of the sierra at Porta Chico. This the round trip takes about four hours but most of the interesting species occur in the first two kilometres or so. There are other tracks off into the

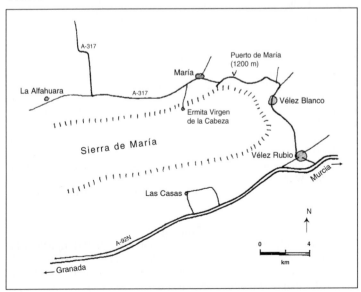

sierra, some of them signposted, but care should be taken when negotiating some of these as they are rather rough in places.

Calendar

All year: Golden Eagle, Bonelli's Eagle, Goshawk, Peregrine, Little Bustard, Stone Curlew, Wren, Black Redstart, Stonechat, Black Wheatear, Blue Rock Thrush, Dartford Warbler, Sardinian Warbler, Blackcap, Long-tailed Tit, Crested Tit, Coal Tit, Short-toed Treecreeper, Southern Grey Shrike, Azure-winged Magpie, Raven, Rock Sparrow.

Breeding: Short-toed Eagle, Booted Eagle, Hobby, Scops Owl, Bee-eater, Roller, Hoopoe, Nightingale, Northern Wheatear, Black-eared Wheatear, Rock Thrush, Melodious Warbler, Subalpine Warbler, Woodchat Shrike.

Winter: Lapwing, Robin, Whinchat (sporadic), Ring Ouzel, Redwing, Mistle Thrush, Common Chiffchaff, Dunnock, Alpine Accentor.

RÍO ANTAS   AL8

Status: No specific protection.

Site description

This site covers the west bank and mouth of the Río Antas. There is abundant reed growth along both margins of the river here as well as a quite ample area of water ringed by reeds, which is easily visible from the mouth itself when it is closed off by a sand bar. The river generally only flows after the scarce rains when the bar breaks and the pent-up water is let out. The breach is usually closed again fairly rapidly by wave action once the rains stop.

Species

Although the range of species is not particularly great, there are some of interest, notably Purple Gallinules which are present in small numbers, as well as the more common Coots, Moorhens and Black-necked Grebes. These last are just as likely to be seen on the sea as in the fresh water. Migrant and wintering seabirds include Balearic Shearwaters, Audouin's Gulls and Lesser Black-backed Gulls. Cetti's Warblers are resident while Spectacled Warblers occur in summer along the edges of the reedbeds in the low scrub. The possibility of the elusive Penduline Tit in the winter is a positive encouragement for the visitor. Recent winters have also often seen the presence of small parties of Glossy Ibises.

Timing

This site is worth visiting at any season although it is best during the winter months and in early spring. In summer and at weekends, visits should be carried out as early as possible in the day because there is intense human disturbance here later.

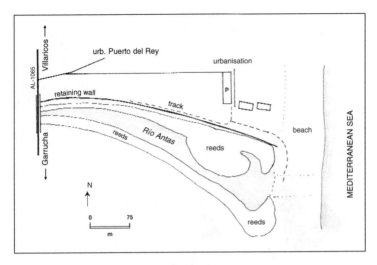

Access
This is at Puerto del Rey, on the AL-1065 local coastal road, between Garrucha and Villaricos. Turn shorewards just north of the bridge over the river, into the urbanisation of Amilcar and Playa Puerto Rey. Keep to the left for some 250 m until you reach a car park. Then follow the river to its mouth.

Calendar
All year: Little Grebe, Purple Gallinule, Pochard, Coot, Moorhen, Yellow-legged Gull, Sandwich Tern, Hoopoe, Cetti's Warbler, Sardinian Warbler, Jackdaw.

Breeding: Reed Warbler, Great Reed Warbler, Spectacled Warbler.

Winter: Black-necked Grebe, Great Cormorant, Little Bittern, Glossy Ibis, Lesser Black-backed Gull, Razorbill, Common Chiffchaff, Long-tailed Tit, Penduline Tit, Black Redstart, Southern Grey Shrike, Jackdaw, Magpie.

Passage periods: Balearic Shearwater, Audouin's Gull.

RÍO ALMANZORA   AL9
Status: No specific protection.

Site description
There are dense reedbeds near the mouth of the Río Almanzora, which only occasionally disgorges into the Mediterranean after rains. The nearby shore includes low, rocky outcrops attractive to waders.

Species

The channel and its reedbeds shelter Little Bitterns, both Grey and Purple Herons, Purple Gallinules and numbers of Coots and Moorhens. Teal hide in the reeds during the winter months. The noisy Cetti's Warblers sing cheerfully here for most of the year. Occasional Kingfishers flash up and down the narrow channels. The fields and scrub along the short walk to the shore itself offer Hoopoes, Dartford Warblers, Linnets, the ubiquitous Goldfinches and Greenfinches and the much less common Tree Sparrows. Pallid and Common Swifts, and hirundines, are often overhead in numbers, especially during migration periods.

Auduoin's Gulls: two juveniles, 2nd summer and adult

Black-necked Grebes, Great Crested Grebes and Razorbills are often to be found on the sea here in winter as well as occasional Red-breasted Mergansers. Gannets and Balearic Shearwaters are also often offshore.

The rocks and shoreline are attractive all year to Kentish Plovers and Sanderlings and a variety of other waders, notably Redshanks, Black-tailed Godwits, Whimbrels and occasional Turnstones. Great Cormorants often hang themselves out to dry on the rocks in winter. Flocks of Audouin's Gulls often rest here, especially in late summer. Numbers of Sandwich and Common Terns occur on migration and Caspian Terns have also been recorded.

Timing

Interesting species may occur at any time of year. Early morning visits are necessary in summer and at weekends to avoid the often intense human disturbance later.

Access

The channelled bed of the Río Almanzora is just to the south of Villaricos on the AL-1065. The river embankments are visible from some distance. Drive seawards for some 250 m along the track along the top of the southern embankment to the wider area at the end. The riverbed can be easily watched from this point and it is only a short stroll down to the beach.

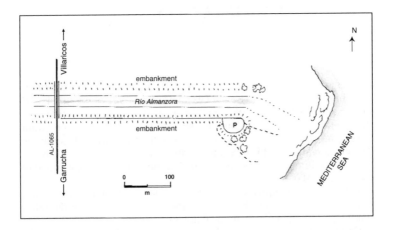

Calendar

All year: Little Grebe, Black-necked Grebe, Grey Heron, Purple Gallinule, Coot, Moorhen, Kentish Plover, Sanderling, Sandwich Tern, Hoopoe, Kingfisher, Dartford Warbler, Magpie, Linnet, Tree Sparrow, Corn Bunting.

Breeding: Little Bittern, Common Swift, Pallid Swift, Red-rumped Swallow.

Winter: Gannet, Great Cormorant, Teal, Red-breasted Merganser, Black-winged Stilt, Redshank, Lesser Black-backed Gull, Razorbill, Crag Martin, Common Chiffchaff, Black Redstart.

Passage periods: Balearic Shearwater, Purple Heron, Ringed Plover, Little Ringed Plover, Grey Plover, Ruff, Whimbrel, Little Stint, Little Gull, Audouin's Gull, Caspian Tern, Common Tern, Little Tern.

EXTREMADURA

The region of Extremadura is now getting much much more attention from birders than used to be the case. Its fame as one of the prime and unmissable birding areas of Spain has at last spread widely both within the country and abroad. Many overseas visitors come to Extremadura in search of birds and we hope and expect that this trend will continue. The conservation of this outstanding region can only be helped by the realisation among the powers-that-be that the wildlife interest is one of its major assets.

Extremadura comprises just two large provinces, Badajoz in the south and Cáceres in the north. Together they offer excellent birds, other wildlife, and peaceful, often unspoilt landscapes.

Conservation of wildlife is the concern of ADENEX, la Asociación para la Defensa de la Naturaleza y los Recursos de Extremadura (Association for the defence of the wildlife and resources of Extremadura), one of the most effective non-governmental organisations of its kind in Spain. Its website (http://mastercom.bme.es/adenex) is most comprehensive and an incomparable taster for any would-be visitor. The English-language version was revised in 2000 by EG. ADENEX has campaigned vigorously and indefatigably for years and has achieved some notable successes, especially the designation of Monfragüe (CC6) as a parque natural. Official interest in conservation has lagged behind and, despite the enormous wildlife interest of many areas, there is still nothing to compare with the comprehensive inventory of officially protected zones which is such a welcome feature of Andalucía. In fact, the contrast between the two regions in this respect is stark. On the other hand, ADENEX has established its own network of reserves and protected areas; most of these are not open to the public but they are nonetheless most valuable as refuges for a wide range of species, although they are mainly of small size.

We hope that this book will help to sustain interest in the region and will contribute to the future protection of the many exciting wildlife communities which it offers.

Why Extremadura? We cannot recommend it too strongly. It really is essentially just one big birding site and interesting species can be encountered just about anywhere. BirdLife International has developed an inventory of important bird areas (IBAs) worldwide. Under their criteria, no less than 74.1% of the area of Extremadura qualifies as IBAs, hugely more than for any other Spanish region.

This is by far the best part of our area in which to find the open-country 'steppe' birds. There are many sites offering excellent opportunities, among the best in Spain, to see both Great and Little Bustards, Stone Curlews, both Pin-tailed and Black-bellied Sandgrouse and a full range of the other species of open terrain. The birds occur in important numbers too. It is not at all unusual to find flocks of over 100 Great Bustards, for example. The same habitats are also used by Cranes. Extremadura is a key wintering area for Cranes and flocks of hundreds or even thousands occur here then.

Plains birds apart, the many forested and rocky sierras support a comprehensive raptor population, with significant numbers of Black-shouldered Kites, Black Vultures and Spanish Imperial Eagles as well as a full range of commoner species. Black Storks occur in good and increasing numbers; the breeding population of at least 150 pairs represents some 70% of the Iberian population. A comprehensive range of smaller species includes good numbers of Great Spotted Cuckoos, Rollers, Azure-winged Magpies, Spanish Sparrows and Rock Sparrows. All these species can be found relatively easily.

Extremadura is an excellent choice for a touring holiday of a week or more. It can also be combined with visits to Andalucía or to regions further north, such as the Sierra de Gredos.

BADAJOZ PROVINCE

Badajoz province provides a mixture of wooded hilly country and large tracts of open land. Much of the latter is rough pasture and it includes the impressive expanse of the plains of La Serena (BA9), one of the best areas of steppe-like habitat in Spain. Bustards and other steppe species are widespread in the province. The river Guadiana flows east to west across the top of the province before turning southwards for the Atlantic. Dams on the river have created a complex of large reservoirs in the northeast of the province (BA11, BA12). The reservoirs have created a guaranteed supply of water in a naturally-parched land and many of them are of ornithological interest, not least because they often house large roosts of Cranes in winter.

A result of the increasing availability of water for irrigation has been a rapid expansion of rice cultivation, chiefly east of Mérida and around Madrigalejo (BA10). The rice paddies attract a good variety of waders and other aquatic birds, chiefly in winter and on migration, although some species also breed there. Badajoz provides ready opportunities to see raptors, plains and some wetland species but it also offers many extensive areas of tranquil and enjoyable country which will reward patient exploration.

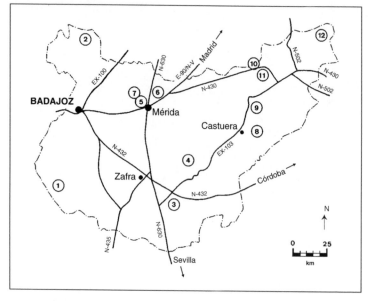

Sites in Badajoz Province

BA1 Southwestern Badajoz
BA2 The western sierras of Badajoz
BA3 Southern Badajoz
BA4 Sierra de Hornachos
BA5 Mérida
BA6 Embalse de Cornalvo

BA7 Embalse de Los Canchales
BA8 Sierra de Tiros
BA9 Plains of La Serena
BA10 The northeastern rice fields
BA11 Eastern Badajoz reservoirs
BA12 Reserva Nacional de Cíjara

Maps

Geocenter International Euromap, Central Spain, 1:300,000.

Mapa de carreteras Plaza & Janes Andalucía, 1:300,000 (includes all but the northernmost part of Badajoz).

Mapa Provincial Badajoz IGN, 1:200,000.

Getting there

The N-630 major trunk road, linking Gijón on the Biscay coast with Sevilla, crosses Badajoz north/south and provides the obvious link with Andalucía. Visitors arriving in Spain via ferry to Santander or Bilbao will also find it convenient for reaching Extremadura generally. Rapid access is also available via Madrid, using the E-90/N-V Madrid/Badajoz toll-free motorway, which crosses Extremadura diagonally.

Where to stay

All the sites are within striking distance of the N-630 along which there are a good number of motels, for example near Zafra and Mérida. Both those cities have paradores and a range of lesser-grade hotels. Visitors to the eastern sites, where early morning/evening visits are often best, may find it useful to find accommodation in Castuera or Puebla de Alcocer. At the former we can recommend: Hostal Los Naranjos, two-stars, Carretera Benquerencia Km 39, Castuera, Badajoz (tel: 924-760888/761054). It offers inexpensive, simple and clean motel-type accommodation and strategically placed for the Sierra de Tiros (BA8) and La Serena (BA9) especially.

SOUTHWESTERN BADAJOZ   BA1

Status: No special protection.

Site description

This is a peaceful corner of Extremadura, somewhat off the beaten track but typical of the region as a whole. The chiefly undulating terrain bordering the river Guadiana (the Portuguese frontier in the west) is devoted to cereal growing, pastureland and olive groves, with woods of encina. Open terrain in the north of the area offers steppe-like habitat, for example near the river at Albala (A) and north and west of La Albuera (B), where bustards now patrol the 1811 Peninsular War battlefield. This latter area has suffered from an intensification of cultivation in recent years, with olive groves making inroads into the steppelands, but good patches of habitat remain. The area from Olivenza to Villanueva, via Cheles (C), offers extensive if rather monotonous encinares. The southern part of the region has better-developed woodland, with mature stands of encinas and cork oaks from Villanueva to Oliva (D) and, especially, in the vicinity of Jerez de los Caballeros (E) where there are some very fine trees. The road from Oliva to Valencia del Mombuey (F) is of more open aspect, with good views across undulating open countryside, with very open encinares giving a park-like aspect.

Species
The region offers opportunities to see the steppeland and woodland species of Extremadura. The former are certainly simpler to locate elsewhere, however, and so the area is not worth visiting if time is limited. White Storks and Cattle Egrets occur in large numbers and a comprehensive range of steppe species inhabits the pastures and cereal fields. Up to several thousand Cranes winter in open habitats in the northern and central parts of the region. The southern part has breeding Black Storks and raptors are very much in evidence.

Timing
Of interest all year round. The largest concentrations of bustards occur in winter, when Cranes are also present.

Access
The region can be visited on a circular course starting from Badajoz or from Zafra, to the east. A gentle drive, visiting all the main habitats and with frequent stops to scan for raptors and steppe species, will take all

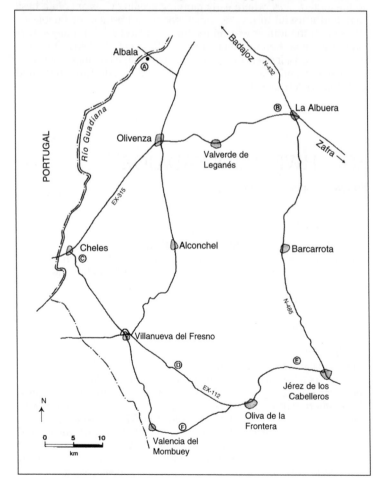

day since at least 200 km will be covered. The minor roads indicated give access to all the main habitats. At Cheles (C) the road marked west of the town is a concrete track which descends 2 km to the River Guadiana. There is no border crossing here but there is access on foot to the riverside habitats, comprising riverine woodland and islets.

Calendar

All year: Cattle Egret, Black-shouldered Kite, Red Kite, Griffon Vulture, Black Vulture, Common Buzzard, Great Bustard, Little Bustard, Stone Curlew, Black-bellied Sandgrouse, Pin-tailed Sandgrouse, Thekla Lark, Woodlark, Crested Tit, Nuthatch.

Breeding season: Night Heron and Little Egret (along the river), Black Stork, White Stork, Black Kite, Short-toed Eagle, Montagu's Harrier, Booted Eagle, Collared Pratincole.

Winter: Greylag Goose and other waterfowl, Crane, Lapwing, Golden Plover.

THE WESTERN SIERRAS OF BADAJOZ

BA2

Status: Much of the area is conserved as private hunting estates; 3217 hectares are designated as a ZEPA.

Site description

This is a sparsely-populated area of low, wooded country to the south-west of the city of Cáceres, mainly comprising a large tranche of north-west Bádajoz province. Much of the region described here falls south of the excellent N-521 Portugal/Cáceres trunk road, and parallel to the road, a line of sierras appears as a long, low green wall. Cork oak wood-lands, with a good understorey of cistus, broom, lavenders and other shrubs, cover these hills. Further south still, the terrain becomes much more open with expanses of cultivation near the towns and villages and large areas of severe, boulder-strewn steppelands, the latter especially north of Alburquerque.

The long ridge in the east of the region, within Cáceres province, is the Sierra de San Pedro. Further west there are a series of parallel ranges, interspersed with small river valleys. Rocky ridges along the sier-ras make them attractive to Black Storks and crag-nesting raptors. Mediterranean forest is exceptionally well developed, with stands of cork oak and encina and matorral of cistus and lavender. Indeed, the area is renowned as an excellently-preserved remnant of the original Mediterranean forest cover of the region. The recent survival here of wolves, the last of their kind in Extremadura, testifies to the quality of the wilderness but their present existence is in doubt. At best, they are very few.

Dotterel

The quiet road along the Portuguese border, via La Codosera, is also worth a visit. This is a region of small isolated villages characterised by stone-walled fields, rustic cottages with Hoopoes on the TV aerials, and a thriving population of misshapen little dogs of untraceable pedigree. Raptors and woodland species are much in evidence.

Species
The whole area is notable for breeding raptors, with good populations of all five eagles as well as Black Storks, Black-shouldered Kites, Black Vultures and Eagle Owls. Black Vultures are particularly common and easily seen overhead. The density of breeding raptors is generally high and soaring shapes are omnipresent over the woodlands. The forests and scrub support a rich community of woodland birds.

Timing
Springtime and early summer visits are recommended but interesting species are present all year round.

Access
The region is easily explored by car, starting either from the N-521 at Aliseda or from the south at Alburquerque. The drive from the N-630 north of Mérida to Alburquerque via the minor roads passing through La Nava de Santiago and Villar del Rey passes through orchards and olive groves which are alive with passerines, especially in winter. Once in the region, a zig-zag route may be followed, stopping frequently to scan the slopes and woodlands or simply whenever interesting looking birds appear, which is very often. Most of the roads are quiet and stopping is easy. However, the Alburquerque/La Herreruela stretch can be busy occasionally but even here there are plenty of farm tracks enabling safe parking off the carriageway.

The minor tarmac road (A) heading southeastwards from the N-521 at Aliseda, past the Sierra de San Pedro, is of interest. For the first 10 km nearest Aliseda the road follows a valley between two low ridges, which should be scanned for soaring raptors. Frequent stops along this road are recommended, with exploration on foot into the adjacent woodlands. The road crosses mature encinares and corkwoods.

The EX-303 road is often productive, especially in the northern sector (B Sierra de la Umbría) and at the bridge across the Río Zapatón (C).

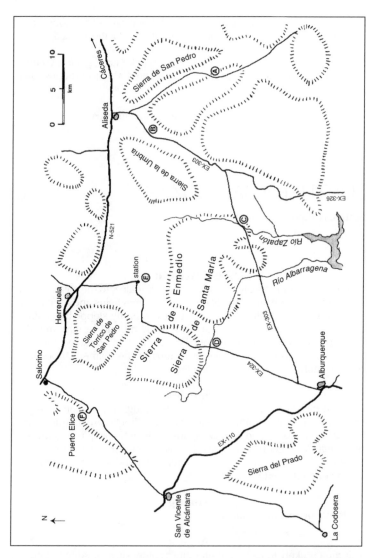

Similarly, stopping on the EX-324 at the south side of the bridge across the Río Albarragena (D) is worthwhile; the woodlands and river may be scanned here and walks along the banks reveal waterside and woodland passerines. Also on the EX-324, panoramic views across the region are available from the disused railway station of La Herreruela (E); follow the signs up the access track to the open area near the station. Panoramic views are also to be had from the Salorino/San Vicente de Alcántara road, at its high point of the Puerto de Elice (F), which overlooks the woodlands and sierras and provides an excellent scanning point for raptors.

Calendar
All year: Black-shouldered Kite, Red Kite, Griffon Vulture, Black Vulture, Goshawk, Sparrowhawk, Commom Buzzard, Spanish Imperial Eagle,

Golden Eagle, Bonelli's Eagle, Eagle Owl, Long-eared Owl, Kingfisher, Thekla Lark, Southern Grey Shrike, Azure-winged Magpie, Rock Sparrow.

Breeding season: White Stork, Black Stork, Black Kite, Egyptian Vulture, Short-toed Eagle, Booted Eagle, Great Spotted Cuckoo, Scops Owl, passerines.

Winter: Red Kite, Crane, Song Thrush, Redwing, finches.

SOUTHERN BADAJOZ   BA3

Status: No special protection.

Site description

Much of the undulating terrain of southern Badajoz, to the east of the N-630 is open country and largely devoted to cereal fields and rough grazing, interrupted by olive and encina groves. Stony steppe-like habitat occupies large tracts in some areas, notably around Usagre and also (west of the N-630) southwest of Fuente de Cantos. Large tracts of 'steppe' are covered by extensive clumps of the feathery broom-like retama: such patches are best avoided.

Species

Open country species, including bustards, sandgrouse and other steppe birds are present if thinly spread. Sparrow flocks are frequent and include both House and Spanish Sparrows, with Rock Sparrows present near Segura de León and likely also elsewhere. Cranes winter in very large numbers, especially east of Llerena. A good selection of raptors will be encountered.

Timing

Visits can be rewarding all year round.

Access

This area is likely to be visited en route to other sites, notably La Serena (BA9). The N-432 between Zafra and Llerena (A) passes through good steppe habitats but, as ever, stopping on main roads is strongly discouraged, except where farm tracks provide lay-bys. The minor roads mapped are a selection of those from which the area can be surveyed at greater leisure. Farm tracks are frequent and allow closer inspection of the more promising pastures. Scanning the open terrain along sections of the EX-202, notably between Segura and Fuente de Cantos (B) and between Usagre and Valencia de las Torres (C), and also along the quiet minor road between Usagre and Hinojosa del Valle (D), is likely to be prove worthwhile. The EX-103 Venta del Culebrín/Llerena road offers a massive colony of Spanish Sparrows in eucalyptus, 13 km from the N-630 (E).

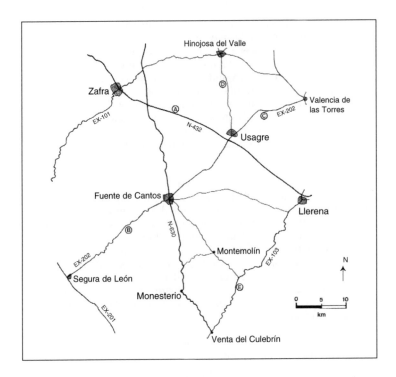

Calendar

All year: Black-shouldered Kite, Griffon Vulture, Black Vulture, Golden Eagle, Spanish Imperial Eagle, Bonelli's Eagle, Great Bustard, Little Bustard, Stone Curlew, Black-bellied Sandgrouse, Pin-tailed Sandgrouse, Calandra Lark, Zitting Cisticola, Southern Grey Shrike, Red-billed Chough, Spanish Sparrow.

Breeding season: White Stork, Black Stork, Black Kite, Egyptian Vulture, Short-toed Eagle, Booted Eagle, Lesser Kestrel, Montagu's Harrier, Great Spotted Cuckoo, Hoopoe, Short-toed Lark, Tawny Pipit, Ortolan Bunting.

Winter: Greylag Goose, Crane, Red Kite, Hen Harrier.

SIERRA DE HORNACHOS   BA4

Status: Local nature reserve of ADENEX (in part). ZEPA 6000 ha.

Site description

Viewed from the N-630, between Almendralejo and Villafranca de los Barros, the Sierra de Hornachos appears as an isolated rocky island above a gently rolling expanse of open country. Approaching from the south, from Hinojosa del Valle, the Sierra reveals a long, grey, flat-topped ridge, with some cliff faces and extensive scree slopes where the dominant cistus scrub seems to have relinquished its grip and slid off the mountain. The red-roofed hamlet of Hornachos reposes against the southern slopes and is surrounded by olive groves. To the east and north there are woodlands of encinas and cork oaks, with a well-developed understorey of cistus, retama and other shrubs. For a change, the Presa de Campillo north of Campillo de Llerena holds back a small lake with good reedbeds. The much larger reservoir south of Hornachos, the Embalse de los Molinos, attracts waterfowl and roosting Cranes in winter.

Species

Hornachos provides another chance to see the raptor community of Extremadura with most species represented. The Sierra is a good site for Egyptian Vultures and both Golden and Bonelli's Eagles. A vulture 'restaurant' run by ADENEX in the northern foothills sometimes attracts numbers of both Griffon and Black Vultures. Woodland passerines are evident. The reservoir and reedbeds at Campillo hold small numbers of waterfowl. White Storks nest on the outlet tower itself. Sparrow flocks around the reservoir include Spanish Sparrows. Cranes, Great-crested Grebes and other waterfowl frequent the Embalses de Los Molinos and de Alange in winter.

Timing

Springtime visits are most productive.

Access

Hornachos is readily reached from the west, turning off the N-630 at Villafranco de los Barros and taking the EX-342 to Hornachos, via Ribera del Fresno. Alternative easy access is from the north, taking the local roads from Mérida to Alange and then continuing to Hornachos along the east shore of the very large reservoir, the Embalse de Alange.

Footpaths from the village allow access to the sierra but the principal species are best located from some distance. Good views are to be had

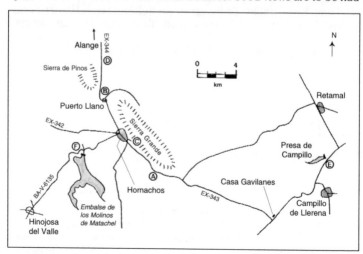

from the roads leading to the village of Hornachos. The EX-343 (A) offers suitable vantage points at many points east of the village. Stop in entrances to the olive groves and other similar 'lay-bys'. The Hornachos/Alange road (EX-344) climbs up the slope to the west of Hornachos, passing between that sierra and the Sierra de Pinos, again giving good views of the area. On this latter road, at Puerto Llano (B), a track gives access to the northern slopes. It is possible to drive along this track, which is in good repair, to scan the steep escarpments on the northern side of the sierra or to explore the woodlands from footpaths.

Hornachos boasts an information centre run by ADENEX but this is irregularly manned; ask in the village for directions to the centre, which lies at the end of a gravelly track just east of the town (C). ADENEX also have an animal 'hospital' and recovery centre (D), where injured birds and other animals from all over Extremadura are taken for veterinary care and rehabilitation. This 'Centro de Recuperación' is magnificently equipped, with an operating theatre and attendant qualified staff. The Centre, northwest of Hornachos is not normally open to the public but visits may be arranged by prior appointment. ADENEX can similarly arrange guided tours of the Hornachos area, again by prior arrangement. Contact the ADENEX headquarters in Mérida (tel: 924-371202; email: adenex@bme.es).

The road from Hornachos to Casa Gavilanes passes through good woodland and offers vistas over the savanna-like encinares. There is a stopping point and 'picnic site' at the reservoir at Campillo (E).

The Embalse de los Molinos (F) is readily viewable from the Hornachos/Hinojosa road, which skirts the northwest of the lake and gives elevated views. The river downstream of the dam is also worth inspecting; the bed is a complex of pools, reedbeds and cane-brakes and there is some riverine woodland of alders and poplars which regularly attracts Golden Orioles.

Calendar

All year: Griffon Vulture, Black Vulture, Common Buzzard, Spanish Imperial Eagle, Golden Eagle, Bonelli's Eagle, Eagle Owl, Thekla Lark, Black Wheatear, Blue Rock Thrush, Azure-winged Magpie, Red-billed Chough, Spanish Sparrow, Rock Sparrow, Hawfinch, Rock Bunting.

Breeding season: White Stork, Black Stork, Black Kite, Egyptian Vulture, Short-toed Eagle, Montagu's Harrier, Booted Eagle, Lesser Kestrel, Great Spotted Cuckoo, Scops Owl, Red-necked Nightjar, Bee-eater, Roller, Hoopoe, Red-rumped Swallow, Rufous Bush Chat, Great Reed Warbler, Subalpine Warbler, Orphean Warbler, Golden Oriole.

Winter: Great Crested Grebe, Great Cormorant, Greylag Goose, Mallard, Wigeon, Gadwall, Teal, Shoveler, Pochard, Tufted Duck, Crane, Alpine Accentor, Bullfinch.

MÉRIDA

Status: No special protection.

Site description
The city of Mérida, on the River Guadiana, is best known for its well-preserved Roman ruins, including the famous amphitheatre and aqueduct.
The old town is attractive but the newer developments south of the river
are less pleasing. No doubt the Roman artefacts will outlive them. The
city offers the usual haven for rooftop birds, although these are more
evident in Cáceres and Trujillo. The Embalse de Montijo, a long thin
reservoir on the river immediately west of the city, has several wooded
islets. The river itself has a variable rate of flow, unsurprisingly given the
number of reservoirs upstream and the frequent droughts of recent
years. The riverbed thus has numerous, generally-exposed gravel banks
with intermediate pools and clumps of rank vegetation, all of them
attractive to birds.

Species
Breeding White Storks, Lesser Kestrels and Common, Pallid and Alpine
Swifts enliven the city. The Puente Romano (Roman bridge) has a
colony of some 30 pairs of Alpine Swifts and some Common and Pallid
Swifts, which are present from March to October. The islets in the reser-
voir support heronries, principally of Cattle Egrets (1,000+ pairs). The
riverside scrub attracts finches and other passerines, notably Red
Avadavats. Numbers of Great Cormorants, Black-headed Gulls and
Lesser Black-backed Gulls feed and roost along the river in winter.

Timing
Spring and summer visits are necessary for many species but the area is
of interest year round.

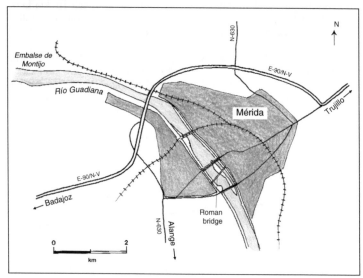

Access
Mérida is at a crossroads between the N-630 and the N-V trunk roads. The river and its birds are easily viewed from promenades along both banks and, especially, from the pedestrians-only Roman bridge. The Embalse de Montijo lies along the river Guadiana, immediately west of the city. It is best viewed from the southern bank, where the road serving the industrial estate provides lay-bys opposite the heronries, about 100 m away in the centre of the reservoir.

Calendar
All year: Little Egret, Cattle Egret, White Stork, Crag Martin.

Breeding season: Night Heron, Lesser Kestrel, Little Tern, Pallid Swift, Common Swift, Alpine Swift, Red Avadavat.

Winter: Great Cormorant, waterfowl, Coot, Black-headed Gull, Lesser Black-backed Gull.

EMBALSE DE CORNALVO   BA6
Status: Parque Natural, 10,740 ha. ZEPA.

Site description
Cornalvo can claim to be a well-established reservoir: the Romans built the original dam and a smaller one to the northwest. The principal interest of the site is the excellent and very accessible woodland of encinas and cork oaks which borders the horn-shaped lake. These woods are a fine example of their kind and shelter a diverse plant and animal community. The southern part of the site is open country.

Species
Breeding species include Black Storks, Lesser Spotted Woodpeckers and a range of raptors including Black Vultures and Black-shouldered Kites. Honey Buzzards have bred. The open country to the south has a high concentration of breeding Montagu's Harriers and Little Bustards, with Great Bustards also present. Several hundred Cranes occur in winter. The reservoirs attract some waterfowl but the Embalse de Los Canchales (BA7) has drawn most of these away in recent years.

Timing
Spring and early summer for breeding species. Winter for Cranes and waterfowl. The site is a mecca for picnickers from Mérida at weekends or on public holidays and is best avoided then.

Access
The reserve lies to the north of the N-V, 18 km northeast of Mérida and 5 km from the town of Trujillanos. It is signposted from the westbound carriageway of the N-V but not from the eastbound carriageway; take

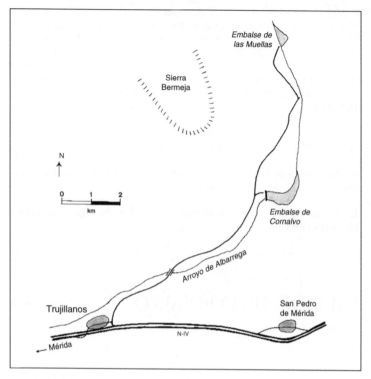

the Trujillanos exit here. Follow the minor road from Trujillanos for 5 km to the dam and explore the reservoir fringe and woodlands on foot. The walk around the entire perimeter of the reservoir, crossing the dam, is a pleasant stroll and takes an hour or two. It is also worthwhile continuing north on the access road, past Cornalvo, for a further 6 km through interesting woodland to a second small reservoir, the Embalse de las Muellas, which also attracts some waterfowl and passage waders.

Calendar

All year: Black-shouldered Kite, Red Kite, Griffon Vulture, Black Vulture, Buzzard, Spanish Imperial Eagle, Golden Eagle, Bonelli's Eagle, Stone Curlew, Little Bustard, Great Bustard, Tawny Owl, Lesser Spotted Woodpecker, Thekla Lark, Southern Grey Shrike, Zitting Cisticola, Rock Sparrow.

Breeding season: White Stork, Black Stork, Honey Buzzard (irregular), Black Kite, Short-toed Eagle, Montagu's Harrier, Booted Eagle, Little Ringed Plover, Great Spotted Cuckoo, Scops Owl, Red-necked Nightjar, White-rumped Swift, Red-rumped Swallow, Rufous Bush Chat, Spectacled Warbler, Subalpine Warbler, Orphean Warbler, Golden Oriole.

Winter: Waterfowl, foraging eagles and other raptors, Coot, Crane.

EMBALSE DE LOS CANCHALES BA7

Status: No special protection.

Site description

This is a quite a new reservoir, dating back to the mid-1980s, serving the city of Mérida. Unlike so many such water bodies, some account was taken of the potential wildlife interest of the site when the reservoir was planned. The plans provided for shallow feeding areas and the construction of islands, to provide secure nesting sites for waterfowl. The result is an interesting reservoir, attractive to birds and birders alike, and well worth a visit.

Species

The reservoir attracts waterfowl all year round but especially in winter when dabbling ducks including Mallard, Teal, Gadwall, Wigeon, Pintail and Shoveler are present in some numbers as well as Pochard, Tufted Ducks and Greylag Geese. Wintering and passage waders are another attraction. Lapwings and Golden Plovers occur in numbers in winter and

Juvenile Montagu's Harrier

a wide range of other species occur both then and in spring and autumn. There is a large Crane roost in winter, when up to 1,000 birds make a fine spectacle as they arrive in the late evening to settle in the marshy pastures along the eastern arm of the lake. The olive groves and open woodlands of encinas surrounding the lake attract the usual passerine community.

Timing

The site is always of interest and may turn up some surprises during passage periods. Bird numbers are highest in winter. The site is popular with local anglers at weekends and gets busy as a picnic site on Sundays and public holidays especially. Hence weekday visits are more peaceful and may well prove more rewarding.

Access

The reservoir lies to the northwest of the city of Mérida. Take the EX-209 west from the N-630 for 15 km to La Garrovilla. A good track leads north for some 7 km to the dam, where there is parking and an information

273

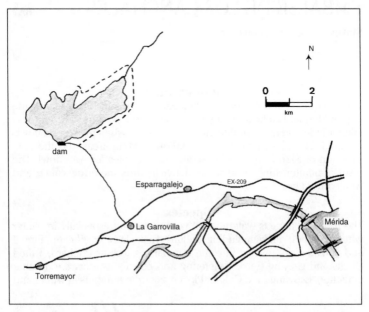

board, showing the site and the location of three blinds, from which the lake may be viewed. A telescope is highly desirable. It is possible to drive around the reservoir to the northern shore on farm tracks but this involves negotiating a shallow ford and some damp stretches which could cause problems to non-4WD vehicles in other than dry weather.

Calendar

All year: Cattle Egret, White Stork, Mallard, Black-shouldered Kite, Coot, Great Bustard, Zitting Cisticola, Southern Grey Shrike.

Breeding season: Black Kite, Marsh Harrier, Collared Pratincole, Gull-billed Tern, Great Reed Warbler.

Winter: Little Grebe, Great Crested Grebe, Little Egret, Greylag Goose, Mallard, Teal, Gadwall, Wigeon, Pintail, Shoveler, Pochard, Tufted Duck, Crane, Black-winged Stilt, Golden Plover, Lapwing, Snipe, Black-headed Gull, Lesser Black-backed Gull.

Passage periods: Spoonbill, Osprey, Avocet, Little Ringed Plover, Little Stint, Curlew Sandpiper, Dunlin, Ruff, Black-tailed Godwit, Spotted Red-shank, Redshank, Greenshank, Green Sandpiper, Wood Sandpiper, Common Sandpiper, Little Tern, Whiskered Tern, Black Tern.

SIERRA DE TIROS

Status: No special protection.

Site description

The Sierra de Tiros forms part of a discrete and abrupt rocky ridge, between the towns of Castuera and Cabeza del Buey. The ridge clearly separates the rolling steppelands of La Serena from the encinares further south. The Sierra itself is rather barren in its uppermost reaches, with occasional vertical rock faces. Lower down there is well-developed scrub and some woodland, with olive groves near the towns. The sierra provides points of vantage over both La Serena to the north and the Dehesas de Benquerencia, the savanna-like open woodlands, to the south.

Species

Breeding species include White and Black Storks, Griffon Vultures and Bonelli's Eagles, as well as the usual woodland and scrub passerines. The steppe species of La Serena (BA9) are present immediately to the north of the sierra. Perhaps the chief attraction of the site occurs in winter when several thousand Cranes cross the area twice daily as they travel to and from their roost at the Embalse del Zújar and their feeding grounds in the open woodlands south of Benquerencia.

Timing

All year, for raptors and steppe species. Winter for Cranes. The Cranes fly south shortly after dawn, traditionally passing through the gaps in the sierra at Puerto Mejoral, just east of Benquerencia, and further east, through a second interruption in the ridge at Almorchón. They return at dusk along the same routes but more especially then at Almorchón.

Access

The EX-104 provides easy access to the southern flanks of the sierra. The road ascends to Benquerencia from Castuera. At Benquerencia the car park on the right when entering the town from Castuera gives fine views over the encinares. The rocky ridge above the town may be scanned for raptors, notably Bonelli's Eagle. The 'Crane Gap' at Puerto Mejoral is obvious as the road descends towards La Nava, just east of Benquerencia. ADENEX have constructed a simple watchpoint (Francisco Carbajo Bird Observatory) south of the road at Puerto Mejoral, which provides an excellent vantage point for watching the flypast of Cranes and other birds through the sierra. The site is marked by a sign (Paso de Grullas) and parking is available next to a telecommunications mast. Follow signs up past the mast to the observatory. Opposite, ADENEX also have an information centre at their nature school in Puerto Mejoral, with exhibits relating to the wildlife of the Sierra de Tiros and La Serena. A resident warden is present here every Friday, Saturday and Sunday afternoon, and on public holidays, during December, January and February. Visits at other times may be arranged by telephoning 924-37 12 02.

The road further east provides plenty of stopping places: entrances to olive groves and farm tracks, from which to scan the sierra. The 'Crane

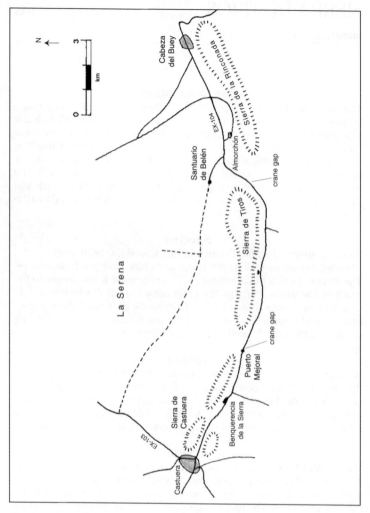

Gap' at Almorchón is marked by the ruined castle of that name, atop an isolated crag. Cranes fly through this gap in the evenings especially. The minor road to the Santuario de Nuestra Señora de Belén, opposite the castle, is the best place to stop here. The same road offers good opportunities to see numbers of Montagu's Harriers in season.

It is also possible to drive past the Santuario to the right and on to a dirt road which is a main access point for the network of farm tracks serving the southern parts of La Serena and from which the full range of steppe species may be seen. The principal track follows a railway line and then heads northwest across the plains for a total of some 20 km, to meet the EX-103 road 8 km north of Castuera. The track is passable to all vehicles in dry weather but the low-lying sectors are apt to become muddy and more challenging in wet weather, when 4WD would be advisable. The trees in the garden of the Santuario house a large mixed colony of both Spanish and House Sparrows.

Calendar

All year: Cattle Egret, Griffon Vulture, Golden Eagle, Bonelli's Eagle, Great Bustard, Little Bustard, Stone Curlew, Black-bellied Sandgrouse, Pin-tailed Sandgrouse, Rock Dove, Eagle Owl, Crag Martin, Black Wheatear, Blue Rock Thrush, Red-billed Chough, House Sparrow, Spanish Sparrow, Rock Sparrow, Cirl Bunting, Rock Bunting.

Breeding season: Black Stork, White Stork, Black Kite, Egyptian Vulture, Short-toed Eagle, Montagu's Harrier, Booted Eagle, Lesser Kestrel, Red-necked Nightjar, Alpine Swift, Red-rumped Swallow.

Winter: Crane, Dunnock.

PLAINS OF LA SERENA   BA9

Status: No special protection, despite being of the greatest interest and importance in harbouring some of the largest concentrations of steppe birds found in Spain. Protected status is urgently required.

Site description

The undulating steppelands of eastern Badajóz province comprise La Serena, some 100,000 ha of rough and often stony pastureland with occasional wheat fields and scattered farmhouses. The region is almost treeless although occasional small clumps of eucalyptus along the roads harbour sparrow colonies and the nests of White Storks. This is the best site of its kind in Spain but the key steppe species are declining, perhaps because of a reduction in habitat quality through over-grazing by sheep and also because of the deleterious effects of periodical spraying with insecticides, used to control the massive and undoubtedly spectacular plagues of large grasshoppers which often occur in spring.

Cranes, adult and juvenile

Species

Breeding steppe species, notably Montagu's Harriers, Red-legged Partridges, Great and Little Bustards, Stone Curlews, Black-bellied Sandgrouse, Pin-tailed Sandgrouse, Rollers and Calandra Larks. Collared
Pratincoles breed locally and Mallard frequent the occasional ponds.
Cranes, Golden Plover and Lapwings occur in winter. Raptors of a wide
range of species occur in small numbers. Birds apart, even the sheep
are apt to provide interest during slack moments; the local merinos
have evolved a curious but no doubt effective strategy to cope with
periods of intense sunlight, huddling together in tight, circular groups of
up to 100 or more, all heads turned towards the centre and tucked
between the legs of the animal in front, rugby-scrum fashion.

Timing

Springtime visits reveal displaying bustards and singing larks and other
passerines. All times of year will provide birds but the heat of the day in
summer can be daunting. Morning and evening visits are recommended and are all but essential in hot weather; the birds are more active
then and are much more easily located. At least half a day should be
allowed to inspect the area since some species can be elusive. Areas
with good densities of the very obvious Calandra Larks are often more
generally productive.

Access

Minor roads crisscross the area and there are numerous tracks leading
to farms which may be negotiated carefully without 4WD in many
cases. Please ask for permission to enter private land whenever possible. A telescope is strongly recommended. Bird numbers are high but
the area is vast and it may be necessary to cover a lot of ground before

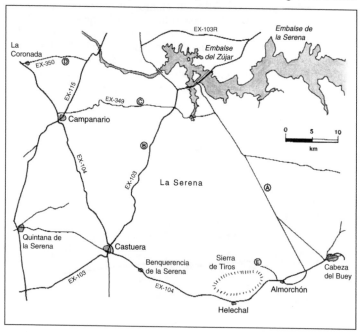

all the typical species are located. Even when birds are not immediately obvious, waiting in suitable habitat very often reveals flocks of sand-grouse flying in or bustards moving between feeding grounds. Rather thoughtlessly, many of the farmers keep pigeons, which may be confused with sandgrouse at first glance, so some care with initial identifications is called for.

The precise location of birds varies as land-use may shift. Typically the bustards like growing crops in which to nest but they are most obvious when searching for grasshoppers and other food on the open stony pastures. This latter habitat too attracts sandgrouse and Stone Curlews.

The road from Cabeza del Buey to the Embalse del Zújar (A) is often the most productive, particularly the southern portions. The whole road has a number of obvious broad sandy tracks leading off across the steppes all of which are worth exploring as far as conditions and your vehicle permit. That leading eastwards from a point 16 km north of the Cabeza del Buey fork is an excellent example of an accessible track which often reveals steppe species.

The road between Castuera and the Embalse del Zújar (EX-103) (B) was straightened and resurfaced in 1993. The adjacent electricity pylons along the southern portion all have large bird boxes attached, most of which are usually occupied by Kestrels or Rollers, although in 2000 many of the boxes were in a state of some disrepair.

In the northwest, the east/west road (EX-349) between the EX-103 and Campanario (C) crosses very stony terrain. Pin-tailed Sandgrouse are characteristic here. Both sandgrouse are also typical of the open grassy steppeland along the east/west road (EX-350) to La Coronada (D), also in the north of La Serena.

There is good access to the southernmost expanses of La Serena from the Santuario de Belén (E) (see BA8).

Calendar

All year: Cattle Egret, Griffon Vulture, Red Kite, Common Buzzard, Common Kestrel, Red-legged Partridge, Great Bustard, Little Bustard, Stone Curlew, Pin-tailed Sandgrouse, Little Owl, Calandra Lark, Spanish Sparrow.

Breeding season: White Stork, Black Kite, Montagu's Harrier, Lesser Kestrel, Quail, Collared Pratincole, Bee-eater, Roller, Hoopoe, Short-toed Lark.

Winter: Hen Harrier, Merlin, Crane, Golden Plover, Lapwing, larks, pipits and finches.

THE NORTHEASTERN RICE FIELDS

BA10

Status: No special protection.

Site description

This region owes much of its interest to the ongoing expansion of rice cultivation, which has seen increasing areas converted to paddy fields and the establishment of reservoirs to irrigate them. Water levels vary with the time of year and the management regime and so there are always some muddy expanses attractive to waders. Drainage channels are often reed-fringed and attractive to warblers and finches. The region is bordered by open encinares to the east and by rolling open pastures to the north, these last attractive to steppe species.

Species

The wetlands attract numbers of waders, notably Black-tailed Godwits, Ruff, Avocets and Black-winged Stilts but also a wide range of other species, especially during passage periods. White Storks, Grey Herons and Cattle Egrets are common. Winter in particular sees numbers of waterfowl, notably Greylag Geese, Mallard, Teal, Shoveler, Pochard and Tufted Ducks. The zone is also noteworthy as a major wintering ground for Common Cranes, up to 3,000 of which are regularly to be found in the encinares to the north of Navalvillar de Pela and also foraging for spilled rice in the paddy fields. Migrating Cranes, which follow the Guadiana river, are often to be seen overflying the area. The rice fields are inevitably a magnet for seed-eaters and large flocks of Spanish and House Sparrows are characteristic. There is also a thriving population of Red Avadavats, which no doubt find echoes of their original Far-Eastern home in the paddies. Resident raptors include Marsh Harriers and Black-shouldered Kites. This is often a particularly good area for the latter species and roosts of over 30 have been recorded in winter.

The pastures to the north, around Zorita within Cáceres province, have good numbers of steppe species, including Great Bustards. They attract flocks of Lapwings, Golden Plovers and Skylarks in winter. Gull-billed Terns, which nest on the reservoir lakes, forage for insects over the pastures in spring and summer.

Timing

The region always offers plenty of interest having, as it does, a wide variety of interesting resident species. Waterfowl and waders are most abundant in winter although the less common wader species occur especially during the spring and autumn passage periods. Common Cranes are only present in winter and their season is a relatively short one, from mid-November to late February. They alone suffice to make a winter visit memorable however. Spring and summer visits are of course necessary to see the breeding species but, as ever, the heat-haze makes visits in the middle of the day in hot weather inadvisable.

Access

A series of major and minor roads traverse the area and it is necessary

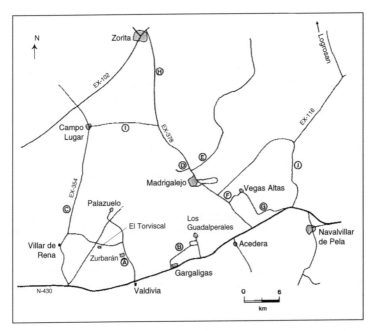

to discover which paddy fields are holding birds at any particular time. Different areas change in attractiveness to waders especially as water levels change and some paddies are flooded and others drained. Stopping along the busy N-430 is sometimes tempting but ill-advised except where farm tracks allow parking right off the road. More relaxed viewing is to be had along the road between Valdivia and Palazuelo (A), the road from Gargaligas through Los Guadalperales (B) and also along the southern part of the Villar de Rena/Campo Lugar road (C).

The vicinity of Madrigalejo offers the best access to the paddy fields. Three sites are particularly productive:

1   Heading north of Madrigalejo, turn left at Km 15.5 (west) just before a clump of eucalyptus trees surrounding a small pool (D). This is the entrance to a network of sandy tracks serving the paddy fields. The car serves as a good hide here. Care should be taken in wet weather since the tracks may become muddy and impassable to other than 4WD vehicles.
2   Also just north of Madrigalejo, turn right (east) into a road running eastwards from the Pension Mayve (E). The rather rough road crosses open fields and encinares before giving access to paddy fields. Common Cranes are often present in winter.
3   Heading south from Madrigalejo take the signposted road left (east) to Vegas Altas (F). The road skirts the town to the east and offers elevated views across the paddy fields. A branch road descends southwards (G) from Vegas Altas to the N-430, giving access to additional large expanses of rice fields.

The steppe species can be seen most readily along the northern half of the Madrigalejo/Zorita road (EX-378, H) and also from the much quieter road to Campo Lugar (I). In winter the road (EX-116) through the encinares for 10 km north from Navalvillar de Pela towards Logrosan (J) is excellent for Cranes.

Calendar

All year: Grey Heron, Black-shouldered Kite, Common Buzzard, Marsh Harrier, Little Bustard, Great Bustard, Stone Curlew, Black-bellied Sandgrouse, Pin-tailed Sandgrouse, Calandra Lark, Zitting Cisticola, Cetti's Warbler, Southern Grey Shrike, Red Avadavat, Spanish Sparrow.

Breeding season: Little Egret, Montagu's Harrier, Lesser Kestrel, Black-winged Stilt, Little Ringed Plover, Collared Pratincole, Gull-billed Tern, Little Tern, Roller, Sand Martin, Short-toed Lark, Tawny Pipit, Black-eared Wheatear, Savi's Warbler, Reed Warbler, Great Reed Warbler, Melodious Warbler.

Winter: Greylag Goose, ducks, Red Kite, Hen Harrier, Crane, Golden Plover, Lapwing (a few may breed), Black-tailed Godwit, Ruff, Penduline Tit.

Passage periods: Spoonbill, Avocet, Redshank, Greenshank, Temminck's Stint, Little Stint, Curlew Sandpiper, Whiskered Tern, Black Tern.

EASTERN BADAJOZ RESERVOIRS   BA11

Status: No special protection.

Site description

The northern steppelands of La Serena (BA9) and the sierras in eastern Badajoz province, are eroded by several rivers whose dammed valleys now comprise a complex of large reservoirs. The Embalses de Orellana, de García Sola, and de Cíjara (BA12) lie along the course of the Río Guadiana. The Embalses del Zújar and de La Serena have been created along smaller rivers to the south of these. The reservoirs provide large bodies of standing water which attract some waterfowl. The waterside vegetation along the reservoirs and feeder streams attracts a range of interesting species. The wooded sierras between the two reservoir complexes, and north of the Embalse de Orellana (Sierra de Pela) also attract a wide range of species.

Species

The Rio Zújar, downstream of the dam of the Embalse del Zújar, has a sizable colony of Cattle Egrets, with some White Stork nests included. Eucalyptus groves nearby hold large colonies of House and Spanish Sparrows. Bee-eaters and Sand Martins have precarious colonies amid the gravel excavations along the river, where Little Ringed Plovers, Common Sandpipers and Little Terns also nest. Breeding passerines include Cetti's, Great Reed and Orphean Warblers and Penduline Tits.

The reservoirs attract Great Crested Grebes, Mallard and other water-fowl in small numbers, especially in winter. The Embalse de Orellana has breeding Gull-billed Terns. Large numbers of Cranes roost regularly at the Embalses de Orellana and del Zújar during the winter months. Griffon Vultures nest above the dam of the Embalse de García Sola, with Crag and House Martins using the dam itself. House Martin colonies are typical of all the dams; that of the Embalse del Zújar has hundreds of nests. The adjacent sierras attract a wide range of raptors and woodland species. The town of Talarrubias has noteworthy and photogenic nest-ing concentrations of White Storks on and around the main church and town square.

Timing

The region has interesting species throughout the year. However, breeding season visits are necessary to find the Spanish Sparrows and other nesting birds along the watercourses. Storks, both Black and White, form pre-migratory gatherings along the Embalse del Zújar and elsewhere in late summer and autumn. Dawn and dusk visits to the Embalses del Zújar and de Orellana in winter (November to February) will reveal concentrations of roosting Cranes.

Access

Limited access to the reservoirs is available from minor roads and the approaches to the various dams. The region is best explored starting from Navalvillar de Pela (perhaps after exploring the nearby wetlands; see BA10) or Orellana, visiting all or some of the following sites: the margins of the Sierra de Pela (A) for raptors, the Presa (dam) de Orellana (B) for wintering waterfowl, the EX-103R road (C) linking Orellana and Puebla de Alcocer, which crosses steppe habitats and the

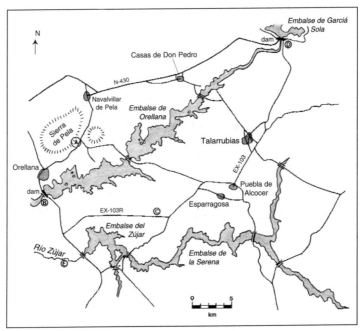

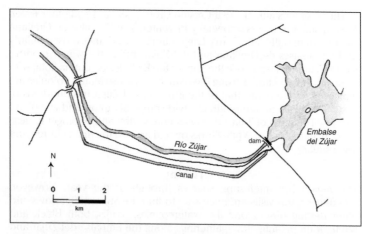

dam at the Embalse de García Sola (D), for waterfowl and also the Griffon Vulture colony and cliff species generally.

The productive region downstream of the dam of the Embalse del Zújar (E) is particularly worth visiting. It is accessible from the minor road following an irrigation channel (Canal del Zújar) along the south bank of the river. The road has obvious stopping places giving access to the frequent pools, riverside scrub and the river itself. The eucalyptus groves, with their sparrow colonies, are along the eastern part of this road, just below the Presa (dam) del Zújar.

Calendar

All year: Little Grebe, Great Crested Grebe, Cattle Egret, Mallard, Red-crested Pochard, Black-shouldered Kite, Red Kite, Griffon Vulture, Black Vulture, Golden Eagle, Moorhen, Coot, Stone Curlew, Common Sandpiper, Eagle Owl, Thekla Lark, Crag Martin, Black Wheatear, Blue Rock Thrush, Penduline Tit, Azure-winged Magpie, Southern Grey Shrike, Spanish Sparrow, Rock Sparrow, Rock Bunting.

Breeding season: Little Bittern, Night Heron, Little Egret, Black Stork, White Stork, Black Kite, Egyptian Vulture, Short-toed Eagle, Booted Eagle, Lesser Kestrel, Little Ringed Plover, Gull-billed Tern, Little Tern, Great Spotted Cuckoo, Scops Owl, Bee-eater, Hoopoe, Roller, Sand Martin, Red-rumped Swallow, Rufous Bush Chat, Nightingale, Black-eared Wheatear, Cetti's Warbler, Great Reed Warbler, Melodious Warbler, Orphean Warbler, Golden Oriole.

Winter: Black-necked Grebe, Great Cormorant, Wigeon, Gadwall, Pintail, Shoveler, Pochard, Tufted Duck, Hen Harrier, Crane, Golden Plover, Lapwing, Black-headed Gull, Lesser Black-backed Gull, Alpine Accentor.

RESERVA NACIONAL DE CÍJARA

Status: Includes a Reserva Nacional de Caza, 25,000 ha. Not otherwise protected.

Site description

This is a sparsely-populated area of rocky wooded hills around the Embalse de Cíjara, in the extreme northeast of the province. It includes a national hunting reserve. The woodlands are of encina with plantations of stone and maritime pines as well as some eucalyptus. There are extensive tracts of matorral, notably gum cistus. The reservoir itself has two main arms, extending up narrow valleys. Rocky outcrops, encrusted with yellow lichens, abound both along the reservoir flanks and as the summits of the ridges of the surrounding sierras. Several islands, also rocky, have been created by the reservoir. Water levels in the lake are often low, which results in temporary reedbeds forming along the valleys, attracting amphibians and their predators.

Species

Black Storks nest on the rocky scarps, including those on islands in the reservoir. A good variety of raptors occur, including Griffon, Black and

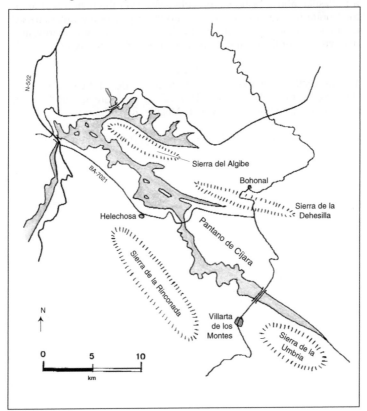

Egyptian Vultures, Golden and Bonelli's Eagles, Hobbies and Eagle Owls. The scrub and woodland house a full range of passerines and others, including Stock Doves and Green Woodpeckers. Rock Sparrows are very common, especially on and near the various bridges on the perimeter road. The area has been relatively little studied ornithologically and may well reward closer investigation. There is a good population of red deer, which are often seen unlike some of the other resident mammals, which include Iberian lynx, wild cat and otter.

Timing

Springtime visits are likely to prove most productive but the site is of interest all year round.

Access

The area is served by minor roads, from which forest tracks allow closer investigation of the passerine community. A drive around the perimeter road (which leaves Extremadura marginally in the north and east, to enter the provinces of Toledo and Ciudad Real), gives access to all the major habitats. The section between Villarta and Bohonal crosses good woodland and includes a crossing of the southern arm of the reservoir on a high causeway, which offers stunning views of the valley. Rock Sparrows are common here and both White and Black Storks may often be seen feeding in the valley below. The rocky outcrops of the Sierra de la Dehesilla, above Bohonal, provide views over the region and are a good point to scan for raptors. The northern part of the drive crosses several scenic bridges, again with Rock Sparrows common nearby, and gives views over the islands in the main body of the reservoir.

Calendar

All year: Cattle Egret, Grey Heron, Griffon Vulture, Black Vulture, Bonelli's Eagle, Golden Eagle, Stock Dove, Eagle Owl, Green Woodpecker, Southern Grey Shrike, Azure-winged Magpie, Rock Sparrow.

Breeding season: Black Stork, White Stork, Egyptian Vulture, Hobby.

CÁCERES PROVINCE

Cáceres province boasts large expanses of wooded sierras, much of the habitat in unspoilt condition. Indeed, some of the large estates have tracts of country which have been pretty well unaltered since medieval times. The terrain is dissected by significant rivers, notably the Río Tajo (Tagus), which have been dammed producing extensive reservoirs. Pasturelands in the province have a steppe-like character and are the home of large populations of bustards and other steppe birds. The province is also well known for the diversity of breeding raptors, which can be seen well at a number of sites but most famously at Monfragüe (CC6). There are also good opportunities to see mountain species, notably on the flanks of the Sierra de Gredos in the Valle del Jerte (CC8) and in the Sierras de las Villuercas (CC4).

Maps

Geocenter International Euromap, Central Spain, 1:300,000.
Mapa de Carreteras Plaza & Janes Madrid-Centro, 1:300,000 (includes all but westernmost Cáceres).
Mapa Provincial Cáceres MOPU/IGN, 1:200,000.

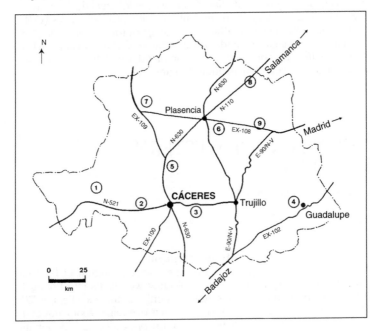

Sites in Cáceres Province

CC1 The plains of western Cáceres
CC2 Steppes of Malpartida de Cáceres
CC3 Cáceres–Trujillo steppes
CC4 Sierras de Las Villuercas
CC5 Cuatro Lugares steppes
CC6 Monfragüe
CC7 Embalse de Borbollón
CC8 Valle del Jerte
CC9 Campo de Arañuelo

Getting there

The N-630 provides north-south access. The N-521 Trujillo/Portugal road crosses the province east/west, branching off the E-90/N-V Madrid/ Badajoz motorway at Trujillo. The EX-108 also crosses the province east/west in its northern sector, linking Plasencia and the N-V and providing easy access to Monfragüe and the northern sites.

Where to stay

Convenient motel-style accommodation is readily available along the major trunk roads. Cáceres, Trujillo, Guadalupe, Plasencia and Jarandilla de la Vera have paradores. The former two cities and other larger towns also offer a range of hotels. Staying in Cáceres overnight on St George's Day (23 April) may be a mistake unless you relish lots of noise and local festivities. St George apparently takes time off from being the patron saint of England to do the same for Cáceres and his memory is commemorated with a pageant (complete with dragon-slaying), a pop concert and a firework display. EG discovered to his cost that you cannot sleep in Cáceres on that night!

Visitors to Monfragüe may stay in Trujillo or perhaps Cáceres but the village of Torrejón el Rubio is an excellent base, lying just to the south of the park boundary. There are several hostales and hotels here, including the recommended four-star Hospedería Parque de Monfragüe, Ctra Plasencia-Trujillo, Km 39.1, 10694, Torrejón el Rubio (Cáceres) (tel: 927-455016). The park itself offers a campsite at Villareal de San Carlos.

Staying in Guadalupe is convenient for visiting Las Villuercas (CC4) and indeed any sites in northeastern Badajoz province, including La Serena (BA9), the Eastern Badajoz reservoirs (BA11) and Cijara (BA12). As well as the parador, which we recommend, Guadalupe offers a full range of accommodation, including a campsite.

THE PLAINS OF WESTERN CÁCERES

CC1

Status: No special protection.

Site description

Westernmost Cáceres province and the adjacent portion of Badajoz province form a spur of territory projecting westwards into Portugal. The northern portion of this region, north of the excellent N-521 Portugal/Cáceres trunk road, has good tracts of encina woodlands and, between the towns of Membrio and Brozas especially, important expanses of rough pastureland and steppe habitats generally. A number of small reservoirs are also of interest.

Species

The steppelands have large numbers of both bustards, both sandgrouse and Stone Curlews. Large numbers of White Storks and colonies of

Lesser Kestrels frequent the towns and villages. A nest box installation scheme between Brozas and Villa del Rey has proved a great success with Rollers, with some 30 pairs occupying most of them each spring. Flocks of Cranes, Golden Plovers and Lapwings are present in winter. The reservoirs attract a range of wetland species also, especially in winter when one or two Temminck's Stints have overwintered in the area in most recent years.

Timing
Interesting species are present all year round.

Access
The N-521 provides easy and swift access to the region. From here a zig-zag route can be followed, starting from near Aliseda, taking-in Brozas, Herreruela, Membrio, Villa del Rey and back to Brozas (see map). This route traverses all the most interesting areas and it will be necessary to stop frequently and scan the plains. Most of the roads are fairly quiet but the EX-302 Herreruela/Brozas link is often busy with fast traffic. Even here, though, there are frequent entrances to farm tracks which allow you to pull off the road safely.

Worthwhile stopping places include the picturesque stone bridge across the Río Salor on the Aliseda/Brozas road (A), where the thin cover of encinas provides a range of woodland passerine species, including Crested Tits. Here too there are small reedbeds where Great Reed Warblers breed. Further north, the road ascends and crosses interesting areas of steppeland, as does the Brozas/Herreruela road (B). Flocks of White Storks, bustards, sandgrouse and Cranes (in winter) can be located here. The road north of Membrio (C) crosses vast expanses

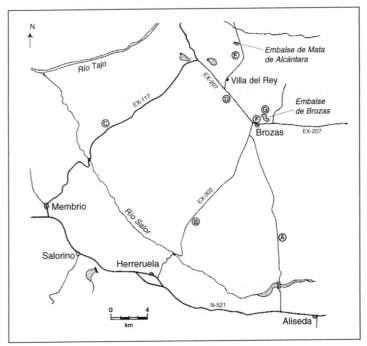

of open country, also requiring frequent scanning to locate the steppe species. White Storks and Montagu's Harriers can be especially abundant here and this quiet road is ideal to enjoy the evocative songs of Quail, Calandra Larks and Corn Buntings in spring. The EX-207 returning towards Brozas (D) is distinguished by the nest boxes which have been attached to the roadside pylons, which accommodate a thriving 'colony' of Rollers. A detour north through Villa del Rey gives access to the Embalse de Mata de Alcantara (E), which attracts waders and waterfowl during passage periods and in winter. It is worth continuing east past Brozas on the EX-207 to view the small pool immediately east of the town (F) and, a short distance further, the Embalse de Brozas (G). Both have ample parking just off the EX-207 and are attractive to waders and ducks in winter.

Calendar

All year: Little Grebe, Cattle Egret, White Stork, Black-shouldered Kite, Griffon Vulture, Black Vulture, Great Bustard, Little Bustard, Stone Curlew, Black-bellied Sandgrouse, Pin-tailed Sandgrouse, Little Owl, Crested Tit, Southern Grey Shrike, Rock Sparrow.

Breeding season: Black Stork, Black Kite, Egyptian Vulture, Short-toed Eagle, Montagu's Harrier, Booted Eagle, Lesser Kestrel, Quail, Black-winged Stilt, Little Ringed Plover, Great Spotted Cuckoo, Roller, Zitting Cisticola, Great Reed Warbler.

Winter: Great Crested Grebe, Black-necked Grebe, Great Cormorant, Wigeon, Gadwall, Teal, Mallard, Shoveler, Pochard, Tufted Duck, Red Kite, Hen Harrier, Crane, Golden Plover, Lapwing, Little Stint, Temminck's Stint (rare), Ruff, Snipe, Redshank, Greenshank, Skylark, Meadow Pipit.

STEPPES OF MALPARTIDA DE CÁCERES
CC2

Status: No special protection.

Site description
Undulating grassy pastures and cereal fields with broad vistas characterise the area northeast of the Sierra de San Pedro, west of Malpartida de Cáceres.

Species
Good numbers of steppe species are present, including Great and Little Bustards, Stone Curlews and sandgrouse. In spring and summer, White Storks are particularly abundant and numbers of Montagu's Harriers are very much in evidence. Vultures and other raptors are regular visitors from the sierras to the south.

Timing
Morning and evening visits in the breeding season are most productive but interesting species are present at all times.

Access
This area offers another opportunity to see the steppe species of Extremadura from easily accessible tracks. Useful access is available from a broad sandy track which extends south from the N-521 at a point about 3 km west of Malpartida de Cáceres or 14 km east of Aliseda. A ruined tower north of the N-521 is just west of the entrance. The track gives access to a network of broad sandy roads across the pastures.

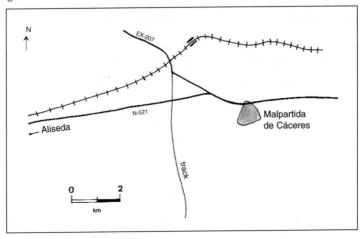

Calendar
All year: Cattle Egret, Red Kite, Griffon Vulture, Black Vulture, Great Bustard, Little Bustard, Stone Curlew, Black-bellied Sandgrouse, Pintailed Sandgrouse, Calandra Lark.

Breeding season: White Stork, Black Kite, Egyptian Vulture, Montagu's Harrier, Booted Eagle, Lesser Kestrel, Hoopoe.

Winter: Crane, Lapwing, larks, pipits, finches.

CACERES–TRUJILLO STEPPES

Status: ZEPA. Parts of the area have been threatened by the application of pesticides intended to cut down on the number of crop-destructive grasshoppers but there are steps being taken to regulate this. Such sprays naturally pose a threat to species as diverse as kestrels and bustards.

Site description

This is an accessible region of steppe-like habitat comprising mainly gently undulating country given over to sheep grazing on rough pastures with areas of wheat cultivation. The pastures are resplendent with their varied flora in spring. A small reservoir, the Embalse del Salor, is attractive to waterfowl, especially in winter. The vicinity of Trujillo is distinctive: the town is centred on a giant rockery of massive boulders and granitic pavements, interspersed with stony pastures.

The towns are picturesque with the characteristic rooftop birds much in evidence. Indeed, to sit in the medieval square of Trujillo on a spring or summer evening, having a drink or a meal accompanied by a dynamic backdrop of swirling clouds of swifts, commuting Lesser Kestrels and storks clattering their greetings on the rooftops, is for many an unforgettable highlight of any trip to Extremadura.

Species

Steppe birds, with notable breeding densities of Montagu's Harriers, Great Bustards (up to 1,000 birds), Little Bustards (2,000+ birds), Stone Curlews, Black-bellied Sandgrouse and Pin-tailed Sandgrouse. Cranes and waterfowl are present in winter. The villages and, notably, the cities of Cáceres and Trujillo have large and conspicuous breeding populations of White Storks, Lesser Kestrels and swifts.

Timing

Birds are obvious all year round but, as with other similar sites, midday excursions in warm weather will be least productive; early mornings and evenings are usually best. Springtime visits are memorable with the harriers visible everywhere quartering the fields. In February, March and into April scattered white 'sheep' prove to be displaying male Great Bustards on closer inspection and the male Little Bustards stand revealing their neck patterns on their territories. The clamour of the Calandra Larks is the most obvious sound but occasional two-tone 'raspberries' can be traced to the Little Bustard males; these uninspiring calls accompany their territorial display. In late spring and early summer particular attention should be paid to areas of recently cut wheat, which often attract sandgrouse flocks. The steppe birds remain in winter, when they form large flocks; wintering Cranes and waterfowl add to the variety then.

Access

The area of interest is traversed by the N-521 Cáceres/Trujillo road. The 18 km nearest Cáceres are dead straight and very busy with fast traffic. Although bustards and other birds can often be seen from this road, indeed they frequently overfly it, stopping here is not advisable. Minor roads, to either side of the N-521, and numerous farm tracks allow access to the fields and pastures. Ask for permission from the local people whenever possible. A telescope is useful for scanning for distant bustards, although the birds generally permit approaches to within 200 m.

Excellent places to try include the tracks north of the village of Torreorgaz, on the EX-206 14 km southeast of Cáceres (A). Here a stone cross on a plinth, and the Bar Extremadura, are directly opposite the entrance to these tracks, which are sandy but in excellent repair. The best track extends for 4 km northwards from Torreorgaz. Stop at the green gate at the end of the road and scan for steppe species or explore further on foot.

Other worthwhile areas include the region on both sides of the Trujillo/La Cumbre road (B) and the Plasenzuela/Botija/Torremocha road (C). North of Torremocha, the latter road gives panoramic views over rolling steppelands and provides excellent vantage points for scanning wide areas. The roads in these areas are all fairly quiet and offer obvious stopping places as well as tracks leading to farms, which may be used for wider exploration.

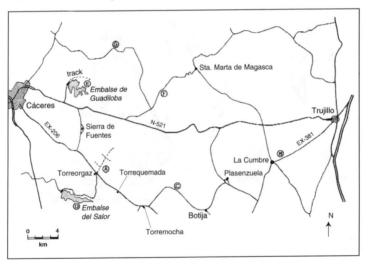

A detour may be made southwards from Torreorgaz to the Embalse del Salor (D). The road follows the northern shore to the dam, which offers good views across the lake. The shallows where the feeder stream enters the river are marshy and often hold waders and the lake itself is attractive to waterfowl, especially in winter. Granite boulders provide islands in the reservoir, which are popular with Grey Herons and waterfowl. The eucalyptus trees fringing the reservoir hold numbers of photogenic White Stork nests.

North of the N-521 and 6 km east of Cáceres a short road leads to a dam, the Presa de Guadiloba, retaining a small reservoir (E). The steppelands around the reservoir may be viewed from this access road, which may be followed left past the dam and then around the northern flanks of the reservoir. Both bustards and other steppe species are again normally present here.

Also north of the N-521, the western road to Santa Marta de Magasca gives views of the steppelands and the usual farm tracks offering closer access (F). The minor road looping from the Santa Marta road and north of the Embalse de Guadiloba, ascends through vast expanses of open pastures and is, again, often productive of bustards and other steppe species (G).

Calendar

All year: Little Grebe, Great Crested Grebe, Cattle Egret, Black-shouldered Kite, Red Kite, Common Kestrel, Great Bustard, Little Bustard, Stone Curlew, Black-bellied Sandgrouse, Pin-tailed Sandgrouse, Little Ringed Plover, Barn Owl, Little Owl, Calandra Lark, Southern Grey Shrike.

Breeding season: White Stork, Black Stork, Black Kite, Montagu's Harrier, Lesser Kestrel, Quail, Black-winged Stilt, Great Spotted Cuckoo, Roller, Pallid Swift, Common Swift, Yellow Wagtail.

Winter: Great Cormorant, Wigeon, Gadwall, Teal, Shoveler, Common Pochard, Tufted Duck, Crane, Golden Plover, Lapwing, Green Sandpiper, Redshank, Lesser Black-backed Gull, larks, pipits and finches.

Lesser Kestrels

SIERRAS DE LAS VILLUERCAS   CC4

Status: No special protection.

Site description

Las Villuercas is the mountainous region of the southeast of Cáceres, in the vicinity of Guadalupe. The parallel rocky ridges which traverse the area enclose narrow and steep-sided valleys, cultivated with olive and almond groves. Elsewhere, the Mediterranean scrub is interrupted by mixed oak and chestnut woods and plantations of maritime pines. In April the heady honey-like scent of gum cistus pervades the whole region. The mountains themselves are craggy and have abundant precipitous escarpments, the rocks attractively splashed with patches of moss and yellow lichens. The highest summit is 1601 m. The local climate is relatively mild in spring and summer and mists and drizzle envelop the mountains in cool weather. Winters are cold.

Species
The area offers a good variety of resident and breeding raptors and passerines.

Timing
Springtime and early summer visits are most rewarding. Nights especially can be cold and suitable clothing for inclement weather is worth having.

Access
The numerous minor roads which cross the area are not busy and offer many opportunities to stop and view the region. Las Villuercas are generally explored by car, on a circuit which should take in Guadalupe, Castañar de Ibor, Retamosa, Navezuelas, Berzocana and Cañamero. Cliffs should be scanned for the nests of Black Storks and raptors. Forest tracks allow access on foot to explore the woodlands for passerines.

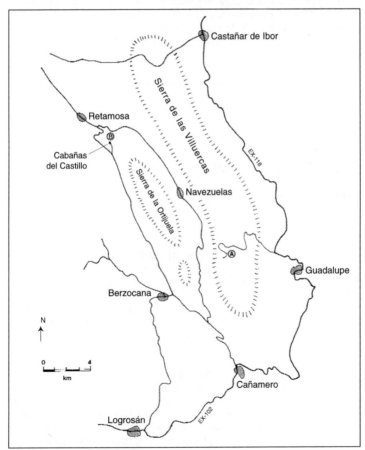

Worthwhile detours include the road to the summit of the Sierra de las Villuercas (A), above Guadalupe, which offers panoramic views. The hamlet of Cabañas del Castillo (B) is also worth visiting. Parking is available at the entrance to the village, where a mirador offers scenic views westwards. The tall rocky outcrops above the village are reached by walking up the steps past the houses and then bearing right to follow the cliff base. The path leads round the back of the ridge and up to the ruined castle on the summit, where there are spectacular views eastwards across the valley to the Sierra de la Ortijuela. Griffon Vultures nest nearby and can be seen at close quarters together with other raptors, such as Bonelli's Eagles. This is a regular site for Alpine Accentors in winter.

Calendar

All year: Red Kite, Griffon Vulture, Black Vulture, Goshawk, Sparrowhawk, Common Buzzard, Spanish Imperial Eagle, Golden Eagle, Bonelli's Eagle, Peregrine, Eagle Owl, Long-eared Owl, Woodlark, Crag Martin, Dipper, Black Wheatear, Blue Rock Thrush, Dartford Warbler, Crested Tit, Nuthatch, Red-billed Chough, Raven, Rock Bunting.

Breeding season: Black Stork, Egyptian Vulture, Short-toed Eagle, Booted Eagle, Hobby, Common Nightjar, Red-necked Nightjar, Alpine Swift, Hoopoe, Crag Martin, Red-rumped Swallow, Northern Wheatear, Melodious Warbler, Subalpine Warbler, Orphean Warbler, Bonelli's Warbler, Ortolan Bunting.

Winter: Dunnock, Alpine Accentor, Fieldfare, Song Thrush, Redwing, Siskin.

CUATRO LUGARES STEPPES CC5

Status: No special protection.

Site description

The rivers Tajo (Tagus) and Almonte enclose an area of steppeland to the north of Cáceres city, between two narrow arms of the massive reservoir, the Embalse de Alcántara. The former is an area of dry-stone walls traversing vast vistas of rough pastureland. By contrast, rather monotonous woodlands of encinas replace the steppes towards the east, from Monroy towards Trujillo. A small reservoir, the Embalse de Talaván, is of interest.

Species

Steppeland species breed in good numbers; they include Montagu's Harriers, Great Bustards, Little Bustards, Stone Curlews, Quail and Calandra Larks. White Storks and Lesser Kestrels from the villages gather here to feed. Cranes are numerous in winter and roost nightly at the Embalse de Talaván. The reservoirs attract large flocks of Cormorants in winter, as well as grebes, waterfowl and thousands of both Black-headed and Lesser Black-backed Gulls. Spanish Sparrows flock in the vicinity. The woodlands have numbers of Azure-winged Magpies and Rock Sparrows among the passerine community.

Timing
Most steppe species are present all year but springtime is most generally productive. Visits to the reservoirs are most rewarding in winter.

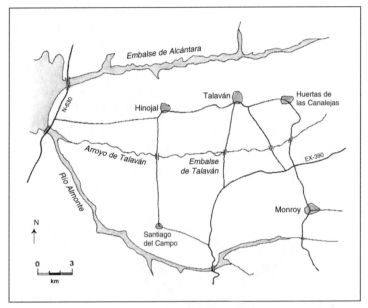

Access
From the minor roads crossing the area. Access to the Embalse de Alcantara is difficult except at a few points off the main road (N-630). The Embalse de Talaván, however, is easily reached from the minor road leading south from Talaván, which crosses the eastern arm of the reservoir. The reservoir is viewable from the minor roads along the south bank and, especially from the dam at the western end, which is the sector favoured by diving ducks and roosting Cranes.

Calendar
All year: Little Grebe, Great Crested Grebe, Cattle Egret, Red Kite, Griffon Vulture, Black Vulture, Great Bustard, Little Bustard, Stone Curlew, Calandra Lark, Southern Grey Shrike, Azure-winged Magpie, Spanish Sparrow, Rock Sparrow.

Breeding season: White Stork, Black Stork, Egyptian Vulture, Short-toed Eagle, Booted Eagle, Montagu's Harrier, Lesser Kestrel, Little Ringed Plover, Roller, Short-toed Lark, Rufous Bush Chat.

Winter: Great Cormorant, Little Egret, Wigeon, Teal, Shoveler, Common Pochard, Tufted Duck, Crane, Golden Plover, Lapwing, larks, pipits and finches.

MONFRAGÜE

Status: Parque Natural, 17,852 ha. ZEPA.

Site description

Monfragüe lies in rugged country at the confluence of the rivers Tiétar and Tajo (Tagus). The rivers have eroded deep gorges, flanked by sheer cliff faces; however, their flow was tamed by dams in the late 1960s and the resulting reservoirs (Embalses de Torrejón and de Alcantara) ensure an abundance of standing water year round.

Monfragüe offers large expanses of unspoilt Mediterranean woodland and scrub. Mixed oak forest predominates, with a characteristic understorey of cistus. Rocky outcrops and ridges divide the area.

The region was under severe threat of development in the 1970s, when there were plans to replace the natural cover with eucalyptus plantations. Some planting was done in the north of the park. However, energetic representations by local conservationists were successful and the park was designated a parque natural in 1979. Today Monfragüe attracts visitors in some numbers and it must be regarded as an essential stop for the ornithologist. The eucalyptus plantations were largely cleared in 2000, to make way for reestablishment of native plant cover.

Sardinian Warbler

Species

This is arguably the prime site of Extremadura offering all the characteristic species, except for the steppe birds, in large numbers. The unrivalled concentration of some 200 pairs of Black Vultures makes this the best site in the world for this spectacular and unforgettable species. All five eagles breed and can be seen with relatively little difficulty; the ten or so pairs of Spanish Imperial Eagles are an obvious attraction. Other breeding raptors include Black-shouldered Kites, Red Kites and very many Black Kites. The cliff faces are populated by easily viewed colonies of Griffon Vultures, as well as Black Storks, Egyptian Vultures,

Peregrines and Eagle Owls. The woodlands support a high density of Azure-winged Magpies among the representative range of passerines.

Timing
Spring visits (April–May) are recommended since the sight of large raptors and Black Storks on their nests is the major attraction of the park. Visits at other times of year will still produce many of the characteristic species.

Access
Monfragüe must once have been very difficult to get at but modern roads provide easy access. A large sector of the park is closed to visitors but the remainder is accessible by car and also on foot, following the several designated foot paths (see map). The visitors' centre at Villareal de San Carlos offers information, an exhibition and the usual car-stickers and similar souvenirs. A campsite (often busy) is adjacent.

A panoramic and productive (birdwise) view is to be had from the top of the Castillo de Monfragüe. Cars may drive up the gravel road and park under the large nettle trees below the castle mount. The views from the top of the tower itself are vertiginous and some care is needed since there are no balustrades and there is a risk of emulating the gipsy who gave his name to the gorge nearby: El Salto del Gitano (Gypsy's Leap). History does not seem to record why the gypsy leapt but at least his mortal remains would soon have been recovered by the inhabitants of the Griffon Vulture colony which occupy the facing escarpment. Black Storks and Egyptian Vultures can also be seen on their nests on

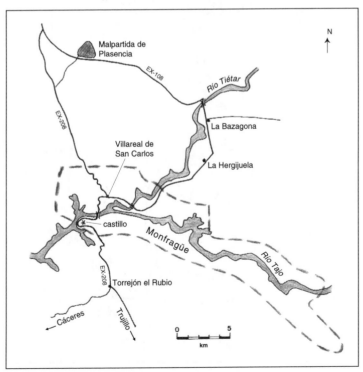

the same cliff face. The castle is a good place to sit and scan the area for raptors; Black Vultures join the Griffons overhead and Golden Eagles are regularly seen here. White-rumped Swifts breed nearby and are often seen in the area in late spring and summer. The woodlands on the south slope are alive with passerines in spring and will repay a patient search.

The Mirador de la Báscula faces rocky wooded slopes favoured by large raptors. Both Black Vultures and Spanish Imperial Eagles may regularly be seen on their nests here.

The roadside continuing northwards from the Mirador de la Báscula, following the River Tiétar gives good views across the narrow reservoir to the low cliffs opposite, where several nests of Black Storks are traditionally placed. A lookout at the Portilla del Tiétar faces the main cliff face, where the nests of a small colony of Griffon Vultures may be clearly seen. Black Vultures nest nearby and are often to be seen perched on the rocks here. Eagle Owls are occasionally visible in the area at dusk.

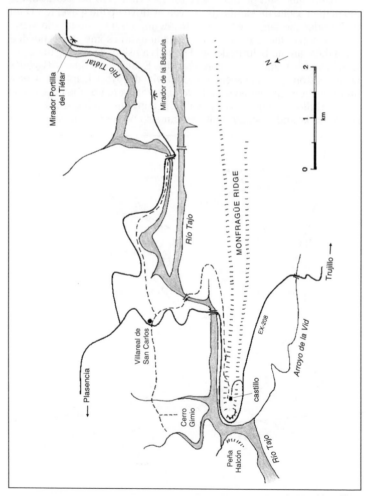

Calendar

All year: Black-shouldered Kite, Red Kite, Griffon Vulture, Black Vulture, Goshawk, Common Buzzard, Spanish Imperial Eagle, Golden Eagle, Bonelli's Eagle, Peregrine, Eagle Owl, Crag Martin, Thekla Lark, Black Wheatear, Southern Grey Shrike, Azure-winged Magpie, Red-billed Chough, Hawfinch, Rock Bunting.

Breeding season: White Stork, Black Stork, Black Kite, Egyptian Vulture, Short-toed Eagle, Booted Eagle, Hobby, Cuckoo, Scops Owl, Red-necked Nightjar, Alpine Swift, White-rumped Swift, Bee-eater, Hoopoe, Red-rumped Swallow, Rufous Bush Chat, Blue Rock Thrush, Spectacled Warbler, Subalpine Warbler, Orphean Warbler, Penduline Tit, Golden Oriole.

Winter: Great Cormorant, Grey Heron, Black-headed Gull, raptors and passerines, including Alpine Accentor.

EMBALSE DE BORBOLLÓN   CC7

Status: The island in the reservoir was a reserve of the Spanish Ornithological Society (SEO), protecting a heronry. It now comes under the auspices of ADENEX. The area in general is not specially protected.

Site description

A dam across the River Arrago encloses the reservoir. The surrounding low undulating hills include rough pastureland and woods of encinas and Pyrenean oaks. Eucalyptus clumps on the island support a colony of 1,000+ pairs of Cattle Egrets.

Species

Breeding Cattle Egrets and Little Ringed Plovers frequent the reservoir. The surrounding pastureland and wheat fields have a population of steppe species: Great Bustards, Little Bustards, Stone Curlews, Pin-tailed Sandgrouse and Calandra Larks. Black-shouldered, Red and Black Kites are among the breeding raptors. Bee-eaters are very common and there is a colony of Spanish Sparrows. Cranes and Black-tailed Godwits occur in winter.

Timing

Springtime for most species.

Access

The reservoir is best viewed from the dam on the south side (telescope advisable). A sandy but drivable track, leading from Villa del Campo eastwards to the reservoir and passing through woodlands, is worth exploring. Eucalyptus clumps along this road near the reservoir hold sparrow colonies in spring.

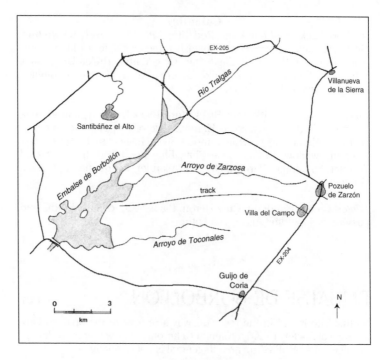

Calendar

All year: Cattle Egret, Black-shouldered Kite, Red Kite, Great Bustard, Little Bustard, Stone Curlew, Pin-tailed Sandgrouse, Calandra Lark, Spanish Sparrow.

Breeding season: White Stork, Black Kite, Montagu's Harrier, Little Ringed Plover, Quail, Bee-eater, Roller.

Winter: Greylag Goose, Crane, Black-tailed Godwit, Golden Plover, Lapwing, Black-headed Gull, larks, pipits and finches.

VALLE DEL JERTE   CC8

Status: Reserva Natural (Garganta de los Infiernos) in the central valley. Otherwise no special protection.

Site description

The valley of the Jerte river is a long, straight canyon descending from the southwestern slopes of the lofty Sierra de Gredos to the historic city of Plasencia. The region offers a contrast with most of the rest of Extremadura, having a temperate rather than a Mediterranean character, with the birds to match. The high tops, easily accessed at the Puerto de Tornavacas (1275 m) and the Puerto de Honduras (1430 m), have a moorland appearance. These upper slopes are rocky but adorned with large tracts of the broom *Cytisus purgans,* whose vanilla-scented flowers provide spectacular sheets of yellow in early summer. Lower down there are extensive woods of Pyrenean oak as well as extensive tracts of black pine and sweet chestnut. The lowest slopes are terraced and heavily committed to the cultivation of cherries. The cherry orchards are a local tourist attraction in spring, when the trees are in blossom. The whole area has the rocky and often snow-capped summits of the Gredos range, which lie outside Extremadura, as a spectacular back-drop. The Gredos sites are described in our sister volume, *Where to watch birds in North and East Spain.*

A narrow reservoir, the Embalse de Plasencia, occupies the lower valley, upstream of Plasencia, which it serves. A much larger reservoir, the Embalse de Gabriel y Galán, some 30 km north of Plasencia, is also of ornithological interest.

Species
The region provides good opportunities to see a range of upland and mountain species, such as Thekla Larks, Alpine Accentors, Dunnocks, Water Pipits, Dippers, Bluethroats, Northern Wheatears, Rock Thrushes, Carrion Crows, Citril Finches and Rock Buntings. The woodlands also attract a range of species which are otherwise local or absent in the southern half of Spain, such as Honey Buzzards, Lesser Spotted Woodpeckers and Garden Warblers. Other breeding raptors include Goshawks and Golden Eagles. The reservoirs attract gatherings of Black Storks in late summer, and waterfowl in winter especially.

Timing
The area requires a full day's birding to do it justice. Visits in good weather in springtime and early summer are the most productive given that many of the valley's attractions are summer visitors. Visits at other times are still enjoyable, again provided that the mountain mists haven't descended, but be aware that the weather may be very cold in winter, with frosts making driving potentially tricky on the minor roads. The passes are occasionally blocked by snow.

Access
The N-110 Plasencia/Avila road gives ready access to the region. The road is moderately busy but there are a number of obvious stopping points. A visit should take in the following sites:

A Embalse de Plasencia (del Jerte)
This long, narrow reservoir is worth a look especially in late summer, when Black Storks often congregate along the shore, and in winter, when there may be small numbers of grebes and waterfowl. Good views may be had from the dam (presa); follow the access road off the N-110 which is signposted 6 km north of Plasencia. The reservoir may also be viewed from the service road below the villas which fringe the eastern shore.

B La Garganta de los Infiernos
Don't be put off by the grim name (The throat of Hell!). This is a new reserva natural featuring a range of marked trails through woodland

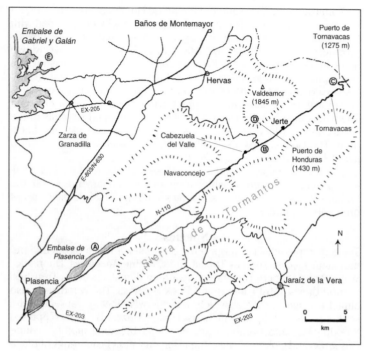

along the Rio Jerte and its tributaries and up the eastern slopes of the valley. Maps and information are available from the splendid reserve centre. Some of the trails involve steep climbs of eight hours' duration — each way. However, much of the bird interest is available without quite such a marathon effort. Honey Buzzards, Lesser Spotted Woodpeckers, Dippers and Garden Warblers, all of them very local species in southern Spain, breed in the area as well as a pleasing variety of other raptors and woodland passerines. The reserve is entered along a short access road located a short distance north of the road to Puerto de Honduras, between the villages of Cabezuela del Valle and Jerte. The entrance is on the right (if you are driving up the valley) opposite and between a conspicuous pottery workshop and craft centre (alabasteria) and a timberyard. Park signs point the way. A short drive leads across the river and to the information centre, from where the trails originate.

C Puerto de Tornavacas

This col lies on the boundary between Extremadura and Castilla y León. There are fine views to be had from the ample car park, right down the Valle del Jerte to Plasencia and north down into Avila province. The col is a natural route for migrant birds, including raptors and passerines and also flocks of Woodpigeons in autumn. These last are the quarry of hunters whose shooting platforms dot the hillside on the northern (Avila) slopes. The area is peaceful in spring and summer when walks up the slopes may reveal the local speciality species: Northern Wheatear, Rock Thrush and Bluethroat. Carrion Crows, a mountain species in southern Spain, are often around the car park. Dartford Warblers and Cuckoos are also characteristic. Raptors overhead frequently include Golden Eagles and Griffon Vultures.

D Puerto de Honduras

The col is reached along a quiet, winding road which climbs upwards from the Valle del Jerte and then descends to the town of Hervas, in the next valley. Starting from the Jerte end, the entrance is signposted some 2 km north of Cabezuela del Valle. The road climbs through the terraced cherry orchards, popular with Azure-winged Magpies and other passerines, to reach open woodlands of Pyrenean oaks and then the moorland above. Traffic is light (although ponies and other live-stock on the road are a minor hazard) and there are abundant stopping places from which to look and listen for woodland species, and also overhead raptors. There are easy walks around the col itself where breeding species include Dunnocks and Rock Buntings. Finches and other passerines often fly over the col and we have seen Citril Finches here. The committed will not be deterred from walking 4 km up to the northern summit, for a good chance of seeing Northern Wheatears, Rock Thrushes and Bluethroats. Once over the top of the col, on the Hervas side, there are some fine old oaks around the first hairpin bend. An easy walk of a few hundred metres through these open parkland-like woods leads to the ridge, giving magnificent views to the north and east. This is an excellent spot to scan for raptors and there is also a good chance of finding Rock Thrushes and Northern Wheatears.

The descent to Hervas is through much denser and more mature woodland, chiefly of Pyrenean oaks and sweet chestnuts, with stands of poplars and a dense undergrowth. There are numerous paths through the woods including the signposted trail 'Ruta Heidi' just above Hervas. The main road itself is so quiet though that it provides ideal access for looking for and listening to the woodland passerines. The town of Hervas provides easy access to or from the N-630.

E Embalse de Gabriel y Galán

This large reservoir is not in the valley but instead lies some 30 km north of Plasencia. Access is from the N-630 and thence west along the EX-205 to Zarza de Granadilla and beyond, where there is roadside access to the eastern and southern shores. The lake attracts wintering Cranes and also waterfowl, the latter also in winter especially.

Calendar

All year: Red Kite, Griffon Vulture, Common Buzzard, Goshawk, Sparrow-hawk, Golden Eagle, Peregrine, Common Sandpiper, Eagle Owl, Tawny Owl, Green Woodpecker, Great Spotted Woodpecker, Lesser Spotted Woodpecker, Woodlark, Thekla Lark, Crag Martin, Grey Wagtail, Alpine Accentor, Dunnock, Nuthatch, Black Wheatear, Blue Rock Thrush, Dartford Warbler, Azure-winged Magpie, Red-billed Chough, Carrion Crow, Raven, Rock Sparrow, Rock Bunting.

Breeding season: Black Stork, Honey Buzzard, Egyptian Vulture, Short-toed Eagle, Booted Eagle, Cuckoo, Red-necked Nightjar, Common Night-jar, Scops Owl, Water Pipit, Bluethroat, Common Redstart, Northern Wheatear, Black-eared Wheatear, Pied Flycatcher, Melodious Warbler, Subalpine Warbler, Whitethroat, Garden Warbler, Bonelli's Warbler, Golden Oriole, Ortolan Bunting.

Winter: Great Crested Grebe, wildfowl, Crane, Siskin, Citril Finch, Bull-finch.

CAMPO DE ARAÑUELO

Status: ZEPA, in part.

Site description

The Campo de Arañuelo is a broad expanse of gently undulating country in the north of Extremadura sandwiched between the rivers Tiétar and Tajo. The Sierra de Gredos forms an imposing, purple-hued and snow-capped backdrop to the whole region. There are excellent tracts of cork oak and encina woodlands, and riverine woodlands, in the north and west of the area. Elsewhere there is much cultivated land, a lot of it given over to tobacco. Indeed tobacco-drying barns, many of them derelict, are a feature of the region. The infamous nuclear power station of Almaráz, long the target of campaigns for closure by ADENEX and others, is in the southeastern corner. Here too is an interesting reservoir, the Embalse de Arroyocampo-Almaráz.

Species

This is an especially good area for seeing the birds of the dehesas. The raptor population is high, not least because the region borders Monfragüe natural park. Griffon and Black Vultures are overhead for much of the day. All five eagles occur, as well as Common Buzzards, Black Kites, Red Kites (which are abundant in winter) and Hobbies. The region is one of the best sites in Spain for Black-shouldered Kites. White Storks are abundant and Black Storks frequently feed along the river channels. Passerines include breeding Sand Martins, Rufous Bush Chats, Tree Sparrows and Hawfinches. The reservoir is one of the few sites in Extremadura inhabited by Purple Gallinules and it also plays host to breeding Marsh Harriers and abundant waterfowl, the latter especially in winter.

Access

The primary access to the region is the EX-108, Plasencia/Navalmoral de la Mata road. The stretch between La Bazagona and Casatejada crosses some interesting woodlands but this is a very busy road, complete with lorries and police patrols and there are few obvious stopping places. The better woodlands may be explored from the quieter roads to the north of the EX-108, leading to and beyond Majadas. The road south from La Bazagona to Monfragüe crosses open country and a small river before passing through some exceptionally fine woodlands, boasting unusually large, very old cork oaks. The roads to Toril, south of the EX-108, are especially quiet and productive.

Beyond Toril there is a network of very good dirt roads crossing excellent woodlands and leading to Monfragüe and Serrejón. The entrances at either end are indicated by signs saying 'Ruta a Toril y Serrejón', adorned with a drawing of a Hoopoe. Stop frequently and scan over the woodlands; some of the cattle here are bullfight material so it is inadvisable to stray beyond running distance from your vehicle.

The Embalse de Valdecañas is reached by driving south from the EX-108 past Casatejada and through Saucedilla. The northern arm of the reservoir (also known as the Embalse de Arrocampo-Almaráz) has fringing reedbeds and is the best area in which to stop and explore.

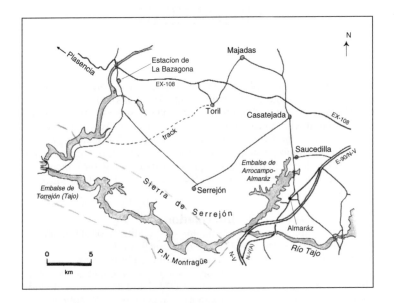

Calendar

All year: Black-shouldered Kite, Red Kite, Common Buzzard, Griffon Vulture, Black Vulture, Purple Gallinule, Water Rail, Southern Grey Shrike, Tree Sparrow, Red Avadavat, Hawfinch.

Breeding season: Purple Heron, Little Bittern, Black Stork, Black Kite, Egyptian Vulture, Booted Eagle, Short-toed Eagle, Marsh Harrier, Lesser Kestrel, Hobby, Gull-billed Tern, Great Spotted Cuckoo, Roller, Sand Martin, Rufous Bush Chat, Savi's Warbler, Great Reed Warbler, Reed Warbler.

Winter: Great Cormorant, ducks, Hen Harrier, Merlin, Common Crane, Golden Plover, Lapwing.

Passage periods: Osprey, Avocet, Black-winged Stilt, Black Tern, Whiskered Tern, hirundines, Sedge Warbler.

GIBRALTAR

This is a really special place which you must visit if you can. At least, one of us (EG) thinks so, probably because he was born there. There can't be many other spots though where you can see a Black Stork sharing a thermal with a Gannet or migrating Fan-tailed Warblers accompanying flocks of Honey Buzzards! Gibraltar is exceptionally well placed for migration watching, of raptors and seabirds particularly. The bird observatory often makes it possible to observe bird-ringing in action, with excellent in-the-hand views available of a whole range of species.

Information

If you are basing your visit on Gibraltar, or spending a lot of time in the area, then the accounts by Cortés *et al.* (1980) and Finlayson (1992) remain informative. A useful resource is the website of the Gibraltar Ornithological and Natural History Society (www.gibnet.gi/~gonhs/). This provides current news about the GONHS and its activities, including the Gibraltar species list, as well as a 'Recent Records' noticeboard in the 'Gibraltar Birds' section (now updated more often than hitherto).

United Kingdom based visitors may contact the Gibraltar Government Office, who will gladly supply tourist brochures, details of car hire companies and similar useful information. Their address is: Gibraltar Government Office, 179 The Strand, London, WC2R 1EH (tel: 0207-836-0777/fax: 0207-2406612).

Flights to Gibraltar are mainly scheduled and operated by GB Airways from Gatwick Airport and Monarch Airlines from Luton. Locally, tourist information is available from the Gibraltar Tourist Board, Duke of Kent House, Cathedral Square, Gibraltar (tel: (350) 74950; fax: (350) 70029; email: tourism@gibraltar.gi).

Where to stay

Gibraltar offers a range of hotels. The Caleta Hotel, on the east side of the Rock at Catalan Bay, is popular with visiting birders. Mr Harry Van Gils of the hotel management is one of Gibraltar's leading birdwatchers and he is always willing to assist visitors. In particular, the hotel offers very significant discounts for birders and they can also arrange car hire at highly competitive rates. It is a good idea to contact Harry if you are planning a visit to the area and especially if you intend to base yourself in Gibraltar. The address is: Caleta Palace Hotel, PO Box 73, Catalan Bay, Gibraltar (tel: 76501; fax: 42143 and 71050).

Camping and caravanning are not permitted but there are numerous campsites in nearby Spain.

The GONHS itself offers accommodation within the Upper Rock Nature Reserve. There are two sites: Bruce's Farm and Jews' Gate Field Centre. Bruce's Farm is a converted army officers' residence, offering twin-room accommodation as well as kitchen, bathroom and other facilities, at the modest charge of £15 per person per night. Jew's Gate only accommodates two persons, at £4.50 per night, in simple but recently refurbished quarters. Bird-ringers will find it ideal since it is only 5 m from the nearest of the mist nets. Accommodation at either site should be pre-booked; contact the society at their website (as above) or by post, email etc.

Sea trips

Pelagic trips are increasing in popularity worldwide, often catering for those wishing to see cetaceans: whales and dolphins. Gibraltar was something of a pioneer in this field since the Dolphin Safari has provided day trips for dolphin watchers for over 20 years now. A number of tour companies now run the same service and the GONHS also has its own vessel, the *Nimo*. Trips on the *Nimo* operate twice daily and cost £15 for adults (£7 for children). None of these trips is pelagic in the strict sense: they operate only in coastal waters, notably in Gibraltar bay. The main attraction is always the dolphins (common, striped and, less often, bottle-nosed), which are more or less guaranteed to appear. The boats do allow a closer look at seabirds such as Cory's and Balearic Shearwaters, and occasionally such exotica as flying fish, sunfish, turtles and sharks, and a trip on one of them is always a pleasant experience. *Nimo* departs from Queensway Quay and other services both from here and the Waterport Marina.

Status: Protected area. There is no hunting and all wildlife is protected from deliberate destruction, although the usual pressures from 'development' arise. Fortunately much new building is on land recently reclaimed from the sea, which has added some habitat for birds incidentally. The whole of the Upper Rock comprises a nature reserve.

Site description

The massive Rock of Gibraltar looms out of the Mediterranean at the western end of the Costa del Sol. Surprisingly many people still believe that Gibraltar is an island but the Rock is firmly attached to the mainland via a broad sand bar (now mainly under the airport, the border posts and other tarmac). Gibraltar covers an area of some 6 km². The northern and eastern sides of the Rock are sheer cliff faces, rising to 426 m (1396 feet) at O'Hara's Battery, the southern end of the summit ridge. The western slopes are more gentle and largely built up on their lower reaches but covered by diverse vegetation higher up. A dense scrub of olives, lentisc, buckthorn and spiny broom is interrupted by numerous firebreaks and other open grassy areas.

Gibraltar has a striking climate which contrasts with that of the Costa del Sol. The prevailing winds are westerly (good for raptors) and easterly, the infamous *levanter*, which often produces a pall of cloud which caps the Rock for days on end. Winter rainfall is considerable, sometimes torrential. Combinations of murk and wetness during passage periods produce falls of migrants.

Species

Gibraltar's claim to ornithological fame is due almost entirely to its strategic position. It is a first-rate viewpoint for raptor migration, which occurs in some form for ten months of the year (February–November). Here raptors can be seen (and photographed) really well at close quarters, which isn't always possible further along the Strait. A good day in spring or autumn will produce 12–15 raptor species, occasionally more. The southern tip (Europa Point) offers excellent year-round seabird watching, with Audouin's Gulls among the regulars and Lesser Crested

Terns if you are lucky. Falls of migrants occur frequently and so the veg-etated areas often harbour a wide variety of small birds; 30 species of warbler have been recorded for example. The high densities of birds and birders mean that rare or vagrant species are detected annually. Recent sightings have included Pintado Petrel, Lammergeier, Pallid Harrier, Spotted Eagle, Grey-headed Gull, Pallas's Warbler, Yellow-browed Warbler, Red-breasted Flycatcher, House Crow, Common Rose-finch, White-throated Sparrow, Dark-eyed Junco, Pine Bunting and Bobolink.

Relatively few species breed in Gibraltar but it is a good site to see Peregrines, Pallid Swifts and Blue Rock Thrushes. The only Barbary Partridges in mainland Europe, most probably the descendants of a long-standing introduction, occur on the Upper Rock. The breeding Shags are also an area speciality; Gibraltar is their only remaining site in southern Spain and they have proved amazingly tenacious, the popula-tion of some five pairs still hanging on in the face of threats from pollu-tion and, especially, disturbance.

Birds apart, Gibraltar is interesting botanically: the limestone flora contrasts with that of the surrounding sandstone hills. Gibraltar can-dytuft is one of the more obvious of the special species. The famous apes are barbary macaques *Macaca sylvana;* like the partridges, they too are probably originally introduced by man. They are much easier to find than the partridges; in fact, they will find you if they think you have anything edible to offer. The apes are of uncertain but mainly malevo-lent temperament and should be treated with discretion.

Timing

Visible migration of soaring birds is obvious from March–May and August–October. The movements mainly involve raptors. Storks and cranes favour Tarifa, further west (CA2). March has large numbers of Black Kites and Short-toed Eagles especially. April is best for all-round variety. May is dominated by vast flights of Honey Buzzards, especially in the first half of the month. The return passage begins in August with Black Kites. The Honey Buzzards mainly return at the beginning of September. Short-toed and Booted Eagles are prominent in September and early October. A trickle of 'northern' species (Sparrowhawk, Com-mon Buzzard, Hen Harrier) continues into November. Raptors pass over Gibraltar mainly in westerly winds; the easterlies displace the flow westwards. However, numbers of Booted and Short-toed Eagles espe-cially, mill about over the Rock in easterly winds in August–October, often flying on a circular course to and from the mainland as they wait for conditions to improve.

Falls of passerine migrants occur from February to May and again from August to November. Bad weather, especially the low cloud and drizzle or thunder associated with the levanter, can cause thousands of migrants to be grounded on the Rock.

Seabird watching is rewarding at all times of year, even in midsum-mer. On bright days, however, viewing from Europa Point is best in the late afternoons and evenings; otherwise the glare from the sun on the water makes life difficult.

Access

Gibraltar airport is one of the obvious arrival points for visitors to our area. Some arrive by sea, mainly by ferry from Tangier. The land frontier provides access from Spain for vehicles and pedestrians; don't forget your passports. The border is plagued by traffic queues at certain times, mainly when commuters enter the Rock in the early mornings and (particularly) when they leave again in the evenings. Avoid these times if possible if crossing the border in a car. Pedestrians and motorcyclists are not usually delayed.

Once in Gibraltar, there are a number of key sites to visit. All of Gibraltar can be 'done' in a day but a visit during good westerly winds in the migration seasons usually means staying for hours at either Jew's Gate or the cable-car station, with perhaps an evening visit to Europa Point. A visit during the winter or during easterly 'fall' conditions in passage periods, needs to take in the other sites mentioned.

A Upper Rock Nature Reserve
The Upper Rock can be reached conveniently by car by driving south along the western side along Europa Road. Follow the signs to the nature reserve. Access is via Queen's Road, which branches off from Europa Road just south of the Casino. There is a toll booth and an entrance fee (£5.00 per person and £1.50 per car in 2000), which includes entry to the 'obligatory' tourist sites such as the limestone caverns of St Michael's cave and the 'apes'' den. However, if you are staying at Bruce's Farm or Jews' Gate, or if you are planning to make several visits during the course of a birding holiday, you should contact the Gibraltar Tourist Board in Cathedral Square who will issue you with a complimentary pass.

All of the Upper Rock is of interest, especially when falls of passerine migrants occur. However, there are a number of notable sites to visit:

A1 Jews' Gate
The Gibraltar Ornithological and Natural History Society have a bird observatory, bird-ringing station and information centre at Jews' Gate, just past the entrance to the Upper Rock Nature Reserve. The centre is often manned by the very helpful local ornithologists and visitors are welcomed. If you are a qualified ringer you may well be able to take part in the bird-ringing there. This is the place to go for information on the latest sightings both in Gibraltar and in nearby Spanish provinces. Jews' Gate is the preferred site for watching raptors in spring; in autumn try the cable-car station on the summit ridge (see A3 below).

A2 Mediterranean Steps
This is a scenic footpath which takes in the highest point of the Rock and which offers spectacular views of the Strait, Spain and Morocco. Park at Jews' Gate and follow the mapped route up the western side to the summit at O'Hara's Battery. The Mediterranean steps descend the eastern side and the path then turns west above Windmill Hill to Jews' Gate once more. It is of course perfectly possible to follow this route in reverse, up the eastern side and down the western side, but the steepness of the eastern climb makes this an option only for the foolhardy or the super-fit. The Mediterranean steps are occasionally frequented by Barbary Partridges and good views of Peregrines and Blue Rock Thrushes are often to be had. Yellow-legged Gulls are abundant, some nesting on the very footpath itself. Alpine Accentors sometimes occur here in winter. The Steps are best visited in the early morning when any grounded night migrants or partridges will still be undisturbed.

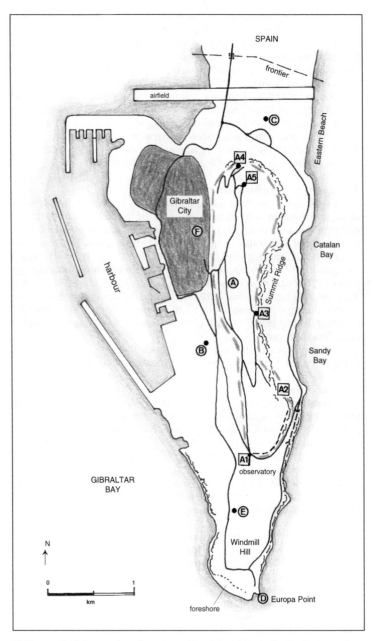

However, in hot weather they are a pleasant place to be in the late afternoons and evenings, when the shadow of the Rock covers the eastern side.

A3 Cable-car top station
This is a good site for raptor-watching, especially during the southward migration (mainly August–October). The cable-car provides a lift there

for those who are lazy or just in a hurry (2000 charge: £4.95 return). Others park at St Michael's Cave and walk. The energetic will walk up the Rock from the town; a leisurely progression taking in the summit ridge will require 3–4 hours, obviously more if there are good birds to delay you. The cable-car station itself has observation platforms and a restaurant and other tourist amenities. Tourists (and those awful apes) may be numerous and most birders prefer to walk a short distance south along the summit ridge and watch in relative peace from the old concrete gun emplacements there.

A4 Princess Caroline's Battery

This is an alternative site for watching southbound raptor migration in August–October. The battery overlooks the airfield. Scan for raptors approaching Gibraltar from the north. This site often offers excellent views of the birds but it misses those which approach the eastern side of the Rock from the northeast. It is possible to drive down to the battery itself. Alternatively follow signs to the Upper Galleries from where viewing platforms give dizzying views down the precipitous north face. A small fig tree, growing in a cleft on the north face some 100 m to the right and below the level of the watchpoint, is a favourite perch for the local Peregrine.

A5 Governor's Lookout

This area of scrub, firebreaks and Aleppo pine groves is attractive to grounded migrants, such as Hoopoes and Bonelli's Warblers, and wintering passerines, such as Firecrests. The firebreaks have a population of Barbary Partridges which can sometimes be seen here at dawn and in the evenings, when they may call noisily. The area can only be explored on foot. Cars may be parked at Princess Caroline's Battery.

B Gibraltar Botanic Garden

The botanic garden at the Alameda is of considerable and increasing floral interest. The beds of aloes, attracting nectar-seeking Common Chiffchaffs and other birds, are a curiosity in December and January. At other times, the gardens hold grounded migrants, notably Hoopoes, chats and warblers. Park in Grand Parade, next to the cable-car station. There is no entrance fee although donations are welcome and are a contribution to the botanical conservation work which is underway here. There is a shop and information centre. The garden is under the supervision of Dr John Cortés, who is also General Secretary of the Gibraltar Ornithological and Natural History Society, and an invaluable source of local information. (The management also have a Nature Shop in Casemates Square, at the north entrance to Main Street; both shops are useful sources of maps, field guides and books.)

C North Front Cemetery

The public cemetery, below the vertical precipices of the north face of the Rock, is also excellent for grounded migrants during 'fall' conditions. Turn north off Devil's Tower Road into Cemetery Road. The cemetery is open to the living during daylight hours but is much disturbed by visitors, who tend to frighten the birds away completely. Morning visits are therefore best.

D Europa Point

This is the southern tip of the Rock, marked by the conspicuous light-house. Europa Point is one the best seawatching sites in the region, offering excellent views from an elevated position. Raptors and other landbirds can also often be seen arriving here into Europe from Africa in spring. Park by the lighthouse and watch from the observation plat-form at the cliff edge. A telescope is an asset but not essential; some fly-bys of Audouin's Gulls and other key species are very close indeed. It is also possible to follow the coastal promenade westwards to where a wooden flight of steps descends to the rocky and sparsely-vegetated foreshore. The lee of a small hut here provides some shelter on windy days and the foreshore itself receives passerine migrants in some num-bers at times.

E Jacob's Ladder

This area of open scrub is sheltered from the east winds by the cliffs of Windmill Hill. It is worth searching for passerine migrants during 'falls'. At other times it often holds Barbary Partridges, especially in the evenings in summer and autumn when they may be seen sitting on the walls above the cliff edges. (Windmill Hill itself often holds large num-bers of migrants but it is off-limits as a military zone and is frequently much disturbed by shooting on the army ranges. GONHS may be able to arrange visits.)

F Gibraltar City

The city has a large and noisy population of both Pallid and Common Swifts. Sunny evenings from April to July provide excellent opportuni-ties to compare these two confusing species in excellent light. The rooftop-nesting population of Yellow-legged Gulls is a relative novelty; the birds are an overspill from the fully-tenanted sites on the cliffs and scree slopes of the Rock. The first nests appeared in the late 1980s and some dozens of pairs now attempt to nest in the city each year, if they are allowed to get away with it. Some human town-dwellers find their swooping defence of the nests rather intimidating and the gulls' habit of spraying generous splashes of excreta over the washing on clothes lines has done little for their public image.

Calendar

All year: Cory's Shearwater, Balearic Shearwater, Gannet, Shag, Lesser Kestrel, Common Kestrel, Peregrine, Barbary Partridge, Great Skua, Audouin's Gull, Yellow-legged Gull, Little Owl, Wren, Blue Rock Thrush, Blackbird, Sardinian Warbler, Blackcap, Blue Tit, Great Tit, Spotless Starling, House Sparrow, Chaffinch, Serin, Greenfinch.

Breeding season: European Storm-petrel (offshore only), Common Swift, Pallid Swift, Alpine Swift.

Winter: Leach's Storm-petrel, Common Scoter, Mediterranean Gull, Little Gull, Black-headed Gull, Lesser Black-backed Gull, Kittiwake, Sandwich Tern, Razorbill, Puffin, Crested Lark, Crag Martin, Meadow Pipit, Grey Wagtail, Pied Wagtail, Alpine Accentor, Robin, Black Redstart, Stone-chat, Zitting Cisticola, Common Chiffchaff, Firecrest, Short-toed Tree-creeper, Rock Bunting.

Passage periods: Greater Flamingo, Black Stork, White Stork, Honey Buzzard, Black Kite, Red Kite, Egyptian Vulture, Griffon Vulture, Short-toed Eagle, Marsh Harrier, Hen Harrier, Montagu's Harrier, Sparrow-hawk, Common Buzzard, Booted Eagle, Osprey, Merlin, Hobby, Eleonora's Falcon, Quail, Pomarine Skua, Arctic Skua, Gull-billed Tern, Caspian Tern, Lesser Crested Tern, Common Tern, Black Tern, Turtle Dove, Great Spotted Cuckoo, Scops Owl, Common Nightjar, Red-necked Nightjar, Common Swift, Pallid Swift, Alpine Swift, Kingfisher, Bee-eater, Hoopoe, Wryneck, Short-toed Lark, Skylark, Sand Martin,

Barbary Partridges

Crag Martin, Barn Swallow, Red-rumped Swallow, House Martin, Tawny Pipit, Tree Pipit, Yellow Wagtail, Rufous Bush Chat, Nightingale, Blue-throat, Common Redstart, Whinchat, Stonechat, Northern Wheatear, Black-eared Wheatear, Rock Thrush, Ring Ouzel, Song Thrush, Redwing, Mistle Thrush, Zitting Cisticola, Grasshopper Warbler, Reed Warbler, Olivaceous Warbler, Melodious Warbler, Dartford Warbler, Spectacled Warbler, Subalpine Warbler, Orphean Warbler, Whitethroat, Garden Warbler, Bonelli's Warbler, Wood Warbler, Iberian Chiffchaff, Willow Warbler, Spotted Flycatcher, Pied Flycatcher, Golden Oriole, Woodchat Shrike, Chaffinch, Brambling, Serin, Greenfinch, Goldfinch, Siskin, Linnet, Ortolan Bunting, rarities.

Records

The Gibraltar Ornithological and Natural History Society keeps a database of records of birds observed in Gibraltar and in nearby provinces. They would be most grateful to receive news of your observations, which should be sent to:

The Records Officer, GONHS, PO Box 843, Gibraltar (tel: (350) 72639; fax: (350) 74022; email: gonhs@gibnet.gi).

The Society publishes quarterly bird observatory reports, a newsletter and an annual report *Alectoris*. Any published records will be fully acknowledged.

A SYSTEMATIC LIST OF THE BIRDS OF SOUTHERN AND WESTERN SPAIN

This list outlines the status of all those species which occur regularly in Andalucía and/or Extremadura. The English names will be recognisable to all. They are largely the familiar ones used in the *Handbook of the Birds of the Western Palearctic* (Cramp & Simmons, 1977 *et seq.*). Spanish names are those currently approved by the Sociedad Española de Ornitología. The list shows the main periods when each species occurs in the region but it excludes marginal dates for which there are only a few records. Those additional species which are vagrants or occur very rarely are listed separately in the following chapter. Species marked * are those which are on the SEO rarities committee list.

Red-throated Diver   *Gavia stellata*   Colimbo Chico
A very scarce winter visitor, December–February, along the Atlantic coast. Rare in the Mediterranean.

Black-throated Diver   *Gavia arctica*   Colimbo Artico
A very scarce winter visitor November–March, along the Mediterranean coast. Rare in the Atlantic and inland.

Great Northern Diver   *Gavia immer*   Colimbo Grande
A very scarce winter visitor November-March on the Atlantic coast, most often reported from Cadiz Bay (CA12). Rare in the Mediterranean and inland.

Little Grebe   *Tachybaptus ruficollis*   Zampullín Común
A common breeding species on reed-fringed lakes. Mainly resident.

Great Crested Grebe   *Podiceps cristatus*   Somormujo Lavanco
Breeds commonly on larger lakes. More widely dispersed in winter.

Black-necked Grebe   *Podiceps nigricollis*   Zampullín Cuellinegro
Locally common as a breeding species on reed-fringed lakes. Numbers are increased by migrants in winter, when some also occur on the coast in sheltered inshore waters, as in Gibraltar Bay.

Cory's Shearwater   *Calonectris diomedea*   Pardela Cenicienta
Present offshore all year round but very scarce in winter, although some are seen in the Strait then. Most frequent in summer in the Mediterranean; scarcer off the Atlantic coast. Large, and at times spectacular, movements occur through the Strait; westwards in late October–November and eastwards in February–March. These involve the Mediterranean populations moving to and from winter quarters in the south Atlantic.

Great Shearwater   *Puffinus gravis*   Pardela Capirotada
Present off Atlantic coasts and in the Strait and seen occasionally from the shore. Accidental in the Mediterranean. Late August–December

Sooty Shearwater   *Puffinus griseus*   Pardela Sombría
Present off Atlantic coasts and in the Strait and seen occasionally from the shore. Accidental in the Mediterranean. Chiefly September–November but it has been seen off Doñana (H5) in January.

Balearic Shearwater   *Puffinus mauretanicus*   Pardela Balear
Present offshore all year round, chiefly in Mediterranean waters. Numbers migrate into the Atlantic through the Strait in June–August, returning from late September–March.

Levantine Shearwater   *Puffinus yelkouan*   Pardela Mediterránea
Until the 1970s, large flocks used to be present in Málaga Bay and the Strait in late summer,

when the birds moult. Gatherings of up to 2,000 were also regular then in Gibraltar Bay. Numbers have been small in recent years.

European Storm-petrel *Hydrobates pelagicus* Paíño Europeo
Present offshore, mainly April–September. Most often seen in the Strait but it is common in central Alborán. Infrequently seen from shore.

Leach's Storm-petrel *Oceanodroma leucorhoa* Paíño Boreal
Present offshore in winter, from November to February, and sometimes visible from land in the Strait and from Atlantic coasts, especially after westerly gales. Accidental in the Mediterranean.

Gannet *Sula bassana* Alcatraz Atlántico
Present offshore all year round, although only a few non-breeders remain in summer. The largest numbers are present in winter, from October to March. Conspicuous migration of small flocks occurs through the Strait, birds entering the Mediterranean from September–November and returning from February–June.

Great Cormorant *Phalacrocorax carbo* Cormorán Grande
Common and locally numerous in winter on lakes and reservoirs in Extremadura and in Andalucía. Has bred locally. Mainly small numbers winter on the coast, notably in Huelva, but Cádiz Bay has a wintering population of over 1,000 birds.

Shag *Phalacrocorax aristotelis* Cormorán Moñudo
A tiny resident population (maximum five pairs) breeds on the southeast sea cliffs of Gibraltar and it is also reported from Cabo de Gata (AL1). Very rare elsewhere.

Bittern *Botaurus stellaris* Avetoro Común
A very scarce but widespread winter visitor. Has bred Doñana (H5).

Little Bittern *Ixobrychus minutus* Avetorillo Común
A widespread but inconspicuous summer visitor (April–September), nesting in reedbeds. A few remain in winter.

Night Heron *Nycticorax nycticorax* Martinete Común
A widespread but inconspicuous summer visitor (April–September), nesting in riverine trees, often in mixed colonies with other herons. Some winter in the Guadalquivir valley and occasionally elsewhere.

Cattle Egret *Bubulcus ibis* Garcilla Bueyera
Resident. One of the most obvious and characteristic species of the area, omnipresent with herds of cattle in western Andalucía and Extremadura especially. Less widespread in the breeding season when birds stay closer to the heronries. These colonies are relatively few but can be very large, totalling up to several thousand nests.

Squacco Heron *Ardeola ralloides* Garcilla Cangrejera
Very local but easily overlooked. Mainly a summer visitor, present April–September, chiefly in the Guadalquivir basin. Small numbers remain in winter.

Little Egret *Egretta garzetta* Garceta Común
A common breeding species. Many are migrants, wintering in Africa, but considerable numbers remain in winter, when it is widespread. Nests colonially with Cattle Egrets and other herons.

Great White Egret *Egretta alba* Garceta Grande
Sightings have increased steadily and it is now annual within the area, occurring mainly during the winter months, October–March. Most records come from sites along the lower Guadalquivir, notably Doñana (H4) and the Brazo del Este (SE1), as well as along both the Atlantic and Mediterranean coasts. There are increasingly frequent records from Extremadura. Single birds are most usual but small groups of up to seven individuals have occurred. It seems likely that it will soon be added to the long list of breeding heron species of the region.

Grey Heron *Ardea cinerea* Garza Real
Numerous and widespread on passage and especially in winter, when many arrive from northern Europe. Increasingly common as a breeding species in western Andalucía and Extremadura, the Doñana (H5) colony having exceeded 450 pairs in 1996.

Purple Heron   *Ardea purpurea*   Garza Imperial
A locally common breeding species in large reedbeds, mainly in western Andalucía. Widespread on passage. Summer visitor, present April–October.

Black Stork   *Ciconia nigra*   Cigüeña Negra
Widespread and locally common in Extremadura and in adjacent parts of western Andalucía, typically nesting on cliff ledges. Increasing. Widespread on passage when small flocks converge on the Strait. Mainly a summer visitor, present late February–October. Occasional birds winter.

White Stork   *Ciconia ciconia*   Cigüeña Blanca
An abundant, increasing and characteristic breeding species in western Andalucía and throughout Extremadura, very local or absent further east. Nests on buildings, trees and pylons. Large churches often support small colonies of ten or more nests. Present all year round but most leave Spain in late July and August, returning once the rains arrive, from November to February. Spectacular movements occur across the Strait; the largest gatherings then occur in early August when merging flocks produce flights of up to 3,000 birds.

Glossy Ibis   *Plegadis falcinellus*   Morito Común
Present in small but increasing numbers in Doñana (H5), the nearby Brazo del Este (SE1), along the Huelva coast and occasionally elsewhere, mainly in winter and spring. The wintering flock at the Brazo del Este exceeded 200 birds in 2000/2001. Several pairs nested in Doñana in 1996 and subsequently.

Spoonbill   *Platalea leucorodia*   Espátula Común
Breeds Doñana (H5), Odiel (H4) and, latterly, Cádiz Bay (CA12) where it is resident. Scarce on passage and in winter elsewhere.

⊘ **Greater Flamingo**   *Phoenicopterus ruber*   Flamenco Común
Up to 10,000 pairs nest in most years at the Laguna de Fuente de Piedra (MA1). Regular and common for much of the year at Doñana (H5), Salinas de Cabo de Gata (AL1), Laguna de Médina (CA15) and a few other localities. Flocks can be seen elsewhere in Andalucía at any time of year, moving between these localities as well as from colonies further afield. Very rare in Extremadura.

Mute Swan*   *Cygnus olor*   Cisne Vulgar
Introduced. There is a small feral population in coastal Almería. Occasional elsewhere.

Greylag Goose   *Anser anser*   Ansar Común
Abundant in winter in and near Doñana (H5), where up to 80,000 gather, and very locally elsewhere. Present from late October to early March mainly, peak numbers occurring in December and January. Flocks cross Extremadura and northern Andalucía on passage to and from Doñana.

Shelduck   *Tadorna tadorna*   Tarro Blanco
Common in winter in Doñana (H5) and the Guadalquivir estuary, where flocks of 800+ occur from November–March. Has bred Bonanza (CA17). Elsewhere present in small numbers in winter.

Wigeon   *Anas penelope*   Anade Silbón
Widespread in winter and on passage; present October–March. Locally abundant, notably in Doñana (H5) where peak counts in January may exceed 30,000 birds.

Gadwall   *Anas strepera*   Anade Friso
Small numbers breed in Extremadura and western Andalucía. Common in winter, when hundreds gather on suitable lakes.

Teal   *Anas crecca*   Cerceta Común
Widespread and common in winter and on passage. Locally abundant; peak counts in January at Doñana (H5) may exceed 60,000 birds.

⊌ **Mallard**   *Anas platyrhynchos*   Anade Real
Widespread and common as a breeding species. Numbers are greatly increased by migrants in winter. Peak winter counts at Doñana (H5) exceed 20,000 birds.

Pintail   *Anas acuta*   Anade Rabudo
Widespread and locally numerous on passage and in winter; present November–March mainly. Up to 15,000 winter in Doñana (H5). Has bred Doñana and Las Norias (AL3).

Garganey   *Anas querquedula*   Cerceta Carretona
Commonly encountered in small flocks during passage periods; February–April and August–October, especially in spring. Occasional individuals winter. Has bred rarely.

Shoveler   *Anas clypeata*   Cuchara Común
Common and locally numerous on passage and in winter, present September–April mainly. Counts at Doñana (H5) may exceed 40,000 birds. Breeds sporadically, mainly in coastal sites in Huelva, Cádiz and Almeria.

Marbled Duck   *Marmaronetta angustirostris*   Cerceta Pardilla
A scarce breeding species, nesting in Doñana (H5) and a few lagoons in southern Andalucía, notably Las Norias (AL3). Most numerous in autumn and winter when flocks of up to a few hundred may form in this area.

Red-crested Pochard   *Netta rufina*   Pato Colorado
Widespread as a breeding species on suitable lagoons, especially in Doñana. Flocks of several hundred form in winter. Over 3,000 winter in Doñana (H5).

Pochard   *Aythya ferina*   Porrón Europeo
Small numbers breed, especially in Doñana. Widespread and numerous in winter when large numbers of migrants arrive from the north. Peak counts in Doñana (H5) exceed 7,000 birds.

Ferruginous Duck   *Aythya nyroca*   Porrón Pardo
A very scarce and sporadic breeding species. Individuals may appear at any time on suitable lagoons.

Tufted Duck   *Aythya fuligula*   Porrón Moñudo
Widespread and common in winter in small numbers.

Common Scoter   *Melanitta nigra*   Negrón Común
A common wintering species, present off all coasts mainly from October to April, although a few non-breeders remain in summer. Large numbers (up to 5,000) winter off Doñana (H5) and the Huelva coast.

Red-breasted Merganser   *Mergus serrator*   Serreta Mediana
Widespread offshore in winter in small numbers. Most numerous off the Huelva coast, from October–April.

Ruddy Duck   *Oxyura jamaicensis*   Malvasía Canela
Strays have continued to appear with increasing frequency at the Laguna de Zoñar (CO1), Laguna de Medina (CA15) and in Almería. These are thought to be stragglers from the large feral population in England. Unfortunately Ruddy Ducks and White-headed Ducks are interfertile and cases of hybridisation have already occurred in Spain. A campaign to shoot Ruddy Ducks is being implemented since they are a definite threat to the White-headed Duck population.

White-headed Duck   *Oxyura leucocephala*   Malvasía Cabeciblanca
A locally common breeding species largely confined to the lagoons of Andalucía where it is progressively more widespread. Numbers are increasing and flocks of over 300 occur in winter in favoured localities such as the Laguna de Médina (CA15). Very rare in Extremadura.

o **Honey Buzzard**   *Pernis apivorus*   Abejero Europeo
Abundant on passage and most readily seen near the Strait, where it is by far the most numerous of the migrant raptors. As many as 100,000 fly south there between mid-August and late September, returning from late April to early June. A few breed in Extremadura, chiefly in the north.

Black-shouldered Kite   *Elanus caeruleus*   Elanio Común
A widespread and increasing resident, frequently seen on pylons and other exposed perches. Most abundant in Extremadura where it first bred in 1975 and where the population exceeds 500 pairs. Also common as a breeding species in eastern Huelva province and increasingly frequent elsewhere in Andalucía. Occasional migrants cross the Strait.

Black Kite   *Milvus migrans*   Milano Negro
A very common and locally abundant breeding species in Extremadura and western Andalucía, characteristically near water. Over 50,000 cross the Strait on migration, mainly from February–May and late July–September. A few winter.

Red Kite   *Milvus milvus*   Milano Real
A widespread and common breeding species in Extremadura and western Andalucía but greatly outnumbered by Black Kites. Most numerous in winter when numbers arrive from northern Europe; over 1,000 birds frequent the Doñana area (H5) alone at this season. A few hundred cross the Strait.

Lammergeier   *Gypaetus barbatus*   Quebrantahuesos
No longer breeds in Cazorla (J1), although there are plans to reintroduce the species. Wandering birds are occasionally reported elsewhere and there have been several recent records near the Strait.

Egyptian Vulture   *Neophron percnopterus*   Alimoche Común
A widespread but declining breeding species, nesting on cliffs. A couple of thousand cross the Strait on migration, arriving mainly from February–April and departing from August–October. A few individuals winter.

Griffon Vulture   *Gyps fulvus*   Buitre Leonado
A highly characteristic, common and increasing species. Large colonies occur on many suitable cliff faces and flocks gather regularly at municipal rubbish dumps as well as at livestock carcases. Foraging birds may appear anywhere. Adults seem to be largely resident but considerable numbers of chiefly immature birds migrate cross the Strait southwards in October–November, returning in late spring.

Rüppell's Griffon Vulture*   *Gyps rueppellii*   Buitre Moteado
A recent colonist from tropical Africa. The first was one seen in Cáceres on scattered dates from 7 April 1990 until 1 June 1992, usually in the company of Griffon Vultures *Gyps fulvus*. What may have been the same bird was in Doñana on 21 and 22 October 1992. Since then records have become more frequent so that by autumn 1998 at least five individuals, an adult, a subadult and three juveniles, were present in the region of the Strait alone, with occasional sightings elsewhere. In 1999 one was reported incubating on the Portuguese side of the river Tajo (Tagus) in Extremadura (although the outcome is unknown nor was it established whether a pair was present).

Black Vulture   *Aegypius monachus*   Buitre Negro
Locally common as a breeding species in Extremadura, mainly in Cáceres province, and in northwestern Andalucía, although greatly outnumbered by Griffons. Nests on trees. Resident but individuals wander widely in winter, occasionally crossing the Strait.

Short-toed Eagle   *Circaetus gallicus*   Culebrera Europea
Widespread and locally common as a breeding species. A summer visitor, arriving mainly between late February and April, returning in September–October. Some 4,000 birds cross the Strait on passage and daily counts of several hundred birds are not uncommon there during the peak months of March and September. Occasional individuals winter.

Marsh Harrier   *Circus aeruginosus*   Aguilucho Lagunero
Widespread and locally common as a breeding species, especially in western Andalucía. Mainly resident but migrants from northern Europe occur commonly on passage and in winter. Several hundred cross the Strait, mainly in March–early May and September–October.

Hen Harrier   *Circus cyaneus*   Aguilucho Pálido
Common and widespread in winter, October–March, when it replaces Montagu's Harrier. Small numbers cross the Strait on passage; in February–April and September–November. Has bred occasionally in Extremadura.

Montagu's Harrier   *Circus pygargus*   Aguilucho Cenizo
A common and characteristic breeding species of farmland and steppe. Present from mid-March to early October. A few thousand cross the Strait on passage. Melanistic birds are not uncommon; up to 5% of migrants at Gibraltar are melanistic.

Goshawk   *Accipiter gentilis*   Azor Común
A widespread and locally common breeding species although inconspicuous and easily overlooked. Largely resident.

Sparrowhawk *Accipiter nisus* Gavilán Común
A widespread and fairly common breeding species. Northern migrants increase numbers in winter. A common and increasing migrant; several thousand cross the Strait in March–April and late August–October.

Common Buzzard *Buteo buteo* Busardo Ratonero
Widespread and common as a breeding species. Migrants from the north increase numbers in winter. A few thousand cross the Strait, in March–April and September–November.

Spanish Imperial Eagle *Aquila adalberti* Águila Imperial Ibérica
A scarce and slowly declining species. The world population was only 131 pairs in 1999, down from 148 pairs in 1994. Most are in central Spain, Extremadura and western Andalucía. The Doñana region (H5) holds 14–16 pairs. Generally resident but some individuals disperse more widely in winter, some then reaching Málaga province.

Golden Eagle *Aquila chrysaetos* Águila Real
Present in some numbers in all mountain ranges. Resident.

Booted Eagle *Hieraaetus pennatus* Aguililla Calzada
A widespread and common breeding species, present mainly from March to October. Small numbers winter in western Andalucía. Flocks form at the Strait on migration; a few thousand cross there from March–May and August–October.

Bonelli's Eagle *Hieraaetus fasciatus* Águila-azor Perdicera
Widespread and characteristic of cliffs and broken country. Apparently declining. Largely resident but disperses more widely in winter.

Osprey *Pandion haliaetus* Águila Pescadora
Common on passage, from mid-February to May and again between August and October. Individuals winter regularly in favoured localities such as Cádiz Bay (CA12) and the Strait region, and occasionally along the Mediterranean coast as well as at the Embalse de Valuengo, Badajoz.

Lesser Kestrel *Falco naumanni* Cernícalo Primilla
Locally common and showing some recovery from the catastrophic decline in numbers suffered in the 1980s and 1990s. Nests colonially on cliffs and older buildings, notably on church towers and castles. Many villages and towns in Extremadura and western Andalucía support large colonies. Present mainly from February to October, with some returning to southern colonies as early as December.

Common Kestrel *Falco tinnunculus* Cernícalo Vulgar
Widespread and common as a breeding species. Numbers are increased by migrants in winter and during passage periods, March–May and September–October.

Merlin *Falco columbarius* Esmerejón
A scarce but regular and widespread wintering species, favouring open country where it hunts larks and finches. Small numbers cross the Strait. Present from October to April.

Hobby *Falco subbuteo* Alcotán Europeo
A widespread but very local breeding species, most abundant in Huelva and Cáceres, present from April to October. Common on passage at the Strait in late spring and autumn.

Eleonora's Falcon *Falco eleonorae* Halcón de Eleonora
Single birds and small groups occur regularly at Gibraltar and in the Strait region between March and October, although most occur in August and September. Their origin is unclear and there are no known breeding colonies in the region. Occasionally reported from the Almería and Málaga coasts.

Peregrine *Falco peregrinus* Halcón Peregrino
A widespread and common breeding species, nesting on coastal and inland cliffs. The Doñana area (H5), lacking cliffs, has Peregrines nesting on the ruined Arab watch-towers along the coast. The local birds *F. p. brookei* are resident but a few of the larger and paler northern Peregrines *F. p. peregrinus* also occur widely in winter.

Red-legged Partridge *Alectoris rufa* Perdiz Roja
Widespread and abundant, despite being a prime quarry species of hunters. Resident.

Barbary Partridge *Alectoris barbara* Perdiz Moruna
Only present in Gibraltar where a declining population of perhaps some 30 pairs inhabits what little open scrub remains there. These are probably the descendants of birds introduced from Morocco by man at least 200 years ago. They are the only partridges in Gibraltar.

Quail *Coturnix coturnix* Codorníz Común
A common and widespread breeding species. Present mainly between March and October, but some remain in winter.

Ring-necked Pheasant *Phasianus colchicus* Faisán Vulgar
A small feral population seems to be established in southern Cádiz province.

Little Buttonquail (Andalusian Hemipode) *Turnix sylvatica* Torillo Andaluz
A relict population still survives in the coastal palmetto scrub of western Andalucía but they are rarely recorded and unlikely to be found by a casual visitor.

Water Rail *Rallus aquaticus* Rascón Europeo
Widespread and locally common in suitable habitat. Resident populations are increased by migrants in winter.

Spotted Crake *Porzana porzana* Polluela Pintoja
Small numbers cross the region on passage and some remain to winter. Breeds Doñana (H5).

Little Crake *Porzana parva* Polluela Bastarda
Nests Doñana (H5) where some remain in winter. May occur elsewhere in suitable habitat.

Baillon's Crake *Porzana pusilla* Polluela Chica
Widespread but elusive in suitable habitat, nesting in western Andalucía. Reputed to be a summer visitor but some winter in Doñana (H5).

Moorhen *Gallinula chloropus* Gallineta Común
A common and widespread breeding species. Mainly resident.

Purple Gallinule *Porphyrio porphyrio* Calamón Común
Widespread and probably increasing, both in numbers and geographical distribution. Locally common in marshy habitats and lakeside reedbeds in Andalucía especially. Familiarity with the calls is a great help in finding the birds.

Coot *Fulica atra* Focha Común
A common and widespread breeding species. Thousands frequent Doñana (H5). Nesting birds are dispersive, some crossing the Strait to winter in North Africa. Large numbers of migrants from northern Europe are also present in winter.

Red-knobbed Coot *Fulica cristata* Focha Moruna
A very scarce resident species. The population of at best 30 pairs is confined to Doñana and a few lagoons in western and central Andalucía.

Crane *Grus grus* Grulla Común
An abundant wintering species in Extremadura and at several sites in western Andalucía. Gatherings of thousands can be seen in favoured localities. Some hundreds cross the Strait. Present mainly from mid-October to early March.

Great Bustard *Otis tarda* Avutarda Común
Resident. Locally common in the steppelands of Extremadura, where thousands breed. Scarce and declining in Andalucía.

Little Bustard *Otis tetrax* Sisón Común
Resident. Thousands inhabit the steppelands of Extremadura and it is locally common in Andalucía. Large flocks, of a few hundred birds, form outside the breeding season.

Oystercatcher *Haematopus ostralegus* Ostrero Euroasiatico
Present on passage and in winter on all coasts, in small numbers. Exceptional inland.

Black-winged Stilt *Himantopus himantopus* Cigüeñuela Común
Widespread and locally numerous, breeding commonly in western Andalucía, along the Mediterranean coast and in the rice fields and reservoirs of Extremadura. Mainly a summer

visitor, present from March to October, but up to 1,000 birds winter in Doñana (H5) and along the Huelva coast and also, increasingly, inland.

Avocet   *Recurvirostra avosetta*   Avoceta Común
Small numbers breed, chiefly in western Andalucía, but present in large numbers on passage and especially in winter. Over 5,000 birds winter in the Doñana area (H5)

Stone Curlew   *Burhinus oedicnemus*   Alcaraván Común
A common breeding species in steppe habitats. Flocks form in winter, some of these probably including migrants from northern Europe.

Collared Pratincole   *Glareola pratincola*   Canastera Común
A summer visitor, locally common along the Guadalquivir and Guadiana valleys especially. Present mainly from April to July, departing promptly after breeding.

Little Ringed Plover   *Charadrius dubius*   Chorlitejo Chico
Mainly a summer visitor, present from March to October. Small numbers breed, especially on stony riverbeds. Widespread on passage. Small numbers remain in winter.

Ringed Plover   *Charadrius hiaticula*   Chorlitejo Grande
Common and locally numerous, on passage and especially in winter. Has bred Málaga. Chiefly coastal. Largest numbers are seen between September and April but some non-breeders remain in summer.

Kentish Plover   *Charadrius alexandrinus*   Chorlitejo Patinegro
Widespread and common, nesting on sandy coasts (despite much disturbance) and salt pans. The resident population is increased by migrants during passage periods and in winter.

Golden Plover   *Pluvialis apricaria*   Chorlito Dorado
A winter visitor, locally numerous. Present November to March mainly.

Grey Plover   *Pluvialis squatarola*   Chorlito Gris
Common in winter and on passage in coastal habitats, rarely inland. Mainly present from August to May but some individuals remain all summer.

Lapwing   *Vanellus vanellus*   Avefría Europea
Small numbers nest, chiefly in western Andalucía. Common and often abundant in winter, especially when harsh conditions occur further north in Europe. Most numerous from November to early March.

Knot   *Calidris canutus*   Correlimos Gordo
Widespread on passage in small numbers in coastal habitats, especially in May and September. Rare inland. A few winter.

Sanderling   *Calidris alba*   Correlimos Tridáctilo
Common on passage and in winter on sandy coasts. Rare inland. Present mainly from October to April but some non-breeders remain in summer.

Little Stint   *Calidris minuta*   Correlimos Menudo
Common on passage, both in coastal and inland wetlands, mainly in April and August–September. Small numbers are present in winter.

Temminck's Stint   *Calidris temminckii*   Correlimos de Temminck
A very scarce migrant and winter resident. Recorded from both Atlantic and Mediterranean Andalucía, especially in Doñana (Huelva), the Brazo del Este (Sevilla), Málaga and Almería. A few winter inland in Cáceres province (see CC1).

Curlew Sandpiper   *Calidris ferruginea*   Correlimos Zarapitín
Common and sometimes numerous on passage, both in coastal and inland wetlands, mainly in May and August–September. A few individuals winter.

Purple Sandpiper   *Calidris maritima*   Correlimos Oscuro
A few individuals occur in some winters on rocky coastal headlands, such as Punta Secreta (CA3).

Dunlin *Calidris alpina* Correlimos Común
Abundant on passage, mainly in April and September, and in winter, chiefly in coastal habitats. Small numbers of non-breeders remain in summer.

Ruff *Philomachus pugnax* Combatiente
Common on passage, mainly in March–April and September, and in winter, both in coastal and inland wetlands.

Jack Snipe *Lymnocryptes minimus* Agachadiza Chica
Present on passage and in winter, chiefly on inland wetlands, from October–April. Locally common; some 3,000 are estimated to winter in Doñana (H5) alone.

Snipe *Gallinago gallinago* Agachadiza Común
Common on passage and in winter, chiefly on inland wetlands, from August–April. Locally abundant; some 30,000 are estimated to winter in Doñana (H5) alone.

Woodcock *Scolopax rusticola* Chocha Perdiz
Principally a winter visitor, widespread but inconspicuous. Present October–March.

Black-tailed Godwit *Limosa limosa* Aguja Colinegra
Very common on passage, in April and July–September and in winter, chiefly on the coast but also at favoured inland localities such as the Extremaduran wetlands (BA10). Over 15,000 winter in Doñana (H5). Non-breeders occur in summer in some numbers.

Bar-tailed Godwit *Limosa lapponica* Aguja Colipinta
Common on passage, in March and September–October, and in winter in coastal habitats. Scarcer than the Black-tailed Godwit and usually seen in small parties.

Whimbrel *Numenius tenuirostris* Zarapito Trinador
Common on passage, chiefly on the coast in July–November and March–May. Small numbers winter, most notably in Doñana (H5), and a few non-breeders remain in summer.

Curlew *Numenius arquata* Zarapito Real
Common on passage, July–October and March–April, and in winter, chiefly on the coast. A few non-breeders remain in summer.

Spotted Redshank *Tringa erythropus* Archibebe Oscuro
Common on passage, July–October and March–May, and in winter. Often on freshwater marshes as well as in coastal habitats.

◦ **Redshank** *Tringa totanus* Archibebe Común
A breeding resident in coastal marshes and more locally inland. Numbers are greatly increased by migrants in winter and during passage periods, July–October and March–May.

Marsh Sandpiper *Tringa stagnatilis* Archibebe Fino
A scarce but regular passage migrant, March–April and July–October, usually seen by freshwater. Small numbers winter regularly in Doñana.

Greenshank *Tringa nebularia* Archibebe Claro
Widespread and common on passage, July–October and March–May, mainly on coasts. Significant numbers remain to winter; up to 6,000 along the Atlantic coast.

Green Sandpiper *Tringa ochropus* Andarríos Grande
Widespread and common on passage, especially by fresh water, mainly July–October and March–May. Some remain to winter.

Wood Sandpiper *Tringa glareola* Andarríos Bastardo
Widespread and common on passage, especially in freshwater habitats, July–October and April–May. Significant numbers winter in Doñana (H5).

◦ **Common Sandpiper** *Actitis hypoleucos* Andarríos Chico
Widespread as a breeding species along the major river valleys in Extremadura, in western Huelva and along the upper Guadalquivir. Numerous on passage in both inland and coastal habitats; July-November and March-May. A few remain to winter.

Turnstone *Arenaria interpres* Vuelvepiedras
Widespread in small numbers on passage, July–November and February–May, and in winter, chiefly on rocky coasts.

Red-necked Phalarope *Phalaropus lobatus* Falaropo Picofino
Occasional individuals are reported on passage in coastal habitats. Very rare inland.

Grey Phalarope *Phalaropus fulicarius* Falaropa Picogrueso
Recorded in small numbers irregularly offshore and along Atlantic coasts, especially after westerly gales in late autumn and winter. Very rare inland.

Pomarine Skua *Stercorarius pomarinus* Págalo Pomarino
Regular but scarce on passage along coasts, most records coming from the Strait in March and April and again from August to October. Occasional in winter.

Arctic Skua *Stercorarius parasiticus* Págalo Parásito
Common on passage, July–November and February–May and some remain in winter, especially in the Strait. Occasional individuals also remain in summer

Great Skua *Stercorarius skua* Págalo Grande
Common on passage, September–November and March–June, and in winter, especially in the Strait. Occasional individuals remain in summer.

Mediterranean Gull *Larus melanocephalus* Gaviota Cabecinegra
Common on passage, mainly October–November and March–April and in winter on or near coasts. Flocks of up to several hundred birds form locally especially after stormy weather. Non-breeders occur in summer in small numbers.

Little Gull *Larus minutus* Gaviota Enana
Regular but usually scarce on passage, August–October and March–May. Common in winter, especially offshore in the Mediterranean. Flocks of hundreds sometimes occur in the Strait after easterly gales in winter. Rare inland.

Black-headed Gull *Larus ridibundus* Gaviota Reidora
Small numbers breed locally. Widespread and abundant both inland and on the coast in winter.

Slender-billed Gull *Larus genei* Gaviota Picofina
Small numbers breed locally, notably in Doñana (H5, some 20 pairs) and sometimes at Fuentedepiedra (MA1). Mainly resident but some disperse along coasts. Regular at coastal sites in Almería, such as Cabo de Gata (AL1), especially in spring. Recent records from Cádiz province, of 500 at Sanlúcar on 21 Mar 1998 and 459 at El Puerto de Santa María on 26 Sep 1998, suggest that it is increasing.

Audouin's Gull *Larus audouinii* Gaviota de Audouin
Common on passage along Mediterranean coasts and through the Strait, mainly February–April and August–October. Concentrations of summering immature birds occur in the Strait, Málaga Bay and in Almería. Small numbers winter, especially near the Strait, but most then descend the African coast as far as Senegal and beyond. Usually scarce on Atlantic coasts except near the Strait but concentrations occur at favoured localities; for example, 203 were at San Fernando (Cádiz) on 6 Oct 1997 and c.70 at Odiel (Huelva) on 17 Jul 1997.

Common Gull *Larus canus* Gaviota Cana
Occasional individuals occur in winter along coasts. Very rare inland.

Lesser Black-backed Gull *Larus fuscus* Gaviota Sombría
Common on passage and in winter, but much less numerous along coasts than prior to the 1980s, reflecting an increasing tendency to overwinter in Europe. Hence large numbers now winter inland, notably along the Guadiana River and at reservoirs in Extremadura. Some non-breeders remain in summer.

Herring Gull *Larus argentatus* Gaviota Argéntea
Occasional individuals occur in winter along Atlantic coasts. Accidental in the Mediterranean.

Yellow-legged Gull *Larus cachinnans* Gaviota Patiamarilla
Locally abundant, with large nesting colonies on rocky coasts including many thousands at Gibraltar. Mainly resident but disperses widely along coasts. Uncommon inland.

Great Black-backed Gull *Larus marinus* Gavión Atlántico
Occasional individuals occur in winter along Atlantic coasts. Very scarce in the Mediterranean.

Kittiwake *Rissa tridactyla* Gaviota Tridáctila
Mainly a winter visitor, usually seen between October and April in the Strait and off Atlantic coasts. Large numbers may appear inshore after westerly gales, when some enter the Mediterranean.

Gull-billed Tern *Gelochelidon nilotica* Pagaza Piconegra
Small colonies breed locally, notably in Doñana (H5), at Fuente de Piedra (MA1), at several reservoirs in Extremadura and sporadically elsewhere. Commonly seen hawking insects over fields near the breeding colonies. Seldom seen on coasts on passage except at Gibraltar. Mainly a summer visitor, present from April to October, but there are occasional winter records.

Caspian Tern *Sterna caspia* Pagaza Piquirroja
Mainly a passage migrant and winter visitor in small numbers, occurring coastally, from July to April, especially in Odiel (H4) and Bonanza (CA17). Non-breeders summer in the Guadalquivir and Guadiana estuaries.

Royal Tern* *Sterna maxima* Charrán Real
A migrant from West Africa which reaches the Strait in small numbers, chiefly from late July to December. Seldom seen on the Spanish shore but there are records from Odiel (H4), Doñana (H5), Tarifa Beach (CA1), the Guadalhorce estuary (MA7) and Gibraltar, mainly in summer. A pair were present in the springs of 1970 and 1971 near Sanlúcar de Barrameda (CA17) and may have attempted breeding.

Lesser Crested Tern *Sterna bengalensis* Charrán Bengalés
Small numbers move east through the Strait chiefly in May. They return there between late August and November, but mainly in October. Most often recorded at Tarifa Beach (CA1) and Gibraltar. Rarely seen elsewhere.

Sandwich Tern *Sterna sandvicensis* Charrán Patinegro
Common on passage and in winter along coasts. Present mainly from August to April but some non-breeders occur in summer.

Roseate Tern *Sterna dougallii* Charrán Rosado
Occurs on passage off Atlantic coasts but seldom recorded onshore. Recorded occasionally in the Mediterranean as far east as Málaga.

Common Tern *Sterna hirundo* Charrán Común
Common on passage, especially along coasts, in August–October and March–May. Has bred Doñana (H5) and in Almería. Occasional birds winter.

Arctic Tern *Sterna paradisaea* Charrán Artico
Occurs on passage off Atlantic coasts but seldom recorded onshore.

Little Tern *Sterna albifrons* Charrancito
Breeds locally on sandy coasts, especially along the Atlantic shore where it is common. Small numbers breed along the major rivers in Extremadura, chiefly along the R. Guadiana and its tributaries. Widespread on passage. Present April–October.

Whiskered Tern *Chlidonias hybrida* Fumarel Cariblanco
Locally common but generally declining, nesting at a few inland wetlands in western Andalucía. Has bred Extremadura. Widespread on passage. Present March to October.

Black Tern *Chlidonias niger* Fumarel Común
Much scarcer than the previous species as a breeding species, being locally numerous only in Doñana. Widespread on passage, especially in May and August/September, when large numbers occur along coasts. Present April to October.

White-winged Black Tern *Chlidonias leucopterus* Fumarel Aliblanco
A very scarce passage migrant in late April and May, somewhat more frequent but still rare
during the return passage in August–mid October. Usually occurs after prolonged easterly
winds.

Guillemot *Uria aalge* Arao Común
Present in small numbers in winter, chiefly in the Atlantic, although rarely seen from shore.

Razorbill *Alca torda* Alca Común
Common on passage and in winter along coasts. Present October to April.

Puffin *Fratercula arctica* Frailecilo Común
Common on passage and in winter but seldom seen from shore. Most often observed on passage through the Strait; large numbers enter the Mediterranean from November to December, returning from March to May.

Black-bellied Sandgrouse *Pterocles orientalis* Ganga Ortega
A locally common resident in stony steppe habitats, chiefly in Extremadura and, much less
abundantly, in Almería.

Pin-tailed Sandgrouse *Pterocles alchata* Ganga Común
A locally common resident in steppe habitats. Chiefly in Extremadura and also in western
Andalucía, where found notably in the periphery of Doñana.

Rock Dove *Columba livia* Paloma Bravía
Feral birds are common. Wild-type birds are locally resident on rocky coasts and on inland
cliffs, especially river gorges.

Stock Dove *Columba oenas* Paloma Zurita
Small numbers breed locally in Extremadura and western Andalucía. More widespread in
winter.

Woodpigeon *Columba palumbus* Paloma Torcaz
A widespread and common breeding species. Migrants from the north increase numbers in
winter, when large flocks occur.

Collared Dove *Streptopelia decaocto* Tórtola Turca
Widespread and locally common, having completed its colonisation of the entire region in
the mid-1990s. Probably still increasing. Generally associated with urban environments and
farms, particularly favouring city parks.

Turtle Dove *Streptopelia turtur* Tórtola Común
A widespread and common summer visitor and passage migrant, occurring from April to
October.

Ring-necked Parakeet *Psittacula krameri* Cotorra de Kramer
A feral population breeds at the Parador del Golf between Málaga and Torremolinos and
along the Río Guadalhorce. These birds range widely to near Málaga airport and to Torremolinos, where they may also be breeding. Occasional sightings elsewhere and has bred in
Córdoba botanic gardens.

Monk Parakeet *Myopsitta monachus* Cotorra Monje
A feral population, estimated at between 30 and 55 pairs in 1995, breeds in Málaga, notably
at the Parador del Golf between Málaga city and Torremolinos. Reported increasingly elsewhere, with nesting records from Huelva, Sevilla, Cadiz and Almería.

Great Spotted Cuckoo *Clamator glandarius* Críalo Europeo
Confined in the breeding season to areas where its hosts, Magpie and Azure-winged Magpie
breed. Most common in Extremadura and Huelva. Absent from the Mediterranean coastlands except on passage. Some arrive very early, from November to February, departing in
July and August. Widespread on passage.

Cuckoo *Cuculus canorus* Cuco Común
Common and widespread on passage, especially in spring, and in the breeding season.
Present from March to September.

Barn Owl *Tyto alba* Lechuza Común
A common and widespread breeding species.

Scops Owl *Otus scops* Autillo
A common and widespread summer visitor and passage migrant, present from March to October. Some remain in winter.

Eagle Owl *Bubo bubo* Búho Real
A widespread and locally common resident especially in rocky wooded terrain.

Little Owl *Athene noctua* Mochuelo Común
A widespread and common resident, often visible in daytime on telegraph poles and other exposed perches.

Tawny Owl *Strix aluco* Cárabo Común
A widespread and locally common resident in wooded habitats, especially in the more humid parts of western Andalucía.

Long-eared Owl *Asio otus* Búho Chico
A widespread but scarce resident in forested areas. Small numbers probably also occur in passage and in winter.

Short-eared Owl *Asio flammeus* Lechuza Campestre
Small numbers occur regularly on passage and in winter, October–April.

Common Nightjar *Caprimulgus europaeus* Chotacabras Gris
Locally common in summer in open heathland habitats, chiefly in more humid areas as in western Andalucía. Widespread on passage. Present from April to October.

Red-necked Nightjar *Caprimulgus ruficollis* Chotacabras Pardo
Widespread and locally common in summer when associated with open pinewoods. Widespread on passage. Present from April to October, with occasional records in February, March and November.

Common Swift *Apus apus* Vencejo Común
Abundant on passage and numerous in most towns and villages. Birds arrive in early April and depart by the end of September.

Pallid Swift *Apus pallidus* Vencejo Pálido
An abundant summer resident, with colonies in most coastal towns and on some coastal cliffs. More local inland but apparently increasing in Extremadura. First arrivals are in late February and some remain into November.

Alpine Swift *Apus melba* Vencejo Real
A widespread and locally common breeding species, small colonies inhabiting mountains and coastal cliffs. Some nest in buildings in Extremadura, especially on the bridges along the Río Guadiana. Present from March to October.

White-rumped Swift *Apus caffer* Vencejo Cafre
Locally common in small numbers, nesting in old Red-rumped Swallow nests. Increasing in numbers and becoming more widespread. It is still most numerous in Cádiz province but it also breeds widely throughout the region, including in Extremadura. A summer visitor, present from early May until November; exceptionally into December. This African species was first discovered breeding in Spain in 1966 at the Sierra de la Plata (CA5), since when it has become increasingly more widespread.

Little Swift* *Apus affinis* Vencejo Moro
Recorded with increasing frequency in southern Andalucía, with records from Almería, Málaga, Huelva and, especially, Cádiz provinces. Apparently established at the Sierra de la Plata (CA5), the same site which saw the initial colonisation of Spain by the previous species. Groups of up to five have been present there in spring and summer since about 1996 and may be breeding in caves on the sierra, alongside White-rumped Swifts and hirundines. Single birds have been recorded in winter, at the Guadalhorce estuary (Málaga) on 30 January and 16 February 1992.

Kingfisher *Alcedo atthis* Martín Pescador
Frequent on passage and in winter, occurring both inland and on rocky coasts. Breeds locally.

Bee-eater *Merops apiaster* Abejaruco Común
A common and characteristic breeding species, arriving from mid-March and departing by October. Large numbers accumulate at the Strait on migration.

Roller *Coracias garrulus* Carraca
Widespread on passage and locally common in the breeding season, especially in Extremadura, where nest box schemes produce local concentrations. Present from April to September.

Hoopoe *Upupa epops* Abubilla
A widespread and common breeding species and migrant. Most arrive in February and March, departing from August to October. Significant numbers winter, especially in Almería and in Doñana (H5).

Wryneck *Jynx torquilla* Torcecuello
A scarce but widespread breeding species, especially in western Andalucía. Occurs widely on passage and small numbers winter locally.

Green Woodpecker *Picus viridis* Pito Real
A locally common breeding resident.

Great Spotted Woodpecker *Dendrocopus major* Pico Picapinos
A common and widespread breeding species.

Lesser Spotted Woodpecker *Dendrocopus minor* Pico Menor
Very local; largely absent from most of the region but most likely to be encountered in northern Extremadura (CC8) and Cazorla (J1).

Dupont's Lark *Chersophilus duponti* Alondra de Dupont
A very local resident, confined to steppes in eastern Granada and Almería. Some individuals may disperse more widely in winter.

Calandra Lark *Melanocorypha calandra* Calandria
A locally common breeding species. Mainly resident but forming large flocks in winter.

Short-toed Lark *Calandrella brachydactyla* Terrera Común
A summer visitor, widespread and common. Present mainly April–September.

Lesser Short-toed Lark *Calandrella rufescens* Terrera Marismeña
A very local species, largely confined to salt flats in the Guadalquivir estuary (where abundant), the Almería coastlands and dry steppelands elsewhere in southern Andalucía. Mainly resident.

Crested Lark *Galerida cristata* Cogujada Común
Widespread and common, generally in lower-lying and more open, often cultivated country than Thekla Lark. Resident.

Thekla Lark *Galerida theklae* Cogujada Montesina
Common in open bushy country, typically in hilly terrain. Resident.

Woodlark *Lullula arborea* Totovía
A common breeding species. Local birds are probably resident but others occur on passage and in winter.

Skylark *Alauda arvensis* Alondra Común
Abundant on passage and especially in winter. A small number breed on the summits of the Sierra Nevada and other high tops.

Sand Martin *Riparia riparia* Avión Zapador
Widespread and common on passage. Large breeding colonies occur locally, often along major river valleys. Present mainly from March to October but occasional individuals occur in winter.

Crag Martin *Ptyonoprogne rupestris* Avión Roquero
Widespread and common wherever there are cliffs or rocky areas. Numbers are greatly increased in winter by migrants from further north, when large roosts occur locally.

Barn Swallow *Hirundo rustica* Golondrina Común
An abundant breeding species and passage migrant. Present mainly from February until early November but birds are regular in winter in western Andalucía especially, notably in the Guadalquivir valley where roosts of hundreds occur in December and January. These winter records may involve very early-returning migrants rather than actual overwinterers.

Red-rumped Swallow *Hirundo daurica* Golondrina Dáurica
Widespread and locally common, nesting on rocks and under bridges or in roadside culverts especially. Present February to October mainly but some occur in winter, with roosts of up to 100 reported from Sevilla in December and January.

House Martin *Delichon urbica* Avión Común
An abundant breeding species and passage migrant. Most nest on buildings, sometimes in spectacular colonies with hundreds of nests. Present February to October mainly but small numbers occur regularly in winter, especially in western Andalucía.

Richard's Pipit *Anthus novaeseelandiae* Bisbita de Richard
Occasional individuals occur in winter in Doñana and elsewhere in Andalucía, most often at the Guadalhorce estuary (Málaga). One spring record from Torremolinos in April 1996.

Tawny Pipit *Anthus campestris* Bisbita Campestre
A widespread and locally common summer visitor and passage migrant. Present April to September.

Tree Pipit *Anthus trivialis* Bisbita Arbóreo
Large numbers occur on passage, chiefly from March–May and September–October.

Meadow Pipit *Anthus pratensis* Bisbita Común
Common on passage and abundant in winter. Present from September–April mainly.

Red-throated Pipit *Anthus cervinus* Bisbita Gorgirrojo
A very scarce passage migrant and occasional winter resident, reported mainly from near the Strait in March–April and October–November.

Water Pipit *Anthus spinoletta* Bisbita Alpino
Small numbers once bred on the high tops of the Sierra Nevada but there are no recent confirmed records of this. Widespread but scarce on passage and locally common in winter, when it occurs in waterside habitats.

Yellow Wagtail *Motacilla flava* Lavandera Boyera
Widespread and common on passage and locally common in the breeding season. Present mid-February to October. Birds of the subspecies *M. f. iberiae*, *M. f. flava* and *M. f. flavissima* are regular but others, such as *M. f. cinereocapilla* occur occasionally. A male of the distinctive black-headed race, *M. f. feldegg**, was recorded from Torremolinos and the Río Guadalhorce ponds (MA8) on 20 and 27 April 1996.

Grey Wagtail *Motacilla cinerea* Lavandera Cascadeña
A common breeding species, frequenting rocky watercourses. More widespread on passage and in winter.

White Wagtail *Motacilla alba* Lavandera Blanca
Common on passage and abundant in winter, when numbers frequent roadsides. Present mainly October–March but there is a relatively small breeding population.

Dipper *Cinclus cinclus* Mirlo Acuático
Very local in mountainous areas, occurring along boulder-strewn, fast-flowing streams. Resident.

Wren *Troglodytes troglodytes* Chochín
A widespread and common resident.

Dunnock *Prunella modularis* Acentor Común
Small numbers breed locally in the sierras of northern Extremadura (CC8). A pair bred in the Sierra Nevada (GR1) in 1998. Widespread but inconspicuous on passage and in winter.

Alpine Accentor   *Prunella collaris*   Acentor Alpino
A breeding population inhabits the summits of the Sierra Nevada (GR1) and Valle del Jerte (CC8). Often reported at lower levels in winter, notably in Extremadura, in the Sierra de Grazalema (CA19) and at Gibraltar, November–February.

Rufous Bush Chat   *Cercotrichas galactotes*   Alzacola
Widespread on passage and locally common in the breeding season, frequenting low scrub along watercourses and prickly pear hedges, as well as olive and citrus groves. Present April–September.

Robin   *Erithacus rubecula*   Petirrojo
A common resident species in more humid woodlands especially, often in mountains. Migrants occur widely on passage and it is abundant in winter.

Nightingale   *Luscinia megarhynchos*   Ruiseñor Común
An abundant and characteristic summer visitor, frequenting watercourses especially. Present March–October.

Bluethroat   *Luscinia svecica*   Pechiazul
A scarce but regular migrant, in March–May and September–November. Small numbers winter, generally near water, especially in southern Andalucía and along the Guadiana valley. The breeding population of the Sierra de Gredos in central Spain extends into the upper levels of the Valle del Jerte (CC8).

Black Redstart   *Phoenicurus ochruros*   Colirrojo Tizón
Locally common as a breeding species in rocky hills. Widespread and abundant on passage and in winter.

Common Redstart   *Phoenicurus phoenicurus*   Colirrojo Real
A local summer resident in well-wooded, humid mountainous areas, notably in the Sierra Morena in Huelva. Widespread and numerous on passage. Present March to October.

Whinchat   *Saxicola rubetra*   Tarabilla Norteña
Common on passage, crossing the area in numbers from late March–May and in August–October.

Stonechat   *Saxicola torquata*   Tarabilla Común
An abundant and characteristic species of the region. The large resident population is greatly increased by migrants in winter.

Northern Wheatear   *Oenanthe oenanthe*   Collalba Gris
Widespread and common on passage. A montane breeding species, widely distributed but especially characteristic of the highest mountain tops in southern Andalucía, as in the Sierra Nevada (GR1). Present late February–November but there are occasional winter records.

Black-eared Wheatear   *Oenanthe hispanica*   Collalba Rubia
An abundant and widespread passage migrant and summer resident. Present March–October.

Black Wheatear   *Oenanthe leucura*   Collalba Negra
Resident and locally common in rocky mountainous areas.

Rock Thrush   *Monticola saxatilis*   Roquero Rojo
A local summer resident inhabiting rocky slopes at high altitudes. More widespread on passage. Present April to October.

Blue Rock Thrush   *Monticola solitarius*   Roquero Solitario
A widespread and common resident, inhabiting coastal and inland cliffs, generally below 1700 m.

Ring Ouzel   *Turdus torquatus*   Mirlo Capiblanco
Widespread on passage, in March–April and October–November. Small numbers remain in winter in the southern mountains.

Blackbird   *Turdus merula*   Mirlo Común
An abundant and widespread resident species. Migrants from northern Europe may increase the population in winter.

Fieldfare   *Turdus pilaris*   Zorzal Real
Occurs on passage and in winter but generally very scarce. Present October–March.

Song Thrush   *Turdus philomelos*   Zorzal Común
An abundant passage migrant and winter resident, present from October–April. Small numbers nest locally, notably in the western Sierra Morena in Huelva province and in northern Extremadura.

Redwing   *Turdus iliacus*   Zorzal Alirrojo
Regular and sometimes common on passage and in winter. Present October–March.

ℰ **Mistle Thrush**   *Turdus viscivorus*   Zorzal Charlo
A widespread and common breeding species. Mainly resident.

Cetti's Warbler   *Cettia cetti*   Ruiseñor Bastardo
Widespread and common, typically in the dense vegetation of watercourses but also in reedbeds. Resident.

Zitting Cisticola   *Cisticola juncidis*   Buitrón
A common species of open grassy habitats. Mainly resident but some cross the Strait.

Grasshopper Warbler   *Locustella naevia*   Buscarla Pintoja
Widespread on passage but easily overlooked. Birds pass through in April–May, returning from August–October.

Savi's Warbler   *Locustella luscinoides*   Buscarla Unicolor
A very local summer resident, chiefly in Doñana (H5) and the lower Guadalquivir, nesting in reedbeds. Widespread but inconspicuous on passage. Present from April–September.

Moustached Warbler   *Acrocephalus melanopogon*   Carricerín Real
A very local species, nesting in reedbeds. The population is centred on the coasts of eastern Spain and it may only occur irregularly in our area.

Aquatic Warbler   *Acrocephalus paludicola*   Carricerín Cejudo
Very scarce but possibly regular on passage, March–April and October.

Sedge Warbler   *Acrocephalus schoenobaenus*   Carricerín Común
Regular on spring passage but much scarcer in autumn, March–May and August–October.

Reed Warbler   *Acrocephalus scirpaceus*   Carricero Común
A summer resident, nesting locally in colonies in reedbeds. Widespread and common on passage. Present early April–October.

Great Reed Warbler   *Acrocephalus arundinaceus*   Carricero Tordal
A summer resident, nesting locally in colonies in reedbeds. Widespread on passage. Present early April–October.

Olivaceous Warbler   *Hippolais pallida*   Zarcero Pálido
A scarce summer resident in dry scrub, and in bushes, especially tamarisks, along dried-up watercourses. Also found in olive groves. Typical of hot, low-lying areas, mainly in coastal and southeast Andalucía and along the lower Guadalquivir valley (SE3). Present May–September.

ℰ **Melodious Warbler**   *Hippolais polyglotta*   Zarcero Común
A widespread and common summer resident. Often numerous on passage. Present April–October.

Dartford Warbler   *Sylvia undata*   Curruca Rabilarga
Widespread and common in low scrub. Mainly resident, but migrants are detected regularly at Gibraltar.

Spectacled Warbler   *Sylvia conspicillata*   Curruca Tomillera
Locally common in extremely low scrub, such as *Salicornia* salt flats, and typical of the Mediterranean coastlands and arid inland regions, as in Almería. More widespread on passage. Mainly present March–October but some remain in winter.

Subalpine Warbler *Sylvia cantillans* Curruca Carrasqueña
Common in tall scrub and the understorey of open woodlands, chiefly in hilly or mountainous terrain. Absent from the larger river valleys. Migrant, present from February–October.

Sardinian Warbler *Sylvia melanocephala* Curruca Cabecinegra
Widespread and common in scrub and dry woodland, as well as in olive groves, orchards and gardens. Mainly resident.

Orphean Warbler *Sylvia hortensis* Curruca Mirlona
Widespread and common in open woodland. A summer visitor, present from April–October.

Whitethroat *Sylvia communis* Curruca Zarcera
A widespread but very local breeding species in low scrub, notably in western Andalucía but also in the Sierra Nevada (GR1) and the mountainous fringe of Extremadura. Many migrants cross the region. A summer visitor, mainly present from March–October.

Garden Warbler *Sylvia borin* Curruca Mosquitera
Breeds locally in tall scrub and humid, open woodlands in western Andalucía and in the mountains of northern Extremadura. Widespread and common on passage, April–May and August–October.

Blackcap *Sylvia atricapilla* Curruca Capirotada
A widespread and common resident species, nesting in scrub, gardens and open woodlands. Local birds are joined by large numbers of migrants in winter, when it is abundant in olive groves.

Bonelli's Warbler *Phylloscopus bonelli* Mosquitero Papialbo
A summer visitor, nesting commonly in open mixed woodland usually in the sierras. Present from April–September.

Wood Warbler *Phylloscopus sibilatrix* Mosquitero Silbador
A scarce but regular migrant which is widespread on passage across the area in April–May. Rare in autumn.

Common Chiffchaff *Phylloscopus collybita* Mosquitero Común
Common on passage and abundant in winter, often occurring in open country far from any trees. Present October to April.

Iberian Chiffchaff *Phylloscopus brehmii* Mosquitero Común Iberico
A summer visitor but very locally distributed in our area, being most typical of humid and riverine woodland in western Andalucía and also in woodlands on north-facing mountain slopes further east. It is best located by its 'Chiffchiff' song: a monotonous but distinctive repetition of one syllable. Present April to August mainly.

Willow Warbler *Phylloscopus trochilus* Mosquitero Musical
Migrant, crossing the region in large numbers from March–May and August–October.

Goldcrest *Regulus regulus* Reyezuelo Sencillo
Scarce and perhaps irregular on passage and in winter. October–April. May breed in mountain conifer forests in northern Extremadura on the fringes of the Gredos range.

Firecrest *Regulus ignicapillus* Reyezuelo Listado
A locally common species of open mixed woodland in southern Andalucía, chiefly in Cádiz, Málaga and Granada. Common in the corkwoods of the Cádiz lowlands (CA6) but chiefly a mountain species further east and also in northern Extremadura. The resident population is increased by migrants on passage and in winter, when it is more widespread.

Spotted Flycatcher *Muscicapa striata* Papamoscas Gris
Common on passage and widespread in the breeding season, often near water. Present April–September.

Pied Flycatcher *Ficedula hypoleuca* Papamoscas Cerrojillo
Migrant, common and widespread on passage. A few breed very locally in mountain woodlands. Present April–October.

Bearded Reedling *Panurus biarmicus* Bigotudo
Occasional in large reedbeds in eastern Andalucía. Irruptive and may occur elsewhere.

Long-tailed Tit *Aegithalos caudatus* Mito
Locally common in oak woodlands, especially in Cádiz, in the Sierra Morena and in Cáceres. Resident.

Crested Tit *Parus cristatus* Herrerillo Capuchino
Common in the Sierra Morena and southern Andalucía but local in Extremadura. Occurs in open evergreen woodland, especially of cork oaks, as well as in conifers. Resident.

Coal Tit *Parus ater* Carbonero Garrapinos
Locally common in coniferous woodlands and hence principally a mountain species, typical of the Sierra Nevada, western Sierra Morena and northernmost Extremadura. Resident.

Blue Tit *Parus caeruleus* Herrerillo Común
A widespread and common resident.

Great Tit *Parus major* Carbonero Común
A widespread and common resident.

Nuthatch *Sitta europaea* Trepador Azul
Widespread in mature, open woodland in the sierras of Extremadura and in the Sierra Morena. More local elsewhere in Andalucía. Resident.

Short-toed Treecreeper *Certhia brachydactylata* Agateador Común
Widespread and common in woodland. Mainly resident but birds wander in winter.

Penduline Tit *Remiz pendulinus* Pajaro Moscón
An occasional breeding species but widespread in winter when it frequents reedbeds and rank vegetation along watercourses.

Golden Oriole Oriolus oriolus Oropéndola
A summer visitor, nesting commonly in mature open and, especially, riverine woodland, as well as in poplar plantations. Present from April–September.

Southern Grey Shrike *Lanius meridionalis* Alcaudón Real Meridional
Widespread and common. Mainly resident.

Woodchat Shrike *Lanius senator* Alcaudón Común
A summer visitor, widespread and common. Present from mid-March to October. There are occasional winter records.

Jay *Garrulus glandarius* Arrendajo
Widespread and common in woodlands, especially where oaks are present. Resident.

Azure-winged Magpie *Cyanopica cyanus* Rabilargo
A characteristic and locally common species of the evergreen oak woodlands of Extremadura. Also common in open pinewoods in western and central Andalucía.

Magpie *Pica pica* Urraca
Widespread and common in Extremadura and Huelva and also in eastern Andalucía, except along the Mediterranean coast. Inexplicably absent from most of Cádiz, Sevilla, Málaga and Córdoba provinces however. Resident.

Alpine Chough *Pyrrhocorax graculus* Chova Piquigualda
Small flocks have been recorded infrequently on migration at Gibraltar, usually in April, and elsewhere.

Red-billed Chough *Pyrrhocorax pyrrhocorax* Chova Piquirroja
Widespread and locally common, principally on cliffs in mountainous country. Resident.

Jackdaw *Corvus monedula* Grajilla
Widespread and locally common. Colonies favour bridges, ruined castles and similar buildings as well as cliffs. Resident.

Carrion Crow *Corvus corone* Corneja Negra
Scarce and local, principally in the mountains of northern Extremadura (CC8), the Sierra Nevada (GR1) and Cazorla (J1). Resident.

🗢 **Raven**   *Corvus corax*   Cuervo
Widespread and common, nesting on pylons as well as on cliffs. Large flocks form on farm-land in winter. This is the common black crow of the region. Resident.

Common Starling   *Sturnus vulgaris*   Estornino Pinto
Migrant, wintering in the area in very large flocks. Present from October–April; numbers vary greatly between winters.

🗢 **Spotless Starling**   *Sturnus unicolor*   Estornino Negro
Widespread and common, nesting in holes in trees and on buildings. Mainly resident but some cross the Strait.

🗢 **House Sparrow**   *Passer domesticus*   Gorrión Común
Widespread and common, nesting colonially in trees in open country as well as in towns and villages, where holes in buildings are used. Resident.

Spanish Sparrow   *Passer hispaniolensis*   Gorrión Moruno
Locally abundant in Extremadura and western Andalucía. Large colonies in eucalyptus plantations near water are typical. Present all year but some cross the Strait in March–April and September–October.

Tree Sparrow   *Passer montanus*   Gorrión Molinero
Widespread but local. Present all year but some cross the Strait in March–April and September–November.

🗢 **Rock Sparrow**   *Petronia petronia*   Gorrión Chillón
Widespread but local in open woodland in Extremadura and in the rocky hills of Andalucía. Resident.

The following nine species have recently been recorded in the area and most of them have bred. All or most of them are likely to have originated in captivity (see Introduction) but the apparent success of some species in establishing themselves makes them of interest.

Red-billed Quelea   *Quelea quelea*   Quelea Común
Introduced to Doñana from sub-Saharan Africa, but very scarce. Found in agricultural areas of the marismas and around buildings, generally with sparrows. Two records of single birds at Gibraltar: on 27 August 1989 and 6 May 1991.

Yellow-crowned Bishop   *Euplectes afer*   Euplectes Amarillo
One at the Brazo del Este (Sevilla) on 8 September 1998 and a flock of seven, four males and three females at Alhaurín de la Torre (Málaga) 10 October 1998. (Sub-Saharan Africa.)

Red Bishop   *Euplectes orix*   Euplectes Rojo
A pair possibly nested at Las Norias (Almería) in 1998 and successful breeding occurred at the Brazo del Este (Sevilla) in 1999, when two males were present and a female and two juveniles were seen. (Sub-Saharan Africa.)

Black-winged Bishop   *Euplectes hordeacea*
A male was at Las Norias (Almería) on 24 and 28 July 1997. (Sub-Saharan Africa.)

Black-rumped Waxbill   *Estrilda troglodytes*   Pico de Coral Colinegro
Reported as breeding in September 1988 near Lora del Río (Sevilla). The population there was estimated at 20 birds. Subsequently recorded from the Guadalhorce valley (Málaga; bred 1993 and 1996), the Velez valley (Málaga; 9 on 17 September 1998) and the Brazo del Este (Sevilla; bred 1999 and probably in 1997). (Sub-Saharan Africa.)

Common Waxbill   *Estrilda astrild*   Pico de Coral Común
An introduced and naturalised species. Often reported in small groups in reedbeds, mainly near the coasts or along major river valleys. Probably resident but groups wander widely. (Sub-Saharan Africa.)

Orange-cheeked Waxbill   *Estrilda melpoda*   Carita de Naranja
Two breeding records: two adults with one juvenile on the Guadalquivir river in Sevilla city on 19 October 1996 and two adults with two juveniles at the Guadalhorce estuary (Málaga) on 26 October 1996. (Sub-Saharan Africa.)

Zebra Waxbill *Amandava subflava* Bengalí Rayado
Two at the Guadalhorce estuary on 31 October 1998. (Sub-Saharan Africa.)

Red Avadavat *Amandava amandava* Bengalí Rojo
A small feral population is established near Málaga and breeding has been reported from other localities along the Mediterranean coast. Large numbers are established along the Guadiana valley in Extremadura. (Tropical Asia.)

Chaffinch *Fringilla coelebs* Pinzón Vulgar
A widespread and common resident species. Large numbers of migrants are also present on passage and in winter.

Brambling *Fringilla montifringilla* Pinzón Real
Scarce but regular on passage and in winter, October–March.

Serin *Serinus serinus* Verdecillo
A widespread and common species. Local birds are resident but large numbers cross the Strait on passage

Citril Finch *Serinus citrinella* Verderón Serrano
Occasionally reported from the tops of the Sierra Nevada (GR1) but there is no evidence that it breeds there. Has bred Cazorla (J1). Occurs on the fringes of the Gredos range in the Valle del Jerte (CC8), especially in winter.

Greenfinch *Carduelis chloris* Verderón Común
A widespread and common resident species. Large numbers of migrants are also present on passage and in winter.

Goldfinch *Carduelis carduelis* Jilguero
A widespread and common resident species. Abundant on passage and in winter.

Siskin *Carduelis spinus* Lúgano
Widespread and common on passage and in winter. Has bred Cazorla (J1) and perhaps sporadically elsewhere. Numbers vary considerably from year to year; October–April.

Linnet *Carduelis cannabina* Pardillo Común
A widespread and common resident species. Large numbers of migrants are also present on passage and in winter.

Crossbill *Loxia curvirostra* Piquituerto Común
A local breeding species, inhabiting coniferous forests, chiefly in the southern Andalucían mountains. Flocks are reported widely in irruption years.

Trumpeter Finch *Bucanetes githagineus* Camachuelo Trompetero
Locally common in the driest parts of Almería (Sierra de Alhamilla (AL6), Desierto de Tabernas (AL5) and Cabo de Gata (AL1)). Occasional elsewhere. Mainly resident.

Bullfinch *Pyrrhula pyrrhula* Camachuelo Común
Very scarce but occasional individuals and small groups occur widely on passage and in winter.

Hawfinch *Coccothraustes coccothraustes* Picogordo
Locally common in open deciduous woodland, chiefly in western Andalucía and northern Extremadura. Mainly resident.

Cirl Bunting *Emberiza cirlus* Escribano Soteño
Widespread and common, especially in southern Andalucía, mainly in open country with bushes in the lower sierras. The resident population is increased by migrants on passage and in winter.

Rock Bunting *Emberiza cia* Escribano Montesino
Widespread and common in rocky areas. Mainly resident but commoner at low levels in winter and some occur on passage.

Ortolan Bunting *Emberiza hortulana* Escribano Hortelano
Migrant, widespread and common, April–September. Breeds very locally in open woodlands in mountains.

Reed Bunting *Emberiza schoeniclus* Escribano Palustre
Very scarce and locally distributed as a breeding species, nesting in reedbeds. The population is increased by migrants on passage and in winter.

Corn Bunting *Miliaria calandra* Triguero
A typical and abundant species of open country and farmland. Mainly resident but flocks wander in winter.

RARE BIRDS IN SOUTHERN AND WESTERN SPAIN

This chapter summarises the records of very scarce and vagrant species which have been reliably recorded in Andalucía, Extremadura and/or Gibraltar. All such records are within the geographical area covered by the Comité de Rarezas de la Sociedad Española de Ornitología (CR-SEO; the Spanish Ornithological Society's Rarities Committee). Rarities seen in Gibraltar are also considered by the Gibraltar Rarities Committee. We have included only those records which have been ratified by either of these bodies, with the exception of some very recent sightings which are pending scrutiny.

Southern Spain is well placed geographically to receive rare birds and the list of species and records is growing rapidly as the number of birders continues to rise. It seems particularly likely that more Afro-tropical species will be recorded in future. The recent spate of records of Rüppell's Griffon Vultures (see p. 320), and the earlier colonisation by White-rumped Swifts, are indications that such events occur. Intra-African migrants, such as Abdim's Stork *Ciconia abdimii* or Woodland Kingfisher *Halcyon senegalensis*, may yet join others such as Allen's Gallinule *Porphyrula alleni* on the short but growing list of overshooting migrants.

Frequent updates on news of rarities from throughout Spain are available on a highly-recommended web site **Rare birds in Spain** (www. terra.es/personal3/gutarb/). If you are lucky enough to come across any rare birds we strongly urge you to submit the details to the Comité de Rarezas. Descriptions should follow the guidelines favoured by *British Birds* rarities committee in Britain. Records may be submitted in English. To contact the Committee write to: Dr. Eduardo de Juana, Comité de Rarezas, Sociedad Española de Ornitología, C/ Melquiades Biencinto, 34, 28053 MADRID (email seo@seo.org).

Descriptions are only required by the Rarities Committee for species which are rarities in Iberia as a whole. Such species are denoted below by an asterisk (*) and the full list, together with the Rarity Record Submission Form, is available on the SEO/Birdlife website (www.seo.org). Records of other scarce species are still welcomed and may be sent to the same address. Annual reports of rare birds, and other interesting records from around Spain, are published in the Spanish Ornithological Society's journal *Ardeola* or in its newsletter *La Garcilla*. All published records are acknowledged.

Slavonian Grebe* *Podiceps auritus* Zampullín Cuellirrojo
Vagrant in winter. Four accepted records from Málaga Bay in winter 1981–82; one unsubmitted record from Gibraltar in December 1989; one accepted record from Doñana on 15 January 1990.

Fulmar *Fulmarus glacialis* Fulmar
One record of a beached bird from Huelva.

Pintado Petrel* *Daption capense* Damero del Cabo
One at Gibraltar on 20 June 1979.

Bulwer's Petrel* *Bulweria bulwerii* Petrel de Bulwer
One record from Alborán on 14 February 1982.

Manx Shearwater *Puffinus puffinus* Pardela Pichoneta
Very scarce. There are very few satisfactory records from the Atlantic sector or the Strait.
Vagrant in the Mediterranean; there is only one record from Alborán.

Little Shearwater* *Puffinus assimilis* Pardela Chica
Very rare, but possibly regular in late summer in the Atlantic and the western approaches to
the Strait. Three accepted records, and several more from Alborán awaiting consideration.
All fall in the period May–November, mainly August–October.

Wilson's Storm-petrel* *Oceanites oceanicus* Paíño de Wilson
Possibly a regular autumn migrant in the western approaches to the Strait of Gibraltar and
waters off Atlantic Andalucía.

Madeiran Storm-petrel* *Oceanodroma castro* Paíño de Madeira
Cited very rarely in coastal waters. There are three winter records of storm-driven birds from
Huelva, at least one being less than satisfactory, and one (well inland!) from Badajoz.

Brown Booby* *Sula leucogaster* Piquero Pardo
There are two accepted records from Málaga Bay; an adult on 28 May 1983 and an immature on 9 September 1986.

Masked Booby* *Sula dactylatra* Piquero Enmascarado
There are two accepted records of adults from within Alborán; on 10 October and 14
December 1985, which almost certainly refer to the same bird. A record from Huelva in
March 1998 is under consideration by CR-SEO.

Cape Gannet* *Sula capensis* Alcatraz de El Cabo
Birds showing plumage features (black secondaries and tails) of this species are occasion-
ally recorded in Alborán and off Doñana but it is unclear whether they really are Cape
Gannets or just an uncommon plumage variant of Gannets *Sula bassana*.

White Pelican *Pelecanus onocrotalus* Pelícano Vulgar
An adult crossed the Strait southwards from Tarifa on 18 August 1996. An immature bird was
in the Marismas del Guadalquivir on 6 and 7 December 1997. Three were together at the
Embalse de los Canchales (Badajoz) on 21 November 1998. The origin of all these birds is
unknown but may be suspect.

Magnificent Frigatebird* *Fregata magnificens* Rabihorcado Magnífico
A subadult female flew past Torremolinos (Málaga) on 22 October 2000.

Western Reef Egret* *Egretta gularis* Garceta Dimorfa
A scarce visitor from west Africa but single birds are seen with some regularity in the Guad-
alquivir salt pans and occasionally elsewhere. A pale-phase bird at the Río Guadalhorce
(Málaga) on 1 May 2000 is under consideration.

African Marabou* *Leptoptilos crumeniferus* Marabú Africano
One in the marismas of El Rocío and other points of Doñana between 27 July and 1 October
1989.

Bald Ibis* *Geronticus eremita* Ibis Eremita
One taken injured in Doñana in July 1958.

Sacred Ibis* *Threskiornis aethiopicus* Ibis Sagrado
One at the Río Guadalhorce estuary (Málaga) on 21 February 1997 and one at the Brazo del
Este (Sevilla) on 8 and 15 July 1997.

Lesser Flamingo* *Phoenicopterus minor* Flamenco Enano
Occasionally recorded at Doñana and Fuente de Piedra. At least some are known to have
been escaped birds and perhaps all are of captive origin.

Fulvous Whistling Duck* *Dendrocygna bicolor* Suirirí Bicolor
A bird was seen irregularly at Fuente de Piedra (Málaga) between autumn 1998 and spring
1999. Record under consideration by CR-SEO.

Bewick's Swan* *Cygnus columbianus* Cisne Chico
An old record from Doñana in February 1910.

Whooper Swan* *Cygnus cygnus* Cisne Cantor
An adult was at Fuente Obejuna (Córdoba) from 28 August until 18 September 1994. The dates make its origin seem suspect.

Geese. The very large numbers of Greylag Geese *Anser anser* which winter regularly in Doñana are accompanied by very small numbers of other species, some of which are regular there. Most such species are rarely seen anywhere else in Spain and as such they are on the CR-SEO list but in practice few records of geese are ever submitted from Doñana, on account of their reputed regularity there. Details of these records are thus not available but it seems clear that Doñana offers the best chance of seeing unusual geese in southern Spain.

Bean Goose* *Anser fabalis* Ansar Campestre
Cited as being the scarcest of the rare geese in Doñana, December–February. Two were at the Embalse de los Canchales (Badajoz) in November 1998.

Pink-footed Goose* *Anser brachyrhynchus* Ansar Piquicorto
Cited as annual in winter in very small numbers in Doñana. One there at Almonte on 2 December 1996.

White-fronted Goose* *Anser albifrons* Ansar Careto Grande
Cited as wintering in the Doñana area with some frequency in very small numbers, October–February. Three recent records from Extremadura.

Lesser White-fronted Goose* *Anser erythropus* Ansar Careto Chico
Cited as a very rare winter visitor to Doñana, December–February

Bar-headed Goose *Anser indicus* Ansar Indio
Annual in winter in Doñana. These are believed to be members of the small population in Scandinavia, which move south with the Greylags. Two recent records from Extremadura.

Snow Goose* *Anser caerulescens* Ansar Nival
Annual in winter in Doñana. These are presumably of feral origin.

Canada Goose* *Branta canadensis* Barnacla Canadiense
Annual in winter in Doñana; October–February.

Barnacle Goose* *Branta leucopsis* Barnacla Cariblanca
Annual in winter in Doñana and also recorded in Cádiz and Extremadura; October–February. Records are normally of single birds, but six were in Doñana in December 1990.

Brent Goose* *Branta bernicla* Barnacla Carinegra
Annual in winter in Doñana; December–February. Birds are nearly always of the pale breasted subspecies *B.b.hrota*. Eleven together at Sancti Petri (Cádiz) on 25 January 1992 is noteworthy. One Extremaduran record.

Red-breasted Goose* *Branta ruficollis* Barnacla Cuellirroja
Vagrant. Cited as having occurred five or six times in Doñana. One shot there in October 1969. Another present there in winter 1984–85.

Egyptian Goose *Alopochen aegyptiacus* Ganso del Nilo
One at Zorita (Cáceres) on 1 September 1993 and two at the Embalse de Arrocampo (Cáceres) on 3 March 2001.

Ruddy Shelduck *Tadorna ferruginea* Tarro Canelo
Formerly a regular visitor, especially to Doñana from August–March, originating from breeding grounds in the Moroccan High Atlas mountains. Rare and irregular at present but some birds do still turn up. A flock of seven at the Salinas de Cabo de Gata (Almería) on 26 June 1993 is noteworthy.

Mandarin Duck* *Aix galericulata* Pato Mandarín
Occasional records in winter from Sevilla, Granada, Córdoba and Cáceres.

American Wigeon* *Anas americana* Anade Silbón Americano
One published record from Doñana in October 1971. Apparently also recorded there since,
but no details available.

Blue-winged Teal* *Anas discors* Cerceta Aliazul
Recorded from Doñana; a male captured in December 1972, single birds in February 1984
and March 1986 (records not submitted) and in May 1988 at El Rocío. There is also an accepted record of a male at the Río Guadalhorce (Málaga), 12 October–15 December 1990,
two (male & female) at the Laguna de la Oscuridad (Cádiz) on 24 March 1990, a male at the
Brazo del Este (Sevilla) on 2 April 1994 and a male at the Laguna de Medina (Cádiz) from
17 to 28 February 1997.

Ring-necked Duck* *Aythya collaris* Porrón de Collar
One at the Laguna del Taraje (Cádiz) in May 1984. Another reported from Doñana in March
1985. A female at the Laguna de Medina (Cádiz) on 31 December 1996.

Scaup *Aythya marila* Porrón Bastardo
A very scarce winter visitor. In recent years birds have been recorded from Adra (Almería)
in January 1988, Laguna de Medina (Cádiz) in spring 1991 and Extremadura (3 records; 8
birds).

Eider *Somateria mollissima* Eider
A very scarce and irregular winter visitor to Atlantic coasts with occasional records from the
Cádiz region. Vagrant in Alborán from where there is a single record from Málaga Bay.

Long-tailed Duck* *Clangula hyemalis* Havelda
One at the salinas de Bonanza (Cádiz) in January 1981. Two records from Roquetas de Mar
(Almería); one in January 1958 and one in October 1986. A group of four females/immatures
was at the Salinas de Cerrillos (Almería) from 8 December 1988 until 6 January 1989. A
female was photographed at Laguna Salada (Cádiz) in July–August 1990, a remarkable time
of year; what may have been the same bird was then on 28 January 1991. One was off the
Parador del Golf, Málaga on 10 February 1992. A female/immature was at the Salinas de
Guardias Viejas (Almería) on 12 November 1993.

Velvet Scoter *Melanitta fusca* Negrón Especulado
A very scarce winter visitor to Atlantic and Mediterranean coasts. Present regularly with
Common Scoters *M. nigra* off Doñana, October–March, and probably also elsewhere along
the Atlantic coasts.

Surf Scoter* *Melanitta perspicillata* Negrón Careto
A first winter male and a female were off Doñana on 6 February 1991.

Goldeneye *Bucephala clangula* Porrón Osculado
An uncommon winter visitor. Almost annual in Doñana; December–March. One at the Laguna de Medina (Cádiz) in January 1989.

Pallid Harrier* *Circus macrourus* Aguilucho Papialbo
A male arrived at Gibraltar from Morocco on 23 March 1992.

Long-legged Buzzard* *Buteo rufinus* Ratonero Moro
Vagrant, although breeding on the Moroccan side of the Strait. One recorded from Doñana
in July 1958. One on 19 August 1974 on the Spanish side of the Strait. One at Gibraltar on 27
July 1985. One at Tarifa (Cádiz) in July 1986. An immature at Punta Secreta (Cádiz) on 7
August 1995. One at Tarifa in September 2000 and another at La Lantejuela (Sevilla) in Jan-
urary 2001.

Rough-legged Buzzard *Buteo lagopus* Ratonero Calzado
Two seen on 31 October 1976 leaving the Spanish side of the Strait southwards.

Lesser Spotted Eagle* *Aquila pomarina* Aguila Pomerana
Cited as being occasionally seen in Doñana, December–February and two recent records
reported from the Strait in autumn, including one on 3 Septmber 2000. All are pending rati-
fication.

Spotted Eagle* *Aquila clanga* Aguila Moteada
Occasional birds winter in Doñana; recent records from there include one which was present from February–May 1987, an immature on 7 March 1994, and adult on 2 Decmber 1996

and an adult on 4 February 1997. Occasional on passage across the Strait; Bernis (1980) gives eight records of single birds there in 1976–77, all in the period 1 August–3 October. One at Chiclana (Cádiz) in November 1981. One arrived at Gibraltar from the Strait on 10 March 1987. One in Doñana on 25 November 2000.

Tawny Eagle* *Aquila rapax* Aguila Rapaz
Status uncertain. Breeds in Morocco and may occasionally cross the Strait.

Red-footed Falcon* *Falco vespertinus* Halcón Patirrojo
A very rare passage migrant with occasional records in May, including at least four from Extremadura. One at Gibraltar on 21 April 1975. Even scarcer in autumn; one in September from Sevilla and one in Doñana in October 1971. There is also a record from Málaga on 9 January 1983 and another from Doñana in January 1987.

Lanner* *Falco biarmicus* Halcón Borni
A scarce visitor from North Africa although bred Doñana in the 19th century. One was captured in Doñana in 1954. Most often recorded at Gibraltar from where there are some 20 records, all in the periods March–April and July–September. One was at Vejer (Cádiz) on 21 October 1994 and another at Cabeza del Buey (Badajoz) on 11 June 1992.

Saker* *Falco cherrug* Halcón Sacré
A bird without jesses seen near the Río Guadalhorce (Málaga) in October 1998 is under consideration by CR-SEO.

Sora Crake* *Porzana carolina* Polluela de Carolina
One shot in Doñana on 30 December 1975 and preserved in the Park collection was the first Iberian record.

Corncrake *Crex crex* Guión de Codornices
Crosses the region on passage but seldom recorded. Noted at Doñana from February–March and late July–September.

Allen's Gallinule* *Porphyrula alleni* Calamón de Allen
Seven records of single birds. Recorded from Granada in 1976; from the Río Guadalhorce (Málaga) in December 1975 and December 1977, and from Doñana; on 15 January 1958, 10 March 1979 and 20 November 1979. Most recently, there was an immature at Laguna Salada (Cádiz) on 31 March 1990.

Demoiselle Crane *Anthropoides virgo* Grulla Damisela
An adult was at Navalvillar de Pela (Badajoz) on 4 and 16 Feberuary 1996.

Cream-coloured Courser* *Cursorius cursor* Corredor
Two accepted records from Almería, in August 1985 and May 1987. One from La Janda (Cádiz) in September 1987. One was with three Dotterels at Esparragosa de Lares (Badajoz) on 25 September 1991. A group of three were at Los Lances beach, Tarifa (Cádiz) on 17 April 2000. (This last is one record in which we really believe since we found them ourselves!)

Dotterel *Charadrius morinellus* Chorlito Carambolo
A very scarce migrant, usually recorded in autumn. There have been several sightings at Los Lances beach (CA1) in September.

American Golden Plover* *Pluvialis dominica* Chorlito Dorado Americano
Vagrant. Four Andalucían records: Algeciras Bay 1953, Tarifa 1972, Málaga 1978 and Málaga 1982.

Pacific Golden Plover* *Pluvialis fulva* Chorlito Dorado Asiático
Vagrant. One was shot at the Guadalhorce Estuary (Málaga) on 17 August 1980.

Sociable Plover* *Chettusia gregaria* Chorlito Social
Vagrant. Four recent records of single birds; from Doñana (Huelva) in January 1971 and February 1984, Jérez de la Frontera (Cádiz) in January 1972 and the Embalse del Celemín (Cádiz) on 17 and 18 Feberuary 1996.

White-rumped Sandpiper* *Calidris fuscicollis* Correlimos de Bonaparte
One at Cabo de Gata (Almería) on 15 and 16 September 1980 and one at the mouth of the Río Velez (Málaga) on 8 November 1996.

Pectoral Sandpiper* *Calidris melanotos* Correlimos Pectoral
One was found dead in Doñana in September 1973 during an epidemic of botulism.

Broad-billed Sandpiper* *Limicola falcinellus* Correlimos Falcino
Two records from Doñana; in May 1988 and in July 1971. One one at the mouth of the Río Velez (Málaga) on 21 May 1994.

Buff-breasted Sandpiper* *Tryngites subruficollis* Correlimos Canelo
One at the Río Guadalhorce (Málaga) in 1977.

Short-billed Dowitcher* *Limnodromus griseus* Agujeta Gris
There is a suspect record of three on 7 April 1964 at Bonanza salinas (Cádiz).

Long-billed Dowitcher* *Limnodromus scolopaceus* Agujeta Escolopácea
One accepted record from Almería in May 1985. There is an unsubmitted record of this species from Doñana in April 1988. There are also accepted records of *Limnodromus* sp. from Málaga in May 1987; Tarifa (Cádiz); a juvenile in August 1988, Doñana, an adult in April 1988 and Salinas de Bonanza (Cádiz); two adults on 3 June 1993.

Slender-billed Curlew* *Numenius tenuirostris* Zarapito Fino
A very rare passage migrant and winter visitor, chiefly recorded at Doñana, from where several records of wintering individuals were claimed in the 1980s and early 1990s. No subsequent reports.

Greater Yellowlegs* *Tringa melanoleuca* Archibebe Patigualdo Grande
One was at Villafranco del Guadalquivir (Sevilla) from 15 to 19 September 2000.

Lesser Yellowlegs* *Tringa flavipes* Archibebe Patigualdo Chico
Single birds recorded from Sanlúcar de Barrameda (Cádiz) in March 1967, Cabo de Gata (Almería) in October 1981, Puebla del Río (Sevilla) in April 1986, Doñana in May 1986 (the latter two were most probably the same bird). There is a December 1998 record from Málaga under consideration.

Terek Sandpiper* *Xenus cinereus* Andarríos de Terek
Single birds at Doñana (Huelva) on 14 May 1974 and 6 March 1982, at Cabo de Gata (Almería) from 14 to 16 September 1980 and from 31 August to 12 September 2000 and at the Río Guadalhorce ponds (Málaga) on 15 May 1991 and in May 2000. Two were at Los Lances (Cádiz) on 9 May 1995. One was at Sancti Petri (Cádiz) on 4 November 2000.

Spotted Sandpiper* *Actitis macularia* Andarríos Maculado
One record from Málaga in May 1982.

Wilson's Phalarope* *Phalaropus tricolor* Falaropo de Wilson
Recorded from Doñana on 28 May 1971 and 1 December 1987, and at Sanlúcar de Barrameda (Cádiz) in December 1985.

Long-Tailed Skua* *Stercorarius longicaudus* Págalo Rabero
May occur occasionally in the western approaches to the Strait from where two were reported in October 1987. One record from Málaga Bay in August 1981. A record from Torremolinos (Málaga) in September 1999 is under consideration by CR-SEO.

Laughing Gull* *Larus atricilla* Gaviota Guanaguanare
Five records of single birds: at Fuengirola (Málaga) in May 1981; at the Río Guadalhorce (Málaga) in July 1985; at Benalmádena (Málaga) in August 1988, Gibraltar in November 1988 and Doñana on 28 and 29 September 2000.

Franklin's Gull* *Larus pipixcan* Gaviota de Franklin
The three accepted Iberian records to date are all from Andalucía; one at Puebla del Río (Sevilla) in May 1978; one at the Río Guadalhorce (Málaga) in October 1983 and another at the Río Guadalhorce in May 1989.

Sabine's Gull* *Larus sabini* Gaviota de Sabine
Accidental on passage. Occasionally recorded in the Strait area in April–May and in late summer and autumn. One autumn record accepted from Málaga. One was at Punta Umbría (Huelva) on 30 December 2000

Grey-Headed Gull* *Larus cirrocephalus* Gaviota Cabecigrís
An adult was present at Doñana (Huelva) from 30 June to 15 August 1971. A juvenile was at Gibraltar on 17 August 1992. The sole Iberian records.

Ring-Billed Gull* *Larus delawarensis* Gaviota de Delaware
A Canadian bird was recovered at Barbate (Cádiz) in January 1965. Three records from Málaga; one at the Río Guadalhorce in January 1986, an adult at Benalmadena on 30 January 1991 and two first winter birds at the Guadalhorce again on 12 January 1991; one of these last remained until 23 March 1991. An adult was at Gibraltar in June 1992. At least three were on the Huelva coast in December 2000

Iceland Gull* *Larus glaucoides* Gaviota Polar
One at Doñana on 6 April 1986. A first-winter bird was present at Gibraltar on 14 and 15 January 1987.

Forster's Tern *Sterna forsteri* Charrán de Forster
One was in the Strait on 27 October 1997.

Sooty Tern* *Sterna fuscata* Charrán Sombrío
One at Doñana in 1963 and one from Málaga in September 1979. There is also an unsubmitted record from Doñana in spring 1987.

Moussier's Redstart

Little Auk *Alle alle* Mérgulo Marino
A very scarce winter visitor. Most records are of beached birds found after winter storms along the Atlantic coast. A flock of 30 off Doñana on 4 April 1988 is exceptional. One February record from Málaga. One off Gibraltar on 26 March 1986.

Laughing Dove* *Streptopelia senegalensis* Tórtola Senegalesa
Two were recorded at the Río Guadalhorce ponds between early 1997 and up to mid 1999. The record is being considered by CR-SEO.

Marsh Owl* *Asio capensis* Búho Moro
An occasional winter visitor to southwest Andalucía until the end of the 19th century. The sole 20th century record was of an injured (shot) female found at Cádiz Bay in December 1998; it died soon afterwards.

Blue-cheeked Bee-eater *Merops superciliosus* Abejaruco Papirrojo
One at Gibraltar on 9 September 1973. A record of three near Mijas (Málaga) in April 1999 is under consideration by CR-SEO.

Shore Lark *Eremophila alpestris* Alondra Cornuda
There is an old recovery of a Swedish-ringed bird near Doñana in October.

Rock Pipit *Anthus petrosus* Bisbita Costero
One recorded at El Rocío (Huelva) in early March 1991. One at Tarifa (Cádiz) in January 1997.

Common Bulbul* *Pycnonotus barbatus* Bulbul Naranjero
Rumoured to have been resident in small numbers around Almuñecar (Granada), but there are no confirmed records.

Moussier's Redstart* *Phoenicurus moussieri* Colorrojo Diademado
A record of a male near the Río Guadalhorce (Málaga) on 26 April 2000 is being considered by the CR-SEO.

Desert Wheatear* *Oenanthe deserti* Collalba Desértica
A male at Chiclana (Cádiz) in April 1985. A male at Gibraltar on 3 September 1987 and another there in March 2001.

White-Crowned Black Wheatear* *Oenanthe leucopyga* Collalba Yebélica
One recorded in Doñana on 20 May 1977 is the only Iberian record.

Paddyfield Warbler *Acrocephalus agricola* Carricero Agricola
A juvenile was mist-netted at the Brazo del Este (Sevilla) on 6 November 1996.

Blyth's Reed Warbler* *Acrocephalus dumetorum* Carricero de Blyth
Two Iberian records; one caught and ringed at Gibraltar on 24 September 1973 and one caught and ringed at El Acebuche (Doñana) in October 1988.

Marsh Warbler *Acrocephalus palustris* Carricero Políglota
A rare passage migrant. Has been ringed in Doñana in autumn.

Icterine Warbler* *Hippolais polyglotta* Zarcero Icterino
A very scarce migrant. One recorded from Doñana in October 1968 and one ringed at Gibraltar on 25 August 1973.

Marmora's Warbler* *Sylvia sarda* Curruca Sarda
There have been a number of sightings reported from Gibraltar and from Málaga province in recent years, the latter especially along the southern edge of the Sierra Blanca, but none of the records have so far been accepted. A pair reputedly bred and was photographed near El Acebuche (Doñana) in May 1986.

Tristram's Warbler *Sylvia deserticola* Curruca de Tristram
One on Windmill Hill, Gibraltar on 10 April 1988 is the sole Iberian record.

Lesser Whitethroat *Sylvia curruca* Curruca Zarcerilla
There is a spring record of one ringed at Gibraltar. Liable to occur exceptionally on passage.

Arctic Warbler* *Phylloscopus borealis* Mosquitero Artico
One reported from Gibraltar on 30 October 1984.

Pallas's Warbler* *Phylloscopus proregulus* Mosquitero de Pallas
One ringed in Doñana on 29 October 1981 was the first Spanish record. There is also a record of one on 17 April 1987 in Cazorla (Jaén).

Yellow-browed Warbler* *Phylloscopus inornatus* Mosquitero Bilistado
The first four Spanish records, all of birds caught and ringed, were from Doñana; three in October–November 1967, the fourth in October 1985. One was caught in Gibraltar on 30 October 1984. One was ringed near Los Barrios (Cádiz) on 27 January 1993.

Radde's Warbler* *Phylloscopus schwarzi* Mosquitero de Schwarz
One in Doñana on 7 November 1966.

Red-breasted Flycatcher* *Ficedula parva* Papamoscas Papirrojo
A very rare passage migrant. One recorded in the Sierra del Algarrobo (Cádiz) on 1 October 1973. There are also two records of single birds from Doñana, in April 1981 and April 1984.

Collared Flycatcher* *Ficedula albicollis* Papamoscas Collarino
A very rare passage migrant. One was in Doñana on 4 April 1972. A male was seen in April 1989 in Torremolinos (Málaga).

Wallcreeper *Tichodroma muraria* Treparriscos
A very rare winter visitor, with occasional reports from Gibraltar, El Chorro (Málaga), Sierra Tejeda (Málaga-Granada) where it has been recorded annually since 1997, Sierra Nevada (Granada), Sierra de Gador (Almería) and Monfragüe (Cáceres). A summer record; one between Algodonales and Grazalema (Cádiz) in July 1993 is apparently unprecedented.

Red-backed Shrike *Lanius collurio* Alcaudón Dorsirrojo
A very rare passage migrant. There are few reliable published records.

Masked Shrike* *Lanius nubicus* Alcaudón Núbico
Two seen in Doñana on 3 May 1956. There are also two old records from Gibraltar; in May 1863 and a specimen labelled 12 January 1883.

Great Grey Shrike *Lanius excubitor* Alcaudón Real Norteño
Occasional individuals may occur in winter.

Black-crowned Tchagra* *Tchagra senegala* Chagra del Senegal
This African species breeds on the southern coast of the Strait but there is only one Iberian record, one near Facinas (Cádiz) on 15 July 1995.

House Crow* *Corvus splendens* Corneja India
One was in Gibraltar from 28 March–4 April 1991. Its appearance coincided with the arrival of a flotilla of warships from the Persian Gulf and so the bird seems likely to have been ship-assisted.

Snowfinch *Montifringilla nivalis* Gorrión Nival
A female/juvenile was recorded on the south side of Sierra Nevada on 16 October 1978.

Scarlet Rosefinch* *Carpodacus erythrinus* Camachuelo Carminoso
Several records of single migrants captured during ringing programmes, all or most them juvenile birds. At La Algaida (Cádiz) on 7 October 1983, El Acebuche (Cádiz) on 15 September 1988, Los Barrios (Cádiz) on 7 November 1986, Alhaurín de la Torre (Málaga) on 24 September 1995 and Gibraltar in autumn 1999.

White-throated Sparrow* *Zonotrichia albicollis* Chingolo Gorgiblanco
One record, an adult present at Gibraltar harbour from 18–25 May 1986. It was caught and ringed. This occurrence is likely to have been ship-assisted.

Dark-eyed Junco* *Junco hyemalis* Junco Pizarroso
One record, an adult male present at Gibraltar harbour from 18–25 May 1986. It was caught and ringed. This occurrence also is likely to have been ship-assisted; it occurred together with the previous species.

Snow Bunting *Plectrophenax nivalis* Escribano Nival
Two records; a female taken within the area of Doñana on 13 November 1955 and another reported from San Roque on 11 November 1982.

Pine Bunting* *Emberiza leucocephalos* Escribano de Gmelin
Vagrant. One record; a male and a female in Gibraltar after strong easterlies on 2 May 1987.

Yellowhammer *Emberiza citrinella* Escribano Cerillo
One recorded in Gibraltar on 7 March 1984. One in Cáceres in July 1989. Also single birds ringed at Doñana (Huelva) on 2 October 1994 and at Rio Gordo (Málaga) on 27 October 1995. This species nests in northern Spain and so it seems likely to have been overlooked in our area.

Rustic Bunting* *Emberiza rustica* Escribano Rustico
Vagrant. One record, a male ringed on 21 December 1987 at Los Palacios (Sevilla).

Little Bunting* *Emberiza pusilla* Escribano Pigmeo
Vagrant. One taken near Málaga in December 1874. Two reported in Cádiz in October 1978; one from Tarifa and the other from Jimena. One was ringed in Doñana in October 1986. One was ringed near Málaga on 10 November 1991

Yellow-breasted Bunting* *Emberiza aureola* Escribano Aureolado
One captured at Chipiona (Cádiz) on 3 October 1969 seems likely to have been an escaped bird.

Red-headed Bunting* *Emberiza bruniceps* Escribano Carirrojo
One recorded in Sanlúcar de Barrameda (Cádiz) in October 1967 seems likely to have been an escaped bird.

Black-headed Bunting* *Emberiza melanocephala* Escribano Cabecinegro
An adult male was at the Río Guadalhorce estuary (Málaga) on 11 October 1996.

Bobolink* *Dolichonyx oryzivorus* Charlatán
One was in Gibraltar from 11–16 May 1984. It was caught and ringed.

APPENDICES

1 SCIENTIFIC NAMES OF PLANT SPECIES MENTIONED

Aleppo pine	*Pinus halepensis*	Lavender	*Lavandula* spp.
Almond	*Prunus dulcis*	Lentisc	*Pistachia lentiscus*
Black pine	*Pinus nigra*	Lusitanian oak	*Quercus faginea*
Agave	*Agave americana*	Maritime pine	*Pinus pinaster*
Asphodel	*Asphodelus albus*	Myrtle	*Myrtus communis*
Black poplar	*Populus nigra*	Oleander	*Nerium oleander*
Buckthorn	*Rhamnus alaternus*	Olive	*Olea europaea*
Canarian oak	*Quercus canariensis*	Orache	*Atriplex halimus*
Cazorla violet	*Viola cazorlensis*	Prickly pear	*Opuntia ficus-indica*
Citrus	*Citrus* spp.	Pyrenean oak	*Quercus pyrenaica*
Common reed	*Phragmites communis*	Retama	*Lygos sphaerocarpa*
Cork oak	*Quercus suber*	Rhododendron	*Rhododendron*
Eucalyptus	*Eucalyptus globulus* etc		*ponticum*
Encina	*Quercus rotundifolia*	Rosemary	*Rosmarinus officinalis*
False esparto grass	*Stipa tenacissima*	Smooth-leaved elm	*Ulmus minor*
Fan palm	*Chamaerops humilis*	Spanish fir (pinsapo)	*Abies pinsapo*
Genista	*Genista* spp.	Spiny broom	*Calicotome villosa*
Giant reed	*Arundo donax*	Strawberry tree	*Arbutus unedo*
Gibraltar candytuft	*Iberis gibraltarica*	Stone pine	*Pinus pinea*
Glasswort	*Salicornia* spp.	Sweet chestnut	*Castanea sativa*
Gum cistus	*Cistus ladanifer*	Tamarisk	*Tamarix africana*
Hawthorn	*Crataegus monogyna*	Thyme	*Thymus* spp.
Halimium	*Halimium halmifolium*	Tree heath	*Erica arborea*
Juniper	*Juniperus phoenicea* etc	White poplar	*Populus albus*

2 GLOSSARY OF LOCAL GEOGRAPHICAL TERMS

Alcornocal	Cork oak wood	Marisma	Tidal flats
Bahía	Bay	Mirador	Viewpoint
Cabo	Cape	Montaña	Mountain
Cascada	Waterfall	Peñon	Rock
Dehesa	Grazing woodland	Playa	Beach
Desembocadura	Estuary	Presa	Dam
Desfiladero	Gorge	Puerto	Mountain pass
Desierto	Desert		(also seaport)
Embalse	Reservoir	Punta	Headland
Encinar	Holm oak wood	Ría	Tidal inlet
Estuario	Estuary	Río	River
Faro	Lighthouse	Rivera	River valley
Hermita	Hermitage	Serranía	Mountain range
Laguna	Lake	Sierra	Mountain

FURTHER READING

Agencia de Medio Ambiente. 1991. *Guía de los espacios naturales de Andalucía.* 2nd edition. Editorial Incafo S.A., Madrid.

Bernis, F. 1980. *La migración de las aves en el Estrecho de Gibraltar (Epoca posnupcial): I. Aves planeadoras.* Madrid. Universidad Complutense.

Chinery, M. 1998. *Collins Wildlife Trust Guide. Butterflies of Britain and Europe.* HarperCollins, London.

Cortes, J.E. *et al.* 1980. *The Birds of Gibraltar.* Gibraltar Bookshop.

Cramp, S. & Simmons, K.E.L. 1977 *et seq. The Birds of the Western Palearctic.*, O.U.P., Oxford.

De Juana, E. (ed.). 1993. *Donde Ver Aves en España Peninsular.* Lynx Edicions, Barcelona.

Finlayson, C. 1992. *Birds of the Strait of Gibraltar.* T. & A.D. Poyser, London.

García, L *et al.* 1989. *Las Aves de Doñana y su Entorno.* Cooperative marismas del Rocío.

Garrido Guil, H. 1996. *Aves de las Marismas del Odiel y su Entorno.* Editorial Rueda S.L., Madrid.

Linares, L., Harper, A. & Cortes, J. 1996. *The Flowers of Gibraltar.* Wildlife Gibraltar Ltd., Gibraltar.

Llandres, C. & Urdiales, C. 1990. *Las Aves de Doñana.* Lynx Edicions, Barcelona.

Molesworth Allen, B. 1993. *A Selection of Wildflowers of Southern Spain.* Mirador Publications SL.

Muddeman, J. 2000. *A Birdwatching Guide to Extremadura.* Arlequin Press, Essex.

Paterson, A.M. 1990. *Aves Marinas de Málaga y Mar de Alborán.* A.M.A.

Paterson, A.M. 1994. *Aves Marinas de Iberia, Baleares y Canarias.* Lynx Edicions, Barcelona.

Paterson, A.M. 1997. *Las Aves Marinas de España y Portugal/Seabirds of Spain and Portugal.* (Bilingual text). Lynx Edicions, Barcelona.

Polunin, O. 1969. *Flowers of Europe.* O.U.P., Oxford

Polunin, O. & Smythies, B.E. 1973. *Flowers of South-west Europe: A Field Guide.* O.U.P., Oxford.

Porter, R.F. *et al.* 1981. *Flight Identification of European Raptors.* T & A.D. Poyser, Carlton.

Rebane, M. 1999. *Where to Watch Birds in North and East Spain.* A & C Black, London.

Rodriguez, J.L. & Blanco, F. 1989. *Guía de Rapaces de Extremadura.* Fondo Natural S.A., Madrid.

Tébar Carrera, J. 1998. *Las Aves de la Bahía de Cádiz.* Wildlife Gibraltar Ltd./ GONHS, Gibraltar.

Viada, C. (ed). 1998. *Areas Importantes Para las Aves en España.* 2nd edition. Sociedad Española de Ornitología. Monograph No.5.

SITE INDEX

INDEX TO SPECIES BY SITE

See also the systematic list (p. 316) for details of commoner species especially. Rarities are listed separately (p. 338). Sites are identified by province titles. G = Gibraltar.

Accentor, Alpine AL7, BA4, BA11, CA2, CA19, CC4, CC6, CC8, CO8, G, GR1, GR2, J1, MA4, MA5, MA10, MA14.
Avadavat, Red BA5, BA10, CC9.
Avocet AL1, AL2, AL3, BA7, BA10, CA1, CA4, CA11, CA12, CA15, CA17, CC9, CO4, H2, H4, H5, J6, MA1, MA8.
Bee-eater, AL1, AL2, AL3, AL5, AL6, AL7, BA4, BA9, BA11, CA2, CA4, CA5, CA6, CA8, CA9, CA10, CA14, CA15, CA17, CA18, CA19, CC6, CC7, CO8, CO9, CO10, CO11, G, GR2, GR4, GR5, GR6, H1, H5, H7, J1, J2, J3, J4, J5, MA1, MA3, MA4, MA8, MA10, MA11, MA12, MA13.
Bittern SE1.
  Little AL3, AL8, AL9, BA11, CA8, CA13, CA14, CA15, CA15, CA15, CA17, CC9, CO12, H3, H4, H5, J6, MA1, MA8, SE1, SE2.
Blackbird G, H5.
Blackcap AL6, AL7, CA6, CA9, CO8, CO10, G, GR1, GR2, H4, H5, H7, J1, J2, J3, J4, J5, MA3, MA10, MA11, MA12, MA13, SE3.
Bluethroat AL3, CA2, CA4, CA7, CA8, CA14, CA15, CA17, CC8, CO1, G, H2, H5, J6, MA8.
Brambling CA2, CO9, G, J3, MA4, MA12.
Bullfinch BA4, CA2, CC8, CO8, H5, J2, J3, MA6.
Bunting, Cirl AL1, BA8, CA2, CA4, CA6, CA9, CA17, CA19, CO8, H5, H6, H7, J1, MA5, MA6, MA11, MA12, MA13.
  Corn AL1, AL9, CA1, CA6, CA9, CO3, CO9, GR6, H4, H5, SE3.

Ortolan BA3, CA2, CA4, CA5, CA6, CA8, CA9, CA10, CA17, CC4, CC8, CO11, G, H4, H5, MA6, MA11, MA12.
  Reed CA7, CA8, CA17, H4, H5.
  Rock AL1, AL5, AL6, BA4, BA8, BA11, CA2, CA6, CA9, CA17, CA19, CC4, CC6, CC8, CO9, G, GR1, GR2, H4, H5, J1, J2, J3, J5, MA3, MA4, MA5, MA6, MA7, MA9, MA10, MA11, MA12, MA13, MA14.
Bustard, Great BA1, BA3, BA6, BA7, BA8, BA9, BA10, CA4, CC1, CC2, CC3, CC5, CC7, CO11, SE3.
  Little AL1, AL6, AL7, BA1, BA3, BA6, BA8, BA9, BA10, CA4, CA17, CC1, CC2, CC3, CC5, CC7, CO5, CO11, GR4, GR6, H5, MA1, MA2, SE3.
Buttonquail, Little H5.
Buzzard, Common, AL3, AL6, BA1, BA2, BA4, BA6, BA9, BA10, CA2, CA5, CA6, CA9, CC4, CC6, CC8, CC9, CO8, CO9, CO10, CO11, G, GR2, GR3, H5, H6, H7, J1, J2, J3, J4, J5, MA3, MA5, MA7, MA8, MA8, MA9, MA11, MA12, MA13, MA14, SE4.
  Honey, BA6, CA2, CA4, CC8, CO8, G, H5.
Chaffinch CO2, CO9, G, G, GR2, GR3, GR5, J1, J2, J3, J5, MA4, MA11, MA12, MA13.
Chat, Rufous Bush, BA4, BA6, BA11, CA2, CA4, CA5, CA6, CA8, CA9, CA10, CA15, CA15, CA17, CC5, CC6, CC9, CO3, CO9, G, H5, MA3, MA13, MA14.
Chiffchaff, Common, AL1, AL5, AL6, AL7, AL8, AL9, CA1, CA6, CA9, CA17, CO8, CO9, G,

GR1, GR2, H4, H5, J1, MA1, MA4, MA5, MA7, MA8, MA10, MA11, MA12, MA13.
  Iberian, CA2, CA6, CA9, G, MA6.
Chough, Red-billed, BA3, BA4, BA8, CA19, CA20, CC4, CC6, CC8, CO8, CO9, GR1, GR2, GR3, GR4, J1, J2, J3, J5, MA3, MA4, MA5, MA6, MA9, MA10, MA11, MA12, MA13, MA14.
Cisticola, Zitting, AL1, AL2, AL3, BA3, BA6, BA7, BA10, CA1, CA2, CA4, CA5, CA6, CA8, CA9, CA15, CC1, G, G, H1, H4, H5, H7, MA1, MA4, MA8, SE3.
Coot AL2, AL3, AL8, AL9, BA5, BA6, BA7, BA11, CA13, CA17, CA18, CO2, CO3, CO4, CO7, H3, H4, H5, J6, MA2, MA8.
  Crested See Coot, Red-knobbed.
  Red-knobbed CA13, CA14, CA15, H5.
Cormorant, Great AL8, AL9, BA4, BA5, BA11, CA7, CA8, CA11, CA12, CA17, CC1, CC3, CC5, CC6, CC9, CO1, CO7, CO12, H2, H4, H5, MA4, MA8.
Crake, Baillon's CA14, CA15, H5, SE1.
  Little H5, SE1.
  Spotted CA8, H5, SE1.
Crane AL1, BA1, BA2, BA3, BA4, BA6, BA7, BA8, BA9, BA11, CA2, CA4, CA17, CC1, CC2, CC3, CC5, CC7, CC8, CC9, CO6, CO11, H5, MA1
Crossbill, CA2, CO8, CO9, GR1, GR2, GR3, GR5, J1, J2, J3, J4, MA4, MA7, MA9, MA12, MA13.
Crow, Carrion CC8, GR1, GR5, J1.
Cuckoo CA1, CA6, CA9, CA17, CC6, CC8, CO9,

CO11, GR4, GR6, H5, SE3.

Crested AL1, AL2, AL3, AL5, CA2, CA17, CO5, CO8, CO9, CO10, CO11, G, GR2, GR4, GR5, GR6, H4, H5, H7, J2, J3, J4, J5, MA1, MA1, MA2, MA3, MA4, MA13, SE2, SE3.

Dupont's AL1, AL6, GR4, GR6.

Lesser Short-toed AL1, AL2, AL3, CA4, CA17, GR4, GR6, H4, H5, SE1, SE2.

Short-toed AL1, AL2, AL3, BA3, BA9, BA10, CA1, CA2, CA4, CA5, CA7, CA8, CA10, CA17, CC5, CO11, G, H5, MA1, SE2, SE3.

Thekla AL1, AL5, AL6, BA1, BA2, BA4, BA6, BA11, CA1, CA2, CA4, CA6, CA9, CA17, CA19, CC6, CC8, CO8, CO9, CO10, GR1, GR2, GR4, GR5, H5, H7, J2, J3, J4, J5, MA3, MA6, MA10, MA11, MA12, MA13, MA14.

Linnet AL1, AL9, CA1, CO9, G, GR2, GR5, H5, J1, J2, J3, J5, MA4, MA14.

Magpie AL8, AL9, CA17, CO9, CO10, GR4, GR6, H4, H5, J1, J2, J3, J4, J5.

Azure-winged AL7, BA2, BA4, BA11, BA12, CA17, CC5, CC6, CC8, CO9, CO10, CO11, GR1, H4, H5, H7, J2, J3, J4, MA6, MA7, SE4.

Mallard AL2, AL3, BA4, BA7, BA7, BA11, CA4, CA13, CA15, CA17, CA18, CA18, CC1, CO1, CO2, CO3, CO4, CO5, CO6, CO7, CO11, H3, H4, H5, J1, J6, MA1, MA2, MA4, MA8.

Martin, Crag AL1, AL5, AL9, BA5, BA8, BA11, CA1, CA2, CA5, CA6, CA6, CA9, CA9, CA10, CA17, CA19, CC4, CC6, CC8, CO8, CO9, G, G, GR2, H4, H5, H7, J1, J2, J3, J5, MA3, MA4, MA9, MA10, MA11, MA12, MA13, MA14, SE4.

House CO8, CO9, G, H5.

Sand BA10, BA11, CA2, CC9, CO9, G, H5, MA13.

Merganser, Red-breasted AL9, CA4, CA8, CA10, CA11, CA12, H2, H4, H5.

Merlin BA9, CA2, CA4, CA5, CA10, CA17, CC9, CO9, CO11, G, H5, MA10, SE3.

Moorhen AL3, AL8, AL9, BA11, CA17, CO2, CO3, CO4, CO11, H3, H4, H5, J6, MA2, MA13.

Nightingale AL5, AL7, BA11, CA6, CA9, CA17, CA18, CO1, CO2, CO3, CO7, CO8, CO9, CO10, CO11, G, GR1, GR4, GR6, H5, H7, J1, J2, J3, J4, J5, MA3, MA4, MA6, MA7, MA8, MA10, MA11, MA12, MA13, SE3.

Nightjar, Common CA2, CA19, CC4, CC8, CO8, G.

Red-necked AL1, BA4, BA6, BA8, CA2, CA4, CA5, CA6, CA8, CA9, CA10, CA17, CC4, CC6, CC8, CO8, CO9, CO11, G, GR4, H5, MA4, MA10, MA13, MA14.

Nuthatch BA1, CA19, CC4, CC8, CO9, CO10, H7, J1, J4, MA10, SE4.

Oriole, Golden AL6, BA4, BA6, BA11, CA2, CA6, CA9, CA19, CC6, CC8, CO8, CO9, CO10, G, GR1, GR2, GR3, H4, H5, H7, J1, J2, J3, J4, J5, MA4, MA13, SE3, SE4.

Osprey AL1, AL3, BA7, CA2, CA4, CA5, CA7, CA8, CA10, CA11, CA12, CA13, CA17, CA18, CC9, CO12, G, H2, H4, H5, J6, MA4, MA8.

Ouzel, Ring AL1, AL7, CA2, CO8, G, GR1, H5, J2, J3, J5, MA6, MA10, MA12, MA13, MA14.

Owl, Barn CA2, CA4, CA15, CA17, CC3, CO9, H5, J5.

Eagle AL1, AL5, AL6, BA2, BA4, BA8, BA11, BA12, CA2, CA4, CA6, CA9, CA19, CA20, CC4, CC6, CC8, CO8, CO9, CO10, GR1, GR2, GR4, GR5, H7, J1, J2, J3, J4, J5, MA3, MA4, MA7, MA9, MA10, MA13, MA14, SE4.

Little AL1, AL5, AL6,

BA9, CA2, CA6, CA9, CA17, CA20, CC1, CC3, CO8, CO9, CO10, CO11, G, GR2, GR4, GR5, H5, H7, J1, J2, J3, J5, MA3, MA4, MA8, MA9, MA10, MA11, MA12, MA13, SE3.

Long-eared BA2, CA17, CC4, CO10, GR4, H5.

Scops AL5, AL7, BA2, BA4, BA6, BA11, CA2, CA4, CA5, CA8, CA10, CA17, CA19, CC6, CC8, CO8, CO9, G, GR2, GR5, H5, H7, J1, J2, J3, J5, MA4, MA7, MA10, MA12, MA13, MA14.

Short-eared, CA2, CA4, CA5, CA17, H5, MA8.

Tawny BA6, CA2, CA6, CA9, CA17, CC8, CO8, CO9, CO10, GR5, H5, H7, J1, J2, J3, J4, J5, MA10.

Oystercatcher AL1, CA1, CA5, CA11, CA12, CA17, H1, H4, H5.

Partridge, Barbary G.

Partridge, Red-legged, AL1, BA9, CA17, CO9, CO11, GR5, H5, J1, MA9, MA11, MA12, MA13, SE3.

Peregrine AL1, AL5, AL6, AL7, CA2, CA5, CA6, CA6, CA9, CA9, CA10, CA11, CA12, CA17, CA19, CC4, CC6, CC8, CO7, CO8, CO10, G, GR1, GR2, GR4, GR5, H5, J1, J2, J3, J4, J5, MA3, MA4, MA6, MA8, MA9, MA10, MA11, MA12, MA13, MA14.

Phalarope, Grey CA1, CA5, CA10, CA11, CA12.

Pintail AL3, AL4, BA7, BA11, CA4, CA15, CA17, CO4, H4, H5, J6, MA1, MA2, MA8.

Pipit, Meadow AL1, AL2, AL5, CA1, CA6, CA9, CA17, CC1, CO8, CO9, CO10, CO11, G, GR4, H4, H5, J4, MA1, MA5, MA8, MA10, MA11, MA12, MA13, SE3.

Red-throated CA2, CA4, CA6.

Richard's H5.

Tawny AL5, BA3, BA10, CA2, CA4, CA5, CA6, CA8, CA9, CA10, CA17, G, GR1, GR2, GR4, GR6, H4, H5, MA10, MA11, MA14.

Subalpine AL5, AL7,
BA4, BA6, CA2, CA6,
CA9, CA17, CA19, CC4,
CC6, CC8, CO8, CO9,
CO10, G, GR1, GR2,
GR3, H4, H5, H7, J1, J2,
J3, J4, J5, MA5, MA6,
MA9, MA10, MA11,
MA13, MA14.
Willow AL1, CA2, CA17,
CO8, CO9, G, H4, H5,
MA10.
Wood CA2, CA15, G.
Waxbill, Common CA8, H5.
Wheatear, Black AL1, AL5,
AL6, AL7, BA4, BA8,
BA11, CC4, CC6, CC8,
CO8, CO9, CO11, GR1,
GR2, GR4, GR6, J1, J2,
J3, J5, MA4, MA6,
MA10, MA11, MA12,
MA13, MA14.
Black-eared AL1, AL2,
AL3, AL5, AL6, AL7,
BA10, BA11, CA2, CA5,
CA6, CA9, CA10, CA15,
CA17, CA19, CC8, CO8,
CO9, CO11, G, GR1,

GR2, GR4, GR5, GR6,
H4, H5, H7, MA3, MA4,
MA6, MA8, MA10,
MA11, MA12, MA13,
MA14.
Northern AL2, AL7, CA2,
CA4, CA17, CA19, CC4,
CC8, CO8, CO9, G,
GR1, GR2, GR6, H4, H5,
MA8, MA10, MA14.
Whimbrel AL1, AL2, AL9,
CA1, CA4, CA5, CA11,
CA12, CA17, H1, H4,
H5.
Whinchat AL1, AL6, AL7,
CA2, CA17, G, H4, H5,
MA8.
Whitethroat CA2, CA5,
CA17, CC8, CO9, G, H4,
H5, H7, MA12.
Wigeon AL3, AL4, BA4,
BA7, BA11, CA4, CA11,
CA12, CA15, CA17,
CC1, CC3, CC5, CO1,
CO2, CO3, CO4, CO5,
CO6, CO7, H4, H5, J6,
MA1, MA8.
Woodcock CA2, CA17, H5.

Woodlark BA1, CA2, CA4,
CA6, CA9, CA17, CA19,
CC4, CC8, CO8, CO9,
CO11, GR1, H5, J1, J2,
J3, MA4, MA9, MA10,
MA13, SE4.
Woodpecker, Great
Spotted CA6, CA9,
CC8, CO10, H5, H6, H7,
J1, J2, J3, J4, MA13.
Green BA12, CA19, CC8,
CO8, CO10, GR5, H5,
J1, J2, J3, J4, MA9,
MA13.
Lesser Spotted BA6, CC8,
J1.
Woodpigeon CO8, CO9,
CO11, H5, J1, J5, MA10.
Wren AL7, CO2, CO9, G,
GR2, GR5, J1, J2, J3,
MA3, MA4, MA5, MA6,
MA10, MA13.
Wryneck CA2, CA4, CA5,
CA14, CA15, CA15,
CA16, CO8, G, H7, J1,
MA13.